History of the Belgians

HISTORY OF THE BELGIANS

by

Adrien de Meeüs

Translated from the French by

G. Gordon

FREDERICK A. PRAEGER
Publisher • New York

BOOKS THAT MATTER

Published in the United States of America in 1962 by
Frederick A. Praeger, Inc., Publisher
64 University Place, New York 3, N.Y.

All rights reserved
© 1962 by Frederick A. Praeger, Inc.
Library of Congress Catalog Card Number: 62-13755

Manufactured in the United States of America

Contents

I

THE PREHISTORIC DAWN

The land which was one day to become Belgium has had a long history, predating the earliest days of human life.

In early prehistoric times, almost the whole country was under water. Only what is now Wallonia had emerged from the sea that still covered Flanders, northern Brabant, and Kempen.

Little by little, Flanders began to emerge, only to be submerged once more in the first century A.D.; during the Middle Ages, northern Belgium remained a land of marshes through which ran streams such as the Senne, the Dyle, the Demer, and the Lys—in those days navigable waterways.

Wallonia in the south was a land of forests. Until the end of the Middle Ages, the forested stretch of the Ardennes harbored wild beasts, which would come down into the towns themselves, and until the sixteenth century the country was a great source of venison, which was exported to cities as far away as Paris. In 1595, the English poet Spenser, writing of a forest "with store of savage prey," added that not even "famous Ardeyn" was "so wide a forest and so waste as this," and Dr. Johnson identified Shakespeare's Forest of Arden with the Belgian Ardennes. According to popular belief, its undergrowth was inhabited by wood spirits—a belief shared by English soldiers in the Hundred Years' War. Centuries earlier, these glades had sheltered the four sons of Aymon and their renowned horse Bayard; in the late fifteenth century, they were the refuge of Erard de la Marck, the "boar of the Ardennes," who rode roughshod over the Liège countryside.

Like the great coal forest, which no longer exists, the Ardennes forest was to retreat in the face of human habitation, until clearings and developments reduced it to its present area.

1

The sea and its inroads, the hills and mountains thus account for much of present-day Belgium, and its rivers have been another dominant influence in the country's history. Flanders is the child of the Schelde, and Wallonia that of the Meuse. Both these rivers flow from south to north, and this explains Belgium's close contact with France and her long period of isolation from Germany. It explains, too, the growth and prosperity of the towns, nearly all of which sprang up around bridges. Belgium was to lie athwart the highways of trade and industry, brought into being by an age-old marriage of the land with the waterways.

There is no basis for the belief that the first inhabitants of Belgium were cave men. They lived in valleys under the open sky, unsheltered, and it has not been proved that they knew fire. Nor is it true that they were clad in skins. Their relics include neither tools for scraping or cutting nor needles nor any other tools for working skins and sewing them together. They probably lived in the nude in a warm climate, making their homes on low-lying ground that offered the security of thick vegetation, plentiful fruits, and an easy escape into the boughs of trees in case of attack by wild beasts.

The Belgian of 150,000 B.C. lived in a tropical climate not unlike that of modern-day Senegal or India, and the flora and fauna he knew would astonish his modern descendants. The fauna, such as the Elephas antiquus and Marck's giant rhinoceros, was those of hot countries.* His oxen, with their enormous eyes, were twice as big as ours; his boars were monsters, as were the herds of giant elephants whose gleaming tusks were straight as lances, instead of curving into the familiar protuberances we know today. His dogs had not yet learned to bark, for barking was not among the accomplishments of these wild creatures.

The man of those days was smaller than his modern counterpart. He stood 5 feet 3 inches at most, but the brain in his 1,400-cubic-centimeter skull was as developed as our own. He was familiar with fire as well as with many primitive tools, including a very heavy axe, shaped and helved, which he used as his chief weapon. He hunted and fished, and, like the Indians of the Amazon, caught his fish with a wooden spear.

* This climate might well recur, for temperature cycles have already repeated themselves two or three times. In the course of 80,000 years, the climate of western Europe has changed from torrid heat to extreme cold. The last glacial period dates back 20,000 years; and the hot period, if this is the right name for what is now beginning, will be at its peak in 35,000 or 40,000 years. Should this happen, our descendants may one day see the ibis nesting in the Schelde and Meuse estuaries, as they do in the Congo of today, with alligators and hippopotamuses cavorting beneath the mangrove trees.

Women were believed to possess magical powers that inspired both respect and fear. He had no inkling of how children are conceived and had not yet learned to connect pregnancy with sex. He equated woman with the other forces of nature—the sun, the water, the earth, and the trees—for she was the fountain of life. The oldest carvings and statuettes show her always heavy with child and with full breasts.

Men and women alike were apt to die young. The Belgian of prehistoric days did not expect to survive much beyond his fortieth year.

Then came the great climatic change, and as the world passed into the period of extreme cold, Flanders slowly emerged from the sea, and the receding water formed its coastline.

More and more, man fled the wet lowlands, seeking shelter on higher ground. On this higher ground, modern archaeologists have discovered the bones and instruments of Belgium's early inhabitants. As the cold grew more intense, early man took refuge in caves, and, quitting the low-lying lands of Flanders, he settled in the Ardennes and in the Meuse valley.

This was the age of the Man of Spy, whose remains were unearthed in 1886, in the Ormeau valley between Gembloux and Namur. The Man of Spy—bowlegged, head hung forward on a short, squat body—was not unlike the present-day Lapp. With his receding forehead, his overdeveloped jaw, his prominent, bushy eyebrows, and his muscular, shaggy body, he was not too unlike an ape. However, he had learned to dress in skins, to hunt the bear and the mammoth, and to break up their bones to eat the marrow. His equipment, made from broken flint, included knives, scrapers, and piercing tools, and he may well have handled many other instruments fashioned of wood or other perishable materials. Unfortunately, no examples of these tools have survived through the ages.

He was the living contradiction of the popular legend which paints primitive man as strong and healthy, living in a state of nature, untouched by the evil and decadence of civilization. In fact, because of the fetid, unhygienic life he lived in his caves, he was forever ill, afflicted with ulcers and eye inflammations.

Then came the last ice age. Western Europe was plunged in polar cold, and high mountains lay beneath a blanket of ice more than a mile thick. The ice cap descending southward covered the sites of present-day London, Berlin, and Odessa. The Man of Spy disappeared, and a new race from the south took his place—Cro-Magnon Man, with his wide, high forehead, his prominent nose, and his long legs. France and Germany became a tundra, and as the sea froze, its level fell a full 300 feet. The Strait of Dover and Gibraltar dried up.

The men of that era lived in bigger caves than their predecessors—in the caves of Chaleux, Furfoz, and Montaigle in the Ardennes—and in bigger groups, less vulnerable to attack by wild beasts. They wore trinkets and necklaces and painted their bodies with red ocher. The communal life in the big caves was instrumental in the birth of art. Magdalenian civilization has left us a multitude of animal figures, drawn in red and brown ocher and manganese black on the walls of caves, but in Belgium the only relics found have been ivory and horn carvings, an art linked to the development of religion and sorcery. Mankind was suffering from lack of game, and man sought to propitiate the gods of the hunt or the spirits of the beasts by creating images related to his ceremonial practices. A wild beast, men believed, could be slain only by those who first gained ascendancy over its spirit. Thus there developed a ritual of exorcism, dances, and incantation—ceremonies of religious or hypnotic intent designed to force the beast into the snare.

The Magdalenians also were the first to practice the primitive ritual of sticking needles into the image of an adversary in order to bring about his death. Yet though they developed their skills as painters and engaged in many forms of collective activity, their civilization failed to develop further. In reaching a degree of perfection they lost their adaptability; they could no longer face new situations, and with the change in climate and the northward migration of the reindeer, their only game, they were unable to survive. This was the first known collapse of a civilization, a collapse resulting not from destruction wrought by external forces, but rather from an innate incapacity to adjust to altered circumstances. Even their art vanished with them, for its purpose was bound up with useful and practical activities no longer required.

Meanwhile, the glaciers were receding, and with them the arctic fauna; in time, the changing climate turned into the climate we now know. The Paleolithic Age was drawing to a close, and the Magdalenians left Belgium at the same time as their game. The sparse population that took their place left the caves and settled in the uplands and in Flanders, which was becoming habitable as the northern part of Belgium emerged from the waters.

It was a time for the emergence of new populations—for people who polished stone instead of cutting it and who developed almost modern techniques and customs—an era marked by three new activities: agriculture, cattle raising, and warfare.

The new race of man was roundheaded, short-nosed, small and dark —the ancestors of the population of Wallonia and France. They came from Asia via Poland or the Balkans in a succession of migrations, and as they came, they carefully surveyed the soil for its fertility to determine whether they should settle down and cultivate it.

Not content with the gathering of wild vegetables, they selected, improved, and modified; of the 247 species of edible plants which are now known, no less than 199 were the product of our Neolithic ancestors, while the rest come from the prehistoric inhabitants of other continents. The invaders tenderized tough plants and made indigestible ones edible, thus transforming many plants into the useful vegetables that we know today. They discovered the leguminous plants— peas, beans, and lentils—and the food properties of tubers and roots— turnips, carrots, and others. They later developed flax, hemp, and cotton, the textile plants which enabled them to clothe themselves. As a matter of fact, their creativeness was so intense that it exhausted the capacities of nature, and since the end of the prehistoric period no new plant species have been discovered although plants indigenous to one region continue to be transplanted to new areas.

The same applies to the domestication of animals. The dog is found close to early Neolithic tombs, and later in Neolithic periods oxen, sheep, the goats and horses were domesticated. Subsequently, the animal stock was improved by selection, and the wild hen, which lays only six or eight eggs a year if left to itself, was bred to produce one hundred or more eggs annually. Altogether about thirty species, including eighteen mammals, ten birds (mostly farmyard species), and two species of insects—the bee and the silkworm—have been handed down to us by Neolithic man, and no additional species of animals has been domesticated since that time. Neolithic man spread his knowledge to surrounding peoples by a system of trade and exchange, thus, by precept and example, communicating his ideas and becoming the agent of his own civilization.

But the outstanding event of the Neolithic period was the first appearance of warfare. Ever since then, war has been a potent instrument for the destruction of civilizations that have ceased to make progress, wiping out those ultraconservative peoples who absorbed, without useful effect, resources needed by the others. In the wake of warfare, mankind began to move—subduing territories, developing them economically, and laying the foundation for future expansion. The Paleolithic period and its slow pace of human evolution had ended; from then on, mankind was forced into the continuous rebuilding of the foundations of its life against a constantly changing background.

It was war which was to reward those peoples who were distinguished for their inventiveness and ingenuity, who could devise new weapons and enslave others. This was to lead to the building of empires and complex social systems that included men of intellect, art, and learning in their structures. Moreover, since defense demanded a constant development of arms, the process of invention was to become a condition of survival for every group of the human race.

This was the beginning of that great adventure of human civilization that has continued through history and which has its roots in six trailblazing innovations—speech, fire, the use of tools, agriculture, the domestication of animals, and metallurgy. The first three date back to the Paleolithic period, but it was Neolithic man who first experimented with and later perfected agriculture, stock breeding, and the use of metals.

But once wars resulted in the creation of empires, mankind began to concern itself with organizing the structure of society. Conflicts between peoples and expansionist migrations strengthened the most youthful and adaptable groups—though not always the most civilized. Communities could no longer live in isolation, and mankind became embarked on a process of continuous development that had its starting point in central Asia and soon reached the region of present-day Belgium.

After the Neolithic period, Belgium was overrun by the Aryans and by the Celts. It was they who introduced the horse and the use of iron, and, thrusting Belgium into the framework of Mediterranean civilization, introduced the customs, culture, and mode of life that have survived until today.

The earliest Belgian Neolithic group known to us are the Omalians, a name derived from the village of Omal near Liège. The Germans have dubbed them the "ribbon potters," because of the shape of their vases. They came from the Danube, reaching Belgium by crossing Germany and the Rhine.

The roots of their civilization are still an enigma. Their tombs have never been found, and nobody knows what they did with their dead. It does not seem likely that they cremated their dead, for had they done so, urns and ashes would surely have been found. And they did not bury them, for they left no graves. They were a peace-loving people, not warriors. Their remains include not even a single flint axe, and it seems that they were almost totally ignorant of the use of arms. Yet they succeeded in surviving on Belgian soil for thousands of years.

How, the reader may ask, did they then defend themselves? There is no answer. At any rate, their civilization failed to develop and they did not assimilate any outside influences. They disappeared quite suddenly, and even their disappearance remains a mystery.

The lesson of the Omalians, however, tallies with what was later learned from the Eskimos and the Tahitians: Warfare is a stimulant frequently resulting in progress, and a society that enjoys continuous peace can easily lose its sense of growth and development, thus condemning itself to stagnation or destruction.*

The dwellings of the Omalians, half underground, were round or oval in shape, a yard high, three or four yards long, and two or three yards wide. They were grouped in villages, and we call them hut foundations, because no trace of their walls and roofs—probably made of timber— has been found. Many tools and articles of excellent workmanship have been found in them: millstones and baked black pottery, richly decorated and equipped with loop handles for hanging.

The Omalians occupied almost the whole of the Hesbaye plateau. They discovered the fertility of the its soil and were the first to cultivate it. But they did not spread out to other parts of Belgium.

The Omalians were succeeded by the Michelsberg people who came from the southeast and were highly skilled in making tools of polished stone. A people of warlike tendencies, they wrought a change in a portion of the world hitherto inhabited by a people who seemed to have held human life sacred. Their weapons were far superior to the equipment of the ancient hunters. They had slender daggers of hard bone, and axes of polished granite or sandstone, reinforced and mounted on handles made of antlers. They operated flint mines, boring through the chalky soil at Flénu, Obourg, Spiennes, Strépy, and Avennes, and they operated a great open quarry at Eysden, on the Dutch frontier. With their polished-stone tools, they manufactured many of the implements we use today—picks, hammers, gouges, shears, chisels, axes, daggers, spearheads, and arrowheads. At the entrance to the mine, they built factories run along modern lines, in which jobs were handed out to a number of workers and where articles were manufactured in successive stages.

This industrial growth was complemented by a complex commercial organization engaging in export, for the goods produced found a wide market.

The Michelsberg people also developed the art of whetting and were able to sharpen their tools and weapons keenly either with sandstone whetstones whose surfaces had been ground with powdered flint, or by using the mortar method, in which one stone turned upon another —the same method by which microscope lenses are produced today. They were also the first to make ceremonial and parade weapons, which they treated with special care for their beauty and elegance rather than for their usefulness.

* This point is emphasized in the writings of Arnold Toynbee.

They tilled the soil and ground grain; they raised herds and domesticated the dog, the pig, the goat, and the sheep—although they remained hunters, pursuing stag, roebuck, and boar. They also used snails for food, as we do today.

It was they who built the first Belgian lake dwellings mounted on piles and protected by drawbridges against wild beasts. Some of these houses, such as the one at Dentergem in Flanders, were still occupied as late as the fifteenth century A.D. They dug mines, sinking their shafts fifty feet into the ground, and the mine galleries extended over an area of 120 acres. They engaged in considerable trade, for by now they knew how to build boats, and Spiennes tools sold as far afield as England.

They were very religious and buried their dead in cave cemeteries. Before burial, the corpse was partly stripped of its flesh, the bones were separated and arranged in orderly rows. Moreover, they made a distinction between temporary and perpetual burial rights; from time to time they dug up long-dead corpses and buried them in a collective trench, in order to make room for their more recent dead.

But the Michelsberg people were not the only inhabitants of Belgium during this period. Other groups, sharing the same civilization, had settled down in other parts of the country and intermingled with the Michelsberg people. Among them were warriors of Spanish origin, known as the people of the bell-shaped cups. Later, they became renowned as the builders of tablestones, and they erected the famous megalithic tombs at Wéris in the valley of the Ourthe. In view of the fact that some of these stones weigh over a ton, it is believed that these early people were organized in large social groups. Originally, the stones were probably set up in underground caves that became exposed by the landslides of later centuries.

These were the first people to set up a social hierarchy, dividing men into two classes—the rich and the poor. Their tombs have produced skeletons whose teeth are intact, indicating that their possessors ate cooked meat; the skeletons of herbivorous peoples reveal bad teeth, even in those who died young. All of them, however, knew only one method of disposing of the dead—by burial. All of them were farmers and stock raisers and possessed the same domestic animals, and they engaged in trading activities, importing various types of hard rock from the Alps—and even from the East—which they used for toolmaking. Among them were such formations as quartzite, phthanite, jadeite, and chloromelanite.

Physically, they seemed to have resembled the present inhabitants of Wallonia, who are probably their descendants and have changed little in the course of time.

This brings us to the period some 4,000 or 5,000 years before the Christian era, when metals began to be used in the manufacture of highly durable tools and implements.

Bronze was first used in Belgium around 1750 B.C. It led to the creation of a new weapon—the sword—while in agriculture the bronze sickle soon replaced the ancient tool of wood or bone with its cutting edge of sharpened flint fragments.

Many new cutting tools were developed, and the life of the human male was revolutionized. For the first time in the history of mankind, beards were cut and shaved. This fashion quickly gained ground, since a clean-shaven man seemed to symbolize an advanced people using the most modern type of equipment. In place of the bone pin came the fibula or safety pin, with which clothes could be adjusted properly and kept in place firmly. Finery and splendor became the order of the day.

We know there was a big commercial community, for some of its secret storehouses have been found. In those insecure times, it was the merchants' custom to interrupt their journeys and store their precious merchandise in secret places until they were ready to pick it up on another trip. Many, however, were killed, and their secrets died with them; but quite a number of these stores have since been found in Hainaut, Brabant, and in the provinces of Antwerp and Namur, particularly at Jemeppe.

At this point civilization was beginning to advance so rapidly that the progress of the next 4,000 or 5,000 years exceeds anything which had happened in the previous 100,000 or even million years.

This was because civilization had found a center—the Middle East, between the Mediterranean and central Asia, the birthplace of all mighty empires. Migrant populations from the area were constantly finding their way to Belgium, bringing with them a continuous stream of inventions and ideas.

The first universal civilization flourished in Mesopotamia between the fifth and fourth millenniums B.C., later radiating in every direction as a result of its trading activities. It was doubtless Mesopotamian merchants who brought bronze to Belgium.

As early as the third millennium B.C., an enormous merchandise transport organization was being created throughout the Near East. The merchant communes or guilds sought and obtained from local princes the right to set up agencies and tribunals to levy taxes on the cloth trade, and to form federations.*

* By 2600 B.C., the Sumerians had invented writing, arithmetic, and astronomy, measured time by a twelve-month calendar and by a year of 360 days, had domesti-

From this time on, the great civilizations of history, in the form of empires and developing societies followed each other rapidly. Their many inventions became the common heritage of humanity, but advancing civilization also brought conflicting tendencies. On the one hand, societies wished to safeguard their achievements; on the other, they sought to destroy the social fabric and institutions of others.

Little by little, they developed political systems which conditioned the individual's relation to his fellow man. Successively, each social structure went into decline, to be replaced by others that rose from the ashes to take up the same task in a different form.

As each empire disintegrated, the barbarians—the apprentices of civilization—would build up new states along the same lines, all of them founded on religions of increasingly universal acceptance: the Egyptian sun worship, the Babylonian and Persian religion of the stars, Greek and Roman polytheism, Asia's Confucianism and Buddhism, and, finally, Christianity and Islam.

Every empire and every nation was born from the ashes of another, so that rise and destruction formed a continuous chain of human rejuvenation, each collapse containing the seeds of a new creation that would reconstitute and transform the social structure.*

Two major concepts of society now confronted one another. The Egypt of the third millennium B.C. had begun by creating a state on a religious foundation, which was to serve as model for all the great empires until our own times. Pharaoh—the king-priest—constituted the predestined intermediary between men and the gods; he could invoke the latter only to obtain from them the sunshine and water necessary for his people, and it was this function that was held to justify his absolute power, the form of which was basic in all the monarchies of the East.

Greece alone set up the cult of man in opposition to the cult of the gods. The system was founded on individualism, as opposed to

---

cated the silkworm, and mastered weaving, chariot making, and shipbuilding. Before long (2328-2220 B.C.) Sumeria's political organization foreshadowed the modern type of state, with unified taxation, a single code of justice, a central administration, and departments dealing with finance, state property, public works, and credit.

* Before the Christian era, the whole of ancient civilization had already perished three times so dramatically and totally that its reconstruction was believed to be impossible. On the first occasion, the destruction was wrought by the Sumerian deluge. On the second, a millennium later, came the cataclysm of the Aryan invasions. The third was the rise of the Dorians and the Peoples of the Sea. Nevertheless, after the flood, the civilizations of the East were reborn and matured to reach their apogee. After the Aryan invasions, the new Egyptian Empire emerged from the destruction of the third millennium B.C. After the catastrophe of the Dorians came the miracle of Greece and the Roman Empire.

the religious royalty which had characterized the Egyptian and Persian systems.

Herodotus tells of a storm at sea when nobles of the court of Xerxes made obeisance in their hour of peril to their sovereign and, at his orders, flung themselves into the water to lighten their vessel, and so died. The king was a god, and the will of man was of no avail before him.

In Greece, on the other hand, it was the individual who counted, and every human life was regarded as precious. The system comprised political institutions founded on equality and freedom, making it the government's duty to serve and educate all its citizens and to seek their happiness and well-being in the name of the commonweal and by all devices within the bounds of knowledge. The doctrine itself had come from Egypt where it had first been nurtured. It led to the reappraisal of all the knowledge and inventions of other peoples, illuminating them with the clear light of reason and stripped of mysticism, so that the spirit of man became the touchstone and universal standard of judgment.

Democracy, born in Phoenicia and adopted by the city-states of Greece, was to become the instrument and motivating force of this doctrine.

Here, then, two great political systems confronted each other. Those that Greece had created, and which were given universal form by the Roman Empire, were still to be found in the social structure of the medieval communes and even survived into our own times.

Greece, however, demonstrates another fact: That democracy is possible only in a world of continual progress, where the work of creation, invention, and renewal is unceasing. Once a society becomes static and loses its sense of movement and initiative, it is no longer viable and enters into a decline.

Democracy, indeed, is founded on human energy. The freedom it guarantees mankind is based on a constant flow of new ideas with which the most enterprising individuals can perfect the structure of the body politic. It is not an ideal form of government that can be thrust artificially upon a people. It is rather the expression of the practical necessities of a period, under a system born of the initiative of a youthful society that has found new fields in which to expand. Democracy becomes nonsense when the source of general enrichment has dried up. When this happens, the ruling minorities become tyrannous, the oppressed masses revolt, sects and parties with mystic slogans emerge, and authoritarian governments are formed. Such governments are apt to incite mankind toward collective and emotional goals—national glory, warfare, religious propaganda, the worship of the past, and so forth. By these means men are made to accept authority, and the end is the creation of oppressive and totalitarian states.

This is the key to the fourth century B.C. in Greece, just as it is the fourteenth century A.D. in Belgium, the sixteenth century in Spain, and the twentieth century in Germany. This mechanism, which has played so great a part in human history, is deeply rooted in human nature. Man was born to waver perpetually between the life of emotion and collective mysticism on the one hand, and the life of action and individuality on the other. The clash between these states of mind may disrupt any social structure when its progress is slackening; or it may be the constructive key in the rise of nations and empires when the wind of new expansion is in their sails.

Society has known only three forms of government: The first is democracy, which, to some extent, is linked with social structures of a mercantile character; the second is mystic or totalitarian government, which is based on the needs of human emotion or religion; and the third is a governmental structure striking a balance between these two extremes, such as the Rome of Augustus, the French monarchy, the English parliamentary system of the eighteenth century, and the Third French Republic of the nineteenth and twentieth centuries.

This is a lesson first taught us by ancient Greece. At that time, 2,000 years ago, at the farthest end of Europe, the framework of what is now Belgium was beginning to take shape, and the days of its annexation to the Roman Empire were imminent.

There are numerous parallels between the structure of ancient Greece and that of modern Belgium. Both these countries were composed of different populations: in Greece, the Achaean mountaineers and the Ionian townsmen; in Belgium, the Flemings and the Walloons. In both cases, the union of the peoples was made possible only by democratic institutions, which provided the bases for freedom and mutuality. In both cases, too, a barren, marshy, rocky landscape was transformed by commercial activity and the development of countless original techniques into a productive land able to feed a growing population. The problems of human government were, in each case, to assume major importance; and in each case, the expansion of industry and trade was to bring with it a flourishing of the arts.

The town halls and cathedrals of Belgium correspond to the Parthenon; Flemish painting of the Renaissance may be compared to the sculptures of Phidias and Praxiteles; and the cosmopolitanism of Antwerp is a modern version of Greek universality. These similarities show, first and foremost, that in both cases we are dealing with one and the same phenomenon. It is a question of the human ideal of which Belgium, in the same way as ancient Greece, is the symbol. The ideal was born 2,500 years ago, and though its growth was for a time impeded by the invading barbarians, it has reappeared and flowered afresh in modern times.

The years passed, and it was only a few centuries before the birth of Christ that a new race of people appeared in Belgium. These were the mysterious urn field peoples. They did not annihilate the earlier inhabitants, but reduced them to submission and made them adopt the civilization they brought. We know almost nothing about them, for they are not mentioned by any of the ancient historians. We know, however, that they cremated their dead and put their ashes in vase-shaped urns, which were deposited in vast burial grounds—the urn fields. We also know that they were Celts; and with them, the Gaulish people make their first appearance in history. Their tumuli, or little mounds of earth, have been found all over Europe. Before long, the Celts invaded England, too, introducing their language, from which the Welsh and the Breton tongues derive. But these early Celts were only an advance guard. Other Celtic peoples were to follow once they possessed a great new weapon—the iron sword—which was to be the instrument of their victories.

Among the rear guard were the Belgae, who crossed the Rhine about the sixth century B.C. By the second century, they had made their home on the soil of present-day Belgium, becoming the Nervii tribe in Brabant and Hainaut, the Eburones in the Liège and Limbourg districts, the Menapii and the Morini in Flanders, and the Treveri in Luxemburg. Shortly thereafter came the Atuatuci in the province of Namur.

These tribes were numerous and active. By modern estimates, there were some 200,000 Nervii, 60,000 Atrebates, 100,000 Morini on the coast, 28,000 Menapii, 76,000 Atuatuci, and 160,000 Eburones, including their allies. The Belgae of the north thus accounted for more than half a million people, and the Belgae tribes as a whole (excluding the Treveri, who were Germans) for more than a million.

Their civilization was an advanced one. By way of the Rhone and Marseilles, and also via the land route to the Danube they themselves had constructed, they were in direct communication with Hellenic civilization. They coined Greek money and worshiped gods who had much in common with the Greco-Roman pantheon. They wore trousers and hooded coats; indeed, their dress was a great improvement on that of the Romans and much more practical, and its principles have been adopted by the whole modern world. Their boats, built with oaken beams, sailed the high seas and called regularly at English ports, which were then a market for their weapons and metal products.

They set up a big iron industry on the site of the present Hainaut coal field, using furnaces to smelt the metal needed for their forges.

Above all, however, they were warriors, and their reputation for bravery, mentioned in a famous passage in Caesar's *Commentaries*, is attested to by their adventurous history.

Before they came to Belgium, they had invaded, or passed through, almost the whole of Europe. They had even reached Asia Minor, where they founded a town called Belgites. Then, with the Gaesatae, who came from the Tongres district, they occupied Italy. Another of their armies invaded England, and there they set up a capital, Venta Belgarum, the modern Winchester. Later they colonized the southern part of the country around Southampton.

It was King Cunobelinus, ruler over the Belgae of southeastern England around the middle of the first century B.C., who became the Cymbeline of Shakespeare. But the clearest traces of the Belgae are to be found in Ireland. The Menapii and the Chauques gave their name to the county of Fermanagh, and many a Belgian warrior—called the *Fir-bolg* in Gaelic—became a figure in the early legends. To Ireland, too, the invaders took their iron swords and also the dreaded *gaesum*, a spear that was typically Belgian and was known in Gaelic as *gai-bolca*. It was so heavy that only Cuchulain, the greatest of the Irish heroes, could handle it, and even he would use it only against enemies he could not conquer with ordinary weapons. Because it had thirty barbed teeth, it could not be withdrawn from the wound it made, and the blow it struck was therefore mortal.

There was a striking similarity between the customs of the Belgae and those of the ancient Irish and Welsh. The Irish are well known for their fondness for conversation and a curiosity that leads them to congregate in fairs and market places. The Belgae had the same thirst for liberty that St. Patrick was to discover in Ireland when he landed there to convert the inhabitants to Christianity. Both were a gregarious, loquacious people given to boasting. In both traditions there are tales of epic challenges, of quarrels picked for the mere pleasure of fighting—expressions of a savage zest for independence.

The language of the Belgae was also very like that of the ancient Irish and Welsh: Most of the names of places and leaders are to be found in the Celtic languages, and they give us a lot of information about the existence of the ancient Belgians. The Morini, for example, were the "people of the sea," which was called *mor* in Welsh; Boduognat means "son of the crow," or de Bordh, the Celtic goddess of war. The Eburones, whom Caesar took for Germans, were the "people of the yew," or the Irish *Ibhar*. They considered the yew a sacred tree, because one of their chiefs, Catuvolcus (Cath-Folg, or "swift in combat") had poisoned himself with yew berries.

The name of the Belgae themselves comes from an old Celtic word meaning "swollen," while many names of places and rivers in Gaul, as in Germany, are of Celtic origin. The Rhine, for example, takes its name from a Celtic word meaning "sea," and the Ardennes comes from the Gaelic *ard*, meaning "high." The same applies to the names of towns, both in Belgium and in France. For example, the Celtic *béber*—"beaver"—is found in names such as Bièvre, Biesne, and Breuvain; *gabro*, "goat," in Gavre and Givry; and *marc*, "horse," in Marquain and Marcel. The Celts had two words for "house": *tig*, which gives us Tillemont, Tignes, and Tige; and *bonna*, which is found in Boulogne and Bonnain. Again, the word *dur*, "fortress," gives us Durbuy and may be the origin of the name Durand.

On the other hand, not a single name of any Belgian place or chieftain is of German origin. Some tribes, indeed, were wont to boast of having a common origin with the Germans, but this meant simply that they had come from beyond the Rhine in the period when Germania was part of Gaul. The very name Germany is Celtic, and it is a known fact that the Belgians originated in Hungary and Bavaria, where they left a number of place names in the local languages. Such, then, were the Belgae whom the armies of Rome found ranged before them in the early days of Caesar's campaigns in Gaul.

In about 56 B.C., Belgium was annexed to Rome after a lightning invasion. Caesar set out from Besançon, decimated the Remi of the Champagne country and, bypassing the Ardennes, invaded Belgium by crossing the Somme at Amiens and proceeding along the Schelde and the Sambre.

The Atrebates of the Artois and the Veromandui of the Oise offered no resistance. Instead, they sought the help of the Nervii, a powerful warrior race with many allies and subject peoples, who controlled a strategically important area. Their chief, Boduognat, gathered his forces and succeeded in taking Caesar by surprise. They fought a battle on the Selle, near Solesmes (Cambrai), on the plateau that contains the sources of the Schelde, the Sambre, the Somme, and the Oise, and which is the strategic key to Belgium and northern France.

It was a mass attack, launched suddenly and with consummate skill. On the slopes of a hill that today carries the sinister name of Mortmont—Mount Death—the Nervii came out of hiding from the woods and caught the Roman army on the march. They thrust into the line of the marching troops before they had time to deploy in battle formation, and Caesar himself had to rush into the field to stay the flying legionaries and restore order, fighting in the ranks of his own army as a common soldier. The tide of battle turned, but the Nervii stayed in the field to be killed to the last man, catching javelins that had missed their mark in mid-air. Caesar himself paid tribute to their bravery, saying: "Of all the peoples of Gaul, the Belgae are the bravest."

The defeat, however, had sealed the lot of Belgium. The Antuatuci, in the Namur region, had not been able to take part in the fight, and now they retreated to their fortress until the Roman siege forced them to surrender. As a warning to the other Belgian tribes, they were reduced to slavery, and soon after all the tribes, except the Menapii and the Morini, surrendered. The Menapii and Morini were not conquered until a year later.

In 54 B.C., Ambiorix, chief of the Limbourg Eburones and a friend and ally of Rome, made a compact with Induciomar, King of the Treveri, for joint attack on the Roman legions. The Roman generals Sabinus and Cotta were slain in ambush, and one and a half legions were wiped out. The next clash occurred near Binche, where Ambiorix fell on the camp of Quintus Cicero. He might have scored yet another victory had not Caesar come up with reinforcements, beaten off the attack, and forced Induciomar to flee westward. Crossing the Meuse, Induciomar was killed, and Ambiorix, beaten, had to take refuge in Germany.

The Romans now held complete sway throughout Belgian Gaul. So strong was their hold that, two years later, the Belgae did not even take part in the abortive revolt led by Vercingetorix.

The Romans let the conquered inhabitants govern themselves and made no changes in their political organization. However, they gave the name of "cities" to the Belgian tribes, each such city being named after its chief center.

In the minds of the ancients, a country was always identified with a town, and no wider system of government than that of a town had been evolved. Thus Plato, telling of his imaginary Atlantis, could only describe it as a city. The Belgae had thirty-five cities, each divided into districts, or *pagi*.

In every region there was a chief town, which served as a marketing center. The population, however, was very sparse, so that even villages were rare, and the inhabitants lived in isolated farms or on large estates. The chief towns had the privilege of self-government, and each town had its own local magistrates who were always elected by twos: two duumvirs, who acted as mayor and judge, and two aediles, who were in charge of police organization and public works. These magistrates were elected by a popular assembly, the comitia, and assisted by an order of decurions, which was a sort of municipal council. They were not remunerated for their work and, moreover, they had to pay for all the things the city itself was unable to finance—games and festivals, ceremonies, and public monuments. None but the rich, therefore, could accept office.

On the other hand, officeholders were granted substantial honors, recognized even in Rome, such as the title of senator or pontiff, or religious appointments; and they often held the same office in several towns simultaneously. A case is known of a Tongres councilor who also held the same position in a town in Hungary; and of a duumvir at Thérouanne, in the country of the Morini, who was at the same time a priest of Rome and of Augustus. The districts had the same elected magistrates as the cities. The local administration was reinforced at the upper levels by a central administration made up of Roman civil servants; and the whole of Belgium was subject to a government with headquarters at Reims. This government encompassed offices dealing with supervision of local authorities, the execution of major public works, the maintenance of roads and bridges, and many other administrative functions.

Only taxation was in the hands of an imperial procurator. His office was at Trèves and his job consisted essentially of preparing the census, which was taken every fifteen years and formed the basis for taxation. Each census was a major undertaking, for upon its results depended taxes for years to come, and the taxpayer had to report for census purposes in his native city. This system prevailed throughout the Roman world, and that is why Jesus of Nazareth was born in Bethlehem. Since very large interests were affected by the census, it was often the practice to put it in the hands of a high-ranking personage, perhaps even a member of the imperial family, as a guarantee of impartiality. The census dealt not only with people, but also with land rights and estates. It was a project that kept a large number of civil servants busy for several years, and it had to be prepared well in advance.

The taxes paid by the Belgians included a turnover tax of 1 per cent on all sales and commercial transactions; a 5 per cent levy on exemptions and inheritances in indirect succession; a general customs duty of 2.5 per cent; and a number of other variable taxes. There were also a number of local levies, and in time the taxation burden weighed increasingly heavily upon the population.

The Belgians also paid a heavy tribute in the form of military service. Unlike other peoples of the Roman Empire, they enjoyed bearing arms and large numbers served in the Roman armies. When Agricola set out for the conquest of England, his armies included seven cohorts of Nervii, one of Menapii, one of Morini, two double cohorts from

Tongres, and others from Condroz and other Belgian districts. More-over, the Roman armies in Germania had a cohort of Belgae, and there was another that was partly Belgian in Dalmatia.

Some of the Belgian officers rose to high rank in the Roman army, and there were also many Belgians in the Imperial Guard, including Stausius, who killed the Emperor Pertinax in 193 A.D. There are inscriptions telling of the exploits of Belgian soldiers on the Rhine, in Italy, in Brittany, on the Danube, and even in Cirenaica and Egypt. During the campaign in Germany, two Nervii, Chumstinctus and Avectius, distinguished themselves and earned a mention in Livy's *History of Rome.* The Menapian Carausius built an empire in England in the third century. Postumus, the Gaulish emperor, was without doubt one of the Atrebates; Maxinthius (350–353), emperor of Rome, probably came from Amiens. Many Belgians also became gladiators and earned distinction in circus combat. Among these was Mirmillon, the man-fish of Tongres, whose name has come down to us from a Roman inscription, and who vanquished all who ventured to fight against him.

The products of Belgian agriculture were appreciated in Rome, despite distance and difficulty of transport. Pliny was appreciative of the asparagus, the pipless apples, and the three-colored cherries from Belgium. The enormous hams from the Menapian country were so popular that in the time of Diocletian their maximum price in Rome had to be fixed at 10 deniers a pound. Latin authors describe to us the long flocks of Morin geese that marched to Italy across Gaul, the tired geese being carefully put at the head of the procession so that they could be pushed forward by the less exhausted geese behind. The Romans, incidentally, ate no part of the goose except the liver—the *foie gras* of future years. They would, however, pluck its feathers twice a year to get at the down; and the legionaries, when they yearned for comfortable pillows, would leave their camp to chase the geese.

The Morini also raised pigs that were so large and so fleet of foot that they could frighten away wolves, and no stranger could come near them save at great peril.

Salt, which the Belgians obtained by a method of pouring sea water over hot bricks, enabled them to manufacture various types of preserved food as well, which were imported into Rome in large quantities. Hunting was another Belgian industry and, according to Pliny, the Ardennes forests contained not only boar and deer, but also bears, which have since disappeared. The ancient Belgians trapped thrushes, a practice still popular in present-day Belgium.

They were also fond of oysters, and the coastal fishermen who caught them shipped them as far inland as Alsace and Switzerland, where their shells have been found.

By all appearances, the Belgians of those days led an intensely active economic life. There was a great demand for grain by the Roman army of the Rhine and Germany, and crops from the rich soil of Hainaut, the Hesbaye, and Condroz were brought in by Belgian merchants and shipped down the Meuse into Holland by Belgian sailors.

These cargoes came to Fectio (or Vechten), near Utrecht, where commercial convoys would meet the vessels carrying Nervian grain by way of the Schelde; together they would move up the Rhine as far as Cologne, where the Nervian merchants had their warehouses. The mariners of the Belgian coast carried their trade into England and were well known in London. The metal industry of Hainaut provided weapons and tools, and Flanders and the Artois region sold their cloth; indeed, in the third century, piecegoods from Arras sold in Rome as luxury items, and the prices listed for them by Diocletian were very high. It is probable that in this period, textiles were the exchange cargo for the Jewish and Syrian merchants who brought the products of the East to Belgium. Goods manufactured in the Entre-Sambre-et-Meuse country included clasps, brooches, and other enameled jewelry.

Belgian trade was not confined to the export of local products, but derived large profits from re-exports and the transit trade, because the route between Germany and England passed across Belgian territory. It enabled traders to avoid the Rhine estuary and shortened the route to the port of Itium, near Boulogne, which had been built by Caesar. London, as a result, became a meeting place of Europe's merchants, and English goods found their way across Belgium. Another route, between Tongres and Fectio, also led to Cologne by way of the Rhine and was the main waterway for the distribution of Belgian agricultural produce.

The importance of Belgian industry, however, was even greater than that of her trade. The textile industry was expanding at Tournai and in the Artois,* and the Belgian metal industry was centered in Wallonia. The Nervii had always been metallurgists, and under Roman rule the industry was expanded and developed. Over a hundred ore bodies were worked to serve the forges and foundries of the Nervii. In the days of Belgian independence, their armor and chariots had been sold as far afield as the Balkans. Now they became suppliers of weapons and tools to the Roman legions, and for five centuries their production of ironware was so great that the waste dumps of the furnace

---

* The Artois, a region of north-central France, was closely linked to life in Belgium until the seventeenth century.

residues were positively mountainous. In the nineteenth century, indeed, it occurred to Belgian iron masters that the slag heaps of the Roman period might still be valuable; and for twenty-five years, from 1860 to 1885, more than a million tons from these dumps was processed in the blast furnaces of the Charleroi neighborhood.

Other industries that throve in the Roman period were glass and ceramics. Belgian potters were able to compete with Italian craftsmen, and the transparent glassware of Cologne (a city then considered Belgian) was found to be vastly superior to the Roman glass vases, employing a creative technique that had no equal. Fine wool cloth of many colors made by the Morin textile industry sold in all parts of the empire, and the textiles of Arras were prized in the elegant world of Rome and Byzantium. The hooded mantles of the Nervii, at once luxurious and practical, gained such renown that attempts to imitate them were made as far afield as Phrygia, particularly in the town of Leodicea. Morin linen and the army uniforms of Tournai helped to spread the fame of those textile products that were to be the fortune of Belgium until our own times.

The improved roads were the main instrument of this prosperity, for Rome's outstanding gift to Gaul had been an organized transport system. The Roman Belgium, like medieval France, was a network of roads between the many camps and strongholds. These roads were all built on the same principle: The foundation consisted of stone blocks, big pebbles, or beams, which were laid to ballast it firmly. Next came a layer of smaller pebbles to spread the load evenly; and finally a surface either of stone slabs or cemented materials, on which the traffic ran. On both sides of the carriageway there was a ditch for drainage purposes. In most cases the soil had been compacted by an earlier roadway, which made the work easier.

The Romans made their roads as straight as possible—not too difficult a feat in a sparsely populated country. The builders also did their best to economize in expensive structural works, such as bridges, viaducts, and embankments.

On the other hand, engineers did not hesitate to build the roads suspended along hillsides on wooden girders and traverses fixed to the rock. Traces of such a road have been found at Leffe in the Meuse valley; its course can be traced by the notches and grooves carved in the rock to support the girders. It is a known fact that one of these roads, the famous Via Mala in the Alps, was still in existence and carrying traffic until the seventeenth century.

The hallmark of the Roman road system was not only solid construction, but also the considerable organization centered on it, including posting inns, guardhouses, and the maintenance service.

Roman roads, like those of Persia in olden times, were planned less for the transportation of goods than as posting roads, enabling orders and messages to be carried with astonishing speed. The one thing that counted was speed of communication, and everything was sacrificed to this.

There were provisions for changing horses every nine miles, and there was a *mansio*, or hostel—with sleeping quarters, stables, and spare chariots—every twenty or twenty-five miles. A huge staff of postmasters, messengers, guards, roadworkers, and others lived at the various stops, and as a result a number of townships were formed around them. Couriers and high officials on urgent missions could cover the ground at the almost incredible speed of 185 miles a day. When the Emperor Tiberius left Mainz to see his brother Drusus, who was dying, he was able to average 175 miles per day, using the posting services.

The fact is that these roads, which impress us by their solidity and by the cost of their construction and upkeep and some of which were to remain in use for a thousand years, were built primarily to keep Rome in constant contact with all points of the empire, while trade was carried mainly by river.

River transport was very advanced, and the waterway sailors, or *nautes*, played an important part. The Romans set to work maintaining and canalizing the rivers; and in Belgium, the tributaries of the Meuse linked with those of the Rhine by a canal 15 or 20 miles long as early as 47 B.C. Another important waterway project linking the Moselle and the Saône was also considered.

The traffic on the roads, however, was very small. Horses were as yet unshod, so that they could not be used to pull heavy vehicles on stony roads. Moreover, the Roman horse was harnessed by the neck rather than by the shoulders, so that he could not pull a total of more than 5 or 6 hundredweight.

The annexation of Belgium to Rome created a new way of life, that of the Gallo-Roman town. Before the Roman conquest, the inhabitants had been country dwellers, and their few urban centers were little more than fortresses, fairgrounds, and market places. The new Belgo-Roman cities, such as Tongres, Arlon, Namur, and Tournai, constituted an economic and social system that Romanized the population and had far-reaching effects on their customs and way of life.

Namur is a good example. It reproduced many features of Italian towns, with the forum in the center of town constituting a market place and surrounded by public buildings and shopping centers. Several of the chief roads ran into the forum, and here the wealthy built their dwellings. The countryside around Namur was dotted with huts and cottages of wood or pisé, roofed with the fine red tiles the Romans used everywhere and fragments of which are still found in the soil. It was populated with smallholders, not unlike those of the Middle Ages. In the center of the cemetery stood a dolmen, which remained there until 1820. It is probable that this was a holy place of ancient Gaul that remained popular even under the Roman emperors.

The Roman city in Namur lay along the banks of the Meuse and the Sambre, at the foot of Le Champeau, the fortified hill where the citadel stands today. The discovery of tens of thousands of Gallo-Roman coins on the banks of the Sambre points to the existence of a bridge or a ford, for it was the custom of the ancients, when they crossed a river, to ensure against the dangers of the crossing by throwing a small piece of money into the water to appease the wrath of invisible powers. During the nineteenth century, these pieces of money were found in the gravel of the Sambre bed in such quantities that the inhabitants were able to sell them to antiquarians by weight or even by the pint; those that were too worn to be of interest to scientists were melted down to make candlesticks. They were found in continuous layers, dating from 48 B.C. until 518 A.D. in the Merovingian period. During these six centuries, every traveler seems to have made an offering to the river gods; had they all been counted, it would be possible to make an exact estimate of the volume of traffic.

The town of Tongres in the Limbourg, the ancient capital of the Eburoni, was a fortified city, one of the main Roman bases for the defense of Belgium. The foundations of its walls, two-thirds of which are still standing, defined a perimeter of 4,700 yards; these walls themselves were sunk 5 yards deep into shifting soil, a construction feat requiring the driving of fourteen oak piles per yard of wall. In other places the foundations consisted of sandstone blocks that were brought from the valley of the Ourthe in the Ardennes foothills. Around the wall, at 100-yard intervals, were circular towers, 33 feet in diameter—colossal structures linked by a double moat of V-shaped sections.

Tongres, like Namur, had its forum, its temples, its theater, and its arenas, but today they are buried beneath the modern city. Only the outer walls have remained, for they were built of the famous Roman cement, a mixture of mortar and pebbles that has become hard and indestructible with time.

Though digging has not been easy, the city has proved a mine of ancient treasures. From the Renaissance on, an incalculable quantity of coins, jewelry, bronzes, pottery, and brass has been brought to light, and has found its way all over Europe. During the eighteenth century, the Tongres antiquaries, by then a rich and powerful corporation, were doing a big business with the antiquaries of England, whom they were inundating with Roman remains and art works.

At the other end of Belgium was Tournai, a Roman city of some forty acres, with its aqueducts, its city wall, and its public buildings, built of brick on foundations of blue stone and faced with valuable stucco or marble.

Tournai commands an important bridge over the Schelde, and this was part of the great road between Tongres and Boulogne. The city's name was evidently derived from Turnus, a great Roman landowner. A number of large cemeteries have been found, including one under the market place, and the tombs date from all the periods that have been studied.

The pottery unearthed at Tournai comes from far afield: from the Rhineland, from Provence, and even from Italy. Here, too, have been found millstone fragments of red sandstone, imported from the southern part of Gaul, which point to the existence of large grain mills. And a first-century limekiln, found in the middle of Tournai, proves that the Belgo-Romans were already aware of the properties of the famous blue stone of Tournai, which can be used alike for the construction of strong buildings and for producing hydraulic lime under the influence of heat. Tournai also was the home of workshops that, until the fifth century, manufactured military uniforms and were the progenitors of the future Flemish cloth industry.

Another important Roman town—or at least road junction—in the extreme south of Belgium was Arlon, where the Tongres road intersected the highway from Reims to Treves. It was called Orolaunum Vicus, and its fortification wall was oval in shape and about 10 feet thick. The turrets around the wall projected inward instead of outward, and many fine works of art have been found in the foundation material.

In a cemetery at Arlon dating back to the Antonines were found the best Roman sculptures in Belgium; the bas-reliefs on the tombs depicted not only the usual naked youths, but also many peasants wearing the garb of their time—the Gaulish hooded mantle, which was to remain in use until the nineteenth century—and the reliefs show them caught, as it were, in the midst of their daily tasks.

A little south of Arlon, still in the land of the Treveri, the 1958 diggings at Buzenol yielded still more exciting discoveries. Here, amid defense works of several periods was a wall that had evidently been thrown up in haste. The builders had utilized, as an improvised measure, the cunningly carved stone blocks that itinerant sculptors had made for the roadside dwellings of the wealthy, by then fallen into disuse and disrepair. Here were lovers hand-in-hand, the serf settling his accounts with the steward of the villa, the farmers trotting their wagons to

market with the untrained horse learning the job beside his more experienced senior between the shafts.

Here, too, was a discovery of first importance; the lost half of an
unexplained fragment found at Arlon a century earlier. When their
kinship was recognized and the two pieces brought together, the
world had its first view—all but complete—of the first mechanical
harvester known to man. The elder Pliny had seen and described it
in this same country of the Treveri, but he died in 79 A.D., when Pom-
peii and Herculaneum were destroyed by a volcanic eruption, and no
relic or picture of this ingenious grain-harvesting method in a remote
part of Gaul has been preserved. Now, however, anyone may see the
patient ass (not the ox mentioned by Pliny) pushing the great chest
mounted on its two wheels; and behind the ass, between the same
shafts, the laborer whose job was to adjust the height of the big iron
comb at the front, designed to tear off the ears and sweep them into
the chest. And in front, to complete the picture, walked the worker
whose task it was to clean the teeth of the comb at every halt, to
prevent excessive clogging.

All over Belgium, the Gallo-Roman cemeteries and tombs have been
mines of artistic treasures. They provide us, too, with striking illustra-
tions of the beliefs and the customs of the people. In the early days
of the empire, cremation was still common practice, but even before
the rise of Christianity, burial of the dead became more and more
widespread. Articles of value and personal treasures, thought to be
useful to the deceased in another world, were buried with the bodies.
Often, too, pieces of money were put into the mouths of the dead,
payment for the fare Charon would charge for passage across the river
Styx, and the type and date of the coins give a clue to the date of
death. This practice, incidentally, is still followed in Rumania.

In addition to the money found in the tombs, there were beautiful
cameos, pieces of pottery, and examples of the gold and silver work,
which give us an idea of the wealth of the country during the first
and second centuries A.D. At Cortil-Noirmont in Brabant was found
a transparent white glass jug, with appliqué work in blue-and-gold
glass thread. This had been made in Cologne, a famous center for
glassware about the year 200. Another discovery, an amber shell
decorated with a capricorn, came from the workshops at Aquilea, near
Trieste. A perforated gold ring and a cameo of Augustus were found
at Tirlemont. Jewelry, it may be concluded, came from all over the
Roman world.

In many cases, mausoleums were erected, like the one at Igel, with
its bas-reliefs, pilasters, and pediments covered by a roof of overlapping
leaves. The bas-reliefs are sometimes portraits and sometimes scenes

from everyday life; they often show the life and work of the departed. There are scenes of vessels being loaded with great bales of merchandise and casks of wine; others are of work in the fields with people digging, forking the ungathered harvest, pulling carts of different types, and weighing the produce as it is brought in. In one of the tombs at Hern Saint Hubert was found the complete working equipment of a painter.

In many cases, the art treasures found, such as the Tirlemont Mercury, the Courtrai Venus, and the Bree Jupiter, probably came from Italy. The discovery of such masterpieces testifies to the unity of Roman culture and the important role of transportation.

The cemeteries and their inscriptions make it possible for us to reconstruct the life of the inhabitants in the Belgo-Roman towns. At Namur, for example, were found the tombs of a number of Belgians of the second century A.D. whose names are both Latin and Gaulish. One of them was called Victor, and his second son Victorius Victorinus; his elder son, whose name was Acceptus, was married to a German whose name was still a barbarian one, Amma.

Victorius was a Roman citizen because he had served in the army, and an assignment as personal assistant to a member of the high command had given him the right of citizenship. His brother Acceptus had remained a Gaul, but most other notables had acquired Roman citizenship. Among the latter were Cassius Pompinus and his son Titus, but Titus had married a lady who still bore the Gaulish name Matta.

Another, Securinus Ammius, lived at the time of Trajan. We know this because his wife, who was of barbarian origin, had taken the name of Ulpia; this name dates from that period and was, in fact, one of the names of Emperor Trajan himself and, as such, was adopted by foreigners who became Roman citizens.

The Securinus family had their favorite slave, Madicua Delicata, buried with them. Her name indicates that she was a barbarian whom they had bought while she was still young. She had been one of the children whom the Romans made a habit of bringing up in their own households, much as we raise puppies and kittens. When they were grown up they were usually sent home, but the Securinus family had evidently become attached to Madicua and kept her with them.

In the cemeteries were found the graves of a number of freed men, slaves, and unenslaved freemen whose names are in some cases Gaulish, though Roman names are somewhat more frequent. The Gaulish Ruso was buried with his son Haldaco and his grandchildren who, however, had the Roman names Victor and Prudens. By this time, about the beginning of the second century A.D., the work of assimilation must have been completed, and no doubt the Latin tongue was replacing the ancient dialects of Gaul.

The habits and customs of the Belgo-Romans of the second century were very different from those of their descendants eighteen centuries later. When it came to food they knew nothing of many of those dishes which are the very foundation of the modern kitchen. They had neither green peas, artichokes, tomatoes, nor beans. In place of the potato, the Romans had only the eggplant and chick-pea. Spirits were nonexistent, and the only alcoholic beverage they knew was wine, either sweet or not so sweet, sometimes flavored with mint.

The women and the more refined men would blow their noses with their fingers. The Belgo-Roman's defense against the cold was not the fireplace or stove, but the hot bath. His means of transport were rudimentary, and it was difficult to bring great quantities of timber or peat into town, so that the ancients were unable to use modern methods of warming themselves. All they had were little portable stoves, not unlike the braziers of today, and it was one of these open stoves that nearly asphyxiated the Emperor Julian. Roman central heating is one of those legends that dies hard.

In most of the big Gallo-Roman villas, there was one room heated by a special device—a double floor of masonry, which served as a chimney for a fire that was lit in the cellar. The hot air, after passing through this space, was expelled through vents in the walls. The room could thus be kept hot enough to serve as a steam room.

There is a certain similarity between these hot-air pipes and those of modern central heating, and this was long believed to indicate that central heating was known to the Romans. This is not the case. In general, the rooms in question were a kind of Turkish bath. They became popular, and after the fall of the empire the Byzantines and the North Africans began to use them and it was they who introduced these chambers to Constantinople. They continued to be used in France throughout the Middle Ages after the crusades, and it was only at the time of the Renaissance that they disappeared.

The Roman cities and towns, however, were only a small part of the Belgium of that period. The majority of the population lived in the country and gained its livelihood from the great rural estates known as villas, in which the life of the people was concentrated.

As many as a thousand peasants lived in each of these villas under the authority of a big landowner. The villa produced almost everything necessary for the sustenance of its inhabitants, who therefore lived completely isolated from the inhabitants of neighboring estates.

The villa was thus a complete economic unit and formed the social cell of the period. (The village, which plays the same part today, did not yet exist.) The villa was a mixed unit including arable land, woods, pasture, kitchen gardens, and workshops grouped around a central building. The latter was a sort of country house and served as residence for the landowner, his family, and his servants. It usually had a long façade and a covered gallery for protection from the rain. At each corner were the wings, forming a courtyard for the various dependencies, such as stables, barns, workshops, and servants' quarters.

In some cases the villa was built as a completely closed cloister, with a big interior court surrounded by a colonnaded walk. The vaulted cellars were large and well stocked, for it was there that provisions were stored for the large population of the villa.

The villa of a rich landowner would usually be decorated with marbles, statues, works of art, and other decorations, which would be placed around the swimming pool and ponds. The statuary and works of art were usually imported from distant countries, perhaps from Italy, or sometimes from North Africa.

The villas comprised not only agricultural buildings, but also bakeries, breweries, wine presses, forges, workshops, and even factories for the manufacture of clothing and sometimes of luxury goods for the inhabitants and also for export to other estates. Each villa, too, was a miniature town, in which every man had his special job and mastered a special skill, such as woodcutting, sheep herding, beekeeping, or masonry.

As a rule, they were built away from the road on a hilltop, or near a spring, the source of drinking water for the inhabitants.

The property was self-contained and self-sufficient. The villa building itself was always centrally located, and the site chosen for it invariably was the best available for overseeing the land and its inhabitants.

The system of big estates served as a powerful instrument for Romanization. Here were servants, tenants, Roman colonizers, immigrant slaves, artisans, and workmen, all speaking different languages and dialects, but all obliged to use Latin as their common tongue—which made it the lingua franca of business and organized life.

Wherever the villa system took root, the population became Roman in language and culture, and neither immigration nor barbarian invasion succeeded in making inroads upon it. The Germanization of the Flemish region may be ascribed to its lack of large estates. Flanders contains neither ruins nor place names like Werlee, Villers, or Ville (which clearly point to the previous existence of villas), nor even names like Mezieres (from the Latin *maceries*—"materials or ruins") current in a later era.

Traces of 400 villas have been found in Belgium. These 400 villas housed practically all the Gallo-Roman population, and it can consequently be concluded that Roman Belgium was ruled by 400 families of landed proprietors upon whom the rest of the population—tenant farmers, colonists, or slaves—was dependent, for the great landowner was the only source of food, organization, and instruction. In time of famine it was from his store that reserves of food would be doled out.

After the great cataclysm of the third century, the last of the free peasantry and independent small landowners gave up their holdings in exchange for the protection of a rich lord. They were, however, given the right to cultivate their lands in perpetuity, subject to a contract of serfdom.

The rural estate was thus to remain the foundation of social life until modern times. It was a society of self-sufficient units, independent of social changes and thus able to resist the destruction that befell the towns at the time of the barbarian invasions. It was a form of organization that spread little by little through the whole of Belgian Gaul, and it was to last until the end of the Middle Ages, and thus almost to our own times.

II

THE DECAY OF ROMAN CIVILIZATION

Christianity was known in Belgium as early as the second century A.D. Irénée of Lyons mentions the presence of Christians in Germania Secunda, the administrative center in the eastern part of Belgium. The first Christian apostles went to the valley of the Rhine and to Holland to combat the Celtic worship of fairies, the Germanic matriarchy, and the goddess Nehalennia.

After 250 A.D., cremation ceased to be practiced, and the dead, even those who were not Christians, were buried in coffins along with their movable effects and personal treasures. Christian emblems were now beginning to appear on pottery, dishes, and glassware.

The first bishop of the Rhineland and Belgium was St. Materne, and his successor (346 A.D.) was St. Servais (Serbatios), Bishop of Tongres. St. Servais was a native of Palestine, so evidently the Christian community in Belgium had not yet become large enough to provide its own priests. His red coat, golden cross, and ivory crook are still displayed in Maastricht. He was present at the synods of Sardis and Rimini (359 A.D.).

During that time, the Frankish population had been moved into the Kempen country at the behest of the Emperor Julian, and it is said that it was St. Servais who transferred the headquarters of his bishopric from Tongres to Maastricht, because its location on the river Meuse facilitated communications.

The Gallo-Roman population had already been forced to evacuate the Rhineland, and in the same period, the present territory of Belgian Flanders was being slowly colonized by the Germanic peoples, who set to work to cultivate the sandy marshy soil. It was in this

29

territory that they made their homes, either as prisoners of war or as soldiers and allies of Rome.

This occupation played an important part in the history of Belgium. Thus, even today, two distinct races, the Flemings and the Walloons, are to be found in Belgium. They are separated by a linguistic frontier that runs straight as a die from Dunkirk to Aachen.

The existence of such a frontier could easily be understood had it been defined by natural obstacles, but in fact the line runs across the free and open plain and, therefore, is one of the enigmas of history. One explanation advanced is the existence of a forest that has since disappeared, the so-called coal forest, which might have halted the infiltration of the Germanic population. This forest, however, stretched from north to south and would not have been an obstacle. Another suggestion is that the frontier was defined by a line of fortifications through which the invaders could not penetrate. However, no trace of this has been found.

It seems, indeed, that the Germanic population infiltrated Belgium peacefully rather than by armed invasion. Their progress into the country seems to have stopped at the point where the existing population was dense. The Germanic immigrants were content to occupy the desert land that had been left unsettled, but they were not able to submerge the highly organized populations concentrated in the Belgian uplands. Thus Wallonia took shape.

Even when the Germanic invaders were most pressing, about 410 A.D., active local chieftains would come to the fore as defenders of the Walloon population. The chieftains were sometimes bishops, sometimes important landlords or civil servants high in the Roman hierarchy. As a result, even when the Walloons were overrun by the Franks, as they had been at Tournai and at Cambrai, the occupation did not take root.

This is the probable explanation of the origin of the Belgian linguistic frontier. It may well be that the same phenomenon occurred in France, defining the line from La Rochelle to Geneva that separates the *langue d'oil* from the *langue d'oc* and bisects the country with the same precision.

The Franks who found their way into Belgium became the ancestors of the Flemings. They were Germanic tribesmen, closely resembling the ancient Gauls in their civilization and way of life, sharing with them many of their beliefs. Their civilization and culture was less advanced than that of the Romans, but it would be wrong to think of them as barbarians.

The Germanic gods had much in common with the Greek pantheon.

Thor, the god of thunder, played the same part as Jupiter; Woden, father of the gods, resembled Saturn; Zin, the symbol of the luminous heaven, approximated Phoebus Apollo; Freya, the goddess of spring, and the other Germanic gods had similar origins and performed the same functions as their Roman counterparts.

The Franks, like the Romans, named the days of the week after their gods, and these names exist today in the Dutch names—*Vrijdag*, or Friday, is the day of Freya; *Woensdag*, or Wednesday, of the god Woden; and *Dondersdag* is Thursday, or the day of Thor.

The towns and villages that they established are for the most part named after tribal chiefs, with the suffix *ghem*, which means "home," or *zele* or *sele*, which means "house." Audergem and Ixelles are examples of this practice.

Contrary to general belief, ethnographic studies show no important physical differences between the Walloons, who are descended from the Gallo-Romans, and the Flemings, whose origin is Germanic. It is easy enough to image the Germans as a blond, blue-eyed race, and the Latins as small, dark, and brown-eyed. In fact, the descendants of the Germanic tribes—the Germans of the Rhineland, the Dutch of the Rhine-Schelde estuaries, and the Flemings of Flanders—can be almost equally divided into fair- and dark-haired types. This is also true of the Walloons and the northern French, among whom the proportion of blue eyes and fair hair is almost as large.

In broad terms, there is only a single human type in the area between the Seine and the Rhine, and the fair-haired and blue-eyed population groups are equally frequent in countries where Romance and Germanic languages are spoken. In northern France, Wallonia, or Flanders, 60 per cent of the people are blue eyed and 40 per cent brown eyed. The highest proportion of black-eyed, brown-haired men is not in Wallonia but in Flanders, in the neighborhood of Zottegem. For Belgium as a whole, the proportion of blonds is reasonably constant—between 58 and 66 per cent—without showing any real distinction between Flanders and Wallonia. To speak of racial differences in this connection is pointless. The difference between these populations is not one of physique, but one of language.

Languages, too, have not been unchanging, for Dutch was long the language of the northern French near Lille, Dunkirk, and Calais; and the people of French Lorraine, whose origin is purely Germanic, spoke German through the Middle Ages, gradually adopting French as their tongue. In Wallonia, too, a number of Germanic colonies were progressively absorbed. This is seen in the Frankish etymology of many place names.

Around 400–10, A.D., there occurred an upheaval that was to mark the dislocation of the Roman Empire. Rome was sacked by the troops of Alaric, in 410, and the frontier armies were recalled to Italy, leaving the Gaulish populations undefended. Some time afterward (430–45), Clodion, a petty chief of the Franks, seized Tournai and the surrounding country. However, both he and his son Meroveus remained in the service of Rome.

Childeric, the son of Meroveus, reigned in Tournai over a tribe known as the Sicambri. He was a mercenary in Roman service. His body was discovered in 1653, encased in gold and lying in a tomb where it had been buried with his war horse. A mantle embroidered with golden bees covered him, and he was surrounded by a treasure of rich Byzantine jewels, swords, and rings, in which his name was carved in Latin—his preferred language—because he had regarded his domain as a part of the Empire. His son Clovis was a bold warrior who, with a tiny army of only 6,000 men, was able to subdue the whole of Gaul in 481.

The Franks of Tournai, like their compatriots, were warriors of renown. They wore no helmets or armor, but they were so swift in action that they were said to fall upon the enemy before their own hurled javelins had reached him. They were armed with a short-handled throwing axe, the *francisc*, which never missed its mark; a broad-headed spear, the *framea*; and a simple shield of reeds. Their hair was red or dyed, and worn knotted at the top of the head—except for the king, whose hair blew free as he was carried high on a shield known as the *pavise*. Every year, picked bands of warriors went forth to pillage. It was their practice to hold a general meeting at which plans were discussed, although, with such armed troops at his command, the king could use force or diplomacy to control the outcome of the deliberations.

All we know of Clovis comes to us through a legend. It is indeed a legend that he was called Clovis, for this name does not appear until the seventeenth century, in the days of Louis XIII. His name was Chlodovech, which is Germanic for "famous battle." It is a legend that his conversion to Christianity was the result of a vow, taken during a battle at Tolbiac against the Alemmani, and just as legendary is his piety, for there was no crime from which he recoiled. The bishops, however, were to throw a chaste veil over his misdeeds. "Much must be forgiven to one who became a propagator of the true faith," was the frank admission of St. Remi.

Clovis was the first barbarian chief to be converted to Christianity, the others having been either Aryans or pagans. It is also probably a legend that St. Remi, when he baptized Clovis at Reims on Christmas day 496 A.D., said: "Bow your head, proud Sicambrian; adore what you have burnt and burn what you have adored." What he probably said was *Depone collam*—"Take off your necklace." This meant "Remove your pagan amulets." The legendary version stems from the translator's error. It is also a legend that the Franks became Christians with Clovis. The great majority of them were still pagans, but this takes nothing from the importance of the alliance between their chief and the Christian church.

Driven by the bishops upon whose support he counted, Clovis gained control of almost the whole of Gaul. Then he transferred his capital from Tournai to Paris. However, he always needed more soldiers, and the only place to find them was among the Franks; in his quest he sought to subdue the tribes in Belgium and the Rhineland by dethroning their chieftains or having them assassinated.

Politically the Frankish state was still organized on Roman lines. There was only one governing class, known as the *Leudes*, composed of the soldiers of Clovis, their chiefs, and the aristocracy formed by the great Gallo-Roman landowners. They were an elite who dressed in rich, Byzantine materials, or in white Dalmatian silk, and they wore jewelry with enormous stones and scarlet cloaks fringed with gold. The kings adopted Roman titles and made Latin their official tongue, while the Gallo-Roman civil servants carried the same titles as their predecessors had, in the days of the empire—referees and councilors—although the Franks who served with them carried new titles—such as constable, marshal, and seneschal—which were to remain in use until the Middle Ages.

The trusted servants of the king, known as the antrustions (Latin, *trustii*), rubbed shoulders at court with the Gallo-Romans who were the "fellow guests." Clovis had the title of Patrician, meaning representative of the Emperor in Gaul, and his successors conferred on themselves the Roman title of Sublimity.

Since the Merovingian world was a Byzantine one, all the ceremonies of the court were Byzantine. All the fashions and customs came from Byzantium, and the civilization of Belgium during the seventh century was Oriental in character. In those times camels walked in the streets, and dates and other fruits of the East were on every table. Silks came from Syria, and even from China, by way of Persia or the Indian Ocean; and here, too, was jewelry, goldsmiths' work, and enamel —everything colored by the sun of Byzantium or the Mediterranean.

Clothing was still of the Roman type, with pleated tunics—the chlamys, pallium, and toga—although all the fashions came from Byzantium, originating at the court of Constantinople. The Frankish and Gallo-Roman aristocracy was busy imitating the fabulous luxury of the basileus, as were their equivalents in Italy, Spain, and North

Africa. The Roman Empire was maintaining its customs and its way of life because of the strength of its economic links.

From Byzantium shone what was left of the sun of civilization, but this Byzantine world was one which had reached its peak; and for nearly 500 years its life and customs did not change.

There is something baffling about this fixity. Nowadays we are accustomed to habits and fashions that are perpetually changing. For example, we can scarcely imagine men today wearing the clothes of Louis XIV, or women in the crinolines of the Second Empire, although these eras are not too remote.

Under the Merovingian kings and their successors, however, habits and fashions were to remain unchanged for a full 500 years. In architecture, furniture, decoration, even in the harnessing of horses, nothing changed. Clovis and Charlemagne lived several centuries apart, but they wore identical clothes. It was only in weapons and military uniforms that the barbarians produced anything new, and even these innovations were to disappear quickly. Merovingian civilization was not only barbaric, but ossified. Progress was so slow that it can hardly be said to have been made.

Life in Belgium during this period was primitive. The peasants gained their sole livelihood from hunting, fishing, and tilling the fields. They lived in thatched wooden houses, often built on raised piles.

Young girls wore their hair loose, but married women wove it into plaits, worn hidden under a soft cap known as the pittus. Men were still dressed in the Roman manner, in a short tunic and breeches that left their knees bare, similar to the trousers of the Bavarian and Tyrolese peasants of today. For hose they wound puttees of wool or linen over the calf and shin, but the wealthy and aristocratic still wore traditional Roman dress.

The people already had tame falcons and well-trained dogs, and even domesticated stags that served as bait for the capture of others. The dogs included hounds and watchdogs; and the horses were grouped into hacks, cart horses, and general workers. Belgians of this time knew the art of poisoning arrows (forgotten during the Middle Ages), and they dug wells and built bread ovens around their houses.

Ritual and symbolism permeated their customs. A thief coming up for judgment had to appear before the court with the stolen goods on his back. A landowner selling a field brought along a piece of soil and presented it to the purchaser. If he sold a coppice, he had to give a freshly cut bough. And the seller of a house had to produce a piece of wood and swear before the judge that he wished to exercise no further rights over it.

There were few workers and tenant farmers and forests fetched much better prices than arable land—1,000 gold sous for wooded land, compared with only 200 for a similar tract in the fields. The herds of geese of Augustan times were still extant, as were the sheep and pigs, and methods of cultivation had not changed. The merchants, towns, industry, and commercial organization of the Roman period had, however, disappeared. Religion had reverted to the pagan and primitive, and the region that today is Catholic Flanders worshiped wooden statues and tutelary spirits almost until the end of the Merovingian period. Conversion to Christianity was for many years to be only a matter of form rather than one of conviction.

The legal system marked the transformation of local customs most strongly. The Salic law had no doubt been drawn up at the end of the reign of Clovis as a guide for civil servants, and it was intended for the Franks, whose customs it embodied. But it was to continue in existence throughout the Middle Ages and formed the basis of most codes and legal systems. It is still of great interest because of the customs and ideas it reveals to the modern reader.

There was, for example, a uniform fine of 30 sous for the murder of a blacksmith, silversmith, vine grower, swineherd, or stableboy, for they were only slaves of little value. More serious, however, was the theft of the bag of a hunter or fisherman. This crime deserved a penalty of no less than 45 sous, while the theft of a slave, horse, or mare involved a fine of 30 sous—the same amount that was exacted for the murder of a man!

"If any person strike another on the head," the law said, "in such manner that the brain appear and that three bones of the skull come asunder, the fine shall be 30 sous." The same penalty was incurred by the criminal who squeezed the arm of a free woman, but he might take her hand for 15 sous, and her forearm below the elbow for 20 sous.

The theft of a falcon carried the high penalty of 45 sous, and the same fine was levied on anyone who stole a swarm of bees.

The legal system also discloses that domesticated stags were used as a lure or bait in hunting, because a high price was set on them if they served that purpose. If not, the forfeit was only 35 gold sous.

Although the penalty was only 30 sous for splitting a man's head or disemboweling him, it cost much more—100 sous—to cut off his hand, his foot, or his nose. The fine, however, was reduced to 63 sous if the extremity was not severed completely. The theft of vegetables was punishable by various fines, the sum being proportionate to the scarcity of each food. For beans, chick-peas, lentils, and turnips, the penalty was only 3 sous, while grapes and flax cost 15. Hay, an essential fodder, was prized above human life, at 45 sous. For the theft of building timber, the penalty was 15 sous; for fire wood, 3.

The value of human life varied according to age; the fine for the murder of a ten-year-old child, for example, was six times that of an adult. There was a carefully drawn table of charges for insults; the fine for the accusation of cowardice or of throwing away of a shield, for example, was 3 sous. Curses and spells were also regulated. A spell or poisoning cost 200 sous if the victim died, but only 3 if he survived.

Serious theft and crime carried smaller penalties than mere peccadilloes, and the scale of penalties was, indeed, founded on the frequency and social importance of the misdemeanors involved. It was natural enough that men should be killed from time to time among a warlike people who were swift to anger and given to brawls. On the other hand, causing the death of a child who endangered no one called for severe punishment. The high penalty for taking a lady's arm was inflicted to prevent a breach of the peace, for such an action might lead to a fatal quarrel with husband or family.

The most important section in the Salic law was Chapter LIX, which was later to be used as the pretext for the Hundred Years' War. It reads: "Land shall never pass by inheritance to a woman, but shall revert to the male sex, represented by the brothers." This clause was included because a woman was physically unable to cultivate the family land herself, and it therefore had to be handed on to the nearest male relative. The rule was applied throughout the Middle Ages to the inhabitants of feudal manors and properties. Later, a legal subtlety extended its application to the Crown of France, when the King of England laid claim to it as an inheritance from his mother.

The language of the Belgians at this time was Frankish, a primitive form of Dutch, which was the lingua franca as far afield as Paris and the Loire. Along with Latin, it was the idiom used by the upper classes. Charlemagne spoke only these two tongues and was altogether ignorant of the Romance or French dialects—not because of any hostility for Roman civilization or fondness for Germanic customs, but because Roman and French were no longer generally spoken. They were heard only in backward districts, used by the uneducated and isolated peasantry. During the reign of Charlemagne, a certain Adélard, who later won fame and riches, was first conspicuous because he understood these seldom-heard tongues.

Latin had become the language of the Church, and Frankish—the future Dutch—the language of administration. Frankish was spoken by politicians, civil servants, and soldiers, and a literature appeared, made up of epic songs that later produced the *chansons de geste*.

It was in the Belgian Ardennes, between the Meuse and the Moselle, that many of these songs had their origin. They include the songs of Ogier le Danois, whose name is a corruption of Ogier l'Ardennois, and they may also have been the source of the German legends of Gudrun and the Nibelungs.

The aristocracy of Wallonia in the barbarian period, like its counterpart in northern France, made Latin or the future Dutch the language of cultivated people. The center of civilization in those days was on Belgian territory, and it was here that future works of French and German literature, such as the *Cantilène de Sainte Eulalie* and the *Ludwigslied*, had their origins.

During the early centuries of the new period, society became more barbaric. Throughout Belgium, people had returned to the worship of pagan idols, trees, rivers, and local gods, which the peasants, although nominally Christian, had never ceased to venerate.

These were times of unimaginable savagery. Queen Brunhilda was slaughtered by being tied to the tail of a wild horse, and the author of the *Life of St. Amand* reports the lynching of a prisoner at his trial. "One Dotton, a Frankish count," he recounts, "had assembled a great number of Franks and sat in judgment. The guards brought before him a criminal whom the entire assembly immediately proclaimed deserving of death. He was then brutally and unmercifully beaten and cruelly wounded, so that he was only half alive. Then Dotton ordered that he be hanged from a gibbet, and when St. Amand was unable to obtain a pardon, the prisoner was hanged, despite his sorry state."

The Merovingian kings, however, could not maintain their authority without the support of the Church, and they therefore sent many missionaries into pagan Belgium, giving them not only privileges and rights, but also detachments of troops to support their teachings by force of arms.

Between 500 and 600 A.D., paganism dominated the Low Countries, and there no longer was a Christian bishop there. In the year 625, however, a missionary from Aquitaine, St. Amand, arrived in Ghent and founded the monastery of St. Bavo. His successor, Omer, who came from Luxeuil, converted the coast dwellers; and two other Aquitainians, St. Eloi and St. Remacle, became the bishops of Tournai and Tongres.

The story of St. Amand is told by a ninth-century writer. "The inhabitants of these regions ran to him," the chronicle says, "and humbly asked that he baptize them. . . . With one accord, all came to the worship of God."

On the other hand, around the year 725, a contemporary tells us of conversions made through fear and by force of arms. In this case, the apostle himself had been insulted and beaten, and even thrown into a river—indeed, knowing how to swim was essential to a missionary at that time. Tired of this treatment, he asked King Dagobert for police powers and a compulsory baptism order. Thus, by royal command, he was able to purify and sanctify anyone who would not consent to his own regeneration with good grace.

The missionary effort was successful, and Belgium again became Christian. Soon Wallonia was covered with abbeys, and the movement began to take root in Flanders. In the days of Charlemagne, there were no less than twenty-five large monasteries, of which three were in Flanders.

The date of Belgium's reconversion is important. It occurred nearly five centuries after the reconversion of France, and, arriving late as it did, Belgian Catholicism was to become the more ardent. In this sense it had much in common with the Catholicism of Spain, another country where conversion was late and, thus, intense.

The *Lives of the Saints* and a cosmography written in Ravenna give us an indication of the chief cities of Belgium about the year 570 A.D. Ghent, then called Ganda, consisting of a few houses grouped at the confluence of the Schelde and the Lys, constituted a small local capital. For a long time, Tournai stood apart from the rest of Gaul, and Gallo-Roman civilization survived there after the town's occupation by Clodion and his Franks in 431 A.D. The people of Tournai still spoke Latin, and the vases they manufactured, unlike Frankish ceramics, had a Gallo-Roman cast.

The smiths of Tournai doubtless made the gold and silver found in the tomb of Childeric. These pieces were wholly or partly made in the town's royal workshops. There, gemstones were engraved and workers fabricated cloisonné enamels, their bright colors separated from one another by sinuous lines of inlaid gold.

At the other end of Belgium, the Meuse had become an important waterway. Along its course lay the diocese of Tongres, the most important see of the period, and the cities of Maastricht, Huy, Namur, and Dinant. The distance between one city and another was about 18 miles, or a day's journey. The cities had landing stages and markets, and each had its own mint. Liège, however, was still a village of small importance. About the year 700, St. Lambert, Bishop of Tongres-Maastricht, made it his habit to seek rest and recreation at his villa near this boatmen's resort, only a day's journey from his palace at Maastricht. The bishop was fond of his Liège holidays. There, and only there, could he get away from the bickerings of civil servants that beset him in the rest of his diocese, where his affairs were confusedly entangled with those of the state.

There was, however, one conflict from which St. Lambert could not escape. Some of his friends had killed various kinsmen of a local grandee, a certain Domesticus Dodon. In September, 705, while St. Lambert was resting in the little village, Dodon's hired assassins came to him by night. Breaking their way through walls and doors, they flung themselves at him; he met them with sword in hand. Giving up all thought of defense, he fell on his knees in prayer. An assassin, standing on the roof, threw the spear that killed him.

The repercussions of this murder were enormous. St. Lambert, considered a martyr, was buried at the place where he was killed. His tomb became the object of pilgrimages; and his successor, St. Hubert, built a beautiful stone basilica that gained fame among connoisseurs of the period. The number of persons coming to Liège increased greatly, the village became a township, and the bishop made it his place of residence. Tradition holds that the bishops, whose duties kept them continually on the move, found ways of passing the greater part of their time at Liège. The city continued to grow until it was the biggest on the banks of the Meuse.

The triumph of the Carolingians in 750 marked the real breach between north and south. The area of present-day Belgium now became the center of the Frankish world, which extended over the estuaries of the rivers on which merchants plied their trade between Germany, England, and Gaul. It is from this country that the Carolingians came.

About the same time, the slow process that was isolating northern Gaul, with its Frankish population, from the Mediterranean seaboard, held by the Visigoth or Burgundian kingdoms, was taking effect. Arab conquests and Saracen forays on the coasts of Italy and Provence had stopped traffic between East and West, ending the commerce on which the Roman Empire had been founded. This was a decisive blow to the civilization of the period. Under the Merovingians (about 700 A.D.), papyrus and silks, camels, weapons, jewelry, and other products of the East, still arrived from Syria or from Constantinople. The Roman world in its truest form—civilization and trade—was still nearly intact. The Merovingians had their own treasury and financial organization; they coined their own money, levied taxes, paid their civil servants, and did their best to help merchants and to expand trade.

Half a century later, in the time of Charlemagne, there was neither gold nor taxation nor civil servants. The government, lacking currency, was no longer able to pay its servants; it became necessary to create a new system of administration, based on direct transactions between people, on mutual service, and on gifts of land. Civilization became wholly agricultural and, lacking roads and transportation, each village became self-contained. There were no aristocrats, no intellectuals, and no teachers, so that the culture, the technical skill, the scholarship, and even the memories of antiquity, disappeared completely.

The reign of Charlemagne, great as it was, was an amazing human adventure. Charlemagne himself was tall, somewhat stout, with lively, piercing eyes that exercised a fascination on those with whom he talked. He was so strong that even his life of perpetual riding and hunting, which—even without his prodigious sexual excesses—would have worn out a lesser man, were not enough for him. He had to use up his surplus energy in gymnastic exercises. He lived amid courtiers who wore golden boots and the purple Byzantine chlamys, fastened with a jeweled clasp. His innumerable daughters lived a life as dissolute as his own, and he tolerated their love affairs because he himself kept them from marriage. He was surrounded by men of learning whom he considered mere civil servants, yet all his life he tried to learn to write, spending his hours of insomnia in struggle with the scribe's art.

He is credited with the so-called Carolingian Renaissance, but this consisted of no more than a few schools intended for the training of civil servants. His chief councilor, Alcuin, wrote scholarly texts, but these were not intended to preserve the culture of antiquity. They were intended to prepare higher government functionaries for their jobs.

It was at Aachen, close to the Belgian frontier, that Charlemagne spent his last years, and there he died. He had always been a lover of hot baths, which were to be found in this city of springs. His biographers say that he forced his daughters and his friends to throw themselves with him into the swimming pools there, so that there were sometimes more than a hundred people in the water. When he died, at the age of seventy-one, of pneumonia contracted during a hunting party, his son, Louis the Pious, discharged his father's ministers, his many concubines, and had his daughters confined to a convent for the rest of their lives.

Charlemagne's outstanding quality was his capacity for activity. He was forever moving, riding from one end of his empire to the other, and in forty-six years he fought in no less than fifty-five campaigns.

His administrative efforts were immense, but not lasting. The empire was held together only by force of arms. Means of communication were poor, and the lack of money and transport made it impossible for a single man to command more than a province. For this reason, Charlemagne had to set up a complete hierarchy of chiefs, bound in fealty to him in such a way as to create a huge military organization whose high standards were maintained by the frequent *missi dominici*, the envoys of the Emperor.

Charlemagne was not trying to re-establish the Roman Empire, as his contemporaries believed. He merely restored the form of an empire as people knew it in his day—the Byzantine Empire, with its absolute basileus and its Oriental theocracy. The most striking thing about the empire of Charlemagne, however, was its economic rather than its political organization. It was this that spurred on the tremendous development of Belgium and the surrounding regions.

The Carolingians used the Low Countries as the center of their Empire. Their capital was at Aachen and the family estates were at Herstal, Jupille, and Liège. They founded numerous abbeys, from Nivelles to Fosse; and Einhard, Charlemagne's historian, restored St. Peter's and St. Bavon's at Ghent, where the Emperor created a port for his fleets.

Victories over the Saxons enlarged the frontiers of the empire until they reached the Elbe; and Belgian trade, which had hitherto been directed southward, took a new direction. By then, the south was plunged deeper and deeper into its decline, but Belgium scarcely felt the effects. She was too busy extending her trade into Germany, and Belgian wool and textiles were to be found on the Rhine, the Weser, the Danube, and the Elbe. This was termed the "Frisian epic." The merchants of Duursteede were becoming Europe's great distributors of Flemish cloth and of the metal products of Wallonia.

By the ninth century, the Court of Norway was dressed in Belgian cloth. Scandinavian warriors, the future vikings or Norsemen, bought swords forged in the valley of the Meuse, which, because Flemish merchants sold them, they called *flamingr*.

Lead from England was used for the roofs of churches and abbeys in Belgium, but those in France and Germany were covered only with timber and they were forever catching fire. Rhenish wine could be found everywhere and so could pepper, which, coming only from the East, was a scarce commodity in other parts of France, since it could only enter through the Languedoc ports, and only one in four was open. It came to Belgium by way of the Adriatic and the Rhine; and in the eighth century, it was found as far afield as Cambrai.

The Low Countries were thus a hive of commercial activity and prosperity, linked by overland routes with Venice and Byzantium. When the Norse invasions began, Belgium was the first objective, not only because penetration was easy via the many rivers and inlets, but still more because it was the richest commercial region of the West.

Yet the world of Charlemagne was still a completely Roman world. Military uniforms were not unlike those of the imperial legions. Nothing had changed since the days of the Merovingians—except perhaps that men who had bared their knees in the days of the caesars now wrapped them round with crossed straps. As in the days of Vercingetorix and Ambiorix, the striped or checkered plaids of the Gauls were still worn; and the women, as in the days of Augustus, wore a double tunic, the one underneath long and simple, the other short and wide, with pleats and wide sleeves. At Court, the dress reflected Byzantine luxury; some garments even were made of peacock feathers. Life went on much as it had gone on in Roman times. The calendar was still Roman, and Charlemagne did not designate dates as we do today, but spoke of "the fourth day of the ides of December," or "the ninth day of the calends of June." Both day and night were divided into twelve hours, as they had been divided in the time of Christ, and the length of the hours varied according to the time of year.

Ordinary handwriting was uncommon. It became the art of calligraphy and was practiced only by the scribes who copied Bibles or drew up capitularies to be read by a few bishops and high dignitaries. There no longer was any need for a rapid, cursive handwriting to serve trade and everyday life.

Although civilization had come to a standstill in the immense Carolingian Empire, it was on the march among the Byzantines, and, more particularly, among the Arabs on the shores of the Mediterranean. Their inventions and devices, which reached Belgium, were destined to transform the life of mankind.

The water mill, essentially a southern device, was now carried slowly northward across Gaul. It soon gained such popularity in northern countries that William the Conqueror listed several thousand of them when he made his inventory of English resources in the Doomesday Book. This suggests that virtually all grain was milled by the motive power of streams and rivers rather than by human labor, and the mill was the first of the mechanical slaves to find a place in history. From earliest times to the fall of the Roman Empire, grain could be milled only with the heavy millstones dating back to the Neolithic period. This method of milling required a substantial supply of manpower, found for the most part in able-bodied slaves. The water mill freed this manpower for many other types of work.

Almost at the same period of the eighth century, another device, destined to promote the growth of the feudal world, found its way to Belgium—the stirrup, which gained added importance through its appearance in conjunction with the first horseshoe. During the preceding 2,000 or 3,000 years, a horseman had been able to stay in the saddle only by a feat of balance; since he had nothing to support him, he could use neither lance nor heavy sword, and he could not wear armor or carry an iron shield. The introduction of the stirrup into Western Europe in the Carolingian period made it possible for a heavily armed horseman to keep his seat. The mounted warrior could caparison himself in metal, and, as a result, the art of warfare became completely revolutionized.

Soon thereafter appeared the coat of mail, designed to protect the fighting man against the sword; and then plate armor, to stop a pointed weapon and make the wearer invulnerable. The horse acquired a cuirasse of his own and was safe against all attack by arrows. When a horse was standing still he could be attacked in the belly or on the hocks, but a charging horse could not be touched. The age of the horse was ushered in, years after Charles Martel led his victorious cavalry. From the time of Charlemagne on, armor progressed from the cloth tunic to the coat of mail to complete armor. Improvements in metallurgy produced better armor, which in turn stimulated men to make better metals. At the same time, there sprang up in Europe a lordly warrior class. A knight in armor could put the yeomanry to flight by the dozen. This was the beginning of the feudal age.

After Charlemagne's death, about 820–30 A.D., there converged upon the Empire a whole series of enemies—the Avars, the Hungarians, the Slavs, the Arabs, and, most dreaded of all, the Norsemen.

The Norse vikings came from Scandinavia. They were part of the nation of the Goths that, under Alaric, had burned Rome and founded the kingdom of the Ostrogoths. Under Theodoric, and with the Visigoths as allies, they had conquered Aquitaine, Spain, and Africa. They were, however, not so advanced a society as some of the other branches of their own race.

They did not go into action until the ninth century, when for reasons that have long been a mystery they spread out in many directions at once. They attacked and subjugated Russia, advancing as far as the Black Sea. They attacked and conquered England, annexed the Faroe Islands, Iceland, and Greenland, and even discovered America, where they penetrated far into the hinterland. Their inscriptions on stone have been discovered far inland.

Their attack was, in reality, a counteroffensive. The wars of Charlemagne against the pagan Saxons awakened the whole Germanic world. The Norsemen, who had hitherto been isolated in Scandinavia, beheld the spectacle of their kindred races being forcibly converted to Christianity and ferociously wiped out.

They had long been trading with Belgium and Gaul via Frisian merchants, using the ports of Quentovic and Duursteede. Their raids, and all the acts of pillage associated with them, were a reply to the Carolingian aggression in Germany. The Norsemen killed priests and burned churches, for their struggle was religious in character. Their fleets were fast-moving and well organized, and their mobility rendered the Belgians helpless.

A viking ship discovered intact in our own times reveals that the vessels had no bridges and no rudders. Their sides were flanked with round, multicolored shields, which offered protection against the waves. Norse craft were small, so that they could sail far up the rivers and reach points well in the interior of a country. They made surprise landings at some point on the coast, burned the first village they found, took possession of the horses, and made off for a raid some sixty miles inland. Then they returned with their booty and re-embarked, before the slow-moving defending armies had time to mobilize.

Defense was possible only where local chieftains commanded mobile troops and fast means of transport. In a country that had no considerable network of roads, local sovereigns were unable to mobilize their armies fast enough for effective defense. The only weakness on the part of the Norsemen was their inability to carry siege material in their boats; this led communities to ask the nobility to build fortifications around their cities. These fortifications were soon put to another use, for they offered the local rulers a means of resistance against the central authorities.

The Norsemen's raids became increasingly more powerful and methodical. Their main effort was directed against the most vulnerable part of Belgium, the network of navigable streams and rivers—including the Rhine, Schelde, Meuse, Somme, Dyle, Sambre, and Yser—which provided openings in all directions.

The population, once so active, was soon exterminated or scattered. By 837, the port of Duursteede had ceased to exist, and in 850, the Norsemen began to settle on the ravaged banks of the Meuse and the Rhine, as they were later to do in Normandy. From then on, the work of destruction was to become absolutely methodical.

The Norsemen established their fortified camps in the very center of Belgian territory, at Louvain. Starting out from fixed bases, they gave up the practice of raids by small isolated bands that could be repulsed by the local rulers and their militias. The invaders now brought in great armies, which wintered in well-protected camps, emerging every spring for far-flung successful expeditions.

The invaders now had siege material and were no longer checked by castles or the walls of fortified centers. As early as 850 A.D., they were ravaging Flanders, and, in 859, they destroyed Brabant and wrought havoc in the valley of the Somme. In 879, a great Norse army set up its camp near Ghent and conducted destructive expeditions, advancing along the Schelde and its tributaries to Brabant, Cambrai, Arras, and Tournai. Later, from a camp on the Meuse, they sacked Aachen, Liège, and the Rhineland. Using the permanent camp they had set up at Louvain as a base, they attacked St. Omer, the Artois, the Somme, the lower Seine (890), and later Metz and the Moselle.

Something had to be done to put a stop to it, and eventually an appeal was made to Arnold of Carinthia, the Emperor of Germany, who succeeded in beating the Norsemen at Louvain in 891.

The surviving portion of the afflicted population had sought refuge in the castles of local lords, but the living standard was very low. The most valuable citizens—the specialist workmen, the intellectuals, and the most indispensable of the artisans—had disappeared, either because they had been killed or because there was no longer any work for them in the changed society in which they found themselves.

The Norse invasions stopped suddenly, although nobody can say why. This, oddly enough, happened at a time when they no longer encountered any resistance. It is possible that the Norsemen had wrought so much ruin and devastation that their expeditions yielded them nothing. We know that in Egypt, after the Aryan invasions of the third millennium, civilization had been entirely submerged by destruction that had continued for nearly a century.

Institutions, customs, habits of mind, commerce, and the very bases of social structure, had perished. There were no longer governments or towns, but only independent feudal lords with their fiefs and vassals. Although the church survived as a universal organization, it did so within the framework of the feudal society and the new forces that shaped it. The world was ripe for rebuilding, but there was no foundation upon which to build.

By the year 900, what was left of the Belgian peoples had emigrated into France and Germany. Belgium itself had become a wasteland in which there was no trade and in which even cultivation of the land had ceased.

Restoration and defense were to go hand in hand. These took the form of the building of urban fortifications, most of which are still in existence. The walls of Bruges were built in 879, those of Cambrai in 881, the Arras walls after 883, and the fortifications of St. Omer in 891. Construction continued after the invasions ended in 895, when the walls of Huy were built; and by 898, when Tournai was fortified, there no longer was any fear of a Norse invasion. Fear and peril had made the inhabitants of Belgium abandon their life of isolation on great rural estates and build fortified cities, which were soon to be duplicated throughout the country.

The emigrant population began to return. They found a new kind of military organization and feudal society, which offered them protection.

Revival began in the valley of the Meuse, which had suffered little damage and quickly became an important traffic artery. As early as the tenth century, chroniclers speak of Huy and Namur and even of Ghent as important commercial centers and storage depots, and English coins have even been found in Maastricht and Liège.

Frisian mariners began a new phase of activity and, about the end of the century, Meuse and Schelde merchants were traveling to England in quest of raw materials and exporting their products to the Rhine. The country had turned its eyes eastward, and this may explain the ease with which the Low Countries and Lotharingia were to be annexed by the German emperors.

The dawn of the new age marks a significant point in human history. Civilization had been destroyed at least three times: once by the Aryan invasion, again by the Dorians, and the third time by the barbarian invasion. Until the days of Charlemagne, however, the Merovingians, and later the Carolingians, had, for better or worse, maintained the old form of social hierarchy and the apparent organization of ancient civilization. The old social structure was considered satisfactory, and this feeling blocked social evolution. It was not until the Western world had fallen prostrate before the Norsemen that new forms were to appear.

What had been the fate of the great revolutionary inventions made by man since the beginning of history, and what was their potential for progress in the future? The scimitars of Toledo and Damascus, which had their origin in India, were still being forged. Writing, however, had all but vanished, for lack of an educated population to use it. The spoken word was the chief medium of communication.

Only agriculture had maintained a rate of progress since the times of Neolithic man, the Egyptians, and the Romans. The essentials of civilization, in agricultural techniques and a rural population, were preserved. Peasants, in fact, constituted 99 per cent of the population at the time.

About the end of the Neolithic period, western Europe had become separated from Asia. The inhabitants of Europe were cultivating their fields on the more advanced lines of mixed farming, in which husbandry and tilling were closely linked. The soil was nursed and its yield improved in a regular cycle of cultivation that began with the land being used for a year as pasture; then winter cereals (wheat, barley, and rye) were sown, which were harvested the following year. The ground was then left fallow for six months, after which time spring cereals were planted for harvest the following autumn. After the harvest, livestock was again pastured on the land, enriching it with their manure. There were no hedges, permitting the beasts to pass easily from field to field.

Each peasant was, according to his legal right, given a strip in each zone—winter wheat, spring oats, and common pasture. Near the houses, a separate strip was kept for vegetables, orchards, and textile or industrial plants such as flax and hemp. This system had already existed in Belgian Gaul and had become general during the Roman period. Despite the barbarian invasions, this method had been continued, and thereby the sustenance of the population was assured.

Man's way of life, however, was changing greatly. Wine was in short supply and the Belgian monks had to petition their sovereigns for the right to own vineyards in the Rhineland or at Laon and to import the wine duty-free.

Roman and Gallo-Roman forms of cooking were disappearing, for they required condiments and ingredients no longer obtainable. Only pepper, an absolute necessity, was still imported from the East. Because of poor transportation facilities, meat and fish often spoiled before they could be used. Consequently, they had to be cooked with highly spiced sauces.

Before the Norse invasions, clothing was very luxurious, and noble lords would vie with one another in displays of splendor. Their garments were covered with gold braid and purple and gold embroidery and they were fastened by golden clasps. Even their slippers were of gold and their colored belts and high boots set with precious stones.

After the invasions, each region had to fend for itself. In this closed economy only land had a stable value. The Norse invaders had indeed made the fortunes of the lords and nobility. While the Norse were massacring priests or putting them to flight, the local chieftains had stolen their property and appropriated their revenues. It was into the hands of the feudal nobles that the enormous wealth and property accumulated by the abbeys in past centuries had now passed. Feudal principalities, among them the County of Flanders, the Duchy of Brabant, and the counties of Namur, Hainaut, and Zeeland, began to spring up.

Continual warfare, pillage, and the shortage of transport, made food distribution difficult. The slightest excess or lack of rain would bring the deaths of hundreds of thousands in its wake. Because of the disorganization, anarchy, and banditry associated with the beginnings of the feudal system, these conditions were probably at their worst around the end of the tenth century.

It was not only among the peoples of Belgium and Gaul that the pattern and tradition of life had crumbled to dust. All Europe had become plastic and unstable. Everywhere people were on the move. Despite existing theoretical political divisions—e.g., the kingdoms of France and Lotharingia and Germany, which were to become the Germanic Holy Roman Empire—there were still invasions to be dealt with. The Hungarians penetrated as far into Belgium as Nivelles. Everything was in a state of flux, each region being settled by a nomadic population. In most cases, these groups differed from the people inhabiting the region today.

In the East, the Byzantine Empire still existed. Its capital was Constantinople, and its emperor, who claimed to be the legitimate heir of Augustus, exercised his sway over Greece and Asia Minor.

Budapest, however, had only just become Hungarian. There were no Rumanians in Rumania, and the future Bucharest was overrun by Tartar horsemen. There were no Russians in Russia, and the wild Moscow region was occupied by the Finns. In Spain, the countryside where Madrid was yet to be built was the haunt of Moorish horsemen from Toledo who were preparing to overwhelm the Christians of Castile. In Germany, Berlin was a Slavonic village, as was Vienna (then called Slovine); East Prussia was occupied by a Lithuanian people; and the Kingdom of Saxony was peopled by Slavs. A few centuries earlier, indeed, there had been neither Bulgarians in Bulgaria, nor Serbs in Serbia, nor a single Anglo-Saxon in England.

III

THE MIRACLE OF THE YEAR 1000

A certain legendary atmosphere has surrounded the horrors of the year 1000; in point of fact, they are not mentioned by any contemporary writer, and allusions to them are not found until two or three centuries later. The source of the legend probably lies in the frightful catastrophes that afflicted Europe during this period.

In the seventy years between 970 and 1040, there were no less than forty-eight years of famine. One of these occurred in the year 1000, sparing no region of Europe and forcing people, in the words of the chroniclers, "to take for food not only the flesh of the filthiest beasts and reptiles, but even the flesh of women and children."

The year 1031 was even worse. Ceaseless rainfall so flooded the whole land that "for three whole years, man found not a furrow in which good seed could be sown." The harvest fell to a sixth of what it had been before, and devastation afflicted even the rich agricultural areas of England, northern Italy, and Gaul. A French writer reports having seen human flesh offered for sale in the market at Tournai, and it is impossible to imagine what must have happened in the poorer regions of Spain and Germany.

Hand in hand with famine went plagues and epidemics. Death beckoned from the empty storehouse and larder, haunting the men of the tenth century. This menace acted as a powerful stimulus on society.

Famine shaped the Middle Ages. Were it not for famine, it would be difficult, if not impossible, to explain the expansion and transformation that took place in the tenth century. Disorganization and misery are not the only results of famine. In such times, a closed world holds the promise of fabulous profits for adventurous spirits enterprising enough to bring food from regions of plenty to those regions where it is scarce.

In the Middle Ages shortages were very seldom universal and a large number of people—the younger sons of good families, escaped serfs, ruined peasants, and others—took advantage of them by becoming merchants or carriers. It was not long before these adventurers realized that there were other shortages besides grain, and they did a thriving trade in jewelry, condiments, devotional images, luxury clothing, and yard goods. They sold their wares at high prices, making door-to-door calls at castles and monasteries. These wandering merchants were not restrained or persecuted. Indeed, the lords of manors welcomed their visits and received them warmly.

The increase in the number of itinerant traders is an important circumstance of the tenth century. Traders were the only source of news from the outside world, and they were able to bring luxuries to lords of manors, who closed their eyes to the fact that most merchants were former outlaws, fugitives, or runaway serfs. During the winter, they met at their "depots"—wharves fitted with store sheds and made available by noblemen who charged handsome prices for their use.

In the course of time this toleration, already a matter of current practice, was embodied in charters. This was the beginning of the communes that appeared throughout Belgium. They were not opposed because they existed to foster trade, and both the nobility and the merchants were interested in profits.

The structure of feudal society was responsible for the enormous price differences between one region and another, and the merchant carriers thus had many ways of making their fortunes. In the *Miracles of St. Bavo* we read of a Flemish merchant who, ruined by shipwreck, came to a church dedicated to St. Bavo to pray for help. Looking up from his prayer, he saw a golden chalice upon the altar. Gold was a rarity and most chalices were made of gilded common metals. The merchant was convinced that the chalice was St. Bavo's answer to his prayer. He stole it, sold it, set himself up in trade once more and, making a fresh fortune, donated to the church objects far greater in value than the chalice he had stolen. Such a sequence of events was then considered normal.

One of the writers of the time is at pains to illustrate the attraction of commerce for the human spirit and the diabolical character he believes to be inherent in commerce. He tells a story about St. Guidon, a sexton of a church at Laeken, who was tempted by the devil in the guise of a Brussels merchant. It was a pity, the devil said, that the sexton was too poor to give alms. The devil advised him that one way of never being short of money was "to abandon himself to commerce."

St. Guidon heard this proposal with horror but, for the sake of the poor,
allowed himself to be persuaded. To everyone's amazement he became
a merchant, which of course meant that he lost his soul. Before he had
time to sin, however, God came to his aid and saved him by a miracle.
His vessel was wrecked on the River Senne, and St. Guidon, filled with
grace, turned his back on the sure road to fortune on which "one could
but seldom walk without regrets."

The merchants of this period must not be thought of as timid and
peaceful burghers. The roads were far from safe, and the merchant
would go forth with sword, helmet, and breast plate ready to fight in
defense of his wares.

The caravan of a merchant of some stature was not unlike the traveling circus of today. With him were his staff in their covered wagons
and a guard of his own armed troops. There were scribes who kept
the accounts, grooms, sailors to sail the ships, and porters, who, like
their counterparts in Africa, would carry precious and fragile goods
on their backs.

The complex trading routes were mapped out in advance. The aim
of this planning was to give the merchants the greatest possible protection against robbers and bandits and to keep the burden of local tolls
and taxes to a minimum. For water transport they used boats that
drew little water, could sail in the smallest of streams, and were light
and easily hauled ashore. They laid down sloping platforms of planks
to haul boats from one navigable stretch of water to another, for in
those days locks were unknown. On the more important rivers, these
platforms were equipped with pulleys and hoisting gear. The smallest
vessels could carry more merchandise than a whole troop of horses
and donkeys and often represented the entire fortune of a small
merchant.

Another consequence of these lean times was a veritable explosion
of energy and initiative. In order to survive, men had to increase the
yield of the soil, to recover land from moors and marshes, and to
broaden the scale of society's resources and activities. It was the seed
of the remarkable transformation that was to turn a region of semi-
desert into a countryside of growing towns.

The transformation of Belgium in this period was much like the
evolution of the cities of prehistoric Sumeria and Egypt. After the
devastation wrought by invasion and famine, society was free to reorganize itself and to try every sort of experiment. This was the background for a phase of prodigious creativeness.

A parallel can be drawn between the world of the tenth century
and that of the nineteenth-century American pioneers. There was

the same explosive energy, the same astonishing development of wild and uncultivated regions. In both cases, men started out with complete political liberty. In both cases, there were centers filled with immigrants, banditry—and similar improvised measures for keeping it down—and armed men and wagons traveled over the roads. Also, there was a similar reign of force, in which the rich held sway until the ordinary people revolted, as part of that process of adjustment and compromise symptomatic of the development of young countries.

In this period, Belgium was taking the leadership of Western Europe, which had become a virgin world in the fullest sense of the term. Tenth-century society had been atomized, and the defeat of the Norsemen had left behind a clean sheet on which man's boundless energy could draw any picture it wished.

In our times, the state is forever putting obstacles in the way of change, intervening to fix the pattern of life, and defending the *status quo* in the name of the public interest. In Belgium, the state had disappeared. In its place stood the feudal system, which encouraged initiative and invention. Swift economic revolution and striking, creative works are possible only in new countries or in those that have become new by surviving cataclysm and disaster.

The movement started in Belgium, where destruction had been greatest and anarchy thus most sweeping. It spread into France, Germany, and England, and even as far as the Baltic and the Balkans, largely as a result of trade, expansion of the communal system, and eastward migration.

About 950, there began an extraordinary demographic revolution, which was to result in a remarkable population increase everywhere.

All Belgian towns were beginning to spread beyond their ancient boundaries. Namur lay on a strip of land near the Meuse. It soon spread northward, beyond the Sambre. A new market hall was built on the site of St. Remi's Church. The hall and its platform, as in all the towns of the region, indicate that merchants lived there. Namur soon stretched for a league around the platform. In the reign of Albert III (1063–1102), it became necessary to build a new city wall, and Namur became a free commune.

Much the same was happening at Liège. In its early days, the city lay in a bend of the River Meuse, facing an island. This is the *quartier de l'isle* of today, and the old bridges across this arm of the river have since become streets. At that time, this city of nine churches had a thousand priests and prelates. Merchants came from afar, bringing the clergy all they needed for their comfort—wine, incense, altar cloths, chasubles, pyxides, and chalices of gold and silver. These merchants built the market quarter, where later the town hall that gave its name to the Rue Neuvice was erected. Near this new part of the city were built the Pont des Arches (1025–1037), and later the Pont des Isles and Pont d'Avroy (1056); further east rose the new Church of St. Bartholomew.

The Liège of this period was one of the intellectual capitals of Germany. It was a breeding ground for theologians, mathematicians, poets, and musicians. About the year 1066, when neighboring Huy received the first communal charter of Western Europe, Liège, too, probably became a commune.

Brussels, or so the legend goes, owes its existence to St. Géry, who was born in France about 540. The name Brussels, however, does not appear until 966, and is probably derived from *brug* (bridge) or *broek* (marsh) coupled with *sele*, which is Dutch for "dwelling." The city, built on ground that was originally marshy, was at first called the "Castle in the Marsh." The first Brussels coins show a bridge, and the city rose at the exact point where the Senne River ceased to be navigable and where a pontoon bridge was built around the year 1000.

About 977, Charles of France, one of the Carolingian lords, built a castle on St. Géry's Isle in the Senne. That island is now the site of the Bourse and Place de Brouckère. It could be isolated inside its four moats, or watercourses, which meant it was formidably defended. It was reached by bridges, including the Mirror Bridge on the site of the present Boulevard Anspach and the Bridge of the Jews (Jodenbrugge). The ghetto was one of the early sights of Brussels.

The marketplace, where the town hall now stands, was in those days a great marsh; and on the site of the present suburbs of Brussels there was a host of little villages such as St. Gilles, Uccle, Forest, Anderlecht, Molenbeek, Laeken, Ixelles, Etterbeek, St. Josse, Schaerbeek, Boisfort, Audergem, and Woluwe. They lay in fertile, rolling country, hard by the coal forest that, in its reduced form, is today's Forêt de Soignes.

In 1047, work was begun on the Church of St. Gudule, on a hill known as Mt. Michael. It thus came to be known—and still is—as the Collegiate Church of SS. Michael and Gudule. The first church was built of timber. Like so many medieval churches, it burned down in 1072, and the work of rebuilding did not begin until 1226.

Soon Brussels was filled with *steens* (castles), such as were to be found in all cities of the Low Countries. Rising high above the wooden houses of the burghers, with high, crenelated towers and moats filled with stagnant water, they were the residences of the aristocracy. The owner of St. Géry's castle built such a residence on the site of the present Place Royale, and others were known by names such as The Boar, and The Children of Sir Hugh. There was a great trade highway running into the lower town, ending at the Bridge of Mirrors.

Brussels had plenty of unused land, and there were meadows and cultivated fields inside the city wall. The streets were often broken by open spaces. Houses were known not by their numbers, but by their sculptured emblems—such as the House of the She-Wolf—or by signs that swung in the wind above the entrances.

The biggest roads were dark, forbidding, and only 15 feet broad; usually they were clogged by heavy carts, oxen, and asses. They pursued a zig-zag course, reaching a dead end or an open space, and after nightfall, only the lights above the little street-corner shrines showed the way.

Although arson was punishable by death, a third of the houses burned down in 1276. Public buildings in the lower town had to be built on piers; and even today, one of the streets is called the Rue du Marais, "street of the marsh."

In southern Belgium, Tournai and its bishop had gradually become independent. The royal estates of the Carolingian monarchs had been ceded to the bishop, who had thus become a bulwark against the Count of Flanders.

In the tenth century, the town shared in the general population increase. After 950, a large number of outsiders settled there; and little by little a commercial district prospered near the site of the old Carolingian market. Saturday was market day, and the people gathered where the Frankish assemblies had met and where May Day was celebrated. In that district there is a street called the Rue de Cologne, which almost certainly is a corruption of Rue de la Colonie Étrangère.

About 1010, the people of Tournai staged the first communal revolt in history. All inhabitants were made burghers and given legal rights that took the demands of commerce and the interests of the prince into account. The complexity of business later made it necessary for the merchants to have courts of their own and the bishop duly permitted their establishment. Merchants traveling to fairs in neighboring countries were armed, so they were authorized to form a large confederation, the Charity of St. Christopher. The primary purpose of this organization was to keep them safe while traveling, but it also enabled them to control the bishop. By 1094, Tournai had become so large a producer of cloth that its products were to be found as far afield as Genoa.

Ghent in those days was the half-way house between Flanders and London. About 900, a nobleman built a castle almost a mile away from the center of the present town. It stood near a bridge over the Lys and became the nucleus of the city. Little streets soon began to branch off the main traffic arteries and the Friday market, scene of so much strife and disturbance during the Middle Ages, was laid out just north of the castle; the grain market was to the south.

St. Bavo's had been consecrated in 1067 and St. Peter's was finished in 1070. The city went on expanding, and about 1100, it stretched along both banks of the Lys out to the edge of the communal pasture lands on the site of the present *Kouter*, on the Place d'Armes.

Ghent was now the biggest, most populous city of the Low Countries. Louvain, which was then the capital of Brabant, extended over no more than 148 acres, and Bruges over 162, but the town of Ghent mushroomed over 198 acres. In 1000, it could have been barely a tenth of this size, thus its enormous expansion occurred in less than a century.

Not far away, the town of Bruges was emerging mysteriously from nothing. It, too, derives its name from a bridge, and in the beginning was merely a crossing at the head of the Zwyn estuary, on the frontier between Flanders and Zeeland. It expanded quickly, being situated amidst dunes and marshes of no value. Since the land was not under cultivation, the count encouraged immigration by tax exemptions and other advantages. The city emerged as both a trading center and a fishing port, and its seamen were to become famous. They made the fortune of Bruges, seeking merchandise in the four corners of the earth and bringing it back to their native city. Its marshy soil, hitherto regarded as untillable, was made fertile through drainage ditches. The spirit of freedom, the dominant note of the community's origins, now made for its further success. Merchants set up their counting houses here, free from prohibitions and regulations, and the city became a true metropolis, with its canals, houses, market halls, and quays built in the middle of the fields. In the early days, buildings were made of timber or loam, but later they were replaced with stonework—a great luxury, since stone, not available locally, had to be brought in from remote areas.

Expansion was rapid. A writer traveling with Queen Emma of England tells us that the Queen, upon disembarking at Bruges in 1037, found a port rich with merchandise. The growth in population brought to Europe a crowd of adventurers, mercenaries, emigrants, and pilgrims who became the agents of Flemish commerce and the creators of trading links with all the countries of the world.

In 1043, there were Flemish adventurers helping the Normans conquer Sicily; in 1081, Flemish or Brabant soldiery, including Raymond, who opened the gates of the town to Alexis Comène, was in the service of the emperors of Constantinople. The stream of emigration continued, and Geraldus Cambrensis tells us of newcomers from Flanders who, he says, were "strong and healthy men, faithful in all things, skilled weavers of wool, experienced merchants, fearless mariners, seeking their profit everywhere."

The people of the Low Countries had become so keen on travel and adventure that one might almost say they had turned into nomads. In 1066, they enrolled by the hundreds in the army of William of Normandy when he sailed to conquer England; for their services they received the fiefs of Yorkshire and Northumberland. Belgian soldiers gained such a reputation for courage that soon professional soldiers were known as Brabançons throughout Europe.

Being used to traveling, Belgian priests and penitents were, from 1000 onward, at the head of every pilgrimage. Almost all the bishops of Liège, from Notger on, made the journey to Rome. In 1054, the prelate Lietbert de Cambrai traveled to Jerusalem; in 1086, Robert le Frison, Count of Flanders, went to Byzantium and promised the Emperor 500 horsemen.

The people of Belgium took part in these pilgrimages, and the conversion of Hungary, under St. Stephen, allowed them to go to Constantinople and Jerusalem by the Danube route. About 1050, a group from Liège emigrated to Hungary and settled at Erlau, where they were given land by King Andrew I. For the following three centuries, large numbers of Belgian colonists found their way into central and eastern Europe. In the tenth century, other groups from Liège took part in the conversion of the Slavs of the Oder region and found their way as far east as Poland. For a long time there was a Walloon district in Breslau made up of people from Liège and Picardy; a Walloon colony at Eger in Hungary; and another at Brünn in Moravia; while Belgian abbeys were set up in Cracow and Lublin. In the twelfth century, all the Belgian nobility took the road to Syria and Palestine and it is likely that they played an important part in these far-off places.

In the meantime, new departures were transforming life on every side, changing the form of ideas, institutions, political and social organization, and spurring technical advances, all expressing the ferment of their time. There were new motive forces: a new horse collar, rudders and vessels for navigation on the high seas, window glass, clocks, the Gothic arch, and many more innovations.

These inventions meant enormous progress, transforming the life of man; slavery disappeared because the new horse collar made it possible to use animals to pull heavy loads. Prior to that, the horse had been almost useless, being strangled by the harness if the burden was a heavy one. A horse could neither pull a cart nor carry unduly heavy burdens, and Roman law prohibited the harnessing of a horse to any vehicle weighing more than 700 pounds. Probably even this limit was never reached, and it was necessary to use human labor for transporting most goods. Under such conditions slavery became almost a necessity. Human labor turned the millstones to grind the corn, worked the soil, and pulled the cart that carried the wealthy. Man performed all heavy work.

Both Aristotle and the Church believed that slavery was permissible because it was the root of civilization. Until the tenth century, the Church itself had slaves. When Pope Gregory the Great saw English children sold in the slave markets of Rome, his thoughts turned to the evangelization of England, not to the abolition of slavery. Slavery seemed to him inevitable.

The harnessing of the horse and the first of the mechanical slaves made human slavery superfluous. About the same time, western Europe saw the invention of a hinged rudder—the sternpost rudder—which facilitated navigation on the high seas. It became possible to increase the size of ships without increasing the risk of breaking the rudder, to sail longer distances, and to carry larger cargoes.

The first clocks were produced, and bells ringing from church belfries introduced a concept of time unknown to ancient man. In this period, the Christian Church gained immeasurable stature. In a world dominated by anarchy and violence, subject to the tyrannies and oppressions of the local nobles, the Church sought to enforce justice and to defend the weak and the helpless. It used the weapon of excommunication and raised up the lowly, because its authority rested on dogma and a moral system that nobody could logically contest.

The conduct of man's life was now mapped out by the Church through its religious services, festivals, calendar, and through the registration of births, marriages, and deaths. Its elective institutions, derived from the world of ancient Greece, became models for the laymen. This contributed to the development of the communal system, in which groups of men, collectively organized under elected chiefs, were gradually to transform the structure of the feudal world.

In the monasteries, all problems were discussed in meetings of the monks—among whom there were "plebeians," or lay brothers, and "patricians," or the priests and dignitaries of the chapter. In these hierarchical communities, decisions were reached by vote, and the debates that centered around them had an enormous effect on public opinion. People followed the discussions with passionate interest and paid close attention to the arguments put forward on either side. The monks, who stood for the ideals of the Gospel, represented the dynamic Church as opposed to the episcopal Church, which was linked to the material world and its interests. The monastery was the prototype of the commune, the bishop was the forerunner of the count, and the pope stood in the king's stead. Thus, the Church provided a new spirit that was to supersede tradition and chance to become an agent permeating and changing the whole of human society.

This young and mobile society was to find yet another outlet for its unstable and dynamic qualities in the crusades, which also absorbed much of its surplus energy and the overflow of its population.

The frequency of famine, and the anxiety resulting from it, had created a state of mind in which external diversion was needed to provide a focus for the population's anger, enthusiasm, and desire for action. A Belgian chronicler of the period, Sigebert de Gembloux, gives a good description of these outbreaks in his naïve, day-by-day account of the First Crusade.

It began with a period of preparation and mounting tension:

1095—Famine, already long with us, is growing worse and makes this year a disastrous one. Many are working despite their hunger, and the poor are plaguing the rich by theft and fire.
   1096—The peoples of the West, afflicted to know that the holy places of Jerusalem have been profaned by infidels and that the Turks have invaded many Christian countries, were now seized by a single aspiration, for many signs had been revealed to them.
   Each man's enthusiasm raised that of his neighbor—dukes, counts, noblemen, and commoners; rich, poor, free, and serfs; bishops, clerics, monks; old and young, boys and even girls; all had the same thought in their hearts. From all sides, without means of transportation, they came; from Spain, from Provence, from Aquitaine, from Brittany, from Scotland, England, Normandy, France, Lorraine, Burgundy, Germany, Lombardy, and every other kingdom.

This collective enthusiasm rallied around various symbols, such as the cross, which was said to have magic qualities. Pogroms ensued:

The virtue of the Holy Cross served them for armor, and having placed it on their banner, they made ready to depart, that they might avenge on the foes of the Christian faith the insults that had been proffered against God. In olden times, men had been induced to fight in the armies of man, but now with one accord they wished to enlist in the army of God.
   Complete peace having been established in all quarters, their next action was against Jews wherever they were, and they forced the Jews to convert to Christianity. Those who refused were deprived of their property, massacred, or driven from the town. Some of them later returned to the faith of Judea.
   Among those to be seen in the army of God were Godfrey, Duke of Lorraine; his brothers Eustace and Baldwin; Baldwin, Count of Mons; and Robert, Count of Flanders.

This account describes all the elements of a revolutionary movement—the disquiet, the first slow preparations, the sudden and contagious enthusiasm, the slogans and badges by which the insurgents could recognize one another, the intolerance, and the ultimate massacre of all who disagree. All the crusades were marked by this collective mysticism. Allowing for the difference of setting, Christian Europe of the eleventh century very much resembled the France of 1789.

Like the French revolutionaries, they had their "days," their sensational developments, and their unexpected decisions. Among these was the famous episode at the Council of Clermont, in 1095. Those present cried out: "It is the will of God!" and forthwith they sewed red crosses on their shoulders. This incident foreshadows the red cap and the revolutionary flag.

The crusades, like the French Revolution, were to have their popular orators and their extremists who went beyond the original aims of the founders of the movement—the Crusade of the Poor and the Children's Crusade, for example. Monks were the propagandists and agitators who kept Europe stirred up for two centuries. They had their splendid failures and sporadic, ill-organized outbursts. The great Crusade of the Crowds swept across Europe, only to be massacred in Anatolia. Only the Crusade of the Princes had political consequences of lasting value, and there were those who turned the crusades to their own advantage. The profiteers, adventurer-generals, and others exploited the circumstances of the time to carve out kingdoms for themselves.

The literature and legends of the crusades gave the peoples of Europe a common ideal that sent them out to conquer Syria, Greece, and Sicily, and to campaign in Spain.

It was natural enough that this collective ferment should be at its peak in Belgium, which was the most advanced region of Europe. It was from Belgium that all the crusades set out, and Belgians played a leading role in them.

The First Crusade (1095–99) began with a mass movement of the peasantry and the poor, accompanied by their wives and children. They were not a fighting force, but they found their way across Europe by dint of theft and pillage, only to be exterminated in Asia Minor.

The next was a crusade of princes commanded by Godfrey of Bouillon, who became the first Christian king of Jerusalem. His brother Baldwin followed him to the throne. The Belgians played a major role in this crusade and many of the lords of the Low Countries—among them Robert II of Flanders, Baldwin II of Hainaut, and others—left their homelands to add the cross to their armorial bearings. Of the five groups in the army, two were composed of Belgians and

Flemings. Peter the Hermit of Picardy organized the crusade, and two knights of Tournai—Engelbert and Liétaud—were the first to set foot on the ramparts of the Holy City.

This crusade was a terrifying mixture of mysticism and horror. In time of famine, the crusaders received blades of grass in place of consecrated wafers rather than forgo the Sacrament. But when they captured Jerusalem, they threw into the streets the bodies of women who had taken refuge on the roof tops.

Godfrey of Bouillon, in a letter to the Pope, boasted that he had ridden fetlock deep in the unclean gore of the Saracens. His companions, disappointed at finding so little gold in the town they had captured, burned the dead to recover the gold they suspected them of having swallowed.

The Flemings again took the lead in the Second Crusade (1147–49), when they stormed Lisbon on their way to the Holy Land. Thierry, Count of Flanders, brought back the relic of the Holy Blood, which is still carried in the annual procession at Bruges. His successor, Philip of Alsace, took part in the Third Crusade (1189–92) in company with Frederick Barbarossa, Philip II of France, and Richard the Lionhearted of England. It was in this crusade that Philip of Alsace was killed (1191).

The Fourth Crusade (1202–04) was commanded by Baldwin of Constantinople, Count of Flanders, who led the whole of the Belgian and French nobility. His successors were his brother, Henry of Hainaut, and his step-brother, Peter of Namur.

The spirit of the crusaders was subtly modified by their contact with the more refined Moslem civilization. They acquired a taste for luxury and new pleasures, diversions, and experience. Fashions and attitudes changed. Within a few years, the Roman type of costume, which had been common in Europe since ancient times despite the Carolingian changes, had disappeared. It was replaced by clothing of the oriental type.

Men who had shaved again began to wear beards and even perfumed them, without realizing that in so doing they were following the example of Mohammed. Women began to wear flowing garments. Castles were decorated with tapestries and curtains, beds were hidden beneath curtains and canopies, and cushions and ornaments were found everywhere. The picturesque character of medieval civilization emerged. Its material aspect offered merchants who imported luxury goods, and towns such as Florence and Bruges which made such goods, great profits.

Life and customs grew increasingly refined. Forks began to appear on tables, coarse footwear was replaced by the elegant handiwork of the Arabs of Cordova; the materials of Mossul, which came to be called muslin, were thrown over the recently coiffured heads of ladies, and across their shoulders lay the veiling of Gaza, which came to be known as gauze.

Arabian ideas and culture brought the peoples of the West the works of antiquity. Among the first of these were Aristotle's, and from his ideas sprang the philosophy of the Middle Ages.

The peoples of northern and southern Europe, long isolated, had found a means of transportation and had begun to travel. There was a great mixing of peoples; frequent intermarriages introduced new and exotic strains. In the twelfth century, when the Flemings went to Portugal to help Alphonse I take Lisbon from the Arabs and make it his capital, he bestowed the hand of one of his daughters on a son of Count Thierry of Alsace. The lady's name was Theresa, but "lest the people of Flanders be shocked by its strangeness," she obligingly changed it to Matilda.

Beyond the closed circle of the Mediterranean, which had been the boundary of the ancient world, a new civilization was growing up under the spell of the East. These were triumphant days in a world of legendary wonder for the Flemish emperors of Constantinople and the French princes of Syria with their exotic names—King Lusignan, Queen Sybille, King Foulques, and his wife, Mélusine, or Mélisande.

A new civilization had been born in Belgium and the rest of Europe. In less than two centuries, after the year 1000, the principal achievements of the ancient world had been discovered. Scholarship was less advanced, but the status of the arts was about the same, and the standard of living markedly higher.

Agricultural yield rose to a point unknown before in history, and there were improvements in metallurgy and transportation. Castles were fitted with glass windows to keep out frost and bad weather, and intellectual life could thus continue throughout the year even in northern climates.

The watermill had already added to Europe's power resources, and a new contribution was made by the windmill. This was an Arab device that took the place of the watermill in flat or marshy country such as Flanders, where streams do not develop sufficient power to turn a watermill.

Although the ancients had burned only wood or charcoal, men now began to mine coal, a much cheaper fuel. There is something peculiar in the contrast between this advanced technology and the archaic moral development of the time. Men and women slept completely naked, and it was their practice to undress in public. Miniatures in illuminated manuscripts show us the pious King St. Louis lying beside his wife with her bosom showing above sheets reaching only to the waist. In the romance of Tristan and Isolde, Tristan sleeps with others of the faithful in the chamber of King Mark, barely a spear's length from the bed where the married couple lie together.

Marriage rites and ceremonies were very different from those of today. There were no veils of tulle and muslin, but the bride, if she was still a virgin, wore her hair loose and flowing over her shoulders. The happy couple was united by the priest after first being covered over with a piece of material referred to as "the frying pan." There is still a reference to this custom in the French expression "holding the cords of the pan," which is equivalent to the English phrase "wearing the pants in the family." When there were illegitimate children, by no means unusual, they were placed under the pan too, which made them legitimate. After the ceremony, the newlyweds went to the cemetery, where they called upon the dead and informed them of their union. That evening, the priest would come to bless the young couple in bed.

It was quite common for women to wear "falsies"—two cushions inserted in the bodice. They wore false hair under their horned coifs and their hips swung as they walked. Frocks were pulled up to show the elegant feet and ankles, and ladies learned to smile with their lips closed lest they show their decayed teeth.

Town houses—in many cases movable—were almost always constructed of timber. Iron was dear and nails rare, so that planks were usually joined with simple wooden pegs. On July 10, 1271, Herbert le Mercier, burgher of Ypres, bought a house from Nicholas of Lille, subject to the latter's undertaking to dismantle it and re-erect it at Ypres at his own expense.

This accounts for a number of peculiar clauses that occur in charters. At Priches, for example, there is a stipulation that "no house may be sold with a view to its removal from the village." Also, because it was the desire of every household to live close to the street, dwellings extended in depth and used only their shortest dimension, the gable-end, for street frontage.

There had been no change in the construction of shops since Roman times. They had no windows; instead, they had shutters, which were cut horizontally and were opened during the day to form a lean-to roof above and a display shelf beneath. The merchandise was thus displayed in the narrow street. This practice prevailed until sidewalks came into use and windowglass had become so cheap that windows protecting an indoor stock became feasible.

Taverns were important to the people of the time; they contained neither tables nor chairs, and the floor was covered with fresh-cut grass in summer and dried rushes in winter. Customers sat on the floor to play dice, while eating thirst-inducing snacks, such as salted or smoked fish. Beer as we know it did not exist before the thirteenth century, and the main tavern drink was *cervoise*, a kind of barley beer, a staple drink since Gaulish times. Its name was derived from Ceres, the Roman goddess of grain, and it was made from barley by simple fermentation. The taste, however, was sweet and rather insipid, and it was not until the thirteenth century that brewers began adding hops to produce a bitter tang.

Cooking and eating habits were very different from what we know today. There were no plates; and the meat and other solid foods were served on slices of bread called *tranchoirs*. Food was eaten with the fingers and the *tranchoir* itself, soaked as it was in sauce or gravy, was given to the poor. Condiments were immensely important. All food had to be seasoned with pepper, mustard, or garlic; and the Flemish troops who captured Constantinople in 1204 struck terror into the hearts of the Byzantines by the strong smell of garlic on their breath.

Every dish was served with a special sauce associated with it by long custom. Fresh herrings were served with garlic sauce, mussels or boiled beef with pepper sauce, and white meat with vinegar. Toast was considered a condiment, and a sauce of ground almonds was served with vegetables.

A meal began with bread and wine, followed by hors d'oeuvres, which included pork to stimulate the appetite. The meal ended with fruit, including, in those days, the radish and the horseradish, and even a pine cone to which had been added cinnamon, ginger, or licorice. The wine itself was treated as a food and played its own part, just as bread did, in the composition of a meal. It was carefully prepared in the kitchen, and condiments and spices were added in the cooking process to give it a special bouquet.

Cheese was served as a dessert, and the menu included cheese tarts, custard tarts, and fried cheeses, dishes which still are part of Belgian cuisine. Sauces and minced meat were also sweetened and wine was sometimes added.

Swan's neck was considered a great delicacy for refined palates. *Pâté* was important in the diet, for there were no dentists and most people lost their teeth when they were very young. The first meal of the day was very like an English breakfast, consisting of grilled pork, toasted cheese, and heavy dishes seasoned with mustard. It may be noted in passing that much English cooking has its counterpart in the Middle Ages, including the serving of mint with mutton.

The law was very severe, founded as it was on the old *lex talionis* of Merovingian times. The law of Mechlin, which was to remain in force until the fifteenth century, stipulated that anybody who wounded another person with a prohibited weapon should have his hand cut off. In those days, long journeys were considered so dangerous that they were sometimes ordered as a substitute for the death sentence.

Some of the penalties are defined in humorous terms. For example, the law of Mechlin states that "he who shall have caused a rise in the price of wheat shall be placed on a rush mat and dragged by horses through the town; nothing but eggs shall be thrown at him." The charter law of Priches stipulates (Article 36): "If one woman shall insult another woman, and if the insulted party can bring as witness two men, or one man and one woman, or two women, and so complain to the justice thereof, then shall the culprit pay a fine of 10 sous; or she shall carry hung from her neck from the center of the village to its farthest extremity two stones provided for the purpose." Article 37 says: "If a professional jester shall insult any man in the village, that man shall not go to seek a stick if he has not one with him, but may if he wishes give the jester three blows with his fist. If, however, he have a stick or switch in his hand, he may if it pleases him strike him by whom he is insulted three times. If, however, anyone be insulted in his own house, he may strike him who insults him as much as he will, but without causing his death or the loss of a limb. Afterward he may, if it pleases him, throw him in the mud."

The processes of justice were complex and peculiar. Indeed, justice was not administered in the interest of the people, but was one of the rights of the lord of the manor. The more complicated a law suit, the greater the revenue it would bring the count, and even then it was customary to blame lawyers for spinning out their cases.

The wretchedness of the masses was often terrible. Famine was frequent and after a poor harvest, hundreds of thousands would starve to death. Renier de Liège, who lived in a town renowned for its wealth, with priests and prelates to succor the poor, wrote (1197):

A large number of poor people died of hunger. Animal carcasses were being used as food, and so great was the misery threatening everybody that no one had hope. A hogshead of rye sold for 18 sous on June 11, and the following day for 35. As the time of harvest approached, the price rose, and on July 25, it was 40 sous the hogshead. The poor died in the streets. They came groaning in their death agony, lying before the doors of our churches at matins, waiting for the alms that were given out at the first light of day. This year we have had no wheat since Epiphany [January 6], and after mid-May there was no more wine until vintage time. Ale has been lacking all year, but since we did not wish to make difficulties, we in the convent have been drinking water.

Belgian townspeople were divided into two main categories: burghers and artisans. The latter lived in cottages or huts that were rented to them by the week since they were never given more than a week's work at a time and could not be trusted for a longer lease. On Monday morning, they appeared in great droves in the squares and market places, anxiously waiting for work. On Saturday evening, they were paid their wages and were out on the pavement again.

There was a special artisan's bell to announce the beginning of the working day, the noon meal, and the end of the day. Lateness was severely punished, and there were so many job-hunters that employers did not hesitate to discharge workers, for they could be replaced at once. They owned nothing but the clothes they wore, and as soon as production flagged they lost their jobs and were forced to wander about the countryside as beggars.

The quality of manufactured goods was subject to stringent regulations and an artisan could be punished with exile or even death for minor shortcomings. The sanctity of the home, guaranteed in the town charters, did not exist for him, and inspectors could enter his dwelling at all times. Often the artisan was made to work outdoors in front of his cottage door so that he might be more easily supervised. The majority of the population lived in this wretched state, and it is not surprising that they were renowned for their sober habits.

This regime of strict supervision, however, gave the Flemish artisans a technical skill and virtuosity that gave them a monopoly in making cloth of unsurpassed quality. Most esteemed of all was scarlet cloth dyed with brazilwood extract; they also made brown, blue, striped, or varicolored textiles.

The Flemings of today, as those of the past, have an extremely well developed color sense, and they produce subtly shaded half-tones and delicate contrasts. It has been said that this reflects the richness of the Flemish sky, where the setting sun makes a perpetually changing picture above the misty horizons of the North Sea.

In the Middle Ages, however, art had become part and parcel of ordinary life. It was closely linked with village festivals, the taste for processions and rich clothing, the joyous entries of ruling princes, the cavalcades, and the whole pattern of existence founded on the prosperity of the textile industry.

Walloon towns such as Tournai, which, like its Flemish counterparts, took up weaving, also became cities of painters. But towns like Liège, which specialized in metal carving, made their mark chiefly in the fields of sculpture or music, in which they are still pre-eminent. The same phenomenon may be seen in Italy.

The wives of the burghers of Bruges, say the chroniclers, were "dressed as queens," as richly clad as the ladies of the doges' households in Venice or the great Florentine ladies with their heavy brocades. In both countries, processions and *tableaux vivants* were part of the pattern of life, and this life was the setting for a group of painters who found decor especially important.

It was a sumptuous and cruel world. And during the following century, it was in this world that the Flemish revolutions were to be fought out.*

---

* The reader must remember that half of Flanders of this time was French-speaking. It included towns like Lille and Douai, which have never been Dutch-speaking, just as the Belgian Hainaut includes Valenciennes and the southern part of what is now the French Departement du Nord.

IV

THE REVOLUTION IN FLANDERS

Early in the thirteenth century, Abbé Guillaume le Breton wrote his *Philippide*, showing us a Flanders resembling the pictures Rubens and Jordaens were to paint later—"rubicund of visage and white of flesh" and crowned with splendor. The land had no vineyards or forests, but was rich in countless streams and rivers. Its countryside was covered with the growing grain, and its cows gave an abundance of milk and butter. Its fields, even the marshy or fallow land, yielded an inestimable harvest, as well as peat to warm the hearth. Le Breton sang the praises of the Flemish port of Damme, which he believed meant "damage"; and the people of Flanders, he noted, mixed oats with water to produce a queer potion they called beer.

The countryside was an unbroken checkerboard of tilled fields and pastures. Serfdom was disappearing, and the whole coastline had been redeemed from the sea. Towns and villages were springing up on all sides, and their inhabitants were free citizens, no longer under the thralldom of feudal privilege. We can recognize these settlements today by names ending in *kerke* or *kapelle* (church)—Middelkerke, Mariakerke, Ramskapelle—or by the ending *ster* or *sart* (clearing)—Pepinster or Rixensart.

The population grew so large that Belgians began to migrate eastward. They left the country in great numbers, clearing the land recently conquered by the Slavs in Silesia, Bohemia, and Prussia. Even today, there is many a village in eastern Germany with a Flemish name, and many of their marching songs have come down to us:

> Eastward we would now depart,
> Eastward we would go.

A-welcome we will be.
Eve and morn when we are there
Over beyond the plains,
We will drink the goodly wine.
Eastward we would go.

The counts of Flanders granted all foreigners the highest possible degree of commercial freedom. Bruges became the center of European trade, attracting merchants and bankers from far and wide. In its great market place was found a cosmopolitan crowd of all the races of man—Scandinavians, Portuguese, Spanish, English, French, and, inevitably, the Germans or "People of the East" (*Osterlings*) whose name may have passed into the English monetary system as "sterling."

Flemish coins circulated as far afield as Russia, the Black Sea, and the Caucasus, and Bruges cloth came out of the weaving sheds in runs of 100,000 pieces. It was so cheap that no competition was possible.

The patricians, who were masters of the great towns of Flanders, had set up the London Hansa, through which they alone could command supplies of English wool at the low prices that obtained for purchases in bulk. They commissioned the artisans to weave the wool into cloth, and they were past masters in the arts of trade and distribution to all the markets of Europe.

These same patricians kept the working classes, the "blue-nailed men," in a state of near-slavery, by keeping the threat of unemployment hanging perpetually over their heads. The artisans united into religious societies that, as a defensive measure, were converted little by little into craft guilds or trade unions. The guilds at last enabled the commoners to revolt against their servitude and wretchedness.

The first insurrection occurred at Valenciennes in 1225. There was a fresh outbreak at Douai in 1245, and in 1280, the whole of Flanders was engulfed in revolution. The artisans of Bruges, Ypres, Douai, and Tournai bore arms in the streets, pillaging and massacring, and succeeding for a time in snatching power from the patricians.

Inevitably, the reaction was fiercely repressive. The poor were forbidden to bear arms, to walk in the streets with their tools, to join a society, or to hold meetings of more than seven persons. The patricians created a vast, interurban police force, which pursued migrant workers from town to town and served as a bulwark of the haves against the revolutionary have-nots.

Sons of aristocratic families, on the other hand, incurred no penalty if, even in the very heart of town, they carried off the daughters of burghers; and even their man-servants might with impunity ravish the wives of the common people. This was expressly laid down in the

Keure, the law of Ghent, to the great indignation of the oppressed classes.

The patricians consolidated their power by setting themselves up as a hereditary oligarchy. The famous Thirty-Nine of Ghent governed in three-year relays as alternating groups of thirteen magistrates. Patricians who were sick, even leprous, or too old for their civic duties were nonetheless maintained in office. The Count of Flanders vainly sought to limit their powers. The patricians retorted by challenging his authority and calling on the King of France.

To defend them, the king sent the *ruwaerts,* or "royal guardians," who took the towns under their protection and ran up the fleurs-de-lis on their ramparts, thereby rendering them inviolable. The patricians embroidered the royal fleurs-de-lis on their banners and clothing and became known as the *leliaerts,* or "men of the lily." Against them stood the common people, the *clauwaerts,* or "men of the claw," taking their emblem—easy to draw and easy to embroider—from the heraldic claws of the lion of Flanders.

This does not mean that the men of the lily were traitors. France and Flanders were one nation, and the Count of Flanders had consented to the Treaty of Melun, which gave his nobles the right to revolt against him and to appeal for arbitration to the King of France. In claiming these rights, the patricians had championed independence of the towns. The same rights now drove the oppressed masses into the opposite camp. Flanders was soon divided against itself. Social struggle unleashed hatred and violence, almost civil war.

Faced with this situation, the Count of Flanders, Guy de Dampierre, was at first hesitant. Then he sought the support of the men of the claw and seized the opportunity created by the Franco-English War to revolt against the King of France and call for English aid. Philip the Fair at once ordered the military occupation of Flanders, and against this there was no effective resistance. Guy de Dampierre capitulated, and in 1300, Philip ordered his estates confiscated. In the following year, the king traveled through Flanders and his queen was astonished to behold the wealth and luxury in which the burghers' wives were dressed. "I thought I was the only queen here, but around me I see more than a hundred," she cried. To all appearances, Flanders was peaceful and calm, but the men of the lily were as arrogant as ever, and their imposts and extortions were soon to create another explosion.

The democrats were the really active force in Flanders, and a mystic belief in revolution was stirring them to action. As their leader and organizer they had Peter de Coninck, a simple weaver, and, though one-eyed and sickly, a born orator. News of an unpopular tax fired the tinder and the democrats rose at Bruges, succeeding, for a time, in gaining control of the city. The royal Governor, Châtillon, mustered his troops, recaptured the city, and at once began to render it defenseless by pulling down the city walls.

The men of the claw foresaw ferocious reprisals and sought to do what they could to strike the first blow. Secretly, they brought back to the city Jean de Namur and Guillaume de Juliers as organizers of the resistance, as well as other sons and grandsons of Guy de Dampierre.

On the night of May 17–18, 1302, a handful of exiles cut the throats of the French sentinels and slipped silently into the city. The people rushed into the streets crying *schild en vriend!* (shield and friend), a slogan chosen for its difficulty of pronunciation by anyone but a Fleming. Most of the French and men of the lily were killed in the narrow streets or slaughtered in their beds. Châtillon, almost alone, made his escape in disguise. The news of the "Bruges Matins" was the signal for general insurrection in all of Flanders except Ghent, and the men of the claw seized power everywhere.

Philip the Fair retaliated two months later by mustering all available troops and sending them to Flanders under the command of Robert d'Artois. They met the commoners of Flanders under the walls of Courtrai, in the open country known as the Plain of Groeninghe.

The royal army, composed of many knights from Picardy, Normandy, and Artois, and the flower of chivalry from Hainaut, Brabant, and Flanders in fact consisted of troops from the whole of the Low Countries. The army of the Flemish commoners consisted entirely of rough sons of the people, untrained troops, with only thirty knights to command them.

The battle was fought with all the savagery of civil war. The men of the claw took no prisoners but massacred pitilessly all those who spoke French, including all the Flemish nobility and leaders whose language then was French.

By the ordinary rules of warfare, the outcome of such an engagement should not have been difficult to foresee. Untrained troops automatically should have had little chance against the charge of armed horsemen, and the pointed breastplates and flying hoofs of their mounts should by all odds have broken the commoners' ranks into small groups the horsemen could have cut to pieces.

The commoners, however, had taken advantage of the ditches and bogs of the marshy country, and their army with its motley weapons was drawn up between two streams, giving the mounted attackers little space in which to maneuver. The men were grouped according to the towns and parishes from which they came, so that each man could easily spot anybody he knew. This was the rough and ready solution for the difficult problem of maintaining a coherent battle front throughout the campaign. Most of the men had as their only weapon iron-headed clubs with a hook or spike attached, the famous *goedendags* (good-mornings), with which they unsaddled the horsemen.

The choice of ground was to prove their salvation. Their main outpost was an island formed by three streams, so that the French charge could gather no momentum. On the fourth side, they were protected by the waters of the city moat, and their position could not be broken. The royal cavalry was forced to attack on a narrow front. It could not deploy and was compelled to waste its strength in a succession of useless charges.

Leading the commoners was at least one first-class strategist, Jean de Renesse, a military genius celebrated throughout Europe. He issued precise and detailed orders. No prisoners were to be taken, for they could only cause disorder in the rear. Each man was to remain at his post and under no circumstances was he to seek booty during the battle. Any soldier stooping to pick up treasures was to be slain by his fellows.

The French cavalry threw themselves upon these ranks, each noble horseman on his armored steed, little thinking the rough foot soldiers would offer resistance. The Flemings, however, were using new tactics, and the forces of chivalry were to have the surprise of their lives.

Count Robert d'Artois himself rode in the charge and succeeded in making his way through the Flemish ranks. He got as far as the great banner of Flanders, the sable lion in its golden field, which he wrenched from the standard bearer and proceeded to slash with his sword. The Flemings set upon him, dragging him from his horse; he surrendered, crying his name aloud. Phlegmatically, the commoners replied: "We do not understand French," and killed him where he stood.

The horsemen sought to encircle the Flemings, but their mounts could make no progress and slithered in the mud or sank in the bog. The Flemish ranks were still unbroken and the French soldiers seeing their attacks wreak so little damage, were seized with panic. They felt they were caught in a trap, and this led to their rout. Soon they were in full flight, not stopping until they had reached Tournai. Among the dead left on the field were the heads of seventy-five great families, and all the members of their high command, including Jacques de Châtillon, Pierre Flotte, and Robert d'Artois. This was the Battle of the Golden Spurs.* It took its name from a story that the booty found

* The Battle of the Golden Spurs was fought a dozen years before the Battle of Bannockburn, when Robert the Bruce followed almost exactly the tactics of Jean de Renesse in his choice of ground and in his use of unmounted troops to rout the

on the field included several hundred gilded spurs, the badges of rank of the slain knights. The writers of the period, however, make no mention of these spurs, which have never been found.

Other legends tell of this great battle. One recounts that Count Robert d'Artois himself had sinister premonitions before the attack. His pet wolf, Brun, attempted to prevent him from putting on his armor, or so the story goes. Foiled in this attempt, the wolf is said to have fled into the countryside beyond his master's ken. Another legend has it that the priest who said mass had lost the sacred wafer; and another reports that Robert d'Artois' own war horse had refused to carry him into battle, forcing him to use another mount.

It would be a great mistake to think of the strife between the Flemish communes and Philip the Fair as a national uprising against France. The Flemings at this period considered themselves as vassals of the French king; half their population spoke French and they did not think of the future in terms of political separation. Their struggle was social, not national. The French-speaking parts of Flanders, which did not take part in the Battle of Courtrai, were later to stage their own insurrection under democratic leaders who came into power at Douai and Lille and whose aim it was to establish a new social order.

For long years, the communes of Flanders were galvanized by this mystic ideal, and Flanders was able to put armies into the field, replenishing their ranks with new combatants. The property of patrician families was confiscated, forming a tremendous war-chest into which communes could dip for funds. Their position was not unlike that of the French Republican armies, which, after the Revolution, confiscated the property of *émigrés* to pursue the struggle and drew on the country's soil for new resources to hold all Europe at bay.

The Flemish insurrection was to continue for the next thirty years, despite a succession of truces and the resistance against the Treaty of Athis. Still later it was to enter new phases, with the revolt of coastal Flanders and the uprising of Jacob Van Artevelde in the middle of the fourteenth century.

The Flanders of 1302, however, flushed though she was by her victories, found the balance of forces irresistibly against her. In the eyes of history, the Battle of Courtrai was no more than an accident; the Flemings barely amounted to a twentieth of the whole French population, and it was clear enough that Philip the Fair sooner or later had to get the upper hand.

In the Low Countries themselves, Flanders had to keep France in

---

forces of English chivalry. The Scottish troops, however, were better armed than the Flemings; and the commoners of Flanders lacked the habit and training in warfare that helped to make the clansmen such formidable opponents. (Translator's note.)

check as well as deal with the tenacious hatreds of Holland and Hainaut. The supremacy of the port of Bruges was challenged by the young port of Dordrecht, and the Dutch staged their own version of the "Bruges Matins," massacring the Flemings at Delft. The Flemish fleet was wiped out at Zierickzee, and a French army approaching from the south defeated the Flemish commoners at Mons-en-Pévèle. Robert de Béthune, who had succeeded Guy de Dampierre, realized the hopelessness of the struggle and decided to sign the Treaty of Athis-sur-Orge (1305).

The Treaty of Athis restored Flanders to its count yet left it profoundly troubled. The weavers, still the core of the *clauwaert* party, had succeeded in seizing power in all the towns. They had introduced social reforms to break the patrician monopoly, and the freedom of the artisans and the people had been proclaimed.

At the popular level, however, there was neither capital nor the commercial organization to buy English wool for the weavers and to sell the products of the looms. The newly enfranchised masses were thus still under the economic domination of their former masters, who fixed their wages and were able to reduce them to impotence and unemployment.

The fourteenth century was to be dominated by the drama of the Flemish working class, with its successful seizure of power in the towns and its inability to win real freedom.

The modern solution would be to nationalize industry so that the towns themselves could organize trade. In the fourteenth century, this was impossible, for no nation had reached the point at which it could deal with such a task. The factors of production and the laws of economics were as yet unstudied. In the face of this ignorance, man's efforts were futile.

The weavers, though politically victorious, still had to depend upon their adversaries. The result was a constant desire to revolt. The social ferment produced outbursts of anarchy in which the inchoate masses, seeking to escape from their wretchedness, only succeeded in making it worse.

The first important event of the fourteenth century was an uprising in coastal Flanders. The inhabitants of this region lived on the half-flooded soil along the coast. They were charged by the count with the work of maintaining the dikes and clearing land recovered from the sea for cultivation. They were peasants and small, independent land-owners, free to elect their own assemblies.

After the Treaty of Athis, exiled nobles began returning to Flanders, demanding indemnification for the losses they had suffered. This produced a general irritation, which was particularly acute in the coastal regions where the inhabitants were accustomed to their freedom. An insurrection started under a popular leader named Zannekin who had the support of the peasants. They hoped to drive out the rich, seize the lands of the clergy, create a true rural democracy, and then reorganize society together with the urban workers.

The rising began in 1323, with propaganda and speech-making by countless agitators. They called meetings in country cemeteries to announce the dawn of a new age. In this country of small landholders, the Church appeared the chief obstacle to social progress, and one of the main demands of the agitators was distribution of monastery lands and abolition of tithes paid to the clergy.

An attempt to put down the rising, followed by a general amnesty (1324), had no effect. The movement spread into the towns, and Louis de Nevers, the Count of Flanders, was attacked and taken prisoner by the insurgents during a visit to Courtrai. He was held as hostage and bespattered with the blood of his own councilors, who were executed before his eyes. Ghent, which had become the capital of the *leliaerts*, held out against the revolution, and it was there that the noble and patrician families took refuge.

Before long, the movement fell into the hands of extremists and became more and more anti-clerical. One of its leaders, Jacques Péit, poured derision on Christian ceremonies and proclaimed his desire to see the last of the priests hanging from the gallows. He sought to create an agrarian republic—with no nobles and no clergy—governed by a reign of terror. At the same time, at the opposite end of the Low Countries, the people of Liège were in revolt, and there was unrest in many other towns.

The figure of the Flemish coastal peasant, the *kerel*, or "churl," rose up to loom before the eyes of the terrified nobility. A refugee poet in Ghent immortalized his subject's infectious horror in the *Kerelslied*.*

> Let us sing of the churls.
> Their hordes would make the devil affeared,
> They would subdue the lords.
> They wear an unkempt beard,
> Their ragged clothes are fit for a sty.
> Their hats too small for their heads
> Their hoods are all awry
> Their hose and shoes are worn to shreds.

* From A. A. Barnouw's translation (*Coming After*, New Brunswick, N. J.: Rutgers University Press, 1948).

With bread and cheese, curd and gruel
They all day stuff their guts.
That makes the churl such a fool
He never eats but gluts.

To the kermes goes the lout
Then he thinks himself a duke.
And there he lays about
With a rusty stave or crook.
He starts to drink of the wine,
And in his drunken drawl
He thinks "The world is mine,
City, land, and all."
With bread and cheese, curd and gruel
They all day stuff their guts.
That makes the churl such a fool
He never eats but gluts.

We teach them to be civil
Chasing them over the moors,
They scheme nothing but evil
I know where to send such a boor.
We'll drag and swing them high
And give their beards a shave.
The fellows can't get by
Only force can make them behave.
With bread and cheese, curd and gruel
They all day stuff their guts.
That makes the churl such a fool
He never eats but gluts.

The fourteenth and fifteenth centuries were to be beset by this strife between the "good guys" and the "bad guys," which inspired the famous dialogue between two ultraconservative burghers:

FIRST BURGHER: 'Tis shame that such a sorry rabble
                    Should aim to get a statesman's powers!
SECOND BURGHER: Yet if to war to go they're able,
                    Then we can stick to what is ours.
FIRST BURGHER: For that, it's just as well to know,
                    With what they've got they're never pleased. . . .
SECOND BURGHER: That's why, for sure, they'll soon get teased.

Louis de Nevers succeeded in escaping to Paris. He put the case to Philip VI, King of France, who mobilized an army of French knights and marched against the Flemings on the pretext that the Burgomaster of Bruges, Pieter de Deken, had called for English aid.

The decisive battle was fought at Mt. Cassel, on August 23, 1328, on that part of the Flemish plain that became so strategically important in 1918. This time the miracle of Courtrai was not repeated. The embattled masses of Flemish peasant-soldiers had no military training. Their proper course would have been to hold their positions on the top of Mt. Cassel and await the attack of the French horsemen. Drinking water was lacking, and the army of *kerels* was soon so thirsty that the soldiers lost patience and decided to march on the enemy in three-column formation. The French horsemen waited until the *kerels* were out of breath and their ranks ragged. Then they counter-attacked, cut their way through the ranks, separated the companies from one another, divided them up into isolated groups, and cut them to bits.

It was total disaster. All the towns of Flanders surrendered when they heard the news, and the captains and the commanders of the insurrection were tortured to death. Pieter de Deken was sent to Paris, where he was quartered. All the town fortifications except those of Ghent were destroyed, and the defeat at Cassel also spelled the end of the insurrection in Liège.

Bruges and Ypres had now played their parts, and even the names *clauwaerts* and *leliaerts* disappeared. A single blow, however, could not destroy the mass of the Flemish working class, nor could force put an end to economic and social problems. The victory of Mt. Cassel, therefore, settled nothing, and the spirit behind the revolt of the oppressed classes still existed on the eve of the Hundred Years' War.

These events have their own place in the strife and insurrection that shook the whole of Western Europe. The battle of Courtrai and the victory of Flemish democracy resulted in the revolts of Brussels, Louvain, Mechlin, and, further afield, in the Liège insurrection. The Low Countries were already a single unit. There was the same change everywhere between the social classes: the nobles, the rich capitalists, and the patricians against the artisans, the burghers, and the peasantry.

Hardly ten years after Mt. Cassel, Flanders was again in a state of revolt.

This time, King Edward III of England went to war with France. He was seeking to create a national textile industry of his own. He ordered the blockade of Flanders and prohibited the export of English wool. The Flemish weaving sheds had to stop work, and the unemployed weavers were starving.

It was clear that trouble was brewing. The burghers of Ghent, believing that it would be impossible to keep order, decided to ally them-

selves with the weavers. With this support, the weavers organized a
revolt in 1337 in which the rich and the poor were on the same side.
They created a government composed of burghers' nominees and the
heads of the major craft unions. At its head was Jacob van Artevelde.
He was a patrician, the scion of a *leliaert* family that had taken part
in the municipal administration during the reign of Philip the Fair.
He had held public office at the time of the suppression of the 1325
troubles. Appearing at first to be another simple captain, he soon rose
through his eloquence and energy. A rich merchant and big landowner who occupied a luxurious house in the center of town, he succeeded in rallying all Flanders behind him when the King of England
agreed to lift the wool blockade. His political fortunes depended upon
an alliance with England, designed to enable the people of Ghent to
keep the whole of Flanders in their power. His next step was to declare
war against Philip VI, and a Flemish army, with contingents from
all over the Low Countries, was soon besieging Tournai.

Jacob van Artevelde's power did not rest solely on the English alliance. It was supported by an understanding between the patricians
and the powerful weavers, who were now armed and installed in the
government representing a much more powerful force than the upper
middle class. Flanders of this period was not a state in any ordinary
meaning of the word, but an almost permanent revolution in which
the weavers were by far the most dynamic force. Their only rivals of
any consequence were the fullers,* whom they restricted as far as
possible in order to secure for themselves the best wages. The Flemish
working class was split by this conflict.

On May 2, 1345, the weavers and the fullers came to blows in the
Friday Market in Ghent. The battle raged through the whole of that
Black Monday, and in the end the fullers were massacred. After this,
the power of the Flemish weavers went unchallenged; and Jacob
van Artevelde, as a mere representative of the burgher element, was
no more than a figurehead, barely able to stay in office with the support
of the English King.

The King of England made many gestures of friendship toward the
"ruler" of Ghent, even authorizing his queen to stand as godmother
for Van Artevelde's son.† A final interview at Sluis between these two

---

* The fullers were the workmen whose job it was to mill the cloth underfoot after
weaving, to break it up and make it supple.

† It was in Ghent, too, that Edward's wife, Philippa of Hainaut, bore the infant
John of Gaunt (Ghent). He was the founder of the line of the English House of
Lancaster; and, through his third (Flemish) wife, Catherine Swynford, of the House
of Tudor, which, after the War of the Roses, acceded to the English throne and
became the direct ancestor of the successive reigning dynasties of Stuart, Hanover,
Saxe-Coburg, and the present House of Windsor. (Translator's note.)

leaders came to nothing. Fits of wrath and pride, which were to hasten Van Artevelde's fall, were no doubt part of his reaction to his position in Ghent. He was accused of wanting to deliver Flanders into English hands. Upon his return from Sluis, he had to barricade himself in his Calanderberg mansion, guarded by a troop of Welsh archers. Eventually, the crowds stormed the house and killed him, without giving him a chance to explain his actions. Even his body disappeared and was never found.

The weavers assumed power in his place. The following year, Louis de Nevers was killed at Crécy, leaving his son, the young Louis de Maele, a prisoner of the Flemish commune.

Louis de Maele has gone down in history because of his fondness for buffoons and exotic animals, his frivolity, and his licentious loves; but it is not by these traits that he should be judged. He was an adroit and cunning statesman, reminiscent of the Italian princes of the Renaissance. He loved pomp, was cynical and without scruples, and successfully brought all his opponents to heel. In order to recover authority, he created a new judicial tribunal known as the count's audience, and he shrewdly offered the hand of his daughter Margaret to all neighboring princes to ensure the future independence of Flanders. The first step of his career was to escape from the hands of the communes. He did so in the course of a hunting party, fleeing to Brabant, where he married the daughter of Duke Jean III. From this vantage point, he set out to reconquer Flanders.

By this time everyone was weary of the weavers' power. They were attacked and massacred in Bruges and Ypres in 1348 by members of the other crafts. Even in Ghent they lost ground, although they defended themselves with stubborn energy when they were besieged. They were also afflicted by the plague, which was now making its way across Europe, but their leaders swore they would have no tomb other than the great market place.

On January 13, 1349, a group of émigrés found their way back into the city and decimated the weavers, throwing survivors into the Schelde. All Flanders rallied to the support of Louis de Maele, and a conservative reaction set in. There was special legislation enacted against the artisans, and a number emigrated to Norfolk and Suffolk, where they helped the growth of the new English textile industry, which was to become so powerful a competitor of its Flemish counterpart.

Against this background, the Hundred Years' War was following its course. France was foundering beneath the weight of disaster and civil strife; and Louis de Maele, situated between combatants who were forever seeking his alliance, succeeded in remaining neutral for thirty years.

The Hundred Years' War (1335–1435) is a paradox for any historian. France of the fourteenth century was a country of 20 million inhabitants, and that, for a whole century, it should be attacked, invaded, and beaten by a little country of 2 or 3 million people—the England of Edward III—baffles the imagination. But it was less a war than a succession of revolutions, or at any rate a state of unrest and strife, lasting for generations, for which military defeats and victories were only a backdrop.

But it must be remembered that the Hundred Years' War was not limited to France and England; it was a European phenomenon caused essentially by economic problems. Its origin lay primarily in the great commercial expansion of the thirteenth century that declined with the end of the colonization of eastern Europe and in the social crises that were then threatening the internal stability of every country. War, wrongly considered a remedy for political difficulty, was no more than a bloody manifestation of the decline it aggravated. Since the beginning of the fourteenth century, trade had found no new outlets. The Flemish cloth business had fallen off, and all the great Italian banks were failing. In Germany, eastward migration was checked, and the haven it had offered for surplus populations thus vanished. Conflict and internal tensions increased throughout Europe.

In France, the Champagne fairs, which brought expansion of the towns and revenues to the royal treasury through levies on trade, were on their last legs. Spanish and Italian merchants who frequented the fairs to buy the products of northern Europe had traveled along the Rhone Valley, but now they came directly to the Low Countries by the Rhine route or the new sealanes that linked Bruges with the Mediterranean. France, as a result, was beset by economic and social unrest.

To all this were added the natural disasters of famine and epidemic. One inevitable result was a sharpening of social strife. The resulting violence was coupled with a reduction in popular purchasing power. The ensuing ruin of trade only aggravated the causes of war.

The great plague of 1347 wiped out a third of the adult population of Europe, producing a terrible manpower crisis that disorganized all of society. Living costs rose rapidly, but not because money was abundant and agricultural production was stimulated, but, on the contrary, because production had fallen off and the drop in the standard of living led to general discontent. The peasants alone enjoyed the benefit of high wages, which put them in violent opposition to the lords of the manors and lay at the root of all the rioting and social unrest of France in 1355, and of England in 1380.

In this shifting and unstable world the strength of ideologies and mystical doctrines increased. Class warfare led to a series of revolutions and wars that engulfed almost every country but were nothing more than a form of social self-destruction.

Belgium was fortunate in escaping most of these problems, so that she could continue expanding and adapting to new circumstances. This enabled her, under the dukes of Burgundy, to become one of the first commercial powers of Europe.

Brabant, which stood outside the scene of the Hundred Years' War, was able to use her position to create a powerful textile industry. Her products were exported to Germany, France, and England, and a host of new industries sprang up there as well as in other parts of the Low Countries. In Bruges, the market halls with their belfry were completed. Louvain had 2,400 weaving looms, and Mechlin became a port.

Belgium thus was able to benefit from the technical progress being made, and because her agriculture was the most modern and advanced in the world, its high yield enabled the country to minimize the economic disorganization resulting from the plague. Thus at a time when warfare and commercial crises were ravaging all Europe, the Low Countries were spared. The use of vegetables in the planting cycle, for example, made it possible to treble the crops by rotation—wheat, beans, oats (or clover), and then wheat again.

Although their agricultural and industrial progress kept the Belgians out of the Hundred Years' War, it did not prevent local wars in the Low Countries during the fourteenth century. Most were limited to simple economic goals, such as the ownership of a road or a port. France and England, on the other hand, under the pretext of defending themselves, were thinking only of each other's destruction.

By 1334, many of the streets of Brussels were paved with cobblestones. A whole organization had been created under two civil servants known as the Master of the Highway and the Master of the Mud to clean the roads and enforce health regulations. The town was expanding, and many of the gardens and unused land inside the walls were disappearing. Streets ran into one another, and continuous rows of houses were built.

Markets and market places increased in number and kind. There was a fish market, a mussel market, a tripe market, a chicken market, a cheese market, an herb market, and a milk market—all of which proof that Brussels had already become a place to which people flocked to eat.

Fires were still frequent, and wooden or mud houses were forever being burned down. In 1342, a regulation prohibiting thatched roofs was passed.

City life was extremely noisy. The townspeople were deafened not only by the shouts of passers-by and the grinding wheels of carts and wagons, but also by bells that marked every small event of the day. At dawn, the *Koopklok*, or "trader's bell," sounded to call shopkeepers to their places of business. Stall keepers opened their shutters and vendors of butter, fruit, game, tripe, and clothing loudly hawked their wares. Then the *Werkklok* rang to mark the beginning—as well as the end—of the working day for the laborers; for all serious events, such as executions, riots, or enemy attacks, the tocsin was sounded by the *Stormklok*. The taverns were famous and sold innumerable varieties of beer.

Court life was brilliant indeed. Wenceslas, Duke of Brabant, husband of the Duchess Jeanne, was devoted to good fare and fine horses, elaborate attire, exotic animals, concerts, festivals, and all the other delights of a luxurious and stately life.

> The game of tennis and the dance, the joust,
> Was what the Duke most greatly loved to do;
> And then to pay his court to girls and ladies,
> And all amid the joyfulness of song.

The French poet Eustache Deschamps, who spent three years in Brussels about 1380, composed some sad verses in praise of the charms of life there when he left:

> Beauty and mirth and all delights—farewell!
> In all my frolics, dances, happy songs,
> A thousand times to you my heart belongs,
> Brussels, beside the pools I love so well.
> The cozy warmth, and all the girls so pleasant!
> Beauty and mirth and all delights—farewell!
> Fine rooms, and Rhenish wine, soft beds as well,
> And coney, plover, capons, too, and pheasant.
> Sweet company, and ever-gentle folk,
> Beauty and mirth and all delights—farewell!

The fourteenth century was an age of pomp and circumstance. Fashions changed very quickly and both men's and women's clothes were completely transformed. In the middle of the fourteenth century, Charles V protested in Paris that women's clothes had become so tight that they had to be sewn directly onto their bodies—and ripped when they were taken off. Fashion required that women appear as thin as possible, with their breasts confined by the cloth and their thighs straight. They did, in fact, appear almost naked in the tight, flexible clothes of the period; and men, when they bowed, showed all that was within their hose. Within a few years, however, these clothes were replaced by draped and flowing robes and by skirts that swept the ground. One year, hair styles were as flat as pancakes; the next, they towered so high that castle doors had to be remade to permit women to pass from one room to another.

Some fashions did not change, perhaps because they were the most absurd of all: the pointed shoes of men and the wasp-waists of women —a result of the corset, now making its first appearance in history.

The low-cut neckline, which had not been seen since Roman times and would have been unimaginable in the thirteenth century, reappeared, scandalously taking the form of the "brazen petticoat," a style that left the breasts completely uncovered or barely concealed by a little neckpiece. Men covered themselves less and less, but in their case clothes began to disappear at the bottom. In the thirteenth century, robes had descended at least halfway down the calf, but now they moved progressively upwards, revealing first the knees, then the thighs, and, moving even higher, eventually exposing the hips.

It was in this period that the taste for portraiture made its appearance. During the thirteenth century, people had been content to use anonymous sculpture, bearing little resemblance to their originals, for tombs and statues. We know practically nothing of the features of St. Louis, of Guy de Dampierre, or of Philip the Fair; but we are familiar enough with those of John II and Philip the Bold, for it now became general practice to have one's portrait painted in color. Another matter that contemporaries noted particularly was the growing taste for building zoological gardens—a foretaste of the great maritime discoveries of the Renaissance. Exotic animals of many types were unloaded at Bruges, and people came from afar to buy them. Princes and counts were eager to have a menagerie. Louis de Maele had one, as did the great lords of France. Preparations were even made to import leopards and cheetahs from Africa to be used in hunting lesser game.

Cooking and eating habits were also undergoing a change. Meals now began with hors d'oeuvres, including salads and raw vegetables steeped in vinegar, salted fish, and fruits and sweet dishes, and dinner sometimes began with what we would consider desserts. The hors d'oeuvres included cooked apples, roast figs, purées of peas, herrings, and eels.

Afterward came the roasts, the fish dishes, and the fowl. The repast ended with fruit, waffles, and, finally, hypocras—a mulled wine mixed with ground cinnamon, ginger, muscat, and cardamon beaten with sugar and honey. Hypocras ended every meal, very much like cordials of our time. It signaled the moment for the ladies to withdraw, just as does port in present-day England.

But no vegetables were served. They were not regarded as food and were used only as garnishes. Leeks, for example, decorated beef. Shell-fish were much sought after. Mussels were eaten with vinegar, and snails began to appear on the menu under the name of *limaçons*. Oysters were fried in breadcrumbs and served with a pepper sauce, as they still are in England.

Pork disappeared from the tables of the rich, where it was to be found during the thirteenth century, to go to the scullery under the name of bacon. A similar fate befell the whale, which, caught in great quantities, became the poor man's fish.

With improvements in sailing vessels, a great variety of fish, from salted cod to porpoise (which was prepared in the same way as pork and was considered a welcome change), from whale to herring, became important food items.

The menu of a banquet given by one of the burghers of Valenciennes gives us an idea of what was served at a ceremonial dinner.

The first course consisted of brains and venison. Next came the first of the light dishes—fresh-water lampreys seasoned with cloves and accompanied by various sauces—which alternated with the chief items. The second main course consisted of peacocks, chickens, partridges, herons, and rabbits, all served with their own sauces, and various side dishes. The third course was a blancmange sprinkled with sugar and pomegranate seeds, served with almonds fried in honey, and an aspic jelly made of several varieties of fish. The fourth course was loach, a kind of freshwater carp, fried with garlic buds, and accompanied by an eel *pâté*. Next came a galantine—a jellied, pressed roll of mushrooms and the meat of several fowl—served with peacocks, herons, and chickens. This was followed by the sixth course, crawfish, with boar's head as a side dish. Finally, there was dessert, consisting of apple-like medlars and figs, followed by "claret." This was really a sweet Spanish wine that was made sweeter and more aromatic by mulling it with honey and spices. The meal came to an end with *ronds mestiers*, dry biscuits similar to *petits fours*.

The fourteenth century brought major transformations in Belgian architecture. Town halls, which had been almost unknown a hundred years earlier, were now springing up all over. The town hall at Bruges dates from the latter years of the thirteenth century, but those of Brussels, Louvain, and Oudenaarde, and the cloth hall at Ypres, were yet to be built. Belfries were largely unknown, or, at most, were only one or two stories tall at the time the communes entered their golden age. Monuments as distinctive as the chancel of St. Gudule in Brussels, and the present belfry in Bruges do not date from the century of Van Artevelde, but from the period just before the Renaissance.

The artists of the Low Countries were just beginning to produce sculpture, which was the great medium of artistic expression in the Middle Ages. Some sculpture had always been found in the traditional metalworking region of the Meuse Valley.

In the eastern part of Belgium, relics dating back to the Carolingian period include ivory carvings of Byzantine origin, even Syrio-Egyptian work, like the Tongres diptych of the sixth century. Artists began to imitate these works, and by the tenth century they had produced the Notger ivory—a prince-bishop kneeling in prayer. There were many such works, and they created a style the silversmiths and brassworkers of the Meuse Valley imitated when they began to work in metal.

They soon left their Oriental and Byzantine models behind. Between 1111 and 1118, Renier de Huy carved the baptismal font in the Church of St. Bartholomew in Liège, a masterpiece that echoes the Alexandrian period and seems to bridge the gap between Greek and Renaissance art. It is a work of genuis. The beauty of the figures, the purity of composition, and the delicately modeled lines are almost modern, compared with the stiff, stilted sculpture of the medieval period. Even Renier's contemporaries regarded it as a masterpiece, and for centuries many Walloons, particularly those near Liège, became sculptors.

It is no longer possible to distinguish between Walloon and French artists. Many Walloons sought a career in Paris. Among them were Pépin de Huy, who went into the service of Mahaut d'Artois and worked on the royal tombs in the basilica of St. Denis, and Jean de Liége, who carved the statues of Blanche de France and Charles VI—now in the Louvre—as well as the images of Queen Jeanne d'Evreux and Philippine de Hainaut, now in Westminster Abbey.

Tournai's magnificent cathedral was gradually assuming its ultimate style. It was begun on the site of an earlier basilica about 850, in the style of the Carolingian Renaissance. The older narthex was made into the apse at the western end of the new building, and another church stood close alongside. Between 1110 and 1171, it became, little by little, a Romanesque church. The Gothic chancel, added in the thirteenth century, really represents a lost battle for the innovators.

During 1243-55, the great Bishop Gauthier de Marvis had a plan for the complete demolition of the Romanesque church and its reconstruction as a Gothic edifice. He began with the chancel, which was only a century old and of mediocre quality, and replaced it with the magnificent choir still there today. For want of money, his successors were unable to continue the work.

The five towers of the Romanesque cathedral still stand, and it is the Western world's most gigantic relic from the Middle Ages, equaled only by the Abbey Church of Cluny. Imitations are to be found in all northern French churches, as far afield as Chartres; and Rheims Cathedral itself is in part a copy. The famous cathedral of the coronation of the French kings had, in its original form, seven towers copied from those of Tournai. They remained there until after the time of Joan of Arc, and in 1481, during the reign of Louis XI, they were burned to the ground.

The city of Tournai fell under the direct rule of the kings of France, but in the days of episcopal rule it had claimed to be a free town. When Philip II asked one of the bishops from whom he had received his authority, the reply was:

> From our Lady and God, Sire,
> Like the bishops of old.

The bishop himself, however, was powerless against the growing power of the burghers. He complained to Philip II, who responded by placing the town under his own protection.

The people of Tournai greeted the King of France enthusiastically, for he ruled them from afar, thus giving them the greatest possible degree of liberty. They alone had the right to set up the court known as the King's Chamber and to mount guard over his royal person in time of war. The citizens of Tournai were all "noblemen," and no tax levied on the common people of France could be enforced against them. Their charters proclaimed that they were "the King's friends"; and they enjoyed the remarkable privilege of exemption from all import and export duties on goods. Tournai, on the kingdom's flank, was a clear invitation to the evasion of customs duties.

On the other hand, Tournai was the King's stronghold in the very heart of Flanders. The people of Tournai were so loyal to the French monarchy that they were called "doubly French." It was soon a by-word that "the green lily grows in the roads of Tournai," and devotion to the King was pushed to the most extravagant lengths. In 1299, Tournai canonized St. Louis and erected a chapel dedicated to him.

The inhabitants took part in the Battle of Bouvines in 1214, and it was their participation that won the victory. In 1242, Tournai detachments fought to the last man in the Battle of Saintes. In 1297, under Philip the Fair, they besieged Lille. They took part in the Battle of Mons-en-Pévèle, and in 1328 they were at Mt. Cassel.

Their valor became legendary. At the beginning of the Hundred Years' War, they sent Philip VI a contingent of 1,000 foot soldiers who marched all night without food or drink to reach him. The story holds that when the King saw them, he cried out in the patois of Picardy: "Now we can get on with it. The Tournaisians have come."

During the Hundred Years' War, Tournai naturally fought for the "King of Bourges" against the English. A time came when Charles VII possessed only four important fortresses in his entire kingdom— Mont St. Michel in the west, Vaucouleurs in the east, Orléans in the center, and Tournai in the north.

The city, surrounded as it was by enemies, defied them by cultivating a lily in full flower on the tower of the town hall. Joan of Arc, in a letter, described the Tournaisians as "gentle and loyal Frenchmen." After she fell into English hands, the Tournaisians took up a collection for her. Later they were to aid Louis XI in the capture of Condé.

This tiny city was able to retain its freedom up to the end of the Middle Ages by virtue of the passionate loyalty of its people and the free contract that bound them to the Crown of France.

In the meantime, the other great towns of the Low Countries that were founded in the tenth century continued to grow.

About the middle of the fourteenth century, Ghent had become the true capital of Flanders. Its population numbered about 60,000, an enormous figure for this period, second only to that of Paris. At all times, Ghent was able to field an organized army of not less than 15,000 men, almost as big a force as the entire English army at the battle of Crécy. The poet Boudewyn van der Loren summed up the ideal of the people of Ghent in the words he put into the mouth of a young girl with whom the city was identified: "To live in virtue and freedom is worth more than gold or precious stones."

After the beginning of the fourteenth century, the people of Ghent were fired by an ideal as universal and generous as that of modern revolutionaries. Its weavers were out to create a "new world" and to secure the triumph of social justice and the victory of honesty over corruption. Their successive rebellions were, however, of little consequence. They were, to all intents and purposes, incomprehensible at the time, and all Europe came to hate the city of Ghent as a seat of trouble and destruction. Still, one cannot help admire the indomitable spirit of freedom that inspired the weavers of Ghent, and the inexhaustible energy and tenacity with which, after each of their defeats—their leaders dead and they themselves ground down and terrorized—they prepared for the next uprising.

The city of Ghent, overpopulated because of its expanding industry, could only keep its inhabitants alive by feeding them at subsistence level. There was no solution to the problem, and men struggled with it in vain. The existence of this "red city," governed against a background of recurrent outbreaks, created a vast economic and social drama.

Most of the writers of the time were obsessed by the problem. They thought of Ghent as an "incarnate demon," a town of evil and perversity whose uprisings were a threat to all of human society. It was a child of Satan and of Cain, and its hungry weavers seemed to be possessed of the devil. It was of Ghent that the poet Eustache Deschamps wrote:

> Tree of pride and growth of sin,
>> With every treason rent;
> Born of Canaan, Judas, Cain,
> Mad heretic, in all things vain,
>> Subject to Lucifer's intent . . .
> God has willed your sentence plain,
>> Take heed, false town of Ghent.

In the fifteenth century, the chronicler Georges Chastellain wrote: "Ha! Ghent! Ghent the Bad! Unthankful and unmindful of the gifts of God. Town of blackness and darkness!"

Commynes himself could make nothing of the perpetual spirit of anarchy in "this town where so much evil has befallen, and that is of so little usefulness for the country and still less for the prince. It is not like Bruges, which is a great storehouse of merchandise and a great assembly for foreign nations, so that it would be pity indeed if it were destroyed."

It was the capital of insurrection, the city of Cain, the township of unjustified protest and unmitigated evil, deserving the hatred of mankind. It was cloaked in this gloomy legend for two centuries; whereas in reality it was the scene of a struggle between the restless and impotent poor against the all-powerful rich.

The history of the principality of Liège is bloody and tumultuous; but it was an astonishing human experience. That city, founded on freedom almost 1,000 years earlier, had as long a period of democracy as any town or region could claim.

It was an intellectual center where the influx of students from England, Frisia, Germany, and the Slavic countries contributed to an atmosphere of culture from the eleventh century onwards. The master scholars of Liège found their way as far afield as Ratisbon and Italy, and they triumphed in particular at the University of Paris. It was at Liège that French literature appeared in written form. The texts included *Le Miroir de Vie et de Mort, Les Sept Vies et les Sept Vertus,* and *Le Pélerinage de Vies Humaines,* the oldest morality plays known.

The surrounding country had long been industrialized. The French word *houille,* "coal," is a Liège word first applied to the coal discovered there in the thirteenth century. The collieries were worked by the peasantry, who tilled the fields in summer and mined the coal in winter; metalworking continued and expanded, and the city was filled with bankers and money-changers.

One of the most striking features of Liège's history is the republican character of its government. The prince-bishop was only entitled to administer by agreement with the various population groups, which were known as the "sense of the country." In 1196, a charter given by Bishop Albert de Cuyck proclaimed the freedom of the individual, the sanctity of the home, and the right of every man to be tried in a free court. It was signed nineteen years before the Magna Charta and is the first statement of the English doctrine of habeas corpus.

In the thirteenth century, this industrial town became a financial capital and was able to make loans at interest rates as high as 49 per cent per annum. A rate of 48.57 per cent is recorded for a loan contracted by the Abbé of St. Trond in 1254, and other loans were granted all over Europe. Coal mining, metalworking, and arms manufacture were well-developed industries. A democratic party came into existence, composed of small independent artisans rather than wage earners, as had been the case in Flanders.

Lords—living in castles dominating the countryside—who had been fighting each other for more than a century, struggled in vain to get the better of the people of Liège. When traitors planned to open the city gates to conspirators from without, members of the democratic party heard of the treachery and barred the road with chains while they themselves hid in the meat market.

On August 13, 1312, an armed party of noblemen and patricians came from Huy by night and stole into the city at St. Martin's Gate, which had been secretly opened to them by a traitor. They advanced along the quiet streets until they came to the market place adjoining St. Lambert's Cathedral in the center of town. Here they summoned the remaining conspirators from outside the gates by setting fire to the butchers' hall. The fire could be seen for miles around and it was to proclaim the news that they were masters of the city. But the light brightened the streets and woke the thousands of artisans living in the old houses around the cathedral in the commoners' quarters of the town. They rose, rushed into the market place, and, aided by the canons of St. Lambert's, who had mustered their servants and soldiers, threw themselves on the invaders.

It was a moonless night, but by the light of the flames men fought as though it were high noon. The troops attached to St. Lambert's were first concentrated in the church, but soon they burst open the doors and, torches in hand, rushed out to help the people. More and more artisans gathered from all parts of the city; the fight continued until the burning butchers' hall had become a dark and smoldering ruin and the torches went out one by one. When the night grew blacker, the knights who were still outside the city realized that the attack had failed and prudently remained where they were. The patrician insurgents, now lost in the darkness, did not dare to make a move before dawn.

At dawn they saw that they were trapped and beat a slow retreat toward St. Martin's Gate, through which they hoped to make their escape. They had to fight a rear-guard action and only gained ground step by step in the effort to keep their foes from cutting them off. By this time, reinforcements were reaching the artisans from all sides, and the miners of St. Margaret, armed with their coal picks, were pouring into the city. Just as the patricians were about to leave by St. Martin's Gate, Jean Dupont, the traitor who had opened it, took fright and closed it. The insurgents' only refuge was St. Martin's Church, where they were encircled by their enemies.

Those who tried to escape were slain. The artisans piled straw around the church and set fire to it before the sun was fully up. Those trapped were either burned or suffocated. "The flower of the city is consumed," cried the poet Jean d'Outremeuse, and the day came to be known as Mal St. Martin. It marked the triumph of democracy. The patricians capitulated, signing the Peace of Angleur, which provided for direct government by the people, with a sovereign assembly of the crafts as its main institution.

This was not the end of the civil strife, however. Special laws were passed prohibiting patricians from publicly shouting "Down with the rogues!" and the poor from replying "Down with the fops!" So intense was social hatred that when Prince-Bishop Englebert de la Marck made his ceremonial entry into Liège he was almost frightened into flight by the cries and shouts of thousands of men and women lining his path.

After the Peace of Fexhe (1315) and the Letter of St. James (1343) —the instruments by which the prince-bishop acknowledged the rights of the people—the craft unions became the basis of all political organizations. They alone had the right to sit on the town council; and the patricians and noblemen, if they wished to vote, had to belong to one or another. Class warfare thus disappeared, and thus democracy survived in Liège. Here, the only true form of democracy—simultaneous political and economic democracy—came into being. It is futile to give men political liberty if they are not first given the means of earning their livelihood.

While the rich remained masters of the factories and the means of production in Flanders, Brabant, and the rest of the Low Countries, the population of Liège was made up of independent artisans enjoying political and economic equality. They formed a compact block, and although at times there was opposition between old and young, no other social classes wielded any real power. As in the free towns of Germany, sovereign power was vested in a general meeting of citizens attended by all inhabitants.

The fourteenth century ended with a major social upheaval, and its consequences were felt throughout Europe. Flanders was the cradle of this upheaval.

The vain, cunning Louis de Maele had smashed the system by which industrial towns had controlled the countryside to maintain their routes of commerce. The Flemish textile industry was struggling against competition from Brabant and England. Wages were low and workmen were being reduced to starvation by a steady rise in the cost of living. In 1379, the weavers of Ghent again adopted the white hood as their badge. Their leader, Jean Yoens, used the construction of the Bruges Canal as the occasion for staging a revolt. When the canal workers arrived in the Ghent suburbs, the weavers cut them to pieces. An appeal went out, and all the weavers of Flanders rose to aid their colleagues. Louis de Maele was forced to capitulate; and in Bruges and Ypres, too, the revolution triumphed.

Flanders itself was divided, however. The butchers' and fishermen's corporations, rivals of the weavers, recaptured Bruges and besieged Ghent. The great city, cut off from the outside world, turned to Philippe, a son of Jacob van Artevelde. Before being called, he had led a quiet country life, fishing and raising peacocks, but, overnight, he was transformed into a tribune and popular leader of astonishing force.

The people of Ghent put up a long resistance. In a gesture of bravado, they threw down their gates and, with only their militia to defend them, defied the Flemings to launch an attack. Their starving armies marched on Bruges and surprised the town during the procession of the Holy Blood. The men of Ghent joined battle against a force ten times as great as theirs and won their victory at Beverhoutsvelt (1382). Count Louis de Maele had to flee. He hid out in a working woman's hovel, escaped to Lille, and then went to Paris.

The tale Jean Froissart tells of these events is suspected of embellishment. Nonetheless it clearly expresses the violent enmity between opposing parties.

In Bruges, on the evening of the Battle of Beverhoutsvelt, Count Louis de Maele attempted to lead his troops into the great market place. The men of Ghent were hot on the heels of the enemy and forced them to the market place to form their line of battle.

Louis de Maele at last understood his position and listened to the words of his troops, who said: "The men of Ghent are masters of the town, and if you advance toward the market place, you will be either captured or slain. Even if not, you are in great jeopardy. They are going from street to street in large numbers, seeking out their foes. They have friends who lead them from house to house, to find those for whom they search. You can no longer escape by any of the gates of Bruges. The men of Ghent are masters of them all; nor can you return to your palace for aid. The men of Ghent are marching upon it."

Thus the Count of Flanders remained all alone in great peril. Had he fallen into the hands of the bands from Ghent who were searching the town, he would have been slain without remorse. These bands were searching through all the houses and killing friends of the Count or carrying them off to the market square. In sight of Philip van Artevelde and his lieutenants, these peasants were executed after a kangaroo court-martial.

After creeping through dark alleyways until midnight, while the men of Ghent were all over the city, Louis de Maele decided to knock on the door of a poor woman, to escape capture. It was a poor, small house, blackened by peat and smoke. There was one tiny room with a piece of old cloth to hide the fire. Above, there was a garret, where the woman's children slept on a pallet. When the Count came in, shocked by the house in which he found himself, he said to the frightened woman: "Save me. I am your lord, the Count of Flanders. I must hide from enemies who are pursuing me. I will repay you for sheltering me." The woman knew him well, for she had in the past asked him for alms. She had also seen him when he had gone about the town in pursuit of pleasure.

She immediately told him—for delay would have been fatal—"Sire, go up to the garret and hide beneath the pallet where my children are asleep." He did so, and the woman pretended to tend the fire. Then she took one of her children in her arms. The Count found a place between the floorboards and the straw. He turned his face to the wall and kept still.

Soon the men of Ghent, who were exploring the neighborhood, came to the poor woman's house saying they had just seen a man enter. They found her sitting before the fire, holding her child in her arms. They asked: "Woman, where is the man we just saw enter and shut the door behind him?" "By my faith," she said, "I saw no one, but a few moments ago, I threw out some water and then shut the door again. I have no place where I could hide a man. You can see the whole house. There is my bed, and there lie my children." One of the men then took a candle and mounted the steps so that his head was in the attic and he could see nothing but the pallet and sleeping children. He looked around and then said to his companions: "Come on then, we're wasting our time here and letting the others escape. Poverty can't lie. There's no one here but the children." Then they left and continued their search.

The Count overheard this in his hiding-place. As they spoke, he trembled for his life. What could he have thought or imagined? That morning he may well have said to himself: "I am one of the greatest princes of Christendom." And the very same night he was hiding out and may have thought that the fortunes of this world are unstable. It would be great good fortune for him if he could escape and save his life.

Louis de Maele succeeded in escaping and reaching Paris, where he asked the King of France for help. His son-in-law, Philip the Bold, who had become regent of the kingdom at the death of Charles V, intervened to restore the peace.

The victory of the men of Ghent unleashed a wave of revolution across all Europe. In Rouen, there was the insurrection of the Harelles; in Auvergne and the Languedoc, the Tuchins rebelled; and at Florence, there were the Ciompi. In Paris, the Maillotins seized the mallets stored in the arsenal and massacred the tax collectors. Trouble spread like wildfire throughout the entire kingdom: from Amiens to Béziers, from St. Quentin to Rheims to Orléans. In England, Wat Tyler, the "king of the people," started the great rebellion of 1391 and, with his workers and peasants, seized London.

For five years, the Low Countries remained in a state of permanent insurrection. The towns of Brabant rose, as did those of Liège. At Louvain, democrats threw the patrician aldermen from the windows of the town hall; and the men of Liège marched to the aid of Ghent, which had become the revolutionary capital of Europe. At this point, Philip the Bold led a powerful French army into the Low Countries. They met the Ghent militia at Roosebeke (1382). The battle lasted only a few minutes and was another Mt. Cassel. White hoods, formed in a tight square of 40,000 men, at first stove in the enemy center, but they were soon outflanked and the square was broken. The French lost 43 men, the Ghentians 26,000. The body of Philip van Artevelde was found on the field of battle, the wounded were massacred like dogs. The victors went on to Courtrai and purged the memory of the Battle of the Golden Spurs. Every Flemish town surrendered, with the exception of Ghent, which called the English King, Richard II, to its aid. Philip the Bold was to inherit the title of Count of Flanders after the death of his father-in-law, Louis de Maele. Not planning to ravage and ransack his future estates, he offered Ghent a general amnesty. Its inhabitants at last decided to make peace on December 18, 1385. This was the end of the independence of Flanders. A new power was born in Europe. The century of the Van Arteveldes had come to an end, and the era of the dukes of Burgundy was dawning.

V

THE BURGUNDIAN EPIC

The four dukes of Burgundy are the bright stars in the firmament of the Low Countries. They reigned for a full century, and the states they governed grew continuously in wealth and power while, around them, France and England lived under the shadow of revolution and civil war.

Their very names savor of magnificence—a true index of their worth. Philip the Bold was so called for his courage; John the Fearless gained his title at the battle of Nicopolis against the Turks; Philip the Good was so named for his power rather than his piety; Charles the Bold was formidable or victorious rather than rash or imprudent.

The portraits of the aging Philip the Bold bear a strong resemblance to Goethe. He was a farsighted ruler, and he inaugurated a policy of marriages of state that unified the Low Countries. His son, John the Fearless, succeeded him as master of half the kingdom, heading the somewhat democratic Burgundian Party.

Under Philip the Good, the Low Countries became the richest in Europe. It is said that Duke Philip, on his deathbed, compared his career to a dream. A succession of deaths of princes and princesses had given him undreamed of chances of extending the frontiers of his domain. He brought under his sway all the provinces that are now Belgium and Holland, from Frisia to Zeeland, from Hainaut to the Archbishopric of Utrecht, from Brabant to Luxemburg. Even the principality of Liège came more or less under his protection.

Duke Philip was a dabbler in the arts, a great sensualist, and a ruthless and tenacious politician. His contemporaries nicknamed him Philip the Confident, for nothing disturbed him. He stood straight as an arrow and all who looked upon him were struck by his shaggy eye-

93

brows. These were the barometer of his emotions, for in moments of anger his eyes would flash and "his eyebrows bristled so, they looked like horns." But he easily regained his self-possession and turned again to his pleasures. A great lover of women and amorous adventure, he was proud of his eighteen illegitimate children being raised at his court.

He had, nonetheless, the refined tastes of an artist. He loved jewels and fine materials. Sensualist though he was, he was also a tireless worker. At the age of sixty, he said that if the day should come when he must cease to work, he would gladly die.

According to Guillaume Fillastre, Philip slept little, often went to bed at two in the morning, arising at six. He was forever busy, either reading or exercising, for he was incapable of remaining idle. His appetite was modest, and the fabulous banquets of the Burgundian court were, for him, simply occasions of state. He preferred a slice of ham or salted beef to the partridges and delicate dishes he forced himself to eat at official banquets.

Often he ate nothing until four o'clock in the afternoon, and he could live four days a week on bread and water. He was also exceedingly pious and spent much of his time in prayer, even while his companions waited for him on the eve of combat. His piety, however, did not prevent him from having many mistresses.

His chief characteristic was patience, for he refused to be hurried, and sometimes he carried this trait to the point of seeming neglect of his affairs. He had a horror of making important decisions and could never bring himself to do so until developments forced his hand. It was this very indecision that produced the most important results of his reign, enabling him to weather defeats, disappointments, and abuse without acting imprudently or hastily. His contemporaries admired his equanimity for, except in his brief moments of wrath, his attitude was phlegmatic and unconcerned.

One of his eccentricities was his refusal to hear mass except at two or three o'clock in the afternoon. His entourage found this particularly shocking, but it was in fact sanctioned by a special authorization he had obtained from the Pope.

He scarcely ever sat down, making it a habit to take his meals standing, often without unbuckling his sword. His meals were indeed a spectacle, for everybody watched his refined and elegant gestures as he ate. He walked with imposing grace and majesty, and his conversational style was deliberate and free of coarse expressions. He never showed himself out of humor, but Chastellain records that anybody who irritated him "became an enemy."

On one occasion, in a fit of furious anger provoked by his son, Charles the Bold, he jumped on horseback like a madman and rode out into the forest. A thick fog descended, and the Duke, lost in the forest, wandered about for a whole day and part of the night. Coming at last to a poor peasant's humble cottage, he was not recognized, but was allowed to dry himself before a big log fire and the peasant offered to share his food—"a coarse cottage loaf and skimmed-milk cheese"—with him.

Chastellain, the chronicler, records his astonishment at the difference of character between Duke Philip and his son, Charles the Bold. Philip the Good was cold, slow to act, a slow eater, and rarely alone, for he had a horror of loneliness. He was generous, a lover of luxury, ceremony, and women, and careful in the education of his many illegitimate children. For all this, he was fundamentally an apathetic type. Charles the Bold, on the other hand, was unstable and impetuous, always fiery and excited, a fast eater, taking his meals by himself to save time, a skin-flint having little interest in women, but a man whose schemes were apt to fail because he went off half-cocked. Each man, indeed, was given to excess in his own fashion. It is one of the lessons of history that, while sluggishness may be a defect, success does not always come to the impetuous.

Philip's greatest accomplishment was the organization of the court, which was now considered a tool of reducing the nobility to submission. Within this system, the person of the sovereign was vested with the aura of divinity. All who approached him were required to do so as acolytes, bathed in the splendor of worship, following strict and clearly defined rules. The sovereign could only be served on bended knee, and the least object presented to him—whether towel, brush, an article of clothing, or a letter—had first to be respectfully kissed by a whole series of bearers, since only the really great had the right to hand it personally to the monarch. At mealtimes, his wine had to be carried aloft through the crowd of courtiers, held as high as the carrier's arm extended, lest its bouquet be profaned by human breath—a precaution, incidentally, against any attempt to poison the cup.

The grandees of the court were enthusiastic participants in these ceremonies and intrigued against one another to gain court posts. This system, which continued from Duke Philip's time until the days of Charles V, ensured the loyalty of the nobility and its willingness to collaborate in the government of the country.

Philip the Good also resembled Louis XIV and the Italian princes of the Renaissance in the favors he granted to artists. He paid writers to celebrate his glory, becoming the first prince of northern Europe to have his own propaganda apparatus. The glowing descriptions of his feasts by Chastellain and a whole galaxy of poets served propaganda ends. As storytellers bedazzled the crowds with the Banquet of the Pheasant, and the Tourney of the Swan—complete with their elephants, their actors and actresses, their poets, and their sumptuous displays—they immortalized Philip.

The politics of prestige reached its heights in the creation of the Order of the Golden Fleece. The knights of this order, like those of the Order of the Garter in England, were limited in number. The collar of the order hung from the shoulders, and its device of two threes side by side came to be known as the *Briquet de Bourgogne*, or Burgundian Dog. From the end of the collar hung the golden fleece. The knights were robed in red from head to foot, wearing a cloak lined with white satin. The high standing of the order was maintained by the rule that each of its members must be above reproach by birth, courage, honesty, rectitude, and attainments.

No one could help but admire the sumptuous ceremonies of the Chapter General of the Order of the Golden Fleece held in Brussels at St. Gudule. The knights of the order were arrayed in their "vermilion robes, lined with gray fur, and extending to the knees, over which was thrown a mantle of fine scarlet, fringed with rich orphreys of fine gold. The mantle was long and wide, richly embroidered and bordered with stones and sparkling jewels, fleeces, and the duke's motto—*autre n'aurai*—the whole being lined with the same fur. The hoods hung long behind, and they, too, were scarlet and made in the same cloth. The responsibilities, annuities, and offices of court needed to keep the nobility occupied led to the creation of a hierarchy in which each man had his rank, his rights, and his ceremonial functions. Philip the Good was thus laying the groundwork, though without any set intention, for the absolute monarchy of the future.

What was the purpose and inner meaning of all these ceremonies? The German historians, in particular, have postulated an array of deep-seated philosophical intentions. Pfandl sees in them an astute psychological calculation, a bold attempt to exploit the ignorance and credulity of the masses as well as an attempt to satisfy the taste for luxury and pomp. Others believe Duke Philip was seeking to divert the attention of a restless people from its own lack of freedom and its poverty. For others, the explanation is a "yearning for a finer existence," an aesthetic expression of the people's dream of a better life; a spiritual manifestation that persisted from the days of Philip to those of Louis XIV, and even the Courts of Charles V and Philip II.

The truth, however, is probably less far-fetched. Philip the Good was not the inventor of court ceremonial. By the time he came into power, such ceremonies were well established everywhere in Europe and had become part of aristocratic "snobbishness." A major element was the creation of associations, or orders, whose members considered themselves privileged. They belonged to a social elite and observed rites that, though complicated, satisfied human vanity.

The Duke of Berry and, in particular, the Duke of Bourbon, had trod the same path before the days of Philip the Good. In fact, the device of bringing together the most distinguished members of the nobility in the Order of the Golden Shield had already been done by the Duke of Bourbon.

Duke Philip's father, John the Fearless, was always poorly clad and his tendencies were democratic. His rival, the Duke of Orléans, was organizing sumptuous ceremonials and rallying the faithful to his new Order of the Porcupine, a warlike group organized against the House of Burgundy.

Huizinga has pointed out that these orders were not so much instruments of long-term policy intended to bring the nobility into submission as aristocratic clubs, imposing on their members particular refinements in their style of life and thus separating them from the common herd.

It was as a countermeasure to the Order of the Porcupine that Philip the Good created the Order of the Golden Fleece. It was an order without a specific objective; indeed, no objective was fixed in the rules. It was, however, a pretext for its members to dress up according to detailed rules and to follow a ceremonial that was in itself the reason for the institution. While Philip the Good committed himself to these ruinous extravagances, he did not always do so with a light heart. He was constrained by the opinion of his time, and he practiced scrupulous economies to provide the necessary finances. He avoided useless warfare and purposeless extravagance. He accumulated jewelry and other examples of the goldsmith's art, but he did so less in the spirit of luxury than for the sake of building up a treasury. He spent money judiciously and sought to make his expenditures profitable. Court ceremony, however, reflected the widespread desire for luxury.

The ethics of chivalry were now, like life itself, a dream come true. It had become an obligation for every prince to have his courtiers richly clad, and, at every festival, he would distribute brilliant liveries bearing his own arms. In 1400, Charles VI presented his courtiers with 350 surcoats in the royal colors; and his brother, the Duke of Orléans, in 1404, similarly presented his men with 200 golden headdresses.

It was the custom to require certain functionaries to wear special costumes, more splendid than those worn by their fellows. These officials included chamberlains, gentlemen of the bedchamber, and certain others who alone had the right to approach the person of the prince. There were also secretaries and ladies-in-waiting. It was not only at the Court of Burgundy that festivals became demonstrations of power. This was also the case at such rival courts as those of the Duke of Berry, the Duke of Orléans, and the Duke of Bourbon, where the life of the prince was a brilliant ritual, and where even the serving of meals had the air of a religious ceremony or a performance at the opera.

It was a life of show with an air of sanctity, and the nobility threw itself into it with enthusiasm and fervor. The grave debate as to whether the bread-store keepers and the cup-bearers had precedence over the squires of the trencher, whose job it was to serve the meat, was decided in favor of the former, for were they not concerned with bread and wine, to which the holy office of the Mass had given a mystic character of its own? The meals of the Duke of Burgundy themselves became like the celebration of a Mass, and court life an immense ceremony in which the great nobles, having lost their former power, could find consolation.

Before each festival, the most illustrious personalities met in council to determine the program in all its detail. The taste for ceremonial spread to the masses, who copied it in the festivals of the crossbowmen and in the meetings of the chamber of rhetoric.

Mottoes and symbols were adopted even by the burghers, who carried banners and pennants emblazoned with heraldic signs and coats-of-arms. Snobbery was rampant, and everything was subordinated to the self-glorification of chosen groups. Literature was finding its way into daily life, and the names of the heralds of the Golden Fleece, fixed in the order's own regulations, were copied from the *Roman de la Rose.*

In the course of these festivals, villages were built where masquerades and processions were held. Artificial castles, full of surprises, were constructed. One of Europe's grandest galleries of paintings was the place to which Philip the Good sent his visitors, along with booby traps and surprises—rods and switches that beat them, concealed tubes that covered them with soot or sprayed the ladies under their skirts.

Tournaments now became more important than warfare, and every combatant was required to have at least four noble quarterings to his escutcheon. To prove his breeding, a contestant displayed his arms on the banners that surrounded his tent, and Jacques de Lalaing, at one of these tourneys, exhibited no less than thirty-two quarterings. Banquets had become spectacles, with their presentations of shows and dramas, such as the *Vow of the Pheasant,* in which Philip the Good is shown at the head of a crusade—a commitment he never took seriously for after all it was only a show.

Court ceremonies, however, had another significance. They were designed to ensure the security of the prince by making assassination more difficult. His person being sacred, nobody could approach him, and it became increasingly difficult to poison him. He took his meals separately, surrounded only by the most trusted of his courtiers. Philip II and Louis XIV, when they adopted the same procedures in a later period, did so without suspecting that these had been devised for protection rather than adoration.

This world of the dukes of Burgundy, for all its luxury, was a world of disquiet and contradiction. In none of the portraits of the period is the subject shown smiling, or even relaxed. A taste for blood and torture found its expression in public executions, and scaffolds were permanent features of all cities. This was certainly the case in Ghent during each of its insurrections and in Liège before and after its destruction. It was the case, too, in 1477 and the years following, when heads fell all over Belgium.

A new feature of the life of the time, and an indication of the lack of balance, was an increase in suicides. Between the tenth and thirteenth centuries, suicide had been practically unknown, but during the Burgundian period it became very common.

Morality was nonexistent and license a normal way of life. Commynes describes life at the court of Burgundy as "disorderly frolics with women," which he describes as characteristic of the period. All men of consequence had acknowledged mistresses and bastard children, and great ladies behaved like courtesans. Acknowledged bastards had become an accepted social institution. Philip the Good had at least sixteen of them, while Henri de Gueldre and Jean de Heinzberg, prince-bishops of Liège, had almost as many. Duke John II of Clèves had a record of sixty-three.

Many of the higher dignitaries had themselves been bastards by birth but had been given "letters of legitimacy." This was true of Chancellor Rolin, of the Bishop of Tournai, the President of the Chamber of the Counts at Lille, and the heads of the taxation offices in Hainaut and Flanders. Bastardy was no obstacle to career, and the modern rule that would have prevented a person of illegitimate birth from becoming a bishop did not yet exist.

Immorality became a common practice among all classes of society. Prostitution became a social scourge and public bathing establishments places of debauchery. At the University of Louvain, ladies of the town lured students to their houses under pretense of letting them rooms, and neither the police nor university authorities had any success in mitigating the nuisance.

The general demoralization of the period was evidenced by the number of poisonings. This, in fact, appeared so natural that the most ordinary deaths were ascribed to it. Poison was blamed for the deaths of Michelle de France, wife of the Duke of Burgundy, for those of John of Bavaria and two dukes of Brabant—Philippe de Saint-Pol and John IV—and quite a number of other princes. All this was characteristic of the cruelty of the period.

Human life was now of as little importance as individual freedom and conscience. Dukes of Burgundy put their henchmen to death, without process of law, on the slightest suspicion of unfaithfulness. They also had a way of effecting the disappearance of persons of greater consequence; and if they wished to reward someone for services rendered, they strengthened his estate and inheritance by forcing a rich burgher to offer the hand of his daughter, whether he wished to or not.

The devil himself made a triumphal entry, and the number of prosecutions for witchcraft probably reflects the love for a good show that was part and parcel of social life. Judges dictated the answers to be given by the accused. These answers contained descriptions of witches' rites. The accused would confess to having assisted at the witches' sabbath, perhaps having watched it in the guise of a cat, a dog, or a black cock. The notion of sorcery was closely intertwined with that of heresy. The heretic had to be a sorcerer, since the devil was everywhere.

Even great noblemen were accused of sorcery, the Duke of Orléans among them. It seems that the Duke was a believer in magic and spells and that at times he even conjured up evil spirits.

Joan of Arc herself was one of the victims of this cult of the devil. It was as a witch, not as a faithful servant of Charles II, that Joan was condemned and executed. As recently as the thirteenth century, legends such as those of the witches' sabbath, black magic, and the nightly wanderings of spirits and demons had been matters for scorn and skepticism among theologians, but now they became part of the dogma.

One doctor of theology, Guillaume Edelin, declared in a sermon that there was no such thing as the witches' sabbath, that it was only a fruit of the imagination of overcredulous people. He was at once arrested by the Inquisition and forced to sign a public confession admitting that he himself was a sorcerer, had taken part in the sabbath, and seen the devil, who had persuaded him to deny the whole thing for the sake of deceiving the faithful. In return for this confession, he was allowed to live out the rest of his life in prison.

In the Burgundian period, mass accusation of witchcraft was made against a number of inhabitants of Arras. They were brought before the court and confessed everything. Their lawyers reached an agreement with the judges whereby the accused would be pardoned if they confessed to the slaughter of children, participation in a devil's assembly, sacrilege, and crimes against nature. They gladly confessed all, and they were condemned to death. Thereupon they withdrew their confessions, maintaining that they had lied to save their lives; but their lawyers opposed them and they were executed. It was not until thirty years had passed that their descendants succeeded in having the verdicts reversed.

One of the most magnificent shows put on during the fifteenth century was the triumphal entry into Ghent of Philip the Good and his wife, Isabel of Portugal, after his victory over the people of Ghent in the Battle of Gavere. The Duke had granted a pardon to the insurgent city, and everything was done to show the city's gratitude in a magnificent reception. Minstrels and musicians clad in the colors of the prince and of the town lined the battlements, and all the clergy met at the gate to sing the *Te Deum*. The route of the Duke's procession was lined by platforms on which handsomely costumed actors presented scenes from olden times, including the parable of the prodigal son and Caesar among his senators.

The grandest spectacle of the festival was a platform rising three stories in the center of the market place. Covered with blue cloth, it was hidden behind white curtains. It was a dramatic moment when, as the Duke passed, the veils were lowered revealing a living tableau of the "Adoration of the Lamb," a masterpiece only recently completed by the brothers Van Eyck.

Paper lanterns were hung from the windows of all the houses, and a single night's illumination consumed 22,517 torches. The seven quarters of the city had drawn lots to determine in what order they should present their shows and the theatrical performances were not given until the fourth day.

On the final day, all the games were once more shown in the presence of the Duke, who was so delighted that he had them repeated several times before the prize-giving could begin. The prize for the best show was awarded to the Friday Market district, and the *Fontainistes* received the prize for the best play presented.

The fabulous luxury of the court of Burgundy reached its peak with the wedding of Charles the Bold to Margaret of York. On this occasion, a gigantic wooden house, richly decorated by the greatest artists of Flanders, Brabant, Hainaut, and Artois, was brought down from

Brussels to Bruges by barge. It was full of enormous toys, including a 40-foot-high tower filled with mechanical animals—monkeys, wolves, and boars—who danced and sang. A mechanical 60-foot whale walked about the room. There were thirty 8-foot-high trees, an elephant, and a pelican tossing fish into its ample beak.

Luxury prevailed even in battle. At the siege of Neuss, Charles the Bold had a wooden town with baths, great houses, churches, and richly decorated streets built for his army. There were even festivals.

Display became more and more widespread as great lords strove to imitate the extravagance of their prince. It was during this period that the practice of embellishing clothing with "flying jewelry," i.e., removable jewels that could be sewn on and considered as part of the "outfit," began.

Another sign of the luxury of the times was a zest for travel, and it was a point of honor for great men to make journeys to foreign parts. Guillebert de Lannoy and Bertrand de la Broquière traveled through Prussia, Russia, Egypt, and the Holy Land, returning with many reports about these countries and about mankind in general.

Fashions of the period were expensive and full of excesses. Women wore enormous headdresses designed to elongate their figures and make them appear graceful and slim. These were sometimes conical, garnished with veils of lawn or gauze, and sometimes in the form of two stuffed horns, to minimize the size of the face and make it appear more delicate. License and fashion went hand in hand. Women provoked men with their plunging necklines, while men created a furor with codpieces revealing all anatomical details. It was the fashion for men to pad their shoulders and pinch their waists and make their hips seem narrow.

Philip the Good concealed his baldness beneath a huge turban, and his close-fitting hose caused his enemies to nickname him "long-legged Philip." He was, through it all, a true Renaissance prince, equal in status and stature to the Renaissance princes of Italy. However, he differed from them in one respect. He had a horror of lying and was always faithful to his friends—a characteristic inherited by his son Charles the Bold.

Men wore the doublet, with shoulders padded so stiffly that the wearers needed help in undressing. Beneath the doublet they wore the tight-fitting hose that scandalized the same kind of moralists who, two centuries earlier, had been indignant about long robes. Priests, doctors, and lawyers reacted by keeping their robes as a sign of dignity; and priests, indeed, have retained them through the centuries in the form of present-day cassocks.

Clothes were usually of two colors separated vertically, with blue on the right and red on the left, or green with violet, or orange with pink. Shoes were pointed and as much as half a yard long.

Attention was focused on the face. Plumpness was frowned upon, particularly among the nobility, and it became desirable to look as much like a skeleton as possible. The dukes of Burgundy, except for John the Fearless, were all thin, as were the kings of France—Charles V, Charles VI, Charles VII, and Louis XI—and the personalities painted by the Van Eyck brothers and by Memling and Rogier van der Weyden. Even dogs had to be slim, elegant, and of aristocratic aspect, of some such type as the greyhound. This practice prevailed as far afield as Italy.

By way of contrast, and as a mark of change in the times, the Flemish Renaissance went all chubby-cheeked, full of cherubs, ample-bodied women, and athletes with swelling muscles.

Fashion is so important, and nature so obedient to its dictates, that all the women became blondes, just as in the sixteenth century they were all dark, and in the fifteenth century artists saw them all as slim, even lanky. Yet it is not nature that changes, but art.

The five-pointed star of Burgundian culture now stood high over the Low Countries, and its first point was painting (called Flemish), although many of the masters were Walloons, such as the Tournaisian Roger de la Pasture (also known as Rogier van der Weyden).

The second point was architecture. Outstanding examples are the Brussels Town Hall (by Jan van Ruysbroeck), the town hall of Louvain, finished in 1487, the same year that saw the appearance of the first book, printed by Gutenberg, the Church of Our Lady at Antwerp (Jan and Pieter Appelmans), and St. Rombaut at Mechlin (Wauthier Coolman). Artists and painters of the Low Countries earned fame in Italy, Germany, Spain, and England.

In music, Belgians were the discoverers of polyphony and, with masters such as J. Destrez, Roland de Lassus, and Ockeghem, they became the teachers of other countries.

The fourth point of the star was literature, for the Low Countries had become the refuge of the exiled French poets. From Froissart, born in Hainaut, to the days of the Flemish Commynes, the chief French writers were Belgians. In poetry, the Fleming Chastellain became chief of the rhetoricians; and this school, which included Jean Molinet, and Jean Lemaire de Bavay, is essentially Burgundian in a period when the intellectual life of France itself was stagnating. In the Low Countries, the French and Dutch languages were of equal importance. There was an increase in the number of Ommegangs and chambers of rhetoric. Every town had its own societies for culture, singing, and poetry.

In science expansion was tremendous, particularly after the first printers' workshops were set up in 1473.

Finally, the seamen of Belgium were opening up colonies as far afield as the Azores, thus leading the Spaniards on the road to the Americas.

The University of Louvain was founded in the early reign of Philip the Good (1425) and for a full century it was to play a considerable part in European intellectual life. Thousands of students attended, divided into "nations," and, like the University of Paris, Louvain almost formed a state within a state. Its rector was vested with sovereign powers, a police force, a prison, and a court of law.

Some regulations of the faculty of arts, reminiscent of the Middle Ages and of the universities of England, are well worth quoting. Dress was considered so important that it was mentioned first.

> We therefore enact and order that every student shall present himself in clerk's clothing, neither torn nor cut nor shortened in any indecent manner, nor of hard colors, nor striped, nor in motley or harlequin patterns, and that none shall appear in shoes of different colors or grotesquely arrayed with unbecoming baubles.
>
> Moreover, let none appear in a hood without a tassel, or with the tassel ill-attached, nor with his headdress crowned or ornamented with cords of silk of many colors.
>
> No freshman shall be overwhelmed with curses or blows on his appearance in the university. To liberate himself from the status of a "blue," it shall suffice that he pay one half-griffon to his tutor.
>
> Any student wishing to follow a course at the university shall state on oath that he is fourteen years of age. He shall make a sworn statement, setting forth the exact contents of his purse. The student shall follow the lectures sitting on the ground, not on any chair or stool.
>
> In the case of public debates known as *quolibets*, in which professors and students are mixed together, and which last for eight days, it is hereby permitted that jokes be mixed with the more serious matter, provided that no impropriety, insult, or offensive speech is permitted.
>
> Any professor attending a meeting shall present himself in a decent gown, reaching to his ankles, and otherwise shall have no voice in the discussion.

The University of Paris also had its statutes, reflected in our own day and age in the titles of bachelor and master of arts conferred by English universities.

About 1380 or 1390, when the dukes of Burgundy were first coming into power, the Low Countries were prey to political troubles and three fourths of their trade was destroyed. Great towns such as Ypres, Bruges, Ostend, and Ghent were ruined; the Hansa had left Bruges; and wolves, boar, and other wild animals infested the largely neglected fields.

Fifty years later, under Philip the Good, the Low Countries had become rich and one of the most advanced areas of Europe. Two million inhabitants lived in comfort, even luxury, and there was a great increase in the conveniences of life, such as inside bathrooms, window glass, chimneys, public fountains, paved streets, roads, and canals.

Pleasure, and the joy of living, were almost taken for granted. Progress was exemplified in clothing and social customs. The increased wealth extended not only to the rich and privileged classes, but to the population as a whole. In seeking some form of economic activity to offset the decline in the woolen industry, the country had developed several new resources.

Agriculture saw a considerable increase in stock raising owing to the increasing practice of two-year, as opposed to three-year, crop rotation and the sowing of pastures.

Linen and Flemish lace were beginning to take the place of woolens; and metal-working was becoming an increasingly prosperous industry.

Another growing industry was large-scale fishing for export, made possible by the invention of the barrel (about 1400 A.D.), which was immediately put to commercial use by the Dutch. A special procedure had been devised for preserving herring in barrels, making it possible to sell them all over Europe, particularly Germany.

The port of Antwerp was expanding rapidly, and the first commercial exchange in Europe was founded in Bruges in 1460. The fleets of the Low Countries gained a hold on trade in the Baltic, in the Atlantic, and even in the eastern Mediterranean, presumably the area in which the scheme for Philip the Good's crusade originated.

The history of this period shows how insignificant a decline in trade or changes in the currents of economic activity are compared with human initiative and adaptability, for at this time England was flooding Europe with her cheap woolen cloth; so, one after the other, the towns of Flanders stopped making woolens and began making linen instead.

The technical skill they had acquired in making luxury cloth now made it possible for them to manufacture rare and fine linens, which became yet another European monopoly. Lace and new products such as *sayette*—a mixture of wool and silk—and tapestry again brought export markets within reach of the weavers.

In some cases a town was so set in its old ways and customs that it could not adapt itself to the new conditions. When this happened, some new city would rise to eminence as a competitor and attract the workmen and the industrialists. This was the case with Armentières after the decline of Bruges and Ypres.

Faced by a slackening in the wool trade, each Belgian town reacted in its own way. Antwerp gave up textile manufacture to concentrate on the operation of its port. Louvain offset the decline in its wool exports by concentrating on its university. Mechlin became the seat of a parliament and lived well on the money spent by the legislators and their families. Brussels, the new capital of the Low Countries, took advantage of the presence of the royal court and devoted itself to luxury industry. Ghent offset the decline by trading in grain, on which it was able to secure a hold because of its abundant waterways. Bruges replaced her former industrial power by becoming a banking and financial center. Only Ypres did not adapt. It did not change its methods of work and did not develop new industry.

It has long been believed that the decline of Ypres was the result of the disastrous siege of 1382, in which factories were razed, and the outskirts of the town in which the workers lived were destroyed. In point of fact, however, many other Belgian cities were subjected to the same trials and succeeded in rising above them. The government sought in vain to come to the aid of Ypres by allowing it various tax exemptions and by making it the temporary seat of the Council of Flanders. The inhabitants stubbornly continued to make the same materials as before, although the prices they could command were not profitable. Employers, as one market after another became inaccessible, could think of no better countermeasure than the lowering of wages, so bringing starvation to the workers.

The population continued to decline. More and more houses stood empty and became uninhabitable. Amid the debris stood the textile hall built in the time of the city's greatness. It was to stand useless through the centuries, an empty monument to past glories. It remained standing until 1914, when it was destroyed by German guns. It was rebuilt after World War I, and again after World War II.

By 1470, the population of Ypres had fallen from 100,000 to 10,000; ten years later, one third of the population were beggars. Ypres had become a dead city. It possessed everything to promote a prosperous rebirth. Its workers were skilled, its communications good, the surrounding countryside could provide food, and the sea was near-by. Only energy, initiative, and the willingness to undertake new tasks were lacking.

The city was the prisoner of a past that had been too great; weavers preferred to live on their pride and memories until they starved rather than adapt themselves to the changing pattern of the time. Admittedly, this stubborn pride of craftsmanship contains an element of dignity and nobility, qualities too easily confused with civilization. However, it was nothing more than the path of least resistance, a lazy refusal to face struggle and make the necessary effort. It was an honoring of tradition resulting in waste, an example of the strength of the conservative spirit that prompts men to vegetate in wretchedness rather than try their luck by abandoning the past.

In 1465, when Philip the Good was in his seventieth year and becoming senile, his son Charles the Bold was appointed lieutenant-general of his estates. There are few figures in history so curiously romantic as this young prince, who impressed all his contemporaries by his strange and unusual looks. Athletic, dark-skinned, and black-haired, he had the air of a southerner, a legacy from his mother, Isabel of Portugal, whose influence on him had been so strong that he claimed to be Portuguese.

From his mother he inherited his petulant obstinacy and that baffling and impetuous temperament manifested by frequent sudden outbursts of fury. He loved storms, tempests, and rough seas, and was not only morbidly mistrustful, but also given to superstition, omens, and divinations. These led him to believe that Tuesday was the only day on which he could initiate important undertakings under favorable auspices.

He was highly irritable and continuously overexcited. He bears an odd resemblance to Hitler who, too, did not drink alcoholic beverages, doubtless because he was aware of his own lack of balance and feared stimulants. Moreover, he affected a life of absolute chastity. Women did not interest him, and he was said to be so absorbed in his work and action that he could go whole weeks without sleeping, eating but once a day.

His imagination was so strong he seemed to live in a dream. From his earliest childhood, he never tired of reading about Alexander of Macedon, whose life he fancied was like his own, because he, too, was the son of a Philip. He had been extremely unhappy in his youth and the trials and misfortunes of this period did much to increase the bitterness of his character.

He was terribly disillusioned when his intimate friend Louis XI of France had to be turned out of Philip's Court for trying to play off father against son. It came as a terrible shock to find that his friend "hated him with deathly venom."

As a young man he suffered one of the great humiliations of his life. In 1467, when he arrived in Ghent for his inauguration, he was mocked by the people because he had brought along too small an escort. He was almost a prisoner in the town and had to suffer in silence the insults flung at him by the weavers. It was this affront that made him decide to return from Liège to humiliate the people of Ghent.

On January 8, 1469, he returned for the ceremony of retribution, preceded by an aura of terror created by news of his sack of the city of the prince-bishops. Ambassadors from Cyprus, Livonia, and Moscow were present when, with sadistic magnificence he made the chief citizens of Ghent cringe on hands and knees before him while he tore up their charters.

Commynes commented that this man, who was forever dreaming of splendid or tragic spectacles, so burdened his imagination that in the end it crushed him. His pride made him stubborn before the slightest obstacle, lest any yielding should lose him prestige or bring him into contempt. He believed only in force and imagined he had achieved lasting results when he had only intimidated his opponents. He could not appreciate that force for its own sake is meaningless and that its use always creates a counterforce that becomes its eventual undoing.

At his side were three men, friends and minions as impetuous as he himself—Hugonet, Hagenbach, and Humbercourt. The Chancellor Hugonet threatened the Ghent envoys with decapitation, hoping to provoke a *levée en masse* and crush it. "We will speak fair with your heads!" he told them. He himself was to end his days on the scaffold. Humbercourt, the savage governor of Liège, was to suffer the same fate—by which, as Commynes ironically remarks, he was "much amazed." Hagenbach, the hardest and most brutal of the three, was entrusted by the Duke with the task of spreading terror in Alsace, where he, too, was to be executed, an end not unlike the fate of modern war criminals.

Charles the Bold, feared and hated on all sides, imagined that through these men he was crushing his foes. In reality, he was preparing his own downfall, and between 1467 and 1477 his story is nothing more than a tale of liquidation.

Charles the Bold was a soldier first and foremost. He was a great tactician and a really outstanding leader and organizer. In his *compagnies d'ordonnance* he created the most formidable body of mounted troops in Europe. They were few in number but astonishingly effective in action. Each horseman was fully armed and defended by an imposing bodyguard of soldiers. Each group was composed of a horseman and an admixture of archers, crossbowmen, lancers, pikemen, and musketeers, foreshadowing the composition of the armies and divisions of the twentieth century. These awesome warriors became famous and their names lived on in many marching songs:

> 'Tis brave to see these men-at-arms
> As they advance mounted with their guard.

Charles's artillery, too, was the first in Europe both in quantity and quality, and he was able to lose everything at Granson, without suffering any inconvenience, because of the reserves in his ordnance store. It was his idea, too, to organize a supply train with 1,400 chariots, to supply his troops in the field of battle. He also wanted to build a fleet to rival that of England.

The more powerful and costly his forces became, however, and the greater the temptation of bringing them into use, the more he regarded the army, which should have been merely an instrument of policy, as an end in itself. His whole reign was based on warfare, and it may be said that he organized the destruction and collapse of the state over which he ruled.

Charles succeeded his father in the Low Countries shortly after Louis XI became King of France. His first thought was to stamp out resistance by terror. He found his first pretext in the principality of Liège.

Since the end of the fourteenth century, the people of Liège had established a sort of democratic republic in which the bishop was no more than a president. The city was governed by the crafts through elected magistrates, a governing principle wholly in conflict with the centralized regime the dukes of Burgundy sought to create in imitation of the French policies. In this republic, men of the lowest estate were eligible for the highest honors. In 1407, a simple road worker by name of Badut became Liège's ambassador to the Holy See.

The party in power since the end of the fourteenth century were the *haydroits*, who got their name because they disliked the special rights and privileges of the bishop and the wealthy classes. At the same time, the Liège government was composed of youthful office-holders (apprentices having acquired voting rights from the age of sixteen on) and the population lived in a state of continual unrest fostered by the associations and assemblies.

In the first half of the fifteenth century, Liège passed through an economic transformation. The use of coal became increasingly widespread as more mines were opened, and the metal-working trades, benefitting from the lower-priced fuel, became a powerful iron and armament industry. In the meantime, Philip the Good succeeded in being nominated for the post of prince-bishop for his nephew Louis Bourbon. He appeared to the electorate no more than an agent of the dukes of Burgundy and aroused all the real Liègeois to opposition.

Any pretext was good enough to mock and scoff at the newcomer. He offered the olive branch of conciliation by agreeing to continue ancient customs, but he made the mistake of describing them as

"laudable," instead of using the French word *louables*, "praiseworthy."
One of the leaders, Guillaume de la Violette, cried out, "Good people,
they want to take your freedom away by words you don't understand!
What does laudable mean? Is it Latin? Is it any kind of French?"

As usual, the agitations were led by young people. They took
advantage of social unrest in the countryside and traveled through the
principality wearing in their hats the badge of a man with a club,
which was soon to become their symbol.

Louis de Bourbon fled to Huy in 1458. Then Raes de Heers, a discredited nobleman from the country of Looz, an adventurous and
impetuous personality, took it upon himself to lead the peasant rebellion. He had quarreled with his family and been cast out by the local
nobility because of his wildness. He had become a citizen of Liège by
enrolling as blacksmith and subsequently organized an insurrection.
He was supported by Charles VII, King of France, who sent detachments of the Royal Guard to protect the people of Liège. At a later
stage, Louis XI made a treaty of alliance with them, but by this time
moderate elements were beginning to fear the inevitable war. They persuaded Charles the Bold to lead his army into Liège. The Burgundian
troops were disbanded, but the agitation organized by Raes de Heers
once more became troublesome.

The principality at this time was infested with exiles and outlaws
who remained in the surrounding countryside.

Earlier, the people of Ghent had, in similar circumstances, styled
themselves "the companions of the green tent," and Liège insurgents
adopted the same name. They went through all the provinces, terrorizing other travelers. Bands of young children took possession of Liège,
parading through the streets, breaking up the armorial bearings of the
bishop, and abusing the faithful.

Further up the Meuse, the inhabitants of Dinant, carried away by the
upheaval, revolted. A crowd of exiles and adventurers found their way
into the town, mocking the Duke of Burgundy in masquerades and
processions in which his effigy was carried in the streets, scoffed at, and
labeled "Charloton."

Then Charles the Bold intervened. Philip the Good, old and sick,
was borne in his litter to accompany the crowd that marched on Dinant.
The town, hammered to bits by the Duke's artillery, succumbed on
August 27, 1466, before Liège could come to its aid, and Charles seized
the occasion for terrifying mass executions. The inhabitants were exterminated by hanging or drowning. The town was burned, then razed.
House after house went down, for seven long months.

Yet this frightening example was not enough to intimidate the people of Liège. Their rebellion was fanned by the Dinant refugees, and a

force of 30,000 marched on St. Trond, which Charles was then besieging. At Brustem, 7,000 of the Liègeois were wiped out, and only the marshy country prevented their complete massacre.

Charles next marched on Liège itself, now incapable of putting up a defense. On July 23, one of the leaders of the Green Tent Movement had proclaimed the annexation of the principality to the kingdom of France; at the news of the death of Philip the Good, his effigy had been burned in a bonfire symbolizing the fires of hell. A breach was knocked in the walls; and the Duke, his cloak hiding his shining armor, made a triumphant entry. He rescinded all the freedoms of the city, knocked down its symbol—the perron—and had it carried off to Bruges to ornament the market square.

The burghers of Liège were crushed under enormous fines and the level of taxation rose sixfold. The brutal Humbercourt was appointed Burgundian governor and proceeded to humiliate the inhabitants. Louis de Bourbon, who had now returned, passed his time sailing on the Meuse, not suspecting that fresh tragedy was in the making.

Countless exiles, who were hiding out in forests along the principality's frontiers keeping the agitation alive, united and soon grew into a huge secret army sworn to vengeance and revolt. At last, one band succeeded in creeping into the city and seizing control. A party was sent out to find Louis de Bourbon, who had fled to Tongres, and he was brought back to Liège a prisoner.

The prince-bishop was in a panic, for he well understood the gravity of the impending disaster, and he agreed to go to Charles to ask for mercy. But it was too late, for the Duke of Burgundy had just made Louis XI his prisoner at Péronne, where he heard the news of the city's new revolt. The walls of Liège had been demolished during the governorship of Humbercourt, and the Duke once more directed his march against the city.

So that his intentions might be understood, he forbade his subjects to light victory bonfires until the city had been taken and totally destroyed. Liège had no armament and no means of defense, but with the example of Dinant fresh in their memory, all its inhabitants were seized by a frenzy of self-destruction, and in obedience to an impulse that even Charles had not foreseen, they themselves began firing the city's suburbs—St. Marguerite on October 27, and St. Laurent the following day. Some proposed to set fire to the city itself, so the Duke could never boast of having been its destroyer. Meanwhile, Charles and Louis XI, from their camp on the heights of St. Walburge, looked down on this ravaged but indomitable city. On the night of October 29–30, 1468, 600 men from Franchimont, commanded by Vincent de Bueren and Gossuin de Strailhe, succeeded in making their way as far as the

Prince's tent, attacking by torchlight and almost slaying him. They were quickly overwhelmed. Terrified priests refused sanctuary to the survivors, and the last of them made their escape into the Ardennes Forest. The next day, October 30, at nine o'clock in the morning, the troops of Burgundy entered the city.

Executions began at once. The first people massacred were the peaceful burghers who had stayed behind to cheer the Duke, thinking they had nothing to fear from him. Next, the city was divided into four sections which were pillaged one by one, until the whole was finally set afire on the day of the festival of St. Hubert, the city's patron saint. Its destruction was even more complete than that of Dinant and it went on for seven weeks, each dying fire being rekindled. Even the name of Liège was to disappear, and the fortress built on its ruins was to be called Brabant. Neighboring cities, in their terror, handed over fugitives who had sought refuge with them. Immigrants were hanged or drowned as far away as Maastricht and Huy, and the lords of the Ardennes hunted down the forest fugitives like wild beasts, organizing armed roundups that captured whole bands of the vanquished and handed them over to the Duke. In Germany, Aachen and Cologne, having at first received refugees within their walls, took fright and begged the conqueror for pardon.

Subsequently, Charles proceeded in person to Ghent, where he called the chief citizens together and, defying them from the heights of his throne, solemnly tore up their charters.

Resistance was now no more, and there was none left to oppose the power of absolute rule.

Despite all this, the city of Liège succeeded in rising from its ruins some time before the death of Charles. There could be no better illustration of the futility of destruction and apparent political victory.

In vain, the Duke of Burgundy had destroyed the city house by house, changed its name, and forbidden survivors to return to it. Habit and memory cannot thus be wiped out. Charles, like Frederick Barbarossa when he razed Milan and sprinkled salt on the ruins, had not dared destroy the churches and later could not prohibit priests from celebrating masses in them. Therefore, he had to grant them shelter and make like concessions to the workmen maintaining the buildings. As early as 1470, two years after the destruction, Bishop Louis de Bourbon, a friend of the Duke's, obtained leave to return to Liège.

With this nucleus, the former inhabitants began to return, camping amidst the ruins. They were driven out, but they were far more stub-

born than their adversaries were energetic. Eventually they were accepted and set to work rebuilding the town.

They were helped by the widespread disapproval aroused by Charles's
cruelty, and, in 1475, public opinion waxed so strong that Louis de
Bourbon obtained the Duke's permission for the reconstruction of the
city.

One might think that this would have taken generations, but such
was not the case. The stones of the houses were still there. All that
was necessary was to put them back, one on top of the other; all the
inhabitants devoted themselves to the task, and construction began.

It would seem that Charles would have done better by bringing in
new settlers after having driven out the people of Liège. The reasoning
is sound in theory, but a few years later another incident showed how
difficult such an attempt can be. Only a few months after the death of
Charles, Louis XI was incensed by the resistance of the Artois and
decided to deport all the inhabitants of Arras and replace them with
new settlers. He decreed that every commune in the kingdom appoint
a certain number of its people to come to Arras and live there. Each
commune, of course, chose to get rid of its worst elements, and Arras
became the home of vagabonds and bandits—the dregs of the French
population—men incapable of adapting themselves to the new circumstances and of setting to work. Soon they began to disperse and the
former inhabitants began coming back, one by one, to reoccupy the
town. Louis XI had failed.

Although it is easy enough to repair material ruin, this is not the
case with moral decay, or the resultant violence, hatred, and resent-
ment. The social imbalance—the result of out-of-hand confiscation of
property and destruction of entrenched interests—reduced the wealthy
to proletarians. The exiles who returned to Liège could not reclaim
their fortunes. They were not inclined to accept this expropriation.

The new world was unlike the old. The old political parties were no
more. They had been replaced by parties dedicated to violence and
extremism, groups whose members thought only of revenge. All power
rested with armed bands, and Guillaume de la Marck, Lord of Sedan—
a ruffian—had seized control of the town. His son was to be nicknamed
the "Boar of the Ardennes," because his soldiers had to have a boar's
head embroidered on their red tunics.

Guillaume struck terror into the heart of the prince-bishop, whom
he assassinated on August 20, 1482. The prince-bishop's successor,
feigning friendship, eventually drew Guillaume into a trap, captured
him, and brought him to the scaffold at Maastricht on June 18, 1485.
He died crying vile imprecations. "My head," he screamed, "will be
long bleeding!" His violent end set off a vendetta; his brother, Evrard,

seized Liège three times and massacred Guillaume's opponents. It would seem as if Charles the Bold, although finding it impossible to destroy Liège, had bequeathed it his spirit of violence and left a legacy of half a century of civil strife.

The consequences of Liège's destruction were to be serious, particularly for the Burgundian state.

Charles the Bold used terror as a weapon, launched undertakings on a scale that became ever larger and more costly, and ended a victim of his own policy. His armies, which should have been used only to defend the Low Countries and for whose maintenance he demanded increasing subsidies from the towns, engaged in one offensive after another. In the meantime, wars and destruction continued to disorganize commerce and the wealth of the towns was being depleted. The cost of the armies, the ravages wrought by enemy raids, and the decline in industrial production halted the growth of the population. As a result of the Duke's effort to keep more and more enemies in check, his neighbors formed a coalition against him.

The Burgundian state would have been well advised to concentrate its forces against France, its chief enemy. But instead, Charles mounted an offensive against Gelderland, Lorraine, Alsace, and a number of subsidiary localities, so that he was unable to defeat Louis XI. In view of his possession of the principality of Liège, and given the course of the Meuse, he was drawn toward the Rhineland against a Germany that was, as Commynes says, "a thing so great and so powerful that it can scarce be believed." His success was sufficiently great to cause concern to the Emperor, the Bishop of Cologne, and the dukes of Gelderland, Lorraine, Alsace, and Switzerland. He was opposed by Emperor Frederick III, the Rhineland princes, the Hapsburgs (who controlled Alsace), and the Swiss cantons.

Demanding that the Emperor give him a royal crown, he obtained an interview with Frederick III at Trèves. The Emperor, however, was not anxious to follow in the footsteps of Louis XI at Péronne, and he ran away.

The towns of Alsace chose this moment to rebel against Hagenbach, the Burgundian governor, who fell into the hands of the rebels, was tried, and beheaded as a war criminal. Sigismond of Hapsburg then entered into an alliance with the Swiss to defend the people of Alsace.

Charles, who now had a permanent army, had, by dint of many threats, succeeded in wringing from the towns of Flanders the necessary subsidies and was able to recruit and organize his *compagnies d'ordonnance*—actually an impregnable force of shock troops. The people of the Low Countries, however, attempted to resist his demands for money, thus creating an internal, paralyzing second front. In the end, however, he succeeded in wresting the additional sum of 500,000 crowns from the towns, using this sum to muster a huge army with which to intimidate the Emperor. He laid siege to Neuss, a town near Cologne in the heart of the Rhineland.

All Germany rose up in a storm of patriotism and hatred. The town of Neuss had the full moral support of the empire and succeeded in resisting all assaults. Its walls, destroyed by the Burgundian artillery, were immediately rebuilt by the inhabitants. Charles had promised the English to send his troops to Calais to take part in their invasion of France, but for months the siege kept his men in the Rhineland. When, at last, he decided to lift the siege, his allies had embarked for home and it was too late. Charles, however, could not stay his hand. Having been rebuffed in Germany and in France, he now planned to throw himself upon Italy. He entered into alliances with the Republic of Venice, with Savoy, and with the Duke of Milan, who controlled the Alpine passes. He was dreaming of reconstituting the Lotharingia of old.

For this forerunner of Napoleon, Switzerland was to take the place of Napoleon's Russian campaign. Charles had sworn never to come into conflict with the cantons, but they were disturbed by the occupation of Lorraine, and it was impossible for him to march southward, leaving the cantons in his rear. Although well aware of their military prowess, he found it necessary to attack and, if possible, crush them in a single expedition.

His rear was protected by the truces he had made with Louis XI and with Germany. He entered Switzerland in 1476, stormed the Castle of Granson, and hanged all the defenders from the battlements to avenge the execution of Hagenbach, which had long embittered him. On March 3, 1476, a relief army surprised him on unfavorable terrain, trounced his soldiers, and captured all his artillery.

The Swiss had invented a new method of fighting, their tactics being based on compact squares of men armed with long pikes. These strongholds were practically impregnable. In the Low Countries, squares of this kind could be broken up without difficulty by cannon fire; but in mountain territory, they could neither be dispersed under bombardment nor outflanked. The Duke was baffled by this, since all his previous battles had been fought on level ground.

The Swiss attacked him in a narrow valley where he could neither deploy nor use his artillery. He ordered a retreat as a preliminary to launching a counterattack, but his order was taken as an admission of defeat by his troops. Already demoralized by the Swiss weapons and unexpected tactics, his men broke into headlong flight.

It would have been easy to recover from this reverse, for Charles had immense reserves and only needed to bring them up. Unfortunately, the humiliation he had suffered so enraged him that he announced forthwith that he would take the offensive again within two weeks' time. Though reinforcements were on the way, he did not wait for them but gave the order to attack on the scheduled date. His army, composed of troops of four different nationalities whose leaders were either quarreling with one another or failing Charles, was divided and discouraged. On June 22, 1476, this army was wiped out at Morat.

This time Charles was left without any troops, and most all of his allies had abandoned him. The Duke of Lorraine returned to his duchy and recaptured Nancy. Gelderland revolted. The Flemish cities refused to grant any further supply subsidies, and Louis XI organized a general coalition against him. The Duke's advisers vainly besought him to retire to the Low Countries where he could defend himself indefinitely because of the strength of the communes. He rejected this advice, attributing all his reverses to treason. He lived in an uninterrupted storm of anger, neither eating nor sleeping, and issuing orders for general mobilization at a moment when the people of the Low Countries, thoroughly irritated, were on the point of insurrection.

In the end, Charles seems to have lost all self-control. He was given to attacking people who addressed him. Formerly a teetotaler, he began drinking and using stimulants to keep going. He could not face the collapse of all his plans and became obsessed with the thought of recapturing Nancy.

When the Swiss again marched against him, most of his generals abandoned him. With only 5,000 men under his command, he refused to fall back on Luxemburg where he had large reserves and, like a madman, besieged Nancy in the depth of winter while already encircled by his enemies. At the last moment, his Italian mercenaries deserted, and he went into the decisive battle with only a few hundred men. He threw himself on the enemy, courting death, and on January 5, 1477, mortally wounded, he died in battle.

His body was not discovered until two days later in a frozen pond, disfigured and half eaten by wolves. He was identified only by what was left of his clothes; but for them, he might never have been identified.

At the news of the Nancy disaster, a revolution broke out in the Low Countries. Preparations for it had been in progress for years in all the large towns, because power was in the hands of a class of self-seekers and careerists who, supported by the dukes of Burgundy, had kept the population under control.

As soon as Charles's death became known, the Burgundian regime foundered. In all the great towns the population rose up, high civil servants went into hiding or took flight, and Charles's only daughter, Mary of Burgundy, found herself a prisoner of the Ghent insurgents, without the backing of partisans or army. The great city at once took command of the situation. Ghent at that time was the capital of the Low Countries, residence of the Duke's family and government and meeting place of the estates general. Less than a year before this, Chancellor Hugonet had threatened the deputies that, "if they did anything that might displease the most dreaded and sovereign Prince," he would break "their fat Flemish heads."

Throughout 1476, the people of Ghent had lived in fear of severe repressive measures. When they heard of the Nancy disaster, the crafts at once began an insurrection, the former aldermen were arrested, and the executions began. The estates general had just been called. They re-formed themselves as a constituent assembly, forced Mary of Burgundy to cancel all the Duke's reforms by signing the Great Privilege of 1477, and sought to force her into marriage with the Dauphin of France.

Elsewhere in the Low Countries events were taking a similar course. At Brussels, Antwerp, Mons, Valenciennes, and Ypres, the population was seizing civil servants and magistrates and handing them over to the executioner after trying them before improvised courts presided over by judges who, as often as not, could not even read.

An indication of conditions at the end of the Burgundian period may be found in the trial of Charles's two chief councilors, Hugonet and Humbercourt, at Ghent. A trumped-up charge of conspiracy was brought against them, and they were condemned to death without being given an opportunity to defend themselves. They were beheaded forthwith, despite the tears and prayers of Mary of Burgundy, who, dressed in simple mourning, sought to beseech the crowd to spare them.

Louis XI, however, was only waiting for such a set of circumstances to seize Flanders. Joined by a large number of civil servants and noblemen who were threatened with death by the insurgents, he made ready to dispatch an army to the Low Countries.

The real strength of the Burgundian state, however, lay in public opinion and in the towns rather than in the Duke's troops and centralized governments. At this time, the Low Countries had no army, administration, or political direction. In normal circumstances, they should have collapsed into anarchy and fallen ready prey to the first invader, or permitted themselves to be annexed by the French. Instead, they were to put up a victorious resistance against Louis XI. The estates general at once decided to mobilize an army of 100,000 men. Far from seeking to re-establish the independence of the different provinces, they recognized Mary of Burgundy as common sovereign of Flanders,

Brabant, Hainaut, Namur, Holland, Zeeland, Luxemburg, and the Artois.

When Louis XI invaded the Artois, his supporters included the former civil servants and noblemen of the Duke's party, but all the towns resisted. The King succeeded in taking Arras, but it rebelled against him; and the burghers of Valenciennes burned the suburbs of their town to stop his advance. They hired mercenary troops from Germany, and Louis XI struggled in vain to terrorize the Low Countries by burning the towns and deporting the people. His conduct only further weakened the chances of France.

Within a few weeks, all the provinces had given their support to the marriage of Mary of Burgundy with the Archduke Maximilian, son of Emperor Frederick III, who seemed the only sovereign capable of defending them. The nuptials of the Archduke and the daughter of Charles the Bold were celebrated on August 18, 1477, and the Low Countries passed to the House of Hapsburg. This marriage, which had been decided upon by Charles himself before the Nancy disaster, made the future emperor of Germany, the heir to Austria, the Tyrol, Styria, and Alsace, sovereign of the Belgians. He passed under triumphal arches into his new domain amid the general enthusiasm of the people.

Maximilian and Mary did not know each other's language and could only communicate by signs. Nevertheless, Mary was delighted with the brave, good-looking young Hapsburg, and his credit was good enough for the foreign bankers in Bruges to provide him with the funds needed to raise a large army of mercenaries and German pikemen. In time, the towns of Flanders and Hainaut mobilized and equipped a force of several thousand men and on August 7, 1479, they defeated Louis XI at Guinegate, the last victory ever to be won by communal militia.

The Low Countries were saved for the moment, but it was not long before Mary of Burgundy died after a fall from her horse, and Maximilian's efforts to obtain the regency of the country on behalf of his children were the signal for a savage civil war involving the whole country. Antwerp was on his side, but the town of Flanders rebelled against him and negotiated directly with Louis XI. Maximilian, at the head of his German mercenaries, seized Ghent and beheaded thirty-three of the troublemakers. The city, however, revolted anew under the leadership of Coppenhole and De Rasseghen, entered into an alliance with France, and again began wearing the white hood. Maximilian had proceeded to Bruges, and, entering the town with too small an escort, had been captured. He had, however, ordered his German mercenaries to follow him secretly, and they camped outside the walls. Maximilian arose at dead of night to see that the doors were opened for them, but the burghers were alerted before the troops could seize control of the town. The Archduke was seized and imprisoned in the Cranenburg, a simple grocery store in the market place, and he was made to witness the torture and execution of his partisans.

Maximilian was forced to accept a new constitution drawn up by the insurgent towns, but once at liberty, he promptly went back on his word. He laid siege to Ghent and, with Antwerp as his base, set out to subdue Flanders by force. Ghent had not only been strengthened by a French garrison, but it had also opened the dikes and flooded the surrounding countryside for protection. Thus, it was cut off for forty days and put up fierce resistance, while the various trade corporations within the city fought out their private quarrels. Their leaders sent one another to the scaffold, but in the end victory went to the boatsmen, who favored peace. Coppenhole was executed and the city surrendered. The whole of the Low Countries submitted to Maximilian; and Bruges herself capitulated to him by the Peace of Cadzand in 1492.

The aldermen of the great towns were henceforth to be nominated by the Archduke. He, however, was soon to become Emperor of Germany, handing over the reigns of government of the Low Countries to his son Philip.

At just this time, far away from Flanders on the coast of equatorial Africa, a Belgian in Portuguese pay was exploring the coast south of the Congo estuary; and, further north, Christopher Columbus was preparing the voyage that was to lead to the discovery of America.

The strife between Maximilian and the great towns resulted in enormous devastation in the Low Countries. Brabant was by no means the hardest hit of the provinces, but the number of houses—85,764 in 1472, was reduced to 74,084 in 1480, and to 71,000 in 1486. For the Belgian provinces as a whole, this meant a population loss of at least 20 per cent in less than fifteen years. The population, however, had continued to grow up to the time of the accession of Charles the Bold, when it amounted to more than 2 million inhabitants. About 1 million were in Flanders, 500,000 in Brabant, and 700,000 in the principality of Liège.

Maximilian has been blamed for bringing blood and fire to the country in the attempt to re-establish his authority. But in reality, the strife was caused by economic rivalry. The old towns of Flanders, with their eyes turned toward France, were in conflict with the younger towns of Brabant and Holland, which depended increasingly on the German market.

It was in Antwerp, Mechlin, and Amsterdam that Maximilian had the upper hand; his authority and their interests complemented one another. It was because he could count on the support of these towns that he was ultimately able to subdue the great Flemish communes. The younger, progressive provinces were gradually pushing Ghent and Bruges into the background; and Maximilian was only one element among these forces, which supported him with money and other resources.

The fact that the Archduke was successful in the end, and that for the ensuing three centuries the Low Countries turned their eyes toward Germany, reflects the existence of a large potential market and unlimited possibilities for the future. The regions that had risen and developed during the thirteenth century because of their reliance on France were now condemned to a diminishing prosperity compared with those that had traded with the empire. The most brilliant political triumphs are vain in the face of economic changes, the true determining factors in the enduring destiny of nations.

These events were not devoid of a certain romantic aspect. In later years, Maximilian was to tell the story of his courtship of Mary of Burgundy in terms of the idyll of Tristan and Isolde. He described himself in the third person, walking with the young princess in a garden.

> This same Maximilian was muffled in a great royal robe and crowned with laurel. She, Mary, wore a tall headdress and long tight sleeves from which the tips of her fingers just appeared. And what, then, did they do, these two lovers among the flowers? They taught each other their native languages, she teaching him French and he instructing her in the old German tongue. And the country around them, and the youth that was in their hearts, provided themes for what they said and translated, together with all that human tongue has never translated and never will translate.

When Mary of Burgundy died after her fall from a horse in the forest of Winnendaele, Maximilian recorded his sorrow in a cry of despair. "Never, while I live, will I forget my sorrow for my wife!"

This sovereign, who was to bring blood and fire to the Low Countries and to pass through many trials and tribulations of his own was a spirit above the ordinary. In Germany, he left unforgettable traces. His words won every heart. Those who met him were charmed and delighted, and he brought pleasure wherever he went. He was, above all, an idealist whose dream was to blend the future with the past. He was devoted to everything new, was interested in mathematics, history, the art of warfare, and all other branches of human knowledge. At a more advanced age, he learned to speak Latin, French, Italian, English, and Spanish and became, in some ways, a legendary figure.

Contemporary travelers have given us a good idea of what the great towns of the Low Countries looked like during this period. One of the

travelers, indeed, is famous. He was a Nuremberg doctor, Munzer by
name, who had taken his degree at Pavia about 1480. In 1494, at the
age of thirty-four, he left Germany because of a plague epidemic. In
the course of his travels he went to Italy, then to Spain, and afterward
to the Low Countries. He was a contemporary of Erasmus and Luther,
and he recorded his name in the Latin manner—Monitarius. He was
intelligent enough to understand that flight might be a protection
against the plague, an idea not yet accepted by all men of learning.
Some of them contended that infection was the will of God and that
death was predestined, dogging the footsteps of the fugitive wherever
he might go. This doctor, an exceptionally keen observer, entered the
Low Countries by way of Lille and visited in turn Bruges, Ghent,
Antwerp, and Liège, providing for us a detailed account of his journey,
and he has bequeathed to posterity striking descriptions of the places
he visited, among them this one of the citizens of Bruges:

> The people of this place are very friendly and very sociable. The men are
> handsomely clad, their clothing long, like that worn by churchmen. The
> women are slight of figure and very beautiful, and they often dress in
> bright red. They are much given to love and also to religion, for in these
> regions of the northwest, people are wont to go to extremes—all or
> nothing.

The women, it seems, had many tricks to lure young men into the
traps of love. "They might well," Munzer says, "be known as the
daughters of Venus."

The fact is that, in this town where fortunes were made and unmade
within a few days, where chance and mischance were normal ingredients
of life, the transition from piety to debauch could happen at a moment's
notice, as could the passage from joyfulness to despair. Everything here
was excessive: the exuberance of the people, the violence of their language, and their impetuous habits, which were so to shock Joanna the
Mad. The people of the Low Countries in this period had the air of
southerners; the Spaniards, by comparison, seemed almost northern.

Bruges was a pious town despite, or rather because of, the unin-
hibited morals of its ladies. It had no less than sixty churches spread
over nine parishes, among them the Church of St. Donat, patron of the
town, dazzling with its decorations of silver and gold and black marble
tiles. Some of these tiles were 12 feet long. Notre Dame had the highest
tower in Flanders, rising to about 400 feet, with 300 steps to the summit,
from which one could see the white sails of vessels on the high seas.

In the streets, the first thing that struck the visitor was the fact that
everybody dressed either in red or in black. Memling, in his pictures of
Bruges, always showed women dressed in black or in crimson—wearing
the famous vermilion cloth manufactured in Flanders.

Among the town's innumerable market places was the central square, a fish and vegetable market. Here one could buy cabbages, carrots, and turnips as well as pears, apples, and the "lenten fruits" that came from the South and could not otherwise be found in that region in February and March. Oranges came from Spain and Africa, figs and grapes from the Mediterranean region, and all were a normal part of the local diet.

The Flemings who, in our times, are reputed great trenchermen, were then famous for their moderate habits. All observers agreed that they drank no wine, being content with light beer. Among their vices, however, were avarice, for these merchants were not given to squandering their money. Their fortunes were tied up in the risky sea trade. A shipwreck was a disaster, despite the fact that insurance was already available. The loss of a fleet, as sometimes happened in the storms between December and March, could ruin a considerable number of people. In the town itself, the streets were filled with foreign merchants. The Spaniards, Florentines, Genoese, Venetians, Germans, and the merchants from the Baltic regions could readily be identified by their different manner of dress.

In the great market, known as the bourse, many nationalities rubbed elbows. There were special streets reserved for the Spaniards, others for the Florentines, and others for the Genoese. The same custom prevailed in their own native cities, in which there were special Flemish quarters. The Easterlings had a large house, complete with tower and lobby, where men met to do business. Cellars in the adjacent houses served as warehouses, and sales were conducted where the merchants' stocks were stored.

Business was also done in the great market halls, and the conduct and organization of business was particularly striking to the foreigner. One hall was set aside for the wholesale trade in wool; it was sold by the piece. And at the foot of the hall there was a canal swarming with vessels carrying such goods as chalk, building materials, or fish being shipped to other markets. Another market hall was surrounded by retail shops occupying the ground floors of the buildings. Visitors were impressed not only by the goods themselves and the luxurious decorations of the hall, but also by its general cleanliness and careful upkeep of each room.

Bruges was now a great cosmopolitan port where Baltic products could be exchanged directly for those of the Mediterranean. All merchandise unloaded here was immediately resold and re-exported, and only a fraction of the total remained in the Low Countries. Portugal was busily founding new trading posts on the coasts of Africa, and the part the Portuguese played in Bruges was all the greater because Philip the Good had married a Portuguese princess. The gold mines in the Gulf of Guinea drew their supplies from Bruges, and vessels from far countries unloaded monkeys, lions, and parakeets there to ornament the princely menageries of Europe. The port always harbored a fleet from every country. At one time, there were "three galleys from Venice, a hulk from Portugal, two Spanish caravels, six Scottish ships, forty-two caravels from Brittany, twelve vessels from Hamburg, and a fishing fleet that includes four whalers, and some forty herring vessels."

The city of Bruges had not yet begun to decay, nor had silting yet diminished traffic, for dredgers kept a channel free to Damme and Sluis, where there were large, safe harbors. Bruges was actually two ports: one where ships could drop anchor and discharge their goods, and a second riverport surrounded by a network of canals. The latter was in the city itself, and business was transacted there in complete security.

The Schelde Canal joined Ghent—the waterway terminus for goods coming from Hainaut and the Artois—with Mechlin, to which merchandise from the Meuse and the Rhineland came by overland route. Other canals connected Bruges with Ypres and, by way of Zeeland, with the Rhine estuaries. The port of Sluis was immense and could accommodate 700 or 800 ships at a time.

Bruges was surrounded by 18-ft.-thick stone walls and protected by sixteen 26-ft.-thick towers. The town was so large that its central pasture was large enough for a thousand horses. The rest of the town contained courts and palaces and porches with cisterns. The city gates were made of iron, not wood, as was the general custom. They were considered impregnable and indeed it was only after long sieges that they were ever breached.

Bruges also had a system of distributing running water that was unique in Europe. The town was planned as a circle surrounded by thirty or forty windmills standing on the ramparts and maintaining a flow of water in the ditches. These moats were fed by a wooden sluicegate, a device that impressed the Italian historian and statesman Francesco Guicciardini a century later. The water, however, was not potable. On the south side of the town they had built a big bucket wheel, operated by a horse, to draw fresh water for an enormous cistern. The water was stored in a raised reservoir and found its way through lead pipes into a thousand subconnections that carried the drinking water to the houses.

Bruges was strongly fortified, hence the efforts expended by Maximilian to overcome it. It was surrounded by a wall with recessed gates; the wall extended on each side of the gates forming passages, so that any assault force could be pelted with projectiles. It was no doubt some system of this type that enabled the people of Ghent, when besieged by Philip the Bold, to remove their gates as an act of defiance without running any great risk. The walls of Bruges were further fortified by a large embankment, and beyond that were two successive moats —wide, deep, and always filled. This system of defense was sound against artillery bombardment, for cannon balls, stopped by the embankment, never reached the walls. Maximilian was never able to vanquish this type of town unless he paralyzed its trade, and Bruges capitulated only after it was cut off from the sea by the Peace of Cadzand.

Ghent, however, was still the largest town of the Low Countries. It contained no less than seventy-eight great bridges and some fifty churches and chapels.

As at Bruges, there were windmills on the walls, and its area was equal to that of Paris. In the next century, Charles V was to tell François I, in a famous pun, *"Je mettrai ton Paris dans mon gant."* Paris, indeed, had no more than four bridges over the Seine.

Inside the walls of Ghent, there were many stretches of unoccupied ground. Every house had its courtyard and garden, and the population was scattered. The secret of the city's strength lay in the rapidity with which the surrounding countryside could be flooded. In three hours, it could be made impregnable inside a girdle of water a mile broad. It was built in the form of a star; from its center, roads radiated toward the suburbs and the gates.

It was the meeting place of four rivers, including the Lys and the Schelde. They could be easily distinguished, for their waters were of different colors, the Schelde being the clearer, since the Lys flowed from marshy country. When the rivers were stopped at the town's entrance by closing the gates, ships could sail around through the flooded area; the effect of houses floating on water was quite extraordinary.

The people of Ghent made their livelihood from the traffic in grain from Picardy and the Artois, for the produce had to pass through their city, and the corporation of boatsmen was very powerful. The nobles, the weavers, and the other crafts shared power in the city, but the weavers invariably got the upper hand. The regime was far from stable. "The weavers are hard-headed," travelers would say. "They think only of the present, never of the future. They follow their own desires and their own whims."

The general view was that the town would have been like Milan were it not for so many open spaces. The finest of the churches was St. John's, later to be renamed St. Bavo's, when Charles V transferred monks there from the old Carolingian abbey that had been turned into a fortress from which the population was kept under observation. This is the church that contains the altarpiece of the "Adoration of the Lamb," but nobody knew precisely what it represented. The people called it simply the picture of Adam and Eve. In the time of Philip the Good, cultivated people referred to it as the "Choir of the Blessed," and this was the theme chosen by the rhetoricians of St. Agnes for the tableau presented on the occasion of the Duke of Burgundy's visit to the town.

It had been only a few years since the death of the painter, but already no one could say what he had wished to represent. In the sixteenth century, the picture was to be called "The Assumption," or the "Coronation of the Virgin." It was not until later that people understood that the figures had gathered around the Mystic Lamb, the centerpiece of the picture, in adoration.

Inside the walls of Brussels, hard by the ducal palace, was the land that formed the park called the Garenne or Warande, used in earlier days as a game reserve. The town was filled with fountains and sculptured figures in the squares and at the crossroads. The roof thatching of the dwellings was replaced by slates or tiles. The corporations built their houses in the market place with gable-ended fronts covered with small stone statues and garlands. The towers of St. Gudule, some 230 feet high, were being finished.

In the meantime, the town hall was being transformed. Around the year 1400, it consisted only of its present left wing, beside which stood a belfry of moderate height. The building of the present right wing was begun in 1444, and Charles the Bold laid the cornerstone. The belfry, now in the middle of the building, is raised and crowned with a pierced 300-ft. tower, which in turn is surmounted by a gilded, 16-ft.-high copper statue of St. Michael. It is still there today. The tower is the work of Jan Van Ruysbroeck, the craftsman also responsible for the façade and towers of St. Gudule. Like most artists of his time, he was involved in politics. He was one of the seven democrats who, in 1421, voted in favor of Jacqueline of Bavaria and formed a revolutionary committee. His son William was to become a leader of the Popular Party at the time of the 1477 insurrection.

The Brussels of that era was the scene of intense artistic and political activity. The Tournaisian Roger van der Weyden settled there, did the decorations of the town hall, and became the official city painter. Other Brussels artists, among them Jan Van Eycken, who finished the Gateway of the Lions at Toledo, Jan Van Ruysbroeck, who became the architect for Louis XI of France; and others, working in Ferrara, Bruges, and Antwerp, found patronage all over Europe.

The traveler arriving at Antwerp was always struck by the friendly welcome extended by the inhabitants, who were fond of foreigners and entered easily into conversation. They were a people who loved social life and festivals, of weddings, banquets, and dances. The sound of musical instruments mingled with laughter and song. The traveler was also impressed by the tide of the Schelde River. It rose so high that ships could sail straight into the inner town. The name of the city derives from *ant'werp*, "on the wharf," and is the source of the Dutch name Antwerpen and the French Anvers.

From the church towers the visitor could command a wide view. By climbing the 385 steps of Our Lady, he could see the bell towers of Ghent, the spires of Breda and Mechlin, and, on a clear day, Flushing and the North Sea. Beneath him, beside the Schelde, wide and glittering in the sunlight, lay the town itself, "with its magnificent medley of churches and great houses of well-proportioned roofs and shapely gable-ends, of square and pointed steeples, turrets, and strange façades," as it was to be described much later by Victor Hugo.

The churches were unbelievably rich. In Our Lady there were no less than fifty-one altars with more than 400 finely carved candlesticks. Each of the craft fraternities had built one of these altars at its own expense and strove continuously to embellish it, so it might outshine the altars of rival corporations. In the Lady chapel, the balustrade contained no less than ninety-six bars of copper, then rare and costly. The marble was pierced and carved more finely than metal. There was always music, for the twenty-four canons and fifty chaplains and curates sang continually in the choir. All the churches were correspondingly magnificent, despite the fact that the city was as yet only sparsely inhabited. Its population was, however, growing very rapidly and a citizen who returned after having been away for two years could not recognize it on his return.

Meanwhile, Liège had undergone some changes. The city's reconstruction was still too recent for the population to have been fully reconstituted. The city could be reached only by road, because the Meuse below Maastricht was only navigable by barges and passenger vessels.

The distance from Maastricht to Liège could be covered on foot in one day, provided one left at sunrise. Luckily, the road was safe, which could not be said of the road between Antwerp and Maastricht, a route so infested by bandits and pillaging soldiery that the traveler needed a guide familiar with the side roads. The first sight of Liège was well worth the journey. The city was now delightfully situated, and the eye was at once struck by the twelve great abbeys and collegiate churches surrounding the immense Cathedral of St. Lambert. The hills surrounding the town were covered by vineyards and rich fruit orchards; one of them, known as *petite Bourgogne*, produced a red wine that became famous.

The soil was so rich that the ripening wheat grew "to the height of a horseman." When the harvest had been gathered, it was only necessary to dig holes to extract a heavy clayish soil that could be used as a fertilizer. This procedure astonished many foreigners, for at that time nothing was known of marling and liming.

Part of the region's wealth included its quarries. From them came colored marble and alabaster streaked with black, to say nothing of a dark stone called coal that could be burned. Some believed that the coal had been incandescent but that its brightness had been dimmed in the earth. Mines were "wondrous deep" and it was a matter of astonishment that workmen were willing to risk their lives by going down so far. Softer stones, which hardened with the passage of time, were cut with iron saws and used to build houses.

Although there were still many ruins, Liège had a great deal of atmosphere. A well-known traveler, Sir John Mandeville, after voyaging all over the world, finally settled in Liège, an earthly paradise where he could end his days.

It was indeed the land of *le Bon Dieu*, and everybody agreed that, had it been otherwise, priests would not have chosen to live there. "Pleasant is that place where the clergy settles," says a German proverb, "for Mary chose ever that good part."

Petrarch had said the same thing in 1333: "I have seen the peoples of Flanders and Brabant, who live on wool and its weaving. Moreover, I have seen Liège, which is famous for its priests." He complained, however, that Liège had become so uncultured that he was not even able to buy ink there. Later Guicciardini remarked, "It is a land both fortunate and admirable and indeed it is proverbially called the priests' paradise."

Much the same thing was said about the Rhineland, called "the paradise of Germany," where the Rhine, from its mouth to its source, was no more than a succession of bishoprics—Utrecht, Cologne, Mainz, Trèves (or Worms), Spire, Strasbourg, Basel, Constance, and Coire. Why, then, did so fortunate a people have so tragic a history? Why were the populations massacred so ruthlessly, most recently of all by Charles the Bold?

"The men of Liège are impetuous and prone to rebellion," said Monitarius. "They are sure in their strength and often have they plotted against the people of Belgium. Moreover, they have even set out in sorties against their neighbors." Guicciardini said, in substance: "The people of Liège are ingenious, high spirited, and apt in everything. But it is their evil and inveterate custom to be more usually inclined to hatred and discord than to concord and hard work."

The historian Commynes, hostile as he was to Charles the Bold, commented severely on the city of Liège. "It used every cruel excess against the subjects of the Duke, since the time of his grandfather John the Fearless, without adhering to any agreement or promise they had made. This was the third year the Duke had come in person, and each time they broke the peace the year afterward. They had been excommunicated for years because of the cruel things they had done to their bishop. For all the commandments of the Church, they had neither reverence nor obedience."

Liège had a long anticlerical tradition. This feverishness and instability, however, were only an example of the individualism that was to keep the city independent until our own time.

The Low Countries were to become a center—or perhaps a melting pot—of artistic culture. They even went beyond this by bringing painting into its own. Painting, except for illuminated and illustrated manuscripts, was not known in medieval times.

As early as the fourteenth century, artists from the Low Countries had become skilled in illumination. They entered French schools, and between 1350 and 1420, Flemish names were writ large in the history of French miniature painting.

The Duke of Berry's "Les Très Riches Heures" were illustrated by Flemish artists, as also were "Les Heures" of Chantilly. The first altarpieces were made in the Low Countries, but the work was of low quality. Miniatures were always flat, lacking depth or perspective. There was no variety in the colors, and rivers were painted as unbroken strips of silver.

The first artistic revolution, at the end of the Middle Ages, came in sculpture and portraiture. In Hainaut, during the fourteenth century, André Beauneveu, probably a native of Valenciennes and a fellow countryman of Froissart, became official sculptor and portraitist to three kings of France—Philip VI, John II, and Charles V—whose tombs at St. Denis he decorated. The work of Beauneveu shows progress. Sculpture broke away from the rigid forms of architecture and became a realistic expression of life.

The tumultuous and rather touching prophets on the tower of the Brussels town hall were among the first examples of this new art. They made so strong an impression on Claus (or Claes) Sluter, a young sculptor from Haarlem in Holland, that in 1380, he applied for membership in the stonecutters corporation of Brussels. It was not long before he was entrusted by the dukes with the construction of the Carthusian monastery of Champmol, near Dijon, the "St. Denis of the grand dukes of the West." Here he built his Column of Moses, also known as the Column of the Prophets, the sculptural equivalent of Jan van Eyck's masterpieces. Even the portraits, such as that of Philip the Bold, have unforgettable force and reality.

The Column of the Prophets was not really a column but the plinth of a cross, the upper part of which has been destroyed. Around the stupendous figure of Moses are ranged the five statues of Jeremiah, David, Zacharias, Isaiah, and Daniel. Their faces tell of prophetic inspiration, now eager, now discouraged, forceful or disspirited, and the play of light and shadow upon them provides the sort of contrast and feeling that foreshadows Donatello and Michelangelo.

Life and art were blended in this new technique. In nearby monuments, like the tomb of Philip the Bold and his wife, we can see mourners who express the melancholy, pessimism, and preoccupation with both the ridiculous and death that mark the fifteenth century.

> All I see around are fools,
> The end is coming,
> Sooth to say
> All goes ill.

The revolution soon found its way into painting, whose scope and strength, with Jan van Eyck, became universal. With a single jump, it seemed, painting had reached not only the Renaissance but our own time.

Van Eyck was a genius who "burst beyond the canvas" with his study of perspective. With no predecessors to imitate, he depicted a "total" man, who dominated painting until the twentieth century.

He began by working on illuminated manuscripts, or, at any rate, he grew up in a world where this was the most advanced form of art known. He was born at Maeseyck on the Meuse, the present-day Limbourg, between 1390 and 1400. He set up his studio at Bruges, and in 1425, he entered the service of Philip the Good, Duke of Burgundy.

Scholars have for some time dissociated him from his brother Hubert, whose very existence is questionable. We no longer believe that he was the inventor of oil painting, as the Italian artists did. He used colors consisting of ground mineral powders fixed in egg white. His idea of varnishing the finished painting gave colors a velvety warmth and transparency, not unlike enamel, that was infinitely more sensitive than anything known before.

These technical innovations would have been of little importance if Van Eyck had lacked inspiration. He came into the field, however, with two highly original ideas. The first was to bring the surrounding world into the picture, using space, perspective, the effects of movement, depth, atmosphere, and chiaroscuro. The second was to use the language of feeling and gesture, painting every type of human emotion. Art, in a tiny panel, could encompass all the wealth and variety of a whole cathedral, with its great naves, statues, windows, depth, and multiplicity of color. It was a psychological, plastic means of communication—a new language.

With the art of perspective, representation of open space, and rounded figures thus mastered, "a picture could become a projection of a whole sector of space, with the infinite variety of objects it chances to contain. It was now the image of everything that could be seen in the visual field defined by a rectangular framework and an eye fixed on the horizontal plane" (Hulin de Loo). The picture could be expanded to immense proportions. "A revolution had taken place. Nature was now wholly integrated into the art of painting."

The most striking example of this conception is in the Louvre's "The Madonna of Autun." It was long believed that this painting represented Chancellor Rollin and the Virgin Mary against the background of an imaginary landscape, but it is now known that the subject is Bishop John of Bavaria, and the landscape that of Liège. The landscape starts at the lower edge of the frame and, by the use of perspective, ground patterns, a colonnade, gardens, and a river and bridges, defines a horizon of increasing breadth. It takes the eye past a series of guides and landmarks, thus creating within a small framework a feeling of the immensity and breadth of space. The implacable realism of a brush for which truth was the only objective goes even further than this. It brings out the most minute wrinkle or blemish, seeking to perpetuate every expression in a manner not far removed from cruelty, taking its cue from reality, and giving each model gigantic stature, so that its features portray "the sense of his whole life."

The "Adoration of the Lamb," in St. Bavo's at Ghent, is the *Divine Comedy* of Flemish art and the starting point for all future schools of painting. The picture is at once mystical and material, portraying a world of portraits and landscapes, of colored paints and of real life. It gave painting a scope bordering on the divine and defined its path for centuries ahead.

Not long after, another creative artist came to the fore, Roger van der Weyden, a native of Tournai. He, in turn, found a new pictorial language with which to express his sentiments.

He was born in 1399 or 1400. His achievement was to think of attitudes, gestures, and backgrounds that were to give painting the same motive power as speech or poetry. Like Jan van Eyck, he had a double, the so-called Maître de Flémalle. It is not known whether the latter was his master or if the works attributed to him were not painted by Roger van der Weyden himself in an early period.

These two innovators, Jan van Eyck and Roger van der Weyden (the Italians called them *Il gran' Johannes* and *Il discepol' Ruggero*), were hailed by their contemporaries as the discoverers of a new world. Van Eyck, despite the titles given to his pictures, was not a mystic. He was a lover of life and a passionate painter of its richness and sensual power. Roger van der Weyden, on the other hand, was fascinated by the tragic aspects of human life and sought to paint the souls of his subjects and their inner lives. As he progressed, his subjects became more and more emaciated and disembodied, but the mystical character of his art did not prevent him from painting magnificent nudes.

The work of these two pioneers foreshadows the primitives, the Italian Renaissance painters, Baroque art, and Impressionism. They were followed by a whole crowd of disciples, the first of whom was Petrus Christus, and the next Dirk Bouts, who came from Haarlem and settled at Louvain. It has been said that he was already an Impressionist because of the subtle character of his lighting and atmosphere. His "Last Supper" is a triumph of perspective.

Next came the astonishing Hugo van der Goes, called Hugh of Ghent by his contemporaries, though he had been born in Holland. In later life, he lost his reason and painted his last works in a "systematic and chronic delirium" in the convent of Rouge-Cloître in the forest of Soignes, where he had taken refuge. His was the art of the superman, to be found in such pictures as his "Death of the Virgin," at Bruges, a painting of clenched hands and distraught faces expressing violence and despair. Some of his works seem to mock virtue, showing saints with expressions of cupidity and egoism on their faces. Van der Goes first brought peasants, almost in the wild state, into Flemish painting, particularly in his nativity pictures, and he was apt to give their faces an expression of haggard stupidity.

Soon Hans Memling appeared. His work was a summary and rounding-off of what his predecessors had done. He was born in Seligenstadt, near Mainz, but he had become a citizen of Bruges before reaching the age of twenty-five. Compared with the work of the painters who had preceded him, his work appears to be an elegant synthesis. He was a mystic, like Roger van der Weyden, but he also painted life-sized nudes, like the Stuttgart "Bathsheba," which was a further extension of Jan van Eyck's preoccupation with realistic painting. Memling filled Bruges with his portraits and with the spiritualized faces of his saints, such as those of the famous "Shrine of St. Ursula."

Memling's real successor was Gerard David, another Dutchman. All the masters of the Flemish school, except for Roger van der Weyden, were of northern origin or from the Meuse Valley, but they found the best conditions for artistic growth in the southern part of the Low Countries.

David was appointed official painter to the city of Bruges in 1483. The city authorities of his day drew no hard and fast lines between an artist and an artisan, and his first assignment was to paint the bars of Maximilian's prison cell. His greatest success came later, in works such as "Virgin Among Virgins" and the "Baptism of Christ," at Bruges. In the "Flaying of the Unjust Judge," which foreshadows Rembrandt's "Anatomy Lesson," he associates an element of pathos with a measured softness that already marked him as an academic painter and an imitator of the Italians.

The painter of nightmares, horror, and phantasmagoria was another Dutchman, Hieronymus Bosch, who was born at 's Hertogenbosch (Bois-le-Duc), and in fact never left the town and took its last syllable for his name. His contemporaries thought of him as a moralist, lashing out at the vices of his time, but he was a visionary and a prophet. The figures in his pictures were monsters and their grimaces and shoutings unleashed his "dance of hell." These were the first artistic associations of realistic detail and surrealistic imagination. Bosch was an innovator of astonishing scope, leaving behind him sharply conceived pen drawings, ultramodern color effects and, at the same time, the first examples of romantic landscape.

Flemish art now triumphed in every field. Europe was inundated with Flemish tapestry, altarpieces, engravings, lace, and silver. The great merchant houses of Europe maintained correspondents at Bruges who bought the works of Flemish artists and exported them to every country. Art was becoming an industry.

This creative development was not the product of a united and organized nation. Like Renaissance Italy, it was a divided and politically powerless country. Art depends not on society but on individuals. Admittedly, it thrives when patrons support artists. The essential, however, is genius. After this, the work of one artist grows directly out of that of the others. Artists, in fact, constitute a world of their own, living within the structure of society as a whole.

It is a mistake to interpret the growth of Flemish painting as proof (a "truth by art") that the Low Countries of the fifteenth century were a nation. The same argument could be used to prove the existence of a Florentine or Sienese nation in the same period. What the Low Countries provided was a social medium in which men of genius could work and develop. Five or six of these men of genius, such as Van Eyck,

Van der Weyden, and Memling, were the creators of Flemish painting. After them, the work of each artist logically led to that of the next, each stimulating the others in their continuous efforts to give expression to their vision and inventiveness.

Although the Low Countries were still divided into independent provinces and principalities bordering on France, Germany, and England, they were on the point of creating something of more lasting value than a single nation or a single people. They were about to create a new civilization—a scheme of society that simultaneously staggered the imagination and appeared to bring universal benefits.

VI

THE SPANISH LOWLANDS TAKE
THE LEAD

Philip I (the Handsome), nicknamed "Philip-Take-Advice" because he was a weakling and could do no better than follow the advice of those around him, was the son of Maximilian and father of the Emperor Charles V. He spent most of his reign arranging festivals and engaging in amatory adventures, and he died young. There would be little to say about him if it were not for his marriage.

At the age of eighteen, he married a Spanish princess, Joanna, daughter of Ferdinand of Aragon and Isabella of Castile. She was to become famous under the name of Joanna the Mad. It was not until after her husband's death in 1506 that her madness came upon her, but from the outset she had been an object of scandal in the Low Countries because of her strange appearance, her careless dress, and her indifference to religion.

She was a rebel by nature, and Philip's innumerable infidelities drove her to make violent scenes. Accustomed to the austerity of Spanish customs, she could not understand the license and luxury of the flesh-pots of Flanders. She was subject to fits of morbid neurasthenia that poisoned her life and drove her out of her mind.

A series of unexpected deaths in the three short years between 1497 and 1500 gave Joanna a realm as formidable as has ever been seen. Her brother John's death, in 1497, was followed in 1498 by that of their elder sister, Isabella; Isabella's only son, Don Miguel, died in 1500. Joanna the Mad and Philip the Handsome had a son who was to become Charles V, to whom Joanna thus left Castile and Aragon, Naples and Sicily, Spanish America and the Indies. Through his grandfather Maximilian, Charles V inherited Milan, the Franche Comté, the Low Countries, the Artois, Austria, the Tyrol, and Styria; he also became head of the House of Hapsburg.

The estate that came into the hands of the young prince was composed of most of the Christian world. It included 7 million Spaniards, 3 million inhabitants of the Low Countries, and almost as many Italians and South Germans, not to mention the population of America and the Philippines. It was truly an empire on which "the sun never set."

Not only was France encircled by the Spanish possessions, but all over Europe there were "places of arms"—strategic positions and fortresses controlling and commanding the life of the continent. Germany was ruled from Austria and the Tyrol, the Rhineland from the Low Countries, Western Germany from Holland, Italy from Milan and Naples, and the Mediterranean was firmly held from Sicily and the Balearic Islands. Against this new ascendancy of the House of Hapsburg, the only remaining great power was the Turkish Empire.

In Brussels, Charles V, Duke of Burgundy and sovereign of the Low Countries, was to ascend the throne as King of Spain. The news of the death of the young prince's grandfather Ferdinand of Aragon was directly followed by a great funeral ceremony in St. Gudule. Here young Charles was proclaimed sovereign of Castile and Aragon. Charles was present at the ceremony, dressed in deep mourning and surrounded by princes and ambassadors of foreign powers. In the style of the times, the priest Michel de Pavye delivered a funeral oration for Ferdinand:

"Kings and princes must dance the dance of death," he cried, "for such is the law of our existence. Crown and scepter must come to dust. Forget not, oh forget not, the fate that menaces our joys and festivals, changing them to tears and sorrow."

Then the herald of the Golden Fleece advanced and called in a loud voice: "Don Ferdinand, King of Castile and Aragon!"

Twice he repeated the call, but there was no reply. The herald threw his staff on the flagstones before him, and three times repeated in a low voice: "He is dead!"

The royal standard before the high altar was lowered; then the herald of the Golden Fleece picked up his staff and cried: "Dona Joanna and Don Charles, by the grace of God, Catholic sovereigns, heirs of all these kingdoms and principalities!" The standard of Aragon was raised before the altar, and Charles V appeared on the platform, no longer clad in the hooded mantle of mourning. From the hands of the Bishop of Badajoz he took the Sword of Justice and declared his willingness to accept the titles and duties of the dead king. Then he left the church, amid the acclamation of priests and grandees, burghers and the people.

At first, people were dismayed by young Charles's apparent lack of intelligence. At the age of twenty, he looked sleepy and stupid, spoke with difficulty, and went about with his mouth hanging open. It was only later that he became the wise and majestic sovereign we know from the Titian portraits.

He was no advocate of the divine right of kings, by which the absolute power of the sovereign is vested with religious authority. Instead, he let his people govern themselves and sought to settle most problems by compromise. He thought of himself rather as a final arbiter and allowed his subjects freedom of authority and initiative. In America, his policy of giving a free hand to the *conquistadores* gained him sovereignty over Mexico and Peru. He maintained the prosperity of the Low Countries by relying to a large extent on the nobility, thus making sure of their loyalty. Even when Charles punished the rebels of Ghent, he did so with the idea of assuring the rebirth of the city by giving it leaders and institutions capable of restoring its prosperity. Having been brought up in the Low Countries, Charles understood the customs and way of thinking that prevailed there.

His successor, Philip II, was above all a Spaniard. In his typically Spanish view, Catholicism was a militant religion, a supernatural, mystical doctrine that must triumph. Every sacrifice and devastation was justified by the victory of good over evil.

Despite these differences, both kings failed for similar reasons. Both were suspicious recluses by nature; each deceived himself through fear of being deceived by others. In his youth, Charles V was exploited by his councilors—Chièvres persuaded him to sacrifice the interests of his empire in favor of those of the Low Countries, inciting the revolt of the Spanish *comuneros*. When Charles understood what was going on, he withdrew into himself and became suspicious of everyone. He was convinced that those who advised him did so in their own interest.

In later years he passed on the fruit of his experiences to Philip II, exhorting him to see for himself, judge for himself, and decide issues on his own initiative. As a result many decisions were put off almost indefinitely, and interminable delays in administration ruined the King's plans and led to the foundering of his policy.

This is the drama of absolute monarchy, which must oscillate between the hesitancy of a sovereign fearing to be misled by his councilors, and the errors he commits in seeking to rule by his own judgment. In the end Philip II, with the support of his people, solved the problem by setting himself up as the defender of the intolerant and fanatical religious system that led the Low Countries into ruinous warfare.

By about 1530, Belgium had become the chosen commercial outlet for Germany and the two countries formed a single zone of culture and civilization. France had not yet been able to repair the ravages of the Hundred Years' War, nor to win back her share of trade that had moved eastward and northward, so that Belgium, communicating with Italy by way of the Rhine valley, became the leader of the Renaissance.

The Low Countries were then called "The Ring of the World," for they were the golden circle that united all nations. The policy of Charles V was aimed at flattering and taking care of them, as it was impossible for him to finance his European undertakings without the loans and resources he drew from the Low Countries. For this reason, he did all he could to give them an impression of liberty. He called them "the country where I left my heart," and his personal bodyguard was made up entirely of Belgians. The flower of his army consisted of his Belgian regiments, who saw service in Hungary against the Turks, in Africa against the pirates of Barbary, and in Germany against the Protestants.

One of the victors at Muehlberg, in 1547, was a Belgian, De Buren, whose death was reported by Brantôme in the famous episode of *Death and the Stirrup Cup*:

This Knight of the Golden Fleece suddenly fell sick and was visited by André Vésale, the doctor of the Emperor Charles, who told him frankly that he had but five or six hours to live.

The Count showed no astonishment, but called his two closest friends, Granvelle and the Count of Aremberg. Then, wishing to rise from his bed, he sent for the richest and most sumptuous clothes he possessed and had himself carried into the hall of his mansion.

When he was seated in the great chair, he asked his two brothers-in-law to call before him his captains and officers, that he might bid them farewell. Then there came before him pages, valets, servingmen, stable-men, lackeys, pastry-cooks, wine stewards, muleteers, and many others, and he spoke with them. There even came before him a poor falconer, blear-eyed, hunchbacked, and ill-clad, whom his master thereupon bade be of good cheer, and asked him more particularly after the health of diverse birds for which he was caring.

Then he asked that they drink to the health of the Emperor, his master. After doing so, he made them a fine discourse, telling of his life and the honors he had received, after which he handed the collar of the Golden Fleece to the Count of Aremberg, that he might return it to the Emperor, and drank forthwith the stirrup cup of death.

Thus, proudly clad and armed, he died.

The people of the Low Countries, or the Spanish Lowlands, as they were called, now felt they belonged to a common fatherland, and as such they found their way around the world as merchants and explorers. The Portuguese explorer, Ferdinand Magellan, who made the first trip around the world, organized his expedition with money lent him by an Antwerp banker, and among his crew were five Belgians, including two from Antwerp. It was a Belgo-Dutch fleet that seized Tunis, and merchants from Antwerp found their way as far as China.

Belgian Catholic missionaries carried on their evangelical work in the farthest corners of the Spanish empire. The first Bishop of Cuba, Jean de Witte, was a native of Bruges, and the first Mexican book was published by the Belgian Jean van Dak. Peter of Ghent baptized 300,000 American Indians. Two Belgians, Josse Rycke and Pierre Gossens, were the first to reach the Andes. The father of the science of anatomy was Andreas Vesalius of Brussels, whose real name was Van Weselen. He was bold enough to dissect corpses in the heart of Madrid, despite the orders of the Inquisition, and he may have been sentenced to make the pilgrimage to the East where he died.

The geographer, Gerardus Mercator (Gerhard Kremer), who invented the cylindrical system of map projection that bears his name, was a native of Rupelmonde. His compatriot, Abraham Ortelius, compiled a famous atlas, while the man of widest learning of the period was Gerard Geerts from Rotterdam, who gained lasting fame under the name of Erasmus.

Almost all the great musicians of the time were Walloons, and all over France, Germany, and Italy, the new laws of musical counterpoint were being taught by the Belgian contrapuntists. Roland de Lassus of Mons, who scored musical successes in Vienna, Rome, and Paris, was said to have "recreated the world."

Flemish painting reached its golden age with Quentin Massys, Gossart, Bernard van Orley, Pieter the Elder, and Frans Floris the Incomparable, in whose Antwerp studio there were no less than 120 disciples.

The College of the Three Languages (Hebrew, Greek, and Latin), founded at Louvain by Erasmus, was later duplicated by Francis I, when he set up the College de France in Paris.

The Belgians of the sixteenth century seemed an intellectual elite to all foreigners. The proportion of illiterates was smaller than elsewhere, culture was more widely spread, and art was more fully developed. Although the country's population was only a sixth that of France, it contained at least as many artists and men of learning, and its painters and musicians were of higher caliber. The Belgian art forms were essentially plastic, architectural, and musical, but did not equal the French in literature. France's Ambroise Paré, however, was matched by Vesalius, and Montaigne by Erasmus.

As the intellectual capital and center of new thought and ideas, the Spanish Lowlands held the role that later belonged to Paris, and their main asset was internationalism. Foreigners were welcomed, as were the ideas they brought with them—they were not confronted with the barrier of national tradition that so often masks intellectual laziness. The country's spirit, open and free, and receptive to new things from all sources, was the secret of its greatness during this period. If Bruges was on the decline, it was because she had succumbed to the temptation of self-glorification and had fixed her eyes on the past; if Antwerp was in the ascendant, it was because of the stimulus towards creativeness and self-renewal she had gained from her contacts with Germany and Italy.

The very heart of the ascendancy of the Spanish Lowlands was the spirit of liberty. The political regime was essentially republican and was to remain so for nearly three centuries. There was, indeed, a sovereign prince, but each new sovereign had to be recognized anew by the country. He had no right to demand obedience from his subjects until he had taken the prescribed oath to maintain each province's customs and privileges. And he was only recognized as sovereign after the Estates General had consented to his inauguration, and in Brabant this recognition could be withdrawn at any time.

The Estates alone had stewardship of the public purse. They had their own civil servants, levied taxes, elected a permanent deputation to administer the country, issued loans, built roads and bridges, granted subsidies, and, in certain cases, tax exemptions. In Brabant no foreigner could be naturalized without his consent, nor could any criminal be extradited—a situation that accounts for the fact that so many Frenchmen took refuge in Brussels during the sixteenth and eighteenth centuries. The rights and privileges of the Estates, by which the power of the sovereign was limited, were summarized by the Prince of Orange, in his *apologia*, at the end of the sixteenth century.

> He may not violently constrain any of his subjects to do anything, unless it be in accordance with the customs of the judicial bench of his domicile. He may not, by any ordinance or decree, reorganize his country and he must be content with his ordinary revenues. He may not raise or exact any tax, save at the express will and consent of the country and in accordance with its privileges. He may not bring troops into the country without its consent, and he must not make any change in the money or coinage without the consent of the Estates. He cannot arrest any subject unless information has been laid before a magistrate of the peace: and, having made him a prisoner, he may not send him out of the country.

The powers of the Estates were already very wide, and they were increased by the fact that the smallest authorization, exemption, or tax granted to the prince had to be voted unanimously. Moreover, valid international treaties could not be concluded without the cooperation of the Estates. It was also obligatory to consult them on all matters of justice, for the right to be judged by due process of law was a fundamental liberty of the citizens of the Low Countries.

A good idea of the life of a citizen of Brussels in this period can be gained from our knowledge of the youth of the great doctor Andreas Vesalius. His father, a Brussels pharmacist, lived in a house in the Rue de l'Enfer, which is today the Rue aux Laines in the Minimes quarter near the law courts. In those days it was a refuge for vagabonds, prostitutes, and the destitute. Behind the house there was a stretch of open ground, where the present law courts now stand, that was then called Galgenberg, Gallows Hill. This was the official place for executions, and young Vesalius could look from his father's pharmacy window and see corpses swinging in the wind. Hanged felons had no burial rights, and their flesh was eaten by rats and scavenger birds. When their skeletons fell apart, stray dogs made off with the bones. It was doubtless from familiarity with this spectacle that young Vesalius became interested in the study of anatomy.

On the other side of town he could see the fields and meadows that surrounded the river Senne, and northward the tangle of inns and houses in front of St. Gudule. Southward stretched the houses surrounding the Place du Sablon, beyond which lay the princely houses along Coudenberg and the Montagne de la Cour.

Under Charles V, Brussels became one of the centers of European life. Sometimes there were as many as seven crowned heads at once in Coudenberg Palace, a favorite residence of the Emperor. The town consisted of a group of houses and orchards, with many gardens, meadows, and wooden thickets within the wide compass of the city wall. There were many small bodies of water, and the park had become a garden, occupying several times the area it does today. The town continually expanded. From the mud of the Senne a large marsh was reclaimed and christened the Terre Neuve—which later gave its name to today's Rue Neuve.

Kings and princes mingled with burghers and the common people in sumptuous festivals held for the *Ommegang*, or archery contests, in which the target was the popinjay. The fairs, feasts, jousts, tournaments, motley processions, fireworks, and licentious scenes alternated with famine and wretchedness.

Hunting, or venery as it was then called, was one of the main occupations of a nobleman's life, and almost the only thing deemed worthy of his concern. Maximilian wrote to his grandson Charles V: "We were joyful to learn that our offspring Charles takes such pleasure in the chase, since we must else have thought him a bastard."

The forest of Soignes was twice as large then as it is today, spreading over 25,000 acres. Its capital was at Boitsfort, the administrative seat of the special courts that had judicial competence in hunting matters and always sat in forest country. The tribunals had strange and romantic names, such as the "Consistory of the Trumpet" and the "Tribunal of the Horn." There was one famous hunting party in the forest of Soignes, near the abbey of Groenendael, in which the participants included seven crowned heads, among them the Emperor Charles V and his son

Philip. The Emperor's Spring still flows through the forest, the name a reminder of these rides, and the emperor's hunts were an inexhaustible subject for the painters of pictures and weavers of tapestries.

Many of the local festivities that still take place are not survivals from the Middle Ages, as is generally believed, but date from the sixteenth century. Among these is the famous fight of the Doudou at Mons, at which the brave Sir Giles kills the dragon, the processions of giants, and the Binche carnival, which may be traced to an inspiration derived from the Indians of South America.

At Mons, the skirted "Chin-Chins" line the market place to share in the fight of St. George against the dragon, known as Lumeçon, while devils and savages bound about among the crowd. At Namur, the local passion is for a game (found elsewhere only in the Landes of France) consisting of fights on stilts. These take place in the public squares, where bands of young people on high stilts, like giants, throw themselves upon rival groups in attempts to knock one another over. Each group numbers about fifty contestants and their uniforms are very bright, some of them bearing the imperial eagle of Hapsburg or the cross of Burgundy. Their virtuosity is astonishing and they are able to remain erect in the midst of tremendous melees. Upon the accession of Philip II in Belgium, a stilt show was one of the spectacles of the festival.

A new institution was the post. In 1489, an Italian living in Venice, a certain Janetto de 'Tassis, began carrying letters, and, in 1505, Philip I made an agreement with Franz de Taxis for a postal service between the Spanish Lowlands, Germany, and France. The first mail carried at full speed, with relay points and remounts, was organized in 1516, when Charles V gave the Taxis family the postal monopoly for Spain and the Spanish Lowlands. In 1520, Jean Baptiste de Tour et Taxis became postmaster general, and in 1545 a law was passed that all letters and packets must be entrusted to the official postal service.

There was a great growth in luxury among all classes of society, and clothing fashions changed rapidly. At the beginning of the century, men's doublets had been open at the neck, forming a square across the chest. Under Philip II they were closed and decorated with a ruff, so that the head appeared to have been set on a plate, like that of a beheaded man, and was jokingly compared to John the Baptist.

Little by little fashions from Spain dictated enormous ruffs of pleated and dazzling white linen for both men and women. The fashion was rigorously Catholic, modesty triumphing over the décolleté. Sleeves, doublets, and breeches were worn slashed, with opening through which linings or undergarments were visible. Men now wore long, close-fitting stockings, which came halfway up the thigh, requiring the development of a new and essential craft. Unknown in the Middle Ages, knitting increased in popularity and created in turn a new handicraft, that of the hosier (*bonnetier*), whose trade it was to fashion socks, vests, and what were known as muslin hose. The rise of the knitting trade enabled people to dispense with sewn hose, which fitted poorly and required that children have new sets of clothes as they grew up. It now became possible to wear vests and tights of elastic material, and Henry VIII was the first to wear silk stockings.

Another novelty was the pocket. Although in the Middle Ages money and small objects had been carried in a hanging arm purse, by the sixteenth century puffed pants, with their slits and horse-hair stuffing, made possible the concealment of pockets in their structure. Women, too, wore puffed-out frocks, with stuffing in the sleeves and bodice to hold their rosaries, their comfit boxes, their watches, and, before long, their handkerchiefs.

Beards reappeared. At the close of the Middle Ages, beards were unknown, and everybody in the fifteenth century had a shaven chin. All the dukes of Burgundy, from Philip the Bold to Charles the Bold, were clean-shaven, as were the Emperor Maximilian and his son Philip I. Beginning with Francis I, all the kings of France wore beards or goatees and, among the Hapsburgs, Philip I and Charles V did the same.

The new fashions, however, were slow in reaching the countryside. It might have been assumed that shaving was a sign of luxury and refinement and that the lower classes would be loath to follow it. This in fact is the opposite of what happened; the peasantry, who are always behind fashion, were clean-shaven throughout the sixteenth century.

In the same period, the idea of time became more precise and people began to speak of a half-hour, a quarter of an hour, and similar subdivisions. A German artisan had devised a way of replacing the pendulum of a clock by an alternating balance wheel, operated by springs that could be wound. The production of watches greatly increased, and they became small and strong enough to be carried on the person.

The moment was at hand for the reform of the Gregorian calendar. The Julian calendar had been in use since the days of Caesar, and the official year was getting more and more behind the real or astronomical year. On December 13, 1582, Pope Gregory XIII ordered the reform of the calendar, and December 21 of that year became January 1, 1583. The fact that ten days disappeared altogether from the calendar has left its mark even in the language of today, for the French speak of "a week of four Thursdays" and the English of "a month of Sundays."

Refinements until then unknown were reaching the dining table through the spread of intelligent cookery. For the first time, strawberries and other fruits were served with cream, while a great number of new vegetables were making their appearance—the tomato, which had come from America, beans, artichokes, asparagus, lettuce, the melon, and the large strawberry. Another discovery was the use of distilled spirits, which had been unknown in the old days when drunkenness only proceeded from the wineskin. During this period, however, the Jesuits made *aqua vita* to revive the dying, and the way opened for the making of hard liquors and perfumes.

People still ate with their fingers, carrying morsels from their plates directly to their mouths. Etiquette, however, now demanded that each piece be held with no more than three fingers and that the diner should not use his left hand. No glasses were put on the table, but a filled glass was brought to each guest whenever he asked for it. This resulted in many small observances of courtesy, such as drinking to the health of your neighbor, and turning toward the master of the house when you were on the point of drinking. Increasing use was also made of the table napkin, and each guest spread his napkin, not across his knees in the modern manner, but across his shoulder, or over his left arm, like café waiters of our own time.

It would be wrong to think of the sixteenth century entirely as an age of progress, intellectual freedom, and the spread of science. Culture existed only for the elite, while the masses, and even the middle class, remained in the grip of medieval superstition. Without an appreciation of this primitive atmosphere, it would be impossible to understand the furious and narrow-minded fanaticism of the religious wars.

Jean de Potre, for example, for all that he was a Catholic and cultivated burgher of Brussels, believed that in each year there were thirty-eight unlucky days on which no undertaking of any kind should be started. Children born on these days had no chance of survival, nor did those who fell sick. The cure of jaundice depended on eating yellow food, notably chicken soup made from a yellow-legged cock. Yellow was a lucky color; the fashion for yellow amber from Germany, and the high prices paid for it, sprang from the belief that nobody who wore it could fall ill.

Against such a background, of course, sorcery and spells were widespread, and a great number of prayers and ceremonies were prescribed for exorcisms. In Styria, which, like the Spanish Lowlands, was in the Hapsburg domain, a firm belief persisted that death could be staved off for a day by saying a prayer to St. Christopher. The government made it the duty of every soldier to say this prayer every morning, for the army that had thus found a way of limiting its losses must automatically return victorious.

The Renaissance was now developing in all the more advanced

countries, notably the Spanish Lowlands, western Germany, France, and Italy—those countries that first benefited from the progress and great inventions that were to lead to the modern world. In one sense, however, the Renaissance was the result of three inventions that, although dating from the medieval period, only came into their own later. These were window glass, spectacles, and printing. Invented in Italy during the fifteenth century, spectacles added twenty or thirty years to the normal working life of intellectuals. In the Middle Ages, with the normal deterioration of eyesight with age, people had to give up reading and writing at about fifty, and books printed in large type were rare and costly. The invention of spectacles made possible a greater quantity of books of smaller format, and this was one of the indirect causes of the invention of printing from movable type.

Window glass was to play an even more important part. At first it was installed only in cathedrals, but later, when it was used to keep homes warm, it improved the organization of intellectual life, for it brought the northern peoples into the realm of civilization. In northern climates, where the mean temperature falls below zero for half the year, reading, writing, and even thinking had before then been made difficult by the cold. The writing of a text, the solution of a problem, or the illumination of a manuscript were scarcely possible with fingers paralyzed by cold. Without window glass a house could not be both warm and light; all openings had to be hermetically closed to keep in the heat, and the people inside had to live in comparative darkness, giving up all effective work, except when they went outside for labor of a purely physical character. It has been said that, for countries north of the forty-fifth parallel, the invention of window glass was as important as that of writing.

Since the cost of artificial light was very high it was only available to the rich and privileged, so that artists and men of learning, before the advent of windowpanes, had had to cease work in winter, or take refuge in one of the countries of the south. It was in the Low Countries that the use of window glass spread first to castles and private houses. Pictures and miniatures show us rooms with glazed windows as early as the reign of Philip the Good. The "Annunciation," painted by the Master of Flémalle in 1428, shows windows that are partly glazed and partly closed with wooden shutters. A quarter of a century later, the pictures of Rogier van der Weyden reveal window openings that are entirely glazed; and in the middle of the fifteenth century, Van Eyck and Memling painted windows that opened and closed, like those of our time, by swinging upon hinges.

For all this, medieval civilization was founded on speech and direct action. A St. Bernard, if he wanted to have any real influence, had to travel ceaselessly and write countless letters, each one of which could be read by only a few correspondents. The spread of ideas was limited by the number of listeners. Teaching was almost entirely oral, and the only way by which a doctrine could be propagated, or disciples trained, was to preach, or to found schools or monastic orders. It was possible for reformers to exercise an influence on society by creating new orders, but these ideas could be stopped, or at any rate slowed down, by killing their apostles or putting them in prison.

All this was to be changed by the invention of printing. Ideas, no longer restrained, became all-powerful, for a single man could now communicate with millions of others. Such a man as Martin Luther, hidden in the Wartburg, isolated and forsaken by all, could nonetheless pour out the pamphlets and broadsides that were to throw Germany into disarray and spread the Reformation. From the depths of obscurity he won more adherents to his belief than any of the martyrs and apostles of old.

With the humanists, a new concept of life was beginning to appear. In the Middle Ages, earthly life was a time of trial. Pauperism was cultivated by tempering it with charity, cruelty and misery were tolerated as expressions of the will of God, and the love of mankind was allowed only as a consequence of the love of God.

Renaissance doctrine held that mankind should not yield to evil, but should fight against it by science, education, and culture. Man should strive against ignorance, the source of evil, and love his fellow men and seek their welfare for their own sakes as well as for God's. It was now believed that sickness could be fought by the art of medicine, famine by full granaries and more efficient agriculture, and war by an effort of humanization based on a true religion of humanity.

With the Reformation, however, came the new fact that Christianity, which had previously reconciled man with man under the aegis of the church, now divided men among themselves. Throughout the Middle Ages, religious feeling had restrained violence. This same religious feeling now brought religious wars, launching mankind into savage slaughter and kindling a blaze that set fire to all of Europe.

It was a new phenomenon for religious mysticism to be vested with the power of destruction. Since the change came at a time when the world, stimulated by an improved civilization, was becoming more and more united, the religious wars of the sixteenth century were a cataclysm. The Renaissance, which had begun so hopefully, was to end by unleashing fanatical hatreds which had been unknown in Europe for many years.

At the beginning of the sixteenth century a new elite was beginning to emerge from the ignorant and superstitious masses. Erasmus was the intellectual leader of the movement in the Low Countries, and the outstanding figure of the period. Although he was not Belgian, having been born in Rotterdam, a great part of his life was spent in the southern part of the Low Countries, and he was closely associated with the life of the country. During this period, moreover, there was no real distinction between Dutch and Belgians. They were part of the same people, sharing the same culture and the same ideas, and it could hardly be anticipated that, less than a century later, they would become two separate nations.

Erasmus, moreover, had European stature, because humanism, like the Renaissance itself, was a movement with roots in every country— England, France, Germany, and Italy. Humanism, indeed, was to enjoy universal popularity. Comparing the standards of the time with our own, it is difficult to believe that Erasmus' *Adages* went through sixty editions in thirty-six years, at a time when the number of people who could read was infinitesimal. The reason for his popularity was that he possessed all the characteristics of his age—love of antiquity, multiplicity, a certain superficiality of knowledge, the encyclopedic spirit— and was an admirable expression of them.

During his life Erasmus became a minor canon, a Cambridge don under the protection of Henry VIII of England, and later a servant of Francis I of France. He lived in Venice, Paris, and Basel, forever traveling and leading a nomadic existence. The nearest thing to his real home were the provinces of today's Belgium, for they were the center of his life and activities.

His work in its entirety was published in Latin; *Adagia* (*Adages*) appeared in 1500, *Enchiridion militis christiani* (*Manual of the Christian Knight*) in 1503, *Laus Stultitiae* (the famous *In Praise of Folly*) in 1509, *Institutio principis christiani* (*Education of a Christian Prince*) in 1515, and *Colloquias* (Colloquies) in 1516.

Erasmus was an anti-traditionalist and supporter of the individual, a foe of class distinction, nationalism, and the prejudices of the past— including the celibacy of the priesthood, ignorance, and religious fanaticism.

The aim of the College of the Three Languages, which he founded in 1517 at Louvain, was to liberate knowledge from religion, a revolutionary notion, for until then all teachers, doctors, and men of learning had been priests. The very idea of the college subjected Erasmus to so many attacks that he had to abandon the project in the face of the hostility of the bishops and their supporters among the religious orders and other traditionalist groups. The honor of translating the idea into fact, therefore, belongs to Francis I of France. An absolute monarch, he introduced it in another form.

The life of Erasmus was in itself a human problem. He was the illegitimate son of a priest and a woman of the people, and in his youth was bruised by the stupidity of the teachers who were imposed upon him. Because of his origin, and the ideas of his period, he felt that he had been damaged from the start. After his youthful martyrdom, he saw his covetous guardians forcing him into a monastery so that they could appropriate his inheritance.

His world was essentially a medieval one and it was not long before he rose in protest against it. He recovered his liberty by abandoning holy orders and finally, on the strength of his own intellectual prestige, became councilor and referee to a select world of princes, popes, sovereigns, and grandees.

Despite the eminence of his protectors, however, he was always a restless person, open to suspicion for his bastardy and the fact that he had left the priesthood. His freedom was hampered by the need to earn a livelihood, and by his wretched health with all the precautions and remedies that went with it. He was intensely nervous, sensitive, and emotional, and all who spoke with him were impressed by his immense eyes and their strange and frightening expression. None of the artists who painted his portrait ventured to show him full face, but preferred to show him in profile with his eyes lowered. The effort he had to make to earn his living prevented him from becoming an active revolutionary and one of the leaders of the century in which he lived. This role he left to Luther and to Calvin.

Erasmus may be criticized for being unduly timid, over-prudent, and even self-seeking. His great worth was as a rebel—against the teachers who crushed him, lied to him, and left him to discover the truth for himself, and against the ignorant monks and fanatics who followed their own ideas, denying the true value of scientific inquiry, and thinking only of violent means to silence their opponents.

He fought against such people all his life, pursuing in them the torturers of his youth. Against them, he called on the world of antiquity, the learning and wisdom of the humanists, and the support that the great of the world gave him. He made himself out to be a philosopher, but was swayed by his emotions. His reputation as a man of learning springs from a wholly personal rebellion indelibly stamped on his character by the memories of his childhood.

Although he fought a lifetime battle for justice and tolerance, and dreamed of transforming humanity by science, he was, in the end, forced to leave the Low Countries and retire to Basel in the face of a coalition of his enemies. His life is an outstanding example of the adventures of a sixteenth-century intellectual, with the thousand and one limitations that hemmed it in, but also its greatness amid increasing liberty—for there can be no doubt that a century earlier Erasmus' origin would have necessitated his passing his whole life in the obscurity of a monastery.

It would be a mistake to think of Erasmus and the other humanists as typical of contemporary life in the Low Countries. Their words were only for the few, and the mass of the public did not read them. The public was interested only in processions, or theatrical shows given by the chambers of rhetoric that portrayed the opinions and ideas of the masses, and played an important role in the gradual unification of the Belgian provinces.

How did a small burgher or rich artisan in Ghent or Antwerp live during the early part of the sixteenth century? What was the routine of his daily life and how did he employ his leisure, the best index of the tastes and character of men? What did the artisan or the merchant do once his day's work was over and his shop closed?

Such people were devoted to meetings and parties, a taste that still exists in Belgium. They were forever forming associations and fraternities in which people of the same trade, or living in the same district, could meet together. There were many festivals that played an important part in the life of the time.

Once political and civil strife between the great cities had come to an end, and the Low Countries were united under a central government, people began to find that their only way to prominence and a feeling of self-importance lay in processions and the pomp and circumstance that attended them.

It was not long before everybody who wanted to play a public role had joined the Chamber of Rhetoric in his own town. The possession of such a chamber was a matter of local patriotism and there was great rivalry between one region and another. The rich burgher, artisan, artist, and city fathers were all among the members. All the spirit and vigor of the people found its outlet in great processions, archery contests, and play-acting.

After a time, different towns had the idea of organizing contests, taking turns in sending out invitations. These contests were known as *landjuweel* and became so important that they gained national fame, reaching their height with the *landjuweel* of Antwerp, in 1496. The chambers of rhetoric and their theatrical performances provided a means of expression for public opinion. The part they played was not unlike that of the societies of philosophers in the period leading up to the French Revolution, since they quickly adopted new ideas that gained explosive force through the public attention focused on these great, nation-wide contests. The great development of their critical spirit gave them an essential role in the propagation of the Reformation. It was with some stupefaction that, on the occasion of the great *landjuweel* at Ghent in 1539, the government perceived the fact. In answer to the question, "Which people, in all the world, are the most prone to folly?", the rhetoricians of Tienen (Tirlemont) gave the following answer:

> I've seen the dance of all my fools,
> And none such blockheads, I believe,
> As the heads like stone, tonsure-crowned.
>
> Blind leading blind, they walk about,
> In every action dull and crass,
> Life, clothes, and person of a lout,
> Only lacking the long ears of an ass.

Here is how one of the plays treated the doctrine of indulgences and purgatory:

FIRST SPEAKER:

> If I had earthly goods,
> I could buy the remission of my sins,
> And so escape from purgatory . . .

SECOND SPEAKER:

> No, Man, that would be maligning God . . .
> By doing that you would become guilty.
> Keep closely rather to the gospel's text . . .
> Christ's kingdom doesn't cost a penny.

The authors had complete liberty, and the way the contests were held made any form of attack possible. It was understood, some time later, that the action of the chambers of rhetoric had in effect been revolutionary. The historian Kalff wrote: "Never had literary work been used thus, as an attack against the existing order of things."

Twenty years later, the English traveler, Richard Clough, commented on a visit to the Low Countries: "In this time plays were played such as have cost the lives of thousands of human beings, for the word of God was, for the first time, discussed in public. Moreover, the book of these plays was, and is still, very stoutly defended, as much, indeed, as the books of Martin Luther. These plays were one of the chief causes of the devastation of Ghent."

These festivals created a unique background in the Low Countries for the development of painting and the arts. They trained people to think in terms of painting and painters, and to welcome and appreciate artists. This aided directly the enormous expansion of civilization during the golden age of the Low Countries.

By this time, the framework of life was changing. Medieval architecture was gradually giving way to Renaissance, and even the flamboyant Gothic was going out of fashion. The Italians had revived ancient architectural forms—in favor of these the flying buttresses, pointed arches, tall, slender spires, and elaborate stonework around the stained-glass windows were to disappear.

But the humble life of the artist went on in the midst of all the political adventure, war, and social development of the time. Art itself is a dazzling theater, full of surprises; its sets and creations do not depend on political influences or on the state of society, but simply on the appearance of men of genius.

The most striking aspect of the second half of the sixteenth century is the sterility of painting in the Low Countries by persistent imitation of the Italian school. The exaltation of reality was abandoned in favor of slavish conformity. This happened as early as 1470, when a certain Joos van Wassenhove, a friend of Hugo van der Goes, disappeared from Ghent. Three years later he turned up at Urbino, Italy, where he was known as Iusto di Guanto (Justus of Ghent), and the pictures he was then painting were Flemish. His style gradually changed, becoming Italianate, and in the end some of his works, like "The Liberal Arts," were later attributed to the Italian painter, Melozzo da Forli.

The new Italianism resulted in fashions and public taste that got the better of the inventiveness of creative artists. Flemish painting had performed its task of teaching all Europe the newest and most original form of art, but despite its very richness it showed, during the sixteenth century, a marked decline.

Sixteenth-century Belgian painting is characterized by one particular phenomenon—the center of artistic life moved from Bruges to Antwerp.

The first of the great Antwerp painters was Quentin Massys. He was born before 1500 and thus still had some of the spirit of the fifteenth-century, which may account for the fact that he represents part of the Low Countries' resistance to Italian influence. The enormous prestige of the schools of Florence, Rome, and Venice was creating a sort of international art that was suffocating the creative freedom of artists in much the same way as medieval French art had a century before.

For two centuries, it had been Italy's good fortune—perhaps because of the independence of the different provinces and the opposition between them—to produce a continuous succession of new masters. They gave Italian painting a push forward, with their originality and inventiveness, whenever it seemed on the point of becoming immobile.

Fifteenth-century progress was stimulated by Domenico Ghirlandaio, Sandro Botticelli, and Leonardo da Vinci. In the sixteenth century came Raphael, Michelangelo, and the Venetian school with Giorgione, Titian, and Paolo Veronese. The inventive spirit of such masters was enough to keep painting viable until the end of the century, when the new technical achievements of Caravaggio appeared.

In the same way, Flemish art had lived on revolutions, each associated with the name of an individual artist—Van Eyck, Van der Weyden, Van der Goes, Memling, Gerard David, and Hieronymus Bosch, who followed one another at intervals of only a few years. A period of semi-stagnation was succeeded by the emergence of Bruegel the Elder and Rubens.

Quentin Massys was a friend of Erasmus, and had an acute sense of the expressive power of painting. He imitated Leonardo with exquisite charm in his "Madeleine" at Antwerp; nevertheless, he was always a Fleming and a follower of Roger van der Weyden, and he marks the point of contact between the Middle Ages and the Renaissance. He was less original than Joachim Patinir, a native of Dinant and the Ardennes, whose youth had made him conscious of other landscapes than the Flemish plains. He created a landscape style of his own— compositions with big masses: river estuaries, large stretches of green, and mountain backgrounds. His contemporary, Hieronymus Cock, also painted landscapes that were only half real and that became increasingly reflections of his state of mind.

It was Jan Gossart, known as Jan de Mabuse because he came from Maubeuge, who was the greatest imitator of the Italian style. Mabuse, like the Italians, was caught by the exaltation of the human body and its beauty, of nudity for nudity's sake. He turned his back on the realism of the Flemish school and took the first steps towards Baroque, and essentially intellectual, art from which a direct connection can be traced to the surrealism of our own time. He was both an imitator and a forerunner, seeking to portray against the architecture of the Renaissance, with its columns, arches, and geometrically abstract forms, a world of living beings that were intellectually a part of them.

After this, Belgian painting in the first half of the sixteenth century turned resolutely toward Italy. It was, however, divided into two great schools; the so-called mannerism and the pseudo-classical school of the Romanists.

The aim of mannerism was to develop the details of form. Its greatest exponents included Jan van Cleef, whose work is marked by the excess of gesticulation, and Bernard van Orley, who sought to use Italian inventions to the greatest possible effect. He was, in fact, no more than a specialist in high-class adaptation, scoring his greatest success in imitating the Italian school.

The Romanists gave up Flemish traditions in their entirety. The best known among them were Michel Coxcie and Frans Floris, known as "the incomparable," whose brother Cornelius was the architect of the Antwerp town hall. Frans Floris, who was the leader of the Romanist school, visited Italy and was present at the unveiling of Michelangelo's "Last Judgment," on December 25, 1541. He imitated Michelangelo when he painted the "Fall of the Rebel Angels," now in the Antwerp Museum. He had more than a hundred pupils, and was to exercise a profound influence on Belgian painting, introducing a detailed knowledge of anatomy and seeking a unity of light in the picture. The latter is a characteristic feature of all the pseudo-classical schools that try to substitute design and technical balance for inventiveness.

Much the same may be said of Pieter Pourbus whose "Last Judgment," at Bruges, was inspired by classical marble structures, and the works of Key and Marten de Vos. Their work was elegant but mediocre, and they escaped obscurity only because of their portraiture.

The school did produce one portrait painter of genius. This was Antonis Mor, who was known in Spain as Antonio Moro. In portraiture, he was the foreshadower of Van Dyck and Rubens.

There was only one real genius of seventeenth-century Belgian painting: the "painter of reality," Pieter Bruegel the Elder. Contrary to popular belief, he was neither a thinker nor a peasant painter of humble origins. He was a man who found his own way of appraising reality directly and thus escaped the schools and imitative art. His motto was *naar het leven* ("lifelike"), and while his contemporaries were thronging museums to study the work of others, he went out into the fields to paint nature at first hand. Born between Breda and Antwerp, he paid a visit to Italy, where he discovered not the work of the old masters, but the mountain landscapes of the Alps and the Tyrol, which he later painted into his work. He made a whole collection of sketches and drawings from nature, to fix these landscapes in his mind, and in later years they were to be dubbed "worthy of Titian."

He became an engraver, thinking of himself only as an artisan, and in this capacity he was the official supplier to the famous Shop of the Four Winds, owned by Hieronymus Cock, the great print publisher of the period. He still did a great deal of landscape drawing, but he thought of this as an amusement or a way of taking notes, and refused comparison with the official painters. He thus remained an amateur, and never acquired either the mannerisms, the artificial fashions, or the devices of his contemporaries. He imitated only the highly original and independent satirical work of Hieronymus Bosch.

He was thus a self-educated painter, virtually outside his own period. When he decided to paint only in the last twelve years of his life, he was able to remain entirely original. He composed landscapes and made them the center of his canvases, but in them he sought to integrate man and nature. In his "Fall of Icarus," for example, the subject of the picture is reduced to a small figure in the corner of a magnificent land- and seascape. Bruegel was a painter of simple beings—of peasants, shepherds, and people in general—but he painted them without a trace of mannerism. In "The Seasons," the earth conveys a poignant impression of melancholy, emotion, and tragic power. He "translated the gospels into Flemish," as in the "Census at Bethlehem," in Brussels, and the "Massacre of the Innocents," in Vienna; in all his work, he recreates the world with forms that are both direct and elementary. He stands head and shoulders above the other painters of his time, whose work, by comparison, is either imitative or decadent.

Portraiture, through its imitation of the living model, succeeded in avoiding an academic taint; other creative painting in the Low Countries included the landscape and the still life. Gilles van Coninxloo, a forerunner of Rubens, was the first to see the forest in epic style, with its wildness and great green masses. Paul Bril, too, even before the time of Claude Lorrain, expressed the poetry of space. He was also the first to discover the charm of the Roman countryside.

During this period, tapestry makers were portraying scenes of Maximilian hunting with their great designs of wooded landscapes. Flemish art, indeed, was finding expression in many fields, notably in furniture, lace, tapestry, and the art of the silversmith.

In sculpture, a number of wonderful Italo-Flemish works were created about this time. They include the "Fireplace of the Frank," at Bruges, and Cornelius Floris's astonishing vertical "Tabernacle," slender as a cathedral spire, at Zoutleeuw. In the same period, Jacques du Broeucq of Mons was successfully combining the tradition of Walloon sculpture with the Italian style.

Renaissance art had now become supra-national and was losing in originality what it gained in universal character, becoming as sterile as French art of the fifteenth century. Soon, Belgian artists began to leave their country and find their way throughout Europe, where they were invariably successful.

Among the leaders of the emigrants were Giovanni da Bologna, a Belgian who spent his whole life in Italy; Alexander Colins of Mechlin, who was to become Ghiberti Flamand in Germany and Austria; and Paul Bril, who made his career in Rome. The landscape painter Roland Savery became official painter to the Emperor Rudolph, in Vienna. Many of these artists were no longer known by their original names.

Toeput, for example, was known in Venice as Pozzoserato; it was under the name of Pedro Campana that Pieter de Kempener founded the Seville school and won the admiration of Murillo. Denis Calvaert founded an academy at Bologna; Liége sculptors, such as Delcour and Duquesnoy, also traveled far afield. Thus, by the end of the sixteenth century, the art of the Low Countries had taken on the same general and international character that prevailed throughout the whole of civilized Europe.

Antwerp was in full flower. The city had become a great storehouse to which merchandise flowed from every country in the world, trading goods as different as molasses from the Canary Islands and slaves from Africa and Brazil. Produce was stored here on a tremendous scale. England alone sent in 100,000 pieces of woolen cloth every year, a quantity exceeding the whole production of medieval Flanders; and Portugal consigned for storage as much as 10,000 bales of pepper at a time.

The city expanded on a stupendous scale, continuing to grow at an almost alarming rate to the end of the century. About 1440–60, Antwerp had only 3,334 houses. Half a century later, the number was 6,800, and in 1550 it had grown to 9,000, compared with only 6,000 houses in Brussels at this time. The city's growth would have done credit to any American town in its most dynamic phase, and by now there were 100,000 inhabitants. It continually became necessary to enlarge the ramparts, to lay out new streets, and to open new districts. In this same period, the total volume of business in the city exceeded 3 billion gold francs.

What struck travelers when they came to Antwerp was the absence of the turbulent proletariat that was always making trouble at Bruges. The people of Antwerp knew nothing of riots and disturbances, and their one thought was to collaborate with the immigrant merchants who were the real kings of the city.

The law forbade the arrest of any foreigner, and every merchant was automatically protected by a safe conduct as long as he remained in the city. The Emperor Sigismond ruled that even criminals and traitors exiled from the empire could not be interfered with here. The Church, too, had to take similar action. Interdicts and excommunications affecting the inhabitants of Brabant were suspended at Antwerp during the fairs.

Beyond the market charges, foreigners in Antwerp had no large tax to pay, and they enjoyed complete freedom. The young port now occupied the place Bruges had formerly held, and its inhabitants understood that, if they wanted to attract foreign merchants to their city, they must offer them more freedom than could be found in a rival port. In the middle of the fifteenth century, the English left Bruges and settled in Antwerp. Since the city had no industry, it was not necessary to raise taxes and customs duties. This made it possible for powerful international companies to undertake triangular operations that were impossible at Bruges. On the same day, for example, woolen cloth bought in Antwerp could be resold to merchants from Marseille, then handed over to Florentine merchants, who took delivery at Antwerp, without anyone having to leave the city. Facilities of this kind were one of the causes of the rapid expansion of Antwerp. Nothing of the same kind was available in Bruges, where all sales had to be made through Bruges brokers, who charged a commission on each transaction.

Antwerp was on the way to becoming the capital of European commerce, and its prosperity was continually increasing. With our modern ideas of a great seaport, we may be inclined to think of Antwerp as a harbor of many quays loaded with merchandise, thronged with a jostling crowd of stevedores, bristling with cranes, and set against a background of jetties and warehouses that ran the whole length of the Schelde waterfront. The picture was very different. The quays along the river bank were not accessible because, from one end of the town to the other, stood an immense wall, with its foundations in the river bed. This was the old medieval fortification, built to protect the city against assault, and bristling, not with cranes, but with twenty-one turrets.

The Tripe Hole, the Sandersgat, and the Lisgat were some of the canals which came into the town through holes in the wall. The only berth was a jetty projecting into the water and known as the *werf* (wharf), at the end of which stood the port's only crane, made of wood and mounted on wheels. This crane had a boom, block and tackle, and winch connected to a treadmill powered by several men. They had to use both hands and feet in bringing their weight to bear; the motive power they thus provided was comparable to that of a small steam engine of the nineteenth century.

This crane was enough to handle all the traffic, and it was not until 1546 that a second one, this time a stone-work construction, was erected. Vessels from the high seas could tie up only at the wharf, or at a little quay called the English quay, and they had to wait for the crane until the previous cargo had been discharged. Smaller vessels, on the other hand, were not unloaded at the quayside, but sailed in through the canals and passed through the town in all directions, finding their way eventually to the Schelde through one of the gates.

Oddly enough, this port, sketchy as its equipment seems to us, ranked at the time as one of the best laid out and most convenient in the world. Merchants of the period thought its organization a marvel, for ships were discharged quickly, and the turn-around time was reduced to a minimum. This gave it a standing comparable with such modern ports as New York and London.

The explanation lies in the fact that it was unusual for a seagoing ship to come in to the quayside. Most barques and galleys never came within sight of the walls of Antwerp. They sailed in fleets—the Indies fleet, the English fleet, the Venice fleet, and so forth—and anchored off the mouth of the estuary, not far from Flushing. Little ships would then sail out to them from Antwerp to unload the cargoes and bring them ashore. This procedure sorted out the various goods and they could be consigned to specialized quays and warehouses without extra handling. Usually, a lighter went around the fleet from one ship to another, picking up goods of the same type, and making it possible for the ships to put to sea again with a minimum of delay.

A port organization on these lines provides a ready explanation for the paralysis that later beset the activities of Antwerp, when Flushing and the main estuary became Dutch. The good fortune of the people of Antwerp was not the result of their commercial skill, but of their ready compliance with the requirements of the merchant community. The conditions under which a foreign merchant could work and set up his establishment in Antwerp were extremely favorable, and he was made to feel quite at home. The commerce of the port was not merely Antwerp's trade, for goods that arrived there were bought up by middlemen for re-export to other countries. Indeed, goods often changed hands without any handling. It often happened, for example, that a consignment of bales of pepper from the West Indies unloaded at Antwerp would be sold to German merchants in the morning, to Italians at noon, to the English in the evening, and so forth.

Antwerp did not grow because of its power to satisfy any particular local need; the enormous traffic it handled could have been dealt with equally well anywhere else. All that was necessary was a suitably equipped port, and if all the merchants, bankers, brokers, and commercial agents had been shifted elsewhere *en bloc*, the result could easily have followed. Indeed, this is what happened as a result of the religious wars. It is probable that even if the Dutch had not closed the Schelde, Antwerp traffic would have fallen off in the same way.

One of the most striking things about the great merchants and speculators, who were the governing spirits of Antwerp, was their extreme youth. Antwerp was a world of intensely vital young people who had a way of disappearing if they had not become millionaires by the time they were twenty-five. There were many in charge of very big businesses at twenty. One Portuguese firm appointed its factotum, or general manager, before he was eighteen. At the age of nineteen, the

Antwerp trader Jan van Daele made his will before setting out for Lisbon where he was to handle a number of important deals.

With all these young people around there was of course a brisk and bustling atmosphere. They frequently met at the exchange and it soon became a dangerous place where fights often broke out and people were not infrequently killed. There was indeed a regulation that no person might draw his knife or poignard during an exchange session, on pain of a fine of a hundred florins. In spite of this there were several deaths each year. In 1551, there was the case of the merchant Alféro, who was murdered by Josépho de Ferrare. In the same year another merchant, Déodati, was killed as the result of an affair concerning women. In 1562, the Spanish merchant Pedro Dassario attacked five of his compatriots with a pistol; another merchant, named Ramirio, assaulted an Italian and was himself set upon at night by unknown persons.

These were boom times for hired assassins. Life in Antwerp was singularly free, and a gangster organization soon grew up that would have done credit to Chicago in its palmiest period. The gangsters, of course, had their own world, with the usual pimps and prostitutes among its hangers-on. There were paid killers who would liquidate enemies at your command, and prostitution and brothel keeping became scandalously widespread. In town, residents of a number of special districts were barred from all public office. Adventurers, professional gamblers, and "vice kings" converged on Antwerp from everywhere. Of special fame were the charms of the district known as St. Andrew's, with its taverns frequented by the free friars and ladies of the town.

When Charles V made his "Joyous Entry" into Antwerp in 1520, it is said that women of local high society walked unclad in the procession; and we have an account written by a bishop that the daughter of the Emperor's representative, "a blonde marvel with forty lovers," had had portraits painted of all her suitors by the great artists of the period.

Merchants from southern Europe, born gamblers, were quickly at work in property speculation. They had a monopoly on the sale and resale of buildings, controlled the rents and pushed them sky-high by creating a housing crisis. They worked with notaries to organize life insurance for travelers, and even went so far as to produce false certificates to insure people on their death beds.

Betting was another form of speculation much in vogue. The most popular bets were those on the sex of unborn children. One type of fraud was the payment of money to local women to persuade them to conceal the fact of their confinement until bets had been placed on the child's sex. Public opinion was against fraud of this type, not because betting on a certainty was a form of theft, but because a number of children died without the sacrament of baptism.

Another form of speculation was the sale of patents and secret processes. This led to the setting up of a market in which a thousand-and-one devices were the subject of as many transactions. Among them was a fuel economy device for baking bread; a method of securing quick judgment in lawsuits; even a system of ingenious contrivances for saving the state finances. The purchasers of such schemes were in many cases lured, less by the hope of immediate profit than by the prospect that the judicious publication of their scheme would lead to substantial official recompense or even to patents of nobility.

One of the oldest and most ingenious of the speculators was Gilbert van Schoonbeke, an Antwerp man married to the sister of the rich merchant-financier Dozzi—for the intermarriage of the great merchant families was one of the features of the period. Van Schoonbeke was the inventor of the vertical and horizontal concentration of industry, not for industrial reasons, but because it introduced an element of scientific certainty into property speculation.

One of Van Schoonbeke's achievements was a scheme for building at much lower prices than his competitors. This was a matter of organization that began with the acquisition of peat bogs in northern Brabant where marshy land cost practically nothing. The earth he excavated was sent to the brick-works he had built on the Schelde, and to these also went the other indispensable material—chalk made in the furnaces he had bought in the Meuse valley.

Another of his masterstrokes was to build twenty-four Antwerp breweries and supply them with cut-rate water for brewing. The water came from his famous pump-house and none of the local breweries could compete with it. His competitors' jealousy forced him to flee to Brussels, but he had nonetheless made a fat fortune at an age when many of his compatriots had barely finished their schooling.

About the same time, the expansion of new industries such as lace resulted in a servant crisis throughout the Low Countries. Adroit middlemen, masters of pretty phrases, came knocking at the doors of burghers' houses to strike up a conversation with the servingmaid, offering her high wages to quit domestic work and become a lace-maker. Of course, the middleman secured his commission.

The Antwerp exchange had become the world's financial center and was the prototype of Amsterdam and London. It was in this period of Antwerp's history that sovereign princes came seeking funds to go to war.

An Antwerp financier, Paul van Daele, published a regular list of exchange rates and the buying rates for Italian, French, English, and German commercial bills. Another financier, Jean Impyn, sanctioned and dealt in fictitious exchange operations through the futures market. Rates of interest in the silver market were often as high as sixteen or twenty per cent and money profits were therefore considerable.

Charles V himself had no hesitation in dining at the table of Jan Daens, a financier and simple burgher who had on several occasions provided him with money. On this occasion, he treated the Emperor to a sumptuous repast, then filled the great fireplace of the dining hall with precious woods he set on fire and into which he threw great armfuls of the Emperor's promissory notes. As he watched this vast fortune going up in smoke, he was able to declare that the visit of his imperial guest was payment enough to compensate him for his loss.

Antwerp's initiative was such that it could not be confined within the existing limits of trading with newly discovered America. The merchants of Antwerp were determined to be in the vanguard, and participated directly in financing the explorations, since they knew that their trade would benefit from it. It was from Antwerp that the Fugger and Affaitaidi interests financed the expedition of the Portuguese explorer, Ferdinand Magellan, in 1519. Spanish *conquistadores* and Portuguese discoverers often had Belgian mariners aboard their vessels; and the opinion was widespread that America and the West Indies were better known in Antwerp than they were in Lisbon or Madrid.

Antwerp was the intermediary through which German manufacturers secured the gold and colonial produce that enabled them to corner five-sixths of the Spanish trade and nine-tenths of the trade with America and the West Indies.

It was in Antwerp that tales of exploration were published that drew Europe's attention to the new lands then being discovered. Amerigo Vespucci's book, telling of the discovery of America and giving it his name, was published in Antwerp. Here too lived the great geographers. Ortelius, who printed the first world atlas, was financed by another Antwerp man, a certain Gillis Hooftman. In the field of natural science, a physician, Dodoens of Mechlin, became famous as a botanist. He compiled a dictionary of all Low Countries' plants, and traveled all over Europe to draw up synoptic tables of vegetable species known at this time, classifying them according to their use and physiological form. He settled at Antwerp to supervise the publication of his great *Cruyde Boeck (History of Plants)*, but it was not long before he was attracted to Holland, where he ended his days at the University of Leiden.

If we were to be transported back to sixteenth-century Antwerp we would be impressed by its resemblance to Amsterdam. The metropolis of those days was a checkerboard of closely knit canals and internal waterways with the same quasi-Venetian charm found nowadays in the great Dutch cities. In 1562, there were no less than sixty-two bridges over canals that bore picturesque names indicating the chief merchandise carried on them, among them the Butter Canal, the Cheese Canal, and the Sugar Canal. One of them, known as the Meir, was partly paved over as early as 1541 and was the forerunner of the great central street of Antwerp that bears the same name today. Nowadays the waterways have been filled in, but the names of streets where they once flowed bear names ending in *rui*, "canal," or *vliet*, "brook."

At the beginning of the sixteenth century, when Antwerp's rapid development spread quickly to the suburbs and led to the construction of magnificent public buildings, a law was passed in 1506 prohibiting the throwing of refuse into the canals; and a regulation dating from 1543 saw to it that pigs were no longer allowed to wander in the streets.

The city gates were demolished because they were too narrow for the big carts, loaded with merchandise, that sought to use them. A number of laws were framed to eliminate wooden houses because of the risk of fire; in 1541, and again in 1546, enactments prohibited the repair of such buildings and obliged the owners to rebuild them of brick. About the same time, too, thatched roofs were banned, lest a single spark should create a large fire.

A new town, built of stone and red brick, was rapidly growing up around the cathedral, the market place, and in the new open sectors that had been carefully planned so that traffic might move easily. The Collegiate Church of Our Lady was completed, and the exchange was given a new building near the Meir. The whole town was transformed as mansions and palaces sprang up to serve as residences, offices, and warehouses for foreign merchants.

In this city of many festivals, where money was quickly earned and wealth and luxury were ever increasing, painting and the other arts were soon to become an industry. The buildings and decoration of the many public buildings brought to the town a host of painters, sculptors, and decorators from all over the country.

The labor association of the art fraternity was the Antwerp Guild of St. Luke, and to its roll of membership, between 1491 and 1520, were added the names of no less than 358 new apprentices, of whom 150 were painters, 38 sculptors, and 5 engravers. Their numbers increased and multiplied and in 1549, for the festival of Philip II's ceremonial visit, the city authorities hired 233 painters and 114 sculptors for road decoration work. Even Louis XIV could not have paid out so much money, and it is apparent that the conditions of an artist's life had been altogether transformed. Commissions from the towns and rich burghers were so numerous that the artists were fully independent.

Painting became a mass-production industry, and such was the prestige of Antwerp that paintings and altarpieces were exported in great quantities.

Italy was a large-scale buyer of this merchandise, for the beauty of Flemish landscapes and the charm of the coloring was much admired. In 1535, one consignment numbered no less than 300 pictures, among which was a job lot of 120 bought in a single transaction by the Duke of Mantua. Between 1502 and 1564, the Guild of St. Luke produced 148 masters who gained a European reputation.

Just as Antwerp had its commercial exchange, it also had a permanent picture market, known as the *schilderspand*, in which there was always a great deal going on. Princes, noblemen, and rich burghers came here from all over Europe to buy works to decorate their mansions and palaces. "Men of business and men of art," writes one historian, "were swept along by the same feverish spirit." The fact was that the same forces were at work stimulating the activities of both classes.

Almost every great financier was a Maecenas whose tastes differed from the next man's, thus the variety, independence, and originality characteristic of Antwerp painting. This diversity led to the birth of new schools and skills, and it survived in the seventeenth century workshops of Rubens and Van Dyck. In the sixteenth century, it nurtured such artists as Bruegel the Elder, Quentin Massys, Jan Gossart, Gerard David, Bernard van Orley, Pieter Pourbus, Frans Floris, Joachim Patinir, Joos van Cleef, and many others.

It is not exact to say that Bruges was killed by the competition of Antwerp. In point of fact, the trade of Bruges was well maintained through the sixteenth century. Antwerp's growth did not come from traffic attracted from other ports but from the creation of new traffic that brought an enormous increase in its business. Even at its peak, Antwerp handled only sixty to sixty-five per cent of the general trade of the Low Countries, and Bruges was the leader in handling the remainder.

In 1553, Antwerp exported 600,000 pounds of cloth to Spain, but Bruges still exported 207,000 pounds, a substantial turnover. It was handling, in this period, at least a third as much merchandise as was being exported through Antwerp. In one year, for example, Bruges sold 21,523 pieces of textile material, compared with Antwerp's 58,004.

The Hanseatic merchants remained faithful to Bruges until the eve of the revolution against Spain, for they considered its geographical location far better for the handling of textile goods. Bruges thus kept the Baltic traffic; and the Antwerp monopoly, as befitted a city specializing in new types of goods, extended mainly to produce from the West Indies and southern countries.

Among the industries that found a home in Antwerp, special mention must be made of printing. The cosmopolitan and humanistic world of Antwerp made it a center for the export of books to many countries, despite censorship. To provide for the supervision and identification of every work, printers were obliged by the authorities to date and register all their publications, a practice continued until our own time.

Of the 2,220 works printed in the Low Countries in this period, only 223 came from the towns of Louvain, Bruges, Ghent, and Brussels. Holland, much more advanced, published 796, but more than half the total—1,202—came from Antwerp. Antwerp printing was at its peak about the middle of the century. Book production had assumed an international character, and printers came to Antwerp from all over Europe, even from Germany, Holland, and France.

The most important of them was Christophe Plantin, a native of Touraine, who was born at St. Avertin in 1520. He was fired with the idea that printing might become a great industry with almost unlimited markets, provided it concentrated on works in popular demand, and distributed them in all countries with appropriate fanfare. He brought to printing the same bold spirit and initiative his contemporaries brought to other branches of trade.

The fortunes of an adventurous life led him first to Caen and later to Paris, where he was apprenticed to the great printer Robert Macé. In 1550, at the age of thirty, he set himself up in the Low Countries. He was married to the daughter of his partner Moretus, and among his works was a famous sonnet in which he condensed the experiences of his life along with his century's aspirations to wisdom.

Plantin was both a great printer and a great humanist. In the former capacity, he dazzled all Europe with typographical masterpieces such as the Polyglot Bible; as a humanist, he filled his house with men of learned and inquiring minds and became their propagandist.

He was also a shrewd businessman. When he started work in Antwerp there were already fifty-six printers, the number was growing, and competition was very keen. Luckily, the volume of business was growing even faster, and young Plantin had barely arrived before he was possessed by the restless, go-getting spirit that prevailed. To compete with his rivals, he introduced many new procedures. He hired traveling salesmen to place his books all over Europe; and he went in person to the great fairs held in foreign countries to meet authors whose works he might later print. In short, he made publishing an international business, bringing out his books in every language and engaging in trade with book-sellers, not only in the Low Countries and in France, but also in Spain, Italy, Portugal, England, Scotland, Ireland, Germany, and Poland.

He acquired the printing monopoly for Spain, and later the exclusive printing contract for the missals ordered by the Council of Trent. He printed these in a run of 52,000 copies. This was a figure unheard of at the time and represented a transaction worth 8 million gold francs.

Although Plantin put publishing on the popular level, he continued to cultivate humanists, artists, and men of learning and always sought new talent. It was partly in his bookshop that the young Rubens later secured his education. His house in Antwerp is still open to visitors; indeed, it is one of the finest, and most luxurious of the period—an embodiment of the Renaissance.

In Antwerp the last great contest of rhetoricians was held on the eve of the revolution in 1561; the sensation it caused led to the permanent interdiction of such events. The hosts for the contest were the Antwerp Wallflowers, a famous club. As usual, each of the pieces submitted had to deal with the same theme, and the government had imposed the choice of a subject which appeared innocent enough: "What is it that most urges mankind toward the arts and sciences?" Poets of the different chambers of rhetoric dealt with the subject as France would have dealt with it two centuries later, painting a picture of humanity snatched by science from the prejudices of the past, awakening to its new freedom, and discovering the secrets of nature. Every one of the works submitted was written in the same vein, representing freedom of thought as a condition of all culture.

As the chambers of rhetoric filed into Antwerp, the splendor of the procession surpassed all that had yet been seen. One of the Brussels chambers was represented by 340 men on horseback dressed in velvet and crimson silk, wearing red headdresses shaped like helmets of old, and cloaks embroidered with silver in the Polish manner. Doublets, hose and plumes were white, and their belts were of embroidered silver. From Mechlin came a contingent in rose-red cloaks, with red hats, gold doublets, yellow plumes, and gold ribbons. In all there were 23 great triumphal chariots, 97 smaller vehicles and 1,893 men on horseback.

To welcome the rhetoricians, every house in town was decorated with garlands of foliage, and all the shops, including the exchange and the public buildings, were closed for three weeks. Pomp and magnificence marked the processions, banquets and music, sumptuous parades, and the dancing of male and female buffoons. As was the custom, the contest ended with a "Festival of Folly." There the Prince of Fools, with Mother Fool Alvine at his side, hawked the virtue of a precious ointment that could cure the folly of all his companions "touched by the windmills' sail, feeling the stone of folly, or with the bells in their brain a-jingling."

"Yes," cried Alvine, "but first let's think of our relatives, our friends, and our neighbors."

"Our friends, where are they?"

"Down there, all around, going about in pairs."

"Ahoy there! Get the box of ointment ready. Now then, friends, is the wind good? Is the mill turning as you wish? Good, then let's call up all the dolts we can find." And come they did. Peter the Dolt, Thomas of Dolt Valley, Doltstown Henry, and the rest; and they asked to be cured then and there.

"So be it," said the Prince. "I'm all set to help you, but first draw yourselves up in joyful battle formation."

Then each of the dolts brought his wife forward and began describing her. The gossips had as many faults as their husbands, and their foolishness was reported with tender admiration, every absurdity and idiocy being recounted by the men as a rare and precious quality.

In the end, Doltstown Henry cried out with a laugh:

"Gosh, if we're going to anoint all the fools, we'll need a pot of ointment as big as a Hamburg cask!"

"Well, after all," said the Prince of Dolts, "there's masses of it in every town." Then everyone broke out into jests and punning and nonsense. Waving their caps and bells, the whole company began to dance.

Every fool present, spectators included, was invited to rally round the pole of folly; and the couplets of the song of fools were sung and resung, in the style of the finale of a modern revue.

Thus, amid shouts of laughter, ended the last of the great contests of the chambers of rhetoric. In demonstrating the spirit of freedom, it had given an impetus to public opinion which was to contribute to making the revolution inevitable. Among the spectators there were many already marked for death. Yet none of them could know that the hour of catastrophe and massacre was at hand; that in the days to come, folly would be raising its bloody mast over the Spanish Lowlands.

VII

THE REVOLUTION AGAINST SPAIN

In 1555, Philip II of Spain succeeded the Emperor Charles V as sovereign of the Low Countries.

The new sovereign was one of history's most enigmatic figures; unswervingly Catholic, he let it be known he would rather die than become a king of heretics. There can be no doubting his sincerity.

"If my son were as perverse as you," he cried to a Protestant about to be executed, "I myself would carry the faggots for his burning."

In the Escorial he had his bed placed so that when he awoke he could see the Holy Sacrament safe on the high altar. His palace was dedicated to St. Lawrence, and, in honor of that saint, it was built in the shape of a gridiron. It also commemorated the fact that on St. Lawrence's day the battle of St. Quentin had been won, largely due to the Count of Egmont's heavily armed troops.

For King Philip, the grandeur of Spain and his dynasty were bound up with the Catholic faith. This belief was his justification for the many sacrifices he demanded of his people. Nor did his fervor stop at the frontiers of his own country, for he believed himself entrusted with a universal mission that was the reason for his power, and which demanded that he extend it to the whole of Europe.

In Spain it was easy enough to burn heretics or send them into exile, and this did little damage to the country. In the Low Countries, however, people of heretical disposition and belief were necessary to the country's life. There were so many of them that they could not be exterminated, as the Prince of Orange remarked, "without great spilling of blood and utter ruin." Protestantism, however, was now turning more and more towards Calvinism, taking on itself the character of an organized, dynamic, and revolutionary mysticism.

From 1560 on, these two fanatic and totalitarian ideologies came face-to-face amid the tumult and civil strife in which the blood of all Europe was to be shed. In the Spanish Lowlands, the spirit of freedom and individualism combined with a rising tide of religious passion to cause a terrible tragedy.

The leaders of the Lowlands revolution opposing Philip were the Prince of Orange, known as William the Silent, and Lamoral, Count of Egmont. Against them were the King's chief confidant, Cardinal Granvelle, and Margaret of Parma.

William the Silent had been a favorite of Charles V, and was one of the highest dignitaries of the Low Countries. He was a member of the Council of State and Governor of Holland and Zeeland. His powerful position stemmed from the many estates he owned all over Europe, from the town of Orange, near Avignon, to the principality of Nassau in Germany. His stature made him independent of the King of Spain.

He spoke eight languages with natural eloquence and persuasive power, and possessed extraordinary personal charm. He was always friendly in greeting persons of lesser degree, talking with them naturally, and he never lost his temper, even with his servants. His outgoing personality was all the more striking for the fact that he was the richest man in the Low Countries.

His iron constitution withstood every excess. He ate and drank with his visitors, giving them fabulous banquets, and he even thoughtfully provided luxurious beds for guests who drank themselves into stupors. His conversation was voluble and his nickname, William the Silent, would be difficult to understand were it not that the French word, *taiseux*, can also mean "hesitant." He was given this name because it took him a long time to decide on a course of action. Those who approached him never knew what he would ultimately decide. On the other hand, although hesitant when plans were maturing, he was tenacious and stubborn once his mind was made up.

He was like many modern politicians, not only because of his affability, but also because of his ability to adapt himself to the character and tastes of those to whom he spoke, his air of plain dealing, and his desire to please. He was a prince on an international scale, related to all the great houses of Europe, and the influence he exercised sprang from a character that was always well-balanced and reflective.

The Count of Egmont was a very different type. He was Governor of Flanders and the Artois, a great landowner and immensely rich, and he thought of himself as the real leader of the Low Countries. He was filled with a pride and vanity that stemmed from his victories in the field and from his marriage with Sabina, daughter of the sovereign House of Bavaria. He was impulsive and passionate, often acted very thoughtlessly, and was famous for his fits of anger. In this respect he was like the Count of Hoorn, another impulsive type, who went into a fury whenever anybody spoke the name of Philip II in his presence. Hoorn had been loaded with important duties that had ruined him by obliging him to overspend. These stately noblemen had many imitators, and became the leaders of the Belgian nobility. They were surrounded by poorer nobility and gentry, officers, and poor relations who looked to them for support and the opportunity to win honor and fortune.

The Prince of Orange and the Count of Egmont were, for practical purposes, masters of the state and administrators of the country. Since their most important influence was exercised over the provincial Estates, they molded public opinion. No tax could be voted without their consent, and no measure of importance was taken without consulting them. In their capacity as governors, they controlled the four richest provinces—Holland, Zeeland, Flanders, and the Artois—containing two-thirds of the population of the Spanish Lowlands. The army was under their orders, except for the few Spanish garrisons out in the country; and the gentry, comprising the main part of the national troops, were entirely loyal to them. Their membership in the Council of State simply rounded off this situation.

The nobles were masters of the Council of State, and when Philip II found they were obstructing or opposing his decisions, he was forced to employ guile against them. This took the form of orders to Governor Margaret of Parma to follow the advice of a secret and specially appointed *consulta*, composed of three members with whom the king would be in direct communication. The members were Viglius, Berlaymont, and Cardinal Granvelle.

Granvelle, a man of universal culture, came from the Franche-Comté, and was an adroit courtier and diplomat. He was the son of a minister of Charles V, and had been accustomed from his youth to handling public affairs. He had been made a bishop at the age of twenty-one and enjoyed the complete confidence of the King (to whom he wrote almost every day) and of the Governor. He was a man whose judgment and perspicacity seldom failed.

It was not long before Granvelle had the government under his complete control. The administrator Viglius and the financier Berlaymont were civil servants of the first order, enabling Granvelle to come to the Council of State with plans for action fully prepared and documented. For the most part, there was nothing to do but approve them. This irritated the noblemen, who realized that control of events was slipping from their hands. Granvelle soon became the target for their attacks, particularly since knowledge of the King's support had led him to adopt a haughty attitude, disdaining to say anything in his own defense. He was something of a lady-killer, and his rowdy love-making was sufficiently unbishoplike to become a scandal, enabling his opponents to blacken his reputation.

Even in Naples at the age of sixty, after he had fallen out of favor, he continued to pursue fashionable beauties. Moreover, he continued to act in the interest of the Belgians in Madrid by seeking to influence Philip II toward moderation. He was essentially a sceptic, cultivated and forbearing, who hated blood and violence and preferred to live his life among works of art and precious manuscripts. He was lucid in his appreciation of the situation and he and William the Silent were the only people to foresee exactly what was going to happen in the Spanish Lowlands. Had he been left to advise Margaret of Parma, it is possible that the impending tragedy might have been avoided.

Margaret of Parma, whom Philip II had appointed Governor of the Spanish Lowlands, was herself partly of Flemish origin. She was the daughter of one of the beauties of Oudenaarde who, during the siege of Tournai, had been singled out by Charles V for the distinction of becoming his mistress. Bastard daughter of Charles, the legal daughter of a simple tapestry worker in the neighborhood, Margaret was brought up as a princess.

Margaret grew up in Brussels, first under the supervision of Margaret of Austria and later of Mary of Hungary. Her life was to be both romantic and unhappy. Her first husband was an Italian, Alessandro de Medici, a cruel and corrupt man who was murdered soon after their marriage. It had been his practice to humiliate his young wife— who had been only fifteen when she married him—in the course of his dissolute festivals. When Margaret became a widow, Charles V found a new suitor for her hand in Ottavio Farnese, Duke of Parma.

This time her husband was a child of fourteen. It was a disproportionate marriage that annoyed her so profoundly that for seven years she refused to live with him. It was only when he had reached man's estate that Margaret's confessor was able to persuade her to fulfill her wifely duties. She still detested him however, and her only compensation was that she had a genius for a son; he later became famous as Alessandro Farnese.

Margaret even lost the habit of writing in French; within her were united the refined culture of the Mediterraneans and the robust temperament of the Flemings. She liked her portrait to be painted while on horseback, in her riding habit, or with a horse's bit in her hand.

Because Parma was occupied by Spanish troops, Margaret obeyed Philip's instructions in the hope of recovering control of the duchy. Unfortunately, when she reached Brussels, the country had become ungovernable, partly because of the opposition and partly because of Spain's serious financial problems. The treasury was empty, and Philip II had to humble himself before the provincial Estates in order to gain approval of taxes that would stave off Spain's bankruptcy.

All treasury receipts were mortgaged for several years in advance. Only Antwerp's credit had enabled the Spanish empire to secure the loans and advances that financed her wars. Now these were exhausted. The greater his financial problems, the more Philip found himself at the mercy of the merchants of the Low Countries.

Between 1554 and 1556, the debt had increased fourfold, from 285,000 to 1.4 million livres. Current expenses, including repayments, were about 4 million florins and he owed his troops another 3.5 million florins in back pay. Philip's back was to the wall.

With huge sums of money from Spain, he mounted a force of 56,000 Spaniards, Belgians, and Germans. With them he besieged St. Quentin, and engaged a relief force sent by Henry II under the command of the Constable of Montmorency. The French army was outflanked, routed, and cut to bits by the Count of Egmont's cavalry. St. Quentin fell to Spain, along with all the strongpoints from that citadel to Paris. Philip was about to invade Paris, when he ran out of money, and mutiny and disaster were prevented only by calling the Estates General into session.

The Estates General met first in Valenciennes and later in Brussels. It was very much influenced by the provincial Estates of Brabant, which had led the agitation for some time, and it declared that war expenditure was not its concern. In reply, Philip pointed out that he had brought 12 million florins from his other domains. He argued in vain, for the Estates General dismissed the proposal for a 1- and 2-percent tax that could have set financial matters to rights. The Estates further demanded that the Spanish soldiery be withdrawn, a natural enough demand in view of the irritation caused by their arrogant attitude, not to mention the inevitable pillaging and brawls that went with any military occupation.

There was mutual contempt between the Spaniards and the Belgians. Their differences in temperament were even more pronounced because the Spanish troops were made up of impoverished noblemen whom the officers addressed as "my lords and soldiers." They were, in general, country gentlemen who were ruined when the money lost its value, and who had no recourse but to join the army. There they became soldiers of fanatical courage, proud and difficult to handle.

The King of Spain was absolutely dependent on them, and they formed a state within the state. They brought along with them their wives and children, which explains why, despite their long presence in the Span-

ish Lowlands, there was never any mixture of blood between them
and the Belgians.

They took affront easily, constantly drawing their swords, and their
ostentatious piety scandalized the Belgians.

Philip nevertheless hesitated to recall them. The deficit put him
at the mercy of the Estates General, which took care not to vote funds
to cover it, and he decided to sign the Treaty of Cateau-Cambrésis, in
1559. Under this treaty, all pretext for maintaining Spanish troops in
the Low Countries disappeared. It was impossible to reduce expenditure by a stroke of the pen, and the deficit had reached about 600
million florins annually, with the result that the government became
increasingly subject to the will of the Estates General.

The only hope seemed to lie in the reorganization of bishoprics. The
Spanish government believed that this step would put the financial
situation to rights and re-establish its influence in the Lowlands.

The religious organization of the country, up to this time, had been
that of ancient Gaul. It was more than a thousand years old, and the
Bishops of Thérouanne and Tournai, who were French, exercised juris-
diction over the Flemish clergy, while the Bishops of Liège had ecclesiastical authority as far afield as Antwerp. After long negotiations, the
Pope agreed, in 1559, to divide the Low Countries into eighteen bishoprics, of approximately equal populations. Each diocese was to contain
about 160,000 inhabitants. The new bishops would be appointed directly
by the king from the acknowledged doctors of philosophy and theologians without regard for rank or birth. Since it was necessary to provide the bishoprics with resources, Rome decided to assign them the
property of a number of monasteries.

These measures had long been demanded, but nevertheless they led
to an outbreak of fury, for they involved a threat to a number of interests. The nobles had been accustomed to appoint their sons bishops,
and they complained that the rich bishoprics would now slip out of
their hands to the commoners. The reforms also drew protests from the
monks and clergy who would be deprived of their property.

The people saw that the new bishops would acquire, along with
monastic property, the legal right to appoint clerical delegates to the
provincial Estates and that this would lead to a royalist party. The general wrath focused on Granvelle, who had just been made a cardinal
and was thought to have been responsible for the reform. He maintained
his aloof attitude, despite the many pamphlets in which he was described
as "the red devil," "the Spanish hog," and "the papist scum." The
nobility ran their own campaign against him. It was admirably organized, and the cardinal was represented at the theater surrounded by devils.
The greater nobles kept open house, organizing banquets to which all

and sundry were invited. At their tables could be found local notables, officers of the heavy infantry, lesser nobility, country gentlemen, and the deputies from the Estates. Their criticism and complaints found their way throughout the entire country.

The continuing presence of Spanish troops furnished an excellent pretext for trouble, and, since it could not be justified, in January, 1561, Philip II decided that the troops should be recalled. As a result he found himself disarmed. The only military force left was the heavy infantry that obeyed only the more important noblemen and provincial governors. The Estates of Brabant took a revolutionary attitude and sent delegates to lodge a direct protest with the Pope. The Prince of Orange had ensured himself of European support by marrying, against the wishes of Philip II, the Lutheran princess Anne of Saxony, and he used his marriage to strengthen his links with the German Protestants.

Violent Calvinist agitators, who could no longer remain in France, found their way to the Low Countries. Cardinal Granvelle had been publicly threatened with death, and no longer dared show himself on the streets of Brussels. To ridicule him, the nobility founded a league that wore black livery decorated with red jesters' heads, and they organized masquerades in which devils and vagabonds chased a cardinal in purple robes. (Interestingly enough, the *gueux* later adopted similar dress.) When public sentiment reached its peak, a demonstration was organized.

A triumvirate, formed of the Prince of Orange and the Counts of Egmont and Hoorn, secured approval of the provincial governors and the Knights of the Golden Fleece. They then refused to sit in the Council of State so long as the Cardinal was there, and demanded his immediate recall. Margaret of Parma, overwhelmed by this move, had no choice but to give in. In 1556, Philip II decided that the Cardinal should be recalled. But the nobility, now masters of the Council of State, did not stop there. As the King's troops and confidential ministers were no longer in the country, they required all civil servants to take their orders from the Council. The administration no longer knew where its obedience lay, and conditions soon bordered on anarchy. Provincial governors were acting as if they had become independent, using the public funds for electoral maneuvering by distributing it to their partisans, whom they appointed to all the public offices.

At this point, a new party appeared on the scene. Calvinism, despite the attempts to repress it, had made rapid progress, particularly in Antwerp, where foreign Protestants swarmed in, and in the south, where Calvinist immigrants were entering to escape the civil war in France.

As early as 1561, a number of large towns had fallen into their hands, including Valenciennes and Tournai, where the Calvinists walked eight abreast in processions through the streets, singing psalms. Their pastors dispatched an army of propagandists, trained in special schools at Strasbourg, Lausanne, and Geneva, who could provoke listeners to debate.

Against persecution, they used their own tactics. They met in the open country in camps guarded by their own sentries, and listened to the sermons of the "greensward preachers." The audience was masked to prevent recognition, and the whole company dispersed at the first alarm.

Sometimes Calvinist employers recruited all their workers among Protestants, in order to throw the Catholics out of work. They also closed their shops, throwing workers into the streets to riot when the Inquisitors arrived, without the governing nobles daring to act vigorously against them.

Yet the Protestants who harmed the realm most were the emigrants. In the intense commercial competition between the Low Countries and England, Queen Elizabeth I tirelessly enticed Protestant workers with offers of entire towns, such as Norwich, in which to settle. Their products competed with those of the Low Countries. For the Low Countries this was an economic disaster.

The nobility, once in control of the government, demanded that Philip II call a halt to the Inquisition. Egmont went in person to Madrid in 1565 to press the claim.

Philip, in his Bosco de Segovia, dated October 17–20, 1565, refused this request. In the meantime, the industrial crisis was made worse by a bad harvest and a consequent shortage of grain—conditions similar to those preceding the French Revolution. The price of wheat doubled, and there were outbreaks of rioting. Armed bands made red signs on the doors of merchants to mark them for slaughter.

In this country where the government sorely needed support from the deputies to meet the growing budget deficit, and where all the police forces were in the hands of its opponents, the Protestants easily won over the moderate factions. Then they carefully prepared the next step.

A small group of Calvinist nobles met at Spa, in August, 1565. Led by Jean de Marnix and Louis de Nassau, brother of William the Silent, they drafted a manifesto that seemed moderate, since the signatories simply swore to defend the privileges of the country, cast out the Inquisition, and remain faithful to the king.

During festivals, meetings, and discussions, 2,000 signatures were eventually obtained. These included a large number of ecclesiastical dignitaries and the great majority of the officers of the heavy infantry. The declaration became known as the "Compromise of the Nobles."

The real aim of the organizers was to provoke a revolt, but the Prince of Orange advised them to begin by presenting a formal petition to the Governor. When the manifesto was presented, on April 5, 1566, it was accompanied by a cavalcade of several hundred officers and had the air of a pronunciamento rather than a petition. It had been approved by all of the nobility, as well as by the Council of State and the Privy Council, so that Margaret of Parma was completely isolated. The only thing she could do was to agree to forward the petition to the king, in the meantime suspending application of the repressive decrees known as "placards."

On the evening of April 8, 1566, Brederode, who had placed the "Compromise of the Nobles" in Margaret's hands, attended a banquet with the rest of the party organized by one of their number, Floris van Pallant, in Culembourg Palace. During dinner he distributed a beggar's bowl and pouch to each guest, no doubt with the idea of suggesting that Philip's policy was leading the Low Countries to ruin. "Vive les Gueux!" ("Long live the beggars!"), cried one of the guests, and the slogan was loudly acclaimed on all sides.

The bowl and pouch were adopted as symbols by all the nobility. Men of high standing dressed themselves in beggar's grey, and for easier recognition sported a new style of beard with huge moustaches, in the Turkish manner of the period. Even the burghers pinned on their coats a medal showing two clasped hands, a portrait of Philip, and a beggar's pouch beneath the motto "Faithful to the king, until we're left holding the bag."

It appears that it was Berlaymont who first bestowed on them the name of *gueux*. Supposedly he said to the Governor, when they were handing her the "Compromise": "Goodness, Madam, you need have no fear of such folk. They are but beggars!" For whatever reason, the insurgents were called *gueux*. The name applied to the nobility, the army, and the more eminent burghers, whose aim was to establish an aristocratic republic in the Low Countries, of which they would be the leaders. In their view, victory was assured.

The "Compromise of the Nobles" won momentary triumph, but the Calvinists got out of hand. Emigrants were returning in great numbers from England and Germany, thirsting for vengeance, thinking themselves masters of the country, and alarming the people with the measures they proposed.

Protestants now worshipped in public everywhere, without the authorities daring to take steps against them. Pastors and ministers were even surer of themselves because the Catholics were already compromised in their relationship with the King. They had to obey the hierarchy and rely upon them, lest they be left defenseless before the anger of the King. The Protestants were sure of support from the banking and commercial community of Antwerp. They were the only people who could command sufficient funds to raise enough troops, in Germany, to make a repression impossible. The Catholics had no choice but to come to an agreement with Louis de Nassau. Simultaneously, the beginnings of anarchy caused unemployment, and a revolutionary army was formed. Then the roof fell in.

About the middle of August, 1566, bands of workers came from the industrial region round Armentières. They had long been accustomed to hearing denunciations of the "worship of Satan," and of graven images, and, without any apparent reason, they wrecked the churches and smashed all the statues.

There seemed no cause for this movement, but it grew with startling rapidity. Fathers led their children, carrying little hammers, into churches to find an "idol" to destroy. Magistrates accompanied the rioters and supervised their work without interference. As in France in 1789, the passive attitude of the authorities gave the rioters their strength. Bands of iconoclasts drank the altar wine and put on chasubles to hold masquerades in churches. They did not plunder the churches, however, and the remains of the gold and silver ornaments were scrupulously collected and handed over to the magistrates, who took them into their keeping. Within two weeks, works of art that had taken centuries to collect had been wholly destroyed. The movement spread from town to town like a contagious insanity.

The nobility and the provincial governors allowed all this to continue, trying to prevent the movement from degenerating into a popular revolt. They refused to bring out their troops, and called on the Governor to make enough concessions to put an end to the trouble. She "granted" Protestants freedom of worship, salving her Catholic conscience by declaring that she had been compelled to do so.

This, however, was no way to calm a totalitarian movement. The Calvinists, far from being satisfied by the concessions, went on to proclaim that the ringing of Catholic church bells was a hostile act. The Catholics, having noted how few rioters there had really been, forced Margaret to revoke her concessions, for fanaticism was rising like a tide. Finally, Margaret, counseled by Mansfeld, the Governor of Luxemburg, and a leading Catholic, required the nobles to take a new oath of fealty to the King in terms that would force the Calvinists and the revolutionaries into the open. The Count of Egmont agreed to take the oath; the Prince of Orange and Brederode declined.

The revolutionaries were divided, and Margaret, setting all protests aside, brought in troops from Germany to restore order. She was supported by the Catholics, and banished all foreign pastors. The Protestant army, raised by Louis de Nassau, was the more easily defeated because

William the Silent himself considered the battle lost and refused his support.

When Philip II ordered the Duke of Alba to Brussels with an army recently raised in Italy, order had been restored throughout the country. Long columns of Protestant fugitives, fleeing the punishment they knew was coming, blocked the road to England and Germany. The Prince of Orange himself decided to follow. He tried to take Egmont with him, but the Belgian nobleman refused to abandon his estate and fortune. He had approved the excesses of the iconoclasts, but he nevertheless counted on the clemency of Philip II.

As he bade farewell to William the Silent, it is said that he remarked, "Goodbye, Prince Landless," and that the Prince of Orange replied, "Goodbye, Count Headless."

Orange departed. He had burned his boats, abandoned all his estates in the Spanish Lowlands, and taken refuge in his own principality of Nassau, in Germany.

Egmont remained and the Duke of Alba arrived.

The Duke of Alba marched upon Brussels by short stages. Initially concentrating his troops at Milan, he came north by way of Savoy, the Franche-Comté, and Lorraine. His instructions were to embark on a campaign of implacable repression, and the troops that accompanied him were to make this possible. They were made up of veterans from many countries, their very variety reflecting the grandeur of the Spanish Empire. There were Neapolitans and the dreaded Sicilians. There were men from the Tyrol, south Germans, Castilians, Sardinians, and even horsemen from Albania.

The force was not large. It consisted of only 9,000 men, but their military training and discipline made them invincible. Their religious fanaticism stupefied the Belgians, who looked on aghast when they carried crosses in processions, confessing their sins in loud voices, and indulging in public flagellation. Their women followed them in the baggage wagons, clad in sumptuous apparel that made Brantôme compare them to princesses.

Among the brilliantly uniformed men, the key troops, with powder-horns slung from their crossbelts, carried the heavy harquebus and tripod. Protecting them were pikemen, in steel breastplates and helmets, whose job was to form unbreakable squares around them. The cavalry wore full armor. There were lancers, and pistol bearers who charged in fan-shaped formation, discharged their weapons at the enemy, and then made off to the right and left. To these formidable troops were soon added German and Walloon mercenaries whom the Duke of Alba recruited, giving him an army of 60,000 men.

His first step was to occupy the country, grouping his troops around

Brussels. Then he planned his campaign in detail. He was a fanatical Catholic, a Spanish patriot, and a mystic who hoped to impose his own idea of justice. He was convinced that his task was a holy one, and he pursued it with the somber passion of a man who sees himself as the instrument of God.

Philip had given him detailed instructions for a campaign that would serve both the ends of the state and the Catholic Church. The principal leaders of the opposition were to be exterminated, so that the Spanish Lowlands might once more play their part as a bastion of the true faith. This was especially necessary because the Low Countries were surrounded by the Protestant states of Germany, England, and northern France.

Philip knew that had the French government supported Orange and Egmont it would have been overrun by the Calvinists. The power and financial resources of Spain depended on the Low Countries, and it was absolutely necessary to impose regular taxation to cover the deficit, now more than 600,000 florins annually. This required elimination of their privileges, possible only after a reign of terror.

Margaret of Parma was terrified when she realized what was going to happen, and asked for her recall. This was the signal for the Duke of Alba, armed now with dictatorial powers, to set in motion the huge machinery of repression.

The frontiers were closed so that no one could escape, emigration was prohibited on pain of death, and mass arrests began. The whole country was caught in a gigantic network of espionage and terror. Barely a fortnight had passed after the Duke's arrival when the heaviest blow fell. On September 9, the Counts of Egmont and Hoorn, both of them having legal immunity as Knights of the Golden Fleece, were put under arrest. Suspects were being dealt summary justice by the Council of Troubles; men were condemned with no discussion or defense. The mere fact of having been suspected, or denounced, was enough to warrant the death penalty. Public executions were carried out in batches as they were during the French Revolution. On a single day, January 4, 1568, there were no fewer than eighty-four people executed. On some days as many as 500 people were arrested, and the total ran to somewhere between 10,000 and 20,000, at least as many as occurred in Paris under the Terror.

Every execution was deeply ceremonious, to make it more impressive. Cordons of troops barred the roads, and scaffolds were erected on high platforms in the public squares. There were also symbolic gestures, such as the destruction of the Culembourg Palace, where the "Compromise of the Nobles" had been drafted.

To show that there would be no mercy and that no resistance was possible, Egmont and Hoorn—whose status was such that they could only be judged by the King himself—were condemned and beheaded in the Brussels market place on June 5, 1568. Montigny and Berghes, who had been sent to Spain as ambassadors in the time of Margaret of Parma, disappeared mysteriously. It became known later that Montigny had been kept in prison for three years, and finally executed, without trial, in the dungeons of Simancas Castle.

The goods and properties of the condemned, or of those who had emigrated, were confiscated, accomplishing the Duke of Alba's mission by providing the government with an annual revenue of some 500,000 ducats.

People who perished in this way were not even insurgents, or the King's enemies. At least 100,000 who were the most compromised left the country before the Duke arrived. The great mass of victims were those who were innocent, or stupid enough to remain in the Low Countries because they trusted the King.

The Duke of Alba, however, was not alone against the whole country. He had thousands of spies among the people who supported him. On his side were the Catholic fanatics, the victims of the Protestant excesses and their families, the numerous people who had no wish to be mixed up in politics and supported governments as a matter of principle, and almost everyone in the administration. (It was not without reason that his adversaries soon lumped together in their hatred the Duke and the great majority of the clergy, the nobility, and the more prominent burghers, who were accused of having upheld the Duke because they were afraid of Calvinism.) The protectors and the accomplices of the Protestants had been the great majority of those executed, and people whose first care was for public order refused to be aroused. During the early months, most of the country, instead of being shocked, thought only of getting on with business. It was this spirit of neutrality that resulted in the failure of all attempts at insurrection.

This spawned the unfortunate adventure of the Prince of Orange. He was ill-informed of public opinion and believed that the people would revolt once he raised the standard. He succeeded in raising funds from German Protestants, French Huguenots, the ministers of Elizabeth of England, and even from some of the Antwerp bankers, including a Jew, Marco Perez, who had a business interest in financing the resistance. William raised an army of German mercenaries and invaded the Spanish Lowlands.

The Duke of Alba, who could not hold out against him because he had had to concentrate most of his troops on the French border, retreated and let William the Silent march right across the country.

This proved a master stroke; not a single town rose in the Prince's support. He found their gates closed against him and his armies, in hostile country without supplies, had to take refuge in France. His brother, Louis de Nassau, had attempted a similar maneuver in the north, but he was beaten at Jemgum and forced back into Germany, in 1568.

The Duke of Alba could now boast that he had been successful; the whole country was quiet without violence or arrests. He thought his work was finished and ordered a general amnesty. Protestants railed at the many limitations contained in the pardon, but it had the effect of reassuring those who had not been arrested or otherwise disturbed. In settling the financial problem, he re-introduced the proposals that had been presented in vain to the Estates ten years before. The budget deficit was ended by the acceptance of taxes of the fiftieth, twentieth, and tenth *denier*. This means, in modern parlance, a tax of one per cent on sales of household goods, and ten per cent on all commercial transactions.

The first two of these taxes created no difficulty, but the third was economic heresy. It worked without difficulty in Spain, which was an agricultural country where most of the merchandise was the produce of the earth and was therefore taxed once only, at the source. In an industrial and commercial country, such a tax is multiplied by the number of transactions involved, causing a rapid increase in prices. It had been tried once before, by Charles V, in 1543. On this occasion, a turnover tax of only one per cent had caused an immediate exodus of Antwerp merchants to Hamburg, and the tax had to be abolished hastily.

The tax of the tenth *denier* had scarcely been brought into force, when all economic activity in the Spanish Lowlands came to a stop. Antwerp exporters cancelled their outstanding contracts with industrialists for sales abroad. The rise in prices was such that locally produced goods could not compete in foreign markets; employers reduced their production and workers became unemployed. Merchants began to emigrate. Rents in Antwerp fell from 300 florins to 50 florins. Towns and villages became filled with beggars, and the coastal fishermen, who could no longer sell their catch, set sail for England, or joined forces with pirates preying on Spanish vessels.

The masses understood nothing of this, and believed that their economic ills resulted from a deliberate Spanish plot to ruin them. The political terror and the measures taken against the Protestants had affected only a very small minority in the country, causing little reaction. Now, however, everybody was involved, and a nearly unanimous, passive resistance was offered. In Brussels and Antwerp retailers preferred to put up their shutters rather than pay the taxes, and whole streets of shops were closed. The furniture and effects of defaulting taxpayers were put up for public sale, but the buyers went on strike. Even the sales of beer, the national drink, stopped.

This was when the resistance, and the outlaws who had gone into hiding, became popular. They were most often Protestants, and the title *gueux*, "beggars," applied only to them. In Flanders and Hainaut, they were known as the "Beggars of the Woods," and by the coast, where many of them had succeeded in seizing boats and becoming pirates, they were called the "Beggars of the Sea."

Up to this time they had lived by robbery and plunder, terrorizing the people and pillaging the coast or countryside, without greatly disturbing the government. Now, everyone's enemy was the Duke of Alba, and a great gulf yawned between him and the country. The wrath of the people was turned against the civil servants who gave him their obedience, against the deputies in the Estates who had accepted the new taxes, and, in particular, against the clergy who had held their peace, lest harm befall the Catholic religion. In the face of the terrible misery that had developed, the Protestants incited the people to rebellion with the "Song of the Tenth Denier":

> God helps those who help themselves,
> Throw off the tyrants' chains and locks,
> Oh Lowlands so depressed.
> Already round your throats the rope is knotted,
> Lift up, Oh quickly lift your pious hands.

The Duke of Alba was anxious to back out, but it was too late. He knew that if he were to yield, it would mean an end to all his hopes of settling the financial problem. He was consumed with anger at the resistance offered by the commercial community and threatened to hang everybody. He had incensed a population of 3 million people in a country surrounded by enemies whom he lacked troops to fight. He had had to concentrate his forces at strategic points, leaving Holland and the Zeeland islands ungarrisoned, because he had to keep his eye on France, where Gaspard de Coligny and Charles IX were preparing to attack the Low Countries. The lower coasts of Zeeland were infested by the "Beggars of the Sea," who were being joined by more and more of the fishing population; and, throughout the country, a mass of unemployed and refugees were ready to rally to them at the first sign.

The Count de Boussu, Governor of Holland, had no ships under his command, which explains the ease with which a band of the "Beggars of the Sea" succeeded in securing themselves a port. On April 1, 1572, they surprised and captured the little city of Briel. Neighboring towns, driven wild by hunger and distress, rose in revolt, meeting with no resistance because there was no Spanish garrison. The towns of Zeeland and a great number of Dutch ports came at once under the control of the insurgents: Flushing, at the mouth of the Schelde, went over on April 6; Rotterdam, the great port of the future, on April 8; and Schiedam, two days later. From all over the Low Countries, from the north as well as from the south, unemployed and adventurers rushed to join the insurgent towns. They opened the dikes, flooded the surrounding countryside, and rendered the towns impregnable. It was impossible to wipe them out without a fleet, so that the land forces of the Duke of Alba were useless in dealing with this insurrection. The Prince of Orange now had a piece of free territory from which he could direct his rebellion.

This stroke had been the work of the entire population of the Low Countries. The actual capture of Briel was achieved by a force of 600 insurgents, most of them Walloons and French Protestants under the command of a certain Sire de Lumey, a native of Liége and a descendant of the La Marck family and of the Boar of the Ardennes.

It was principally from the south that people rushed to the rebel towns to establish in Holland the future Republic of the United Provinces. From the outset, this territory was the rallying ground for the cream of the intellectuals and traders of the Low Countries, and its population was unique, with no lack of leaders, soldiers, and organizers. Since they had the support of the maritime towns and their fleets, they were able to monopolize sea trade, giving them enormous resources. They held the estuaries of the Meuse, the Schelde, and the Rhine, and were the only outlet to the sea from Germany. The rebels thus had inexhaustible resources at their command, not only through piracy and the confiscation of clerical property, but also from the markets of the world.

In Holland already lived the most active and energetic people of the Low Countries, who had been taking the lead since the time of Charles V. They now were joined by Protestants from all over the country, as well as by French Huguenots, driven out after the massacre of St. Bartholomew's Day. Holland thus became a sort of international state, organized to serve the Protestant ideal; this new state, founded as it was on freedom and resistance to oppression, was to stand up against Spanish totalitarianism as an incarnation of a new world concept.

The Duke of Alba reacted quickly. The pressure on the French border was relieved, for Coligny and his Protestant friends had fallen as a result of the St. Bartholomew's Day massacre, with the result that the Duke of Alba had the effective use of all his forces. The Prince of Orange had attempted an invasion of the Lowlands from the south,

but he was defeated and forced to flee northward. The Duke immediately made plans for a lightning reconquest of the towns of Holland
and Zeeland. Mercenary troops had been raised in Germany to bring
his army to a total of 40,000 men, and he was in no mood to be held
in check by the approach of winter. Since time was short, he organized
a blitzkrieg in which terror magnified the importance of the military
victories.

The town of Mechlin, in the very center of the Low Countries, was
entirely Catholic. The Duke, however, thought it had not put up a
tough enough resistance against the Prince of Orange, a few months
earlier. Therefore, Spanish troops on their way north occupied the town
and, for three days, tortured and killed the Catholic inhabitants, pillaged the houses, and even sacked the churches and monasteries. This
atrocity caused indignation throughout the Low Countries. The Duke,
however, justified his act by declaring that all he had wanted was to
"terrify the other towns"; and his soldiers, faced with the suggestion
that they would be hated, replied by asking "What good is it to us
to be liked?"

The Duke of Alba next seized Zutphen in Gelderland, where he
hanged all the inhabitants, and his army then triumphantly entered
Holland. The first town to which he laid siege was Haarlem, where resistance was so strong that the Duke understood that a real revolution
was beginning. "If this were but a war against another prince," he
said, "it would be over by now. The marvel is the way that these
traitors increase." The more people were killed, the more there were,
and the insurrection spread like wildfire.

The Duke was then astonished that the inhabitants of the northern
provinces, who had refused to pay their taxes, now offered the Prince
of Orange, without a sign of hesitation, "the whole of their lives and
their property." The towns enthusiastically doubled their taxpayers'
contributions of their own free will. The siege of Haarlem went on for
seven months, and the Duke had to lose the entire winter and tire
his troops. When the famished town at last surrendered, the dictator,
understanding at last that acts of terror only encouraged resistance,
gave the inhabitants an almost universal amnesty.

His clemency, however, served him not at all, for at this very moment the Spanish troops, who had not been paid for many a long
month, rose in revolt themselves. This was the first of the great mutinies that were henceforth to paralyze Spain.

The financial problem, which the Duke thought he had settled by
force, returned anew. Despite further victories, the town-by-town reconquest of the Low Countries was now beyond the forces at the Duke's
command. At Alkmaar, in the far north of Holland, the inhabitants'

resistance could not be overcome, and the Duke had to order a general retreat, abandoning almost all his conquests. There is a Dutch saying: "It is from Alkmaar that victory dates."

From now on, Spain's financial situation caused a military paralysis. The Lowlands had, within a few years, cost Philip II more than 25 million florins. Since the Duke of Alba had arrived in Brussels, it had been necessary to send him 8 million florins from Spain. The fiasco of the tenth *denier* resulted in a sullen and continuous mutiny among the Spanish troops; and authorization to pillage, which it was often necessary to give them, made a final breach between Spain and the inhabitants of the Low Countries.

A Catholic bishop was later to say of the Duke of Alba that he had "done more harm to religion in seven years than ever Luther or Calvin had done." He had, however, done more than this, for his authoritarian reign had destroyed the power of Spain. The financial problem had now become insoluble; on October 15, 1573, Philip recalled him to Spain.

His successor was the elderly Luis de Requesens, governor of Milan. He was a diplomat, moderate in his habits and conciliatory by disposition, but in the Low Countries he found himself in a situation that could not be resolved.

A general mutiny was imminent. The debt to the troops for arrears in pay amounted to 6 million crowns, and military expenditure was running at a rate of 600,000 florins per month. All that Requesens could do was to attempt to calm the troubled spirits by abolishing the tenth *denier* and convoking the Estates General. He declared a general amnesty, but this did not relax the tension. Indeed, tempers were running so high that nobody thought of claiming the pardon. No one believed that victory was possible for Spain, and there were now two rival ideologies face-to-face with their propaganda and counter-propaganda, fanaticism, and intransigent doctrines.

Requesens tried in vain to open negotiations with the Prince of Orange, at Breda. Emperor Maximilian II attempted to act as intermediary, but this proved useless and served only to show that the struggle had now become European. The King of Spain no longer controlled even his own soldiers, for mutinies were continually breaking out and the Low Countries were slowly drifting into anarchy. Requesens had, for a long time, asked for his recall, but it never came, and he died worn out and in despair, without being able to nominate his successor.

At this point Philip II committed a very serious mistake. Instead of promptly nominating a new governor, he hesitated, mistrusting the Council of State, which he left without instructions for several months.

The interregnum and resulting absence of any government were fatal for Spain. Anarchy was spreading rapidly and there were mutterings of revolt in Brussels.

The Spanish troops, who had had no pay for two years, now rebelled openly. In July, 1576, they seized the fortress of Aalst, as much to hold the country for ransom as to provide for their own safety. From this stronghold, they proceeded to levy taxes on their own account, demanding contributions from the towns of Brabant and Flanders. The Estates of Brabant, however, sitting in Brussels, held the Council of State in its power, and forced it to outlaw the Aalst mutineers and to order the mass levy of the national militia. The Spanish troops, frightened, took refuge in Antwerp where, under the direction of their leader, Roda, they set up an independent government.

The Catholics of the south, faced by this menace, were quick to understand that only the Calvinist forces in the north could prevent their towns from being pillaged, and the Prince of Orange hastened to take advantage of this situation. Aided by the commander of the troops in Brussels, Guillaume de Hèze, he organized a coup to subdue the Council of State, encircling it with two companies of musketeers and purging it by arresting several members during the September session of 1576.

This was a crime of lese majesty that compromised the Estates of Brabant, and they now had no recourse but to ask the Prince of Orange for help. They invited the Estates of Flanders and Hainaut to join them in convoking the Estates General at Ghent; together they raised troops who marched on Antwerp to contain the Spanish soldiery. In fact, they forced them into the citadel and the Walloon troops went over *en bloc* to the side of the revolutionaries.

Now that they were threatened by the insurgents, the old Spanish regiments recovered their energy and discipline. Still under the leadership of Roda, they decided to take their revenge by pillaging the town to recover their arrears of pay. At noon on November 4, they marched out of the citadel in three columns, took the town by assault, and set fire to it while the Low Countries' troops took flight. This huge massacre, known as the "Spanish Fury," cost the lives of 7,000 people, and the destruction by fire of 500 houses. It took three weeks to collect and load into wagons the booty acquired from the city, at that time one of the richest in the world.

The ensuing wave of wrath and indignation drove the whole of the Low Countries into a real national union, and the provinces formed a federation. The last hesitations of the Catholics were swept aside, and the Estates General signed the Pacification of Ghent, which provided for a reconciliation between the north and the south.

This was a contract in which the Protestants got the lion's share, for their religion was to be free and unrestricted in the south, while the Catholic religion was still banned in Holland and Zeeland. The people of the south, however, could not do without the help of the Calvinist insurgents, who were the only people with any political and military organization, and the fear of Spanish reprisals kept them dependent upon their allies, despite religious fears and hatreds.

Deputies in the Estates General were forced to vote for the Pacification of Ghent by the shouts of the Ghent rioters, who threatened to slaughter all opponents. Through it all could be heard the cannon of Ghent firing on the Spaniards who were still in possession of the citadel. In reality, Catholics and Protestants hated one another, although none of them yet realized that the Low Countries were in the process of splitting into two separate nations.

At this point the new governor, Don Juan of Austria, took up his new duties. Like Margaret of Parma, he was a bastard child of Charles V, born of the emperor's passing affair with the beautiful and frivolous Barbara Blomberg, a middle-class German from Ratisbon. He was, however, a man of superior type, almost a genius. Eager and attractive, he had already distinguished himself in battle against the Moslems in southern Spain, and in his brilliant naval victory against the Turks, at the Battle of Lepanto. He did not accept his new assignment without stipulating conditions that Philip II took some time to accept.

For all this, however, the new governor's position could not have been more difficult. As soon as he arrived, he found himself faced with the distrust, now prevalent in the Low Countries toward anything that came out of Spain. In the beginning he tried concession. By the Perpetual Edict of Marche, he agreed to the departure of the Spanish soldiery within twenty days, recognized and sanctioned the traditional privileges of the country, and by implication ratified the Pacification of Ghent. His recognition by the Estates General, however, was carried by a majority of only one vote; and with riots now permanently in progress in the streets of Brussels, it became evident that the real master of the Low Countries was the Prince of Orange.

It was not long before Don Juan realized that he, too, was a prisoner of the insurgents. His servants could not leave the palace without being insulted, he had no police force at his command, and he knew that he might be assassinated at any moment. He took advantage of a visit to Namur to seize the citadel and take refuge there. This was considered everywhere as an act of treason. Immediately, there was revolution.

The Prince of Orange made his triumphal entry into Brussels on December 23, 1577, accompanied by countless Calvinist refugees, who were to take charge of the agitation and gain the support of the man in the street for him. He had been called to the capital by a "committee of eighteen," which, like the Paris commune of 1792, had been self-appointed after a day of revolutionary activity. It was made up of delegates from the "nations"—crafts and unions representing the popular element. This committee seized effective power and claimed to be the only representative of the people, as opposed to the deputies of the Estates General, whom they declared to be out of contact with the country because of their wealth and privilege.

The lawyers and fanatical Calvinists who directed the committee now dominated events, and they started a campaign of terror in order to impose their will. They controlled the police and the government, and organized continual riots and popular demonstrations. They sent countless delegations to the tribune of the Estates General, imposed their decisions upon it, insisted upon its being purged of suspect deputies, and dictated the Estates' repudiation of Don Juan, the declaration of war against Spain, and, finally, a vote giving dictatorial powers to the Prince of Orange.

The southern provinces, however, were frightened by the continual progress of the Protestant minority who, although few in number, were better organized. They succeeded in concluding among themselves the Union of Brussels, which gave priority to the defense of the Catholic faith. The southern nobility were still Catholic, and they sought to fight against the increasing power of the Prince of Orange. Their chief was the Duke of Aerschot, Governor of Ghent, who entered into negotiation with Archduke Mathias, one of the sons of the Emperor Rudolph II. His aim was to set the Archduke against both Philip II and the Prince of Orange. He succeeded in bringing him into the Lowlands, but the reply of William the Silent was to organize a day of bloody revolution in Ghent.

The new Protestant party was now called the Patriotic Party, and it armed the vagabonds so that it might have a rebel militia. Two Calvinist leaders, Ryhove and Henbyze, seized power on October 28, 1577, despite the fact that they and their partisans were a very small minority. The Duke of Aerschot and the Bishops of Bruges and Ypres were arrested.

Don Juan, however, who had been proclaimed an enemy of the country by the Estates General, decided now to take the offensive. The leader of the rebel army, the Count of Lalaing, had gone to Brussels to attend a wedding, and Don Juan chose this moment for the attack that brought him a victory at Gembloux on January 31, 1578. This victory restored the Namur district, Limbourg, Hainaut, and southern Brabant to the Spaniards. Don Juan, however, died soon afterwards, worn out and discouraged. His successor was Alessandro Farnese, one of the sons of Margaret of Parma.

The new governor was a political genius, being at the same time a diplomat, an administrator, and a strategist. More Italian than Spanish, he had a suppleness and sense of diplomacy that made him understand that the struggle had become an affair of negotiation and maneuver. He also saw that the absurdity of the revolution was becoming more and more apparent to the people.

The devastated Low Countries were now divided into four distinct sections. In the south was Luxemburg, which had always belonged to the Spaniards, and whose governor, Mansfeld, had been at the head of the Catholic party since the time of Margaret of Parma. This region, with the Namur district, Limbourg, and part of Hainaut, formed a Catholic bloc that supported Philip II.

In the north, Holland and Zeeland, enriched by their expanding commerce and navigation, steadfastly refused to submit to the Estates General and were turning themselves into Protestant citadels. They were in the hands of intransigent Calvinists who were opposed even to the Prince of Orange, whose policy of religious toleration they obstructed. They were not interested in the unity of the Low Countries.

Between these two regions lay the provinces of Brabant and Flanders, held by a Calvinist minority that relied for its support on the popular element, and that maintained its power by a policy of terror that enabled it to dominate the population.

Finally, in the far south, in provinces that are now French—the Artois, southern Hainaut, and southern Flanders (Arras, Lille, Valenciennes, and the surrounding region)—civil war was in full swing. The Calvinists still dominated, but the angry Catholics were willing to rally to the cause of Spain.

The decisive event was the appearance in Hainaut, around the end of 1578, of a revolutionary Catholic party known as the "malcontents." Montigny, their leader, organized an army whose soldiers wore a rosary round their necks and were known as the *paternoster knechten*. Thus reinforced, he entered into negotiation with Farnese.

The die was now cast. All that was necessary was that Philip II, on Farnese's advice, make the concessions necessary to secure agreement between the Spaniards and the Catholics. In vain, the Prince of Orange called the Duke of Anjou, a brother of the French King Henry II, to the Low Countries in an attempt to maintain the union of the insurgent provinces. Anjou tried to seize Antwerp by launching an attack known as the "French fury," and ended by being ignominiously chased away. The southern provinces signed the Peace of Arras on January 6, 1579, to which the northern provinces replied with the Union of

Utrecht on January 23, 1579, a Protestant federation opposed to the Catholic union of the south.

The division was now an accomplished fact, and the revolution had done its work. From the Low Countries of old, two nations had been born; the one Calvinist, under the leadership of the province of Holland; the other Catholic and allied to Spain, the future Belgium.

The reconquest of Flanders and Brabant by Alessandro Farnese was the result of this transformation of a national struggle into a religious one that divided the country in two. Things were moving swiftly, and by 1579, Farnese had seized Maastricht, thus cutting off communications between the Low Countries and Germany. He at once reorganized his army, withdrawing the Spanish soldiers in conformity with the Peace of Arras, which had stipulated that the Spaniards be withdrawn, and replacing them with German mercenaries and "malcontent" troops.

He then took the offensive and seized all the great towns in the south of the Low Countries, initiating siege operations that were both masterpieces of military technique and triumphs of diplomatic ingenuity. In vain the Protestant minorities in power attempted to resist: Tournai fell in 1581; Ghent, where Calvinist chiefs such as Henbyze had been beheaded, in 1584; Brussels in March, 1585; and Antwerp on August 16, 1585.

The principle of all these capitulations was the same. The Catholic religion was re-established and Protestant worship forbidden; but the Calvinists, if they wished to keep their religion, might do so provided they lived inoffensively. If they desired to emigrate, they were given a long interval to sell their property before leaving.

This moderate policy secured Farnese's continued success, because it ensured that the population would rally to his flag. On the other hand, it was an indirect reinforcement for Holland and amounted to a victory for her. The Calvinist inhabitants, using their right to sell property and emigrate, helped reinforce Holland's wealth and power, bringing her an elite population that, active and fanatic as it was, had a high cultural and creative level. The Calvinist departure robbed Catholic Belgium of a large part of her energy and vital strength. Moreover, the migration was equivalent to an exchange of population and created a definite cleavage between the newly constituted countries.

The north was to remain Protestant for centuries, and the south Catholic. This redistribution of the inhabitants sufficed to ensure an extremist triumph in each region. The result was that the two countries were enemies.

Spain was now able to bring the Belgians around to her cause, the defense of European Catholicism. From the Spanish standpoint, the loss of Holland was more than offset by the creation of a Catholic bastion in the southern Lowlands, the Belgium of today.

Alessandro Farnese achieved the greatest of his victories in the siege and capture of Antwerp in 1585. His opposing commander-in-chief was the distinguished writer Philippe Marnix de Sainte-Aldegonde, author of the *Beehive of the Roman Church* and other satirical writings in French and Dutch. The way in which he defended the city was to be a justification of his famous motto *Repos ailleurs*. This siege took precedence over the famous events of Tournai in 1581, when Christine de Lalaing, Princess d'Epinoy, the wife of the absent governor, set herself at the head of a heroic resistance.

Farnese's plan for taking possession of Antwerp included damming the Schelde by means of an enormous chain of boats, 2,400 paces, or over one mile long. He had to dig a new canal across the Waes country, called the Parma canal, to bring in ships and supplies for the besieging forces. All Europe followed this extraordinary siege, in which all the most modern warlike techniques were brought into play, with passionate interest. A ship loaded with explosives was sent out of the besieged city to blow up the floating wall barring the river, and its explosion had much the same effect on the people of the time as the atomic bomb of our day. The incident was described by an eye-witness:

"The infernal vessel, charged with this enormous mine, exploded with so much din that the whole world appeared to have exploded. There were some who thought the last judgment had come, and others that hell was opening beneath them. The waters of the great river Schelde leaped forth from their bed, and those who were standing on the jetty saw the river's bottom exposed and dry. The ramparts of St. Mary's Fort, with a whole company of Germans who were on guard there, were blown into the air with all their artillery and no trace of them was ever found. Farnese himself, who was standing at a little distance, lost his hat and was thrown to the ground with such violence that he remained unconscious for two hours. The trembling of the earth was felt three leagues away. There were many who were knocked silly because the displacement of air was so violent that they were snatched upward from the ground. A number of people died without wounds, killed by the noise. The severed limbs of soldiers were found a good half league away. There were many wounded, and their wounds were most extraordinary, for some had neither arms nor legs. It was a night of horror, with the cries of half-buried wounded adding to the confusion of those who were searching for their friends. On the next day, however, April 5, hope revived."

Farnese patiently set to work on the wall's reconstruction. Antwerp capitulated on August 15, 1585, and made him master of all Brabant as far as the Rhine.

It was now Holland's turn to be invested, according to the Spanish plan for Europe. The Bishop of Cologne, who had become a convert to Protestantism, had come to the aid of the United Provinces. Farnese's first task, therefore, was to neutralize this new attack, for the conquest of Holland was not possible with western Germany hostile.

The Prince of Orange, outlawed by Philip II, was assassinated at Delft on July 10, 1584, by a Burgundian, Baltasar Gérard. The latter was a Catholic fanatic who had acted under the illusion, which he shared with the King of Spain, that this assassination would split the northern provinces. In fact, just the opposite happened. The union became all the closer, and William the Silent became a legend embodying the soul and spirit of the new nation.

Philip has been accused of making a grievous mistake in halting Farnese at the peak of his victories and sending him to fight against France and England, instead of allowing him to conquer the rest of the Spanish Lowlands. After his unbroken record of success, from 1580 to 1585, the total defeat of the insurgents in the north seemed easy enough. All the victories of Farnese, however, had been over outlying towns and provinces, which it had been difficult for the Dutch to help. They had, indeed, gained part of their strength from the aid sent them by Germany and England. Thus Farnese's successes came to an end after he had overcome Brabant, Frisia, and the coast of the Zuider Zee. All that was left to conquer was the small, but immensely wealthy, waterbound territory consisting of the two provinces of Holland and Zeeland.

Elizabeth I of England had allied herself with the Dutch, and Farnese proceeded to Dunkirk to begin preparations for the invasion of England. He brought together, as did the Germans in 1940, barges, flat-bottomed boats, and landing troops who were to support the attack of the "Invincible Armada." The career of the Spanish Armada, however, ended in disaster in 1588, and Farnese had first to seize the Rhineland, lest he be caught in the rear by the Protestants, and then to march off to prevent Henry IV, the King of France, from capturing Paris.

It must not, however, be imagined that these operations were only useless diversions, unrelated to the proposed conquest of Holland. All Farnese's victories, from Antwerp to Frisia, had been won on land, while Holland and Zeeland were sheltered behind their barrier of water, and it would have been almost impossible to conquer them without a fleet. An invading army would have risked attack from the rear by landings in the middle of the flooded zones and would most probably have suffered disaster. Holland was in a fair way to becoming the most important sea power in Europe, and its reduction would have called for a fleet specially equipped and constructed for navigation in estuary waters and the flooded countryside. The Spanish fleet, which had to make its way through the storms of the Atlantic, was composed of ships that drew a great deal of water, quite unusable in the Lowlands.

The conquest of Holland presupposed the domination of Europe, possible only if France and England put their shipbuilding yards at the disposal of Spain. This in turn demanded the subjugation of the two countries, and this is the explanation of King Philip's policy. Experience, however, was soon to show that crushing France and England was beyond the capacity of the Spanish forces. As a result, the conquest of Holland itself had to remain a dream. The capture of the town and port of Ostend alone called for an immense effort from the Spanish armies.

Philip II was thus unable to overcome the United Provinces, and there was nothing left for him to do but to rally the Low Countries and their inhabitants to a common struggle for the defense of the faith. He was now able to make the Belgians accept this role without having to either abolish their privileges or bring them under a dictatorship. All that was necessary was to frighten them with the threat of letting them fall once more into the power of the Dutch, and at the same time to give them partial political autonomy.

A community of beliefs and religious ideals now put the Belgians definitely in the service of Spain. King Philip's victory was more decisive than anything the Duke of Alba had achieved, because Philip won the Belgians to his side and secured their cooperation. He made their territory a bulwark against the Protestant powers of France, Holland, and England and, by protecting Spanish territory against invasion, he secured himself a commanding position in European affairs.

In order to give the Belgians the impression that they were free, Philip established them as an independent domain. This was the object of his action in handing over the Spanish Lowlands to his favorite daughter, the Infanta Isabella, and her husband the Archduke Albert, which, although ostensibly an act of cession, contained secret clauses that allowed Spain to retain control of the country and maintain its civil servants, its troops, and its courtiers there. The result was that the Court of the Archdukes in Brussels appeared to all Europe as "a branch of the Escorial."

Belgium, however, was proud to appear to the world as the defender of the Catholic religion and one of its martyrs. She became a faithful ally of Spain against England, Holland, Germany, and France. Belgians could now face their neighbors with the feeling that they were a single people. They had a common religion, and they were conscious of sharing the same objectives and of being a single spiritual and moral unit. It was at this time that Belgium was born and set about making herself into a nation.

The territory of Belgium had been terribly devastated. In Brabant, the population had diminished by half, in places by three-quarters. Only a quarter of the houses of Grammont were still standing, and only one burgher in six was alive and still in residence. In Gembloux, in 1594, there were only 70 houses standing out of the 170 that had been there previously.

The fields of Flanders were overgrown with brambles. Since 1585 it had been impossible to venture even a few hundred yards out of Ghent for fear of being attacked by wolves. Fifteen years later wolves still infested western Flanders, and it was also infested by so many highwaymen that the woods had to be cut back 700 feet along the rivers and roads to give travelers some security.

Only a tenth of the land was arable, and, in 1592, all comers could cultivate any of the fields that had been left fallow for their own benefit. In towns that had been under military occupation, soldiers had burned furniture and the structural timber of the houses, so that when they had gone the houses were uninhabitable and eventually collapsed.

Trade had almost wholly disappeared. In Antwerp there were now only three Italian merchants, and the exchange had been turned into a library. Belgium was now little more than a desert, both materially and intellectually, and Holland, strengthened by the immigration of the best of the Belgians, was strongly in the ascendant.

Philip II died on September 13, 1598. His reign, begun with immense resources and a virtually unchallengeable freedom of action, ended with a defeat that was to be the beginning of Spain's rapid decay.

The Spanish Lowlands had played a decisive role in Spain's decline. They had been a bottomless pit into which the men and money of the Spanish monarchy had been poured. In the end, there was no denying the fact that Holland had triumphed.

This defeat had not been due to a lack of boldness or fear of large-scale undertakings. King Philip had had all of Europe ranged against him, and after he had beaten the Turks at Lepanto he had still to deal with France, England, Portugal, and the German princes. Nor had he suffered from a lack of able lieutenants. In such men as Don Juan, the Duke of Alba, Granvelle, and Alessandro Farnese, the King had had a galaxy of military and political geniuses at his side. Moreover, there was no lack of military resources, for the Spanish armies of the time were the best in the world; their arms had been bought with gold from America, and their strength was at a level hitherto unknown in Europe.

King Philip was an absolute monarch who had no need to worry about a parliament or a constitution; he held all the reins of power in his own hands. However, the mediocre results that he obtained, and their brief duration, were to be a matter of general comment.

This is a standing confirmation of a law that runs unchanged through all the pages of history: A leader whose power is unlimited must become paralyzed because he cannot resist the pitfall of ideology. In governing, he is forced to rely on ideological concepts, and it is not long before he becomes their slave. Thus he commits his armies and his resources to useless and unwise undertakings, which a government of more restricted powers can generally avoid.

History teaches us that unlimited authority serves only to swallow up the fortunes of a country in the adventurous pursuit of glory and prestige. This is inevitable, because the people will follow a leader unconditionally only if they are carried away by his cause.

It was loyalty, not to Spain, but to the Catholic faith, that led Spaniards to their death at Lepanto, at St. Quentin, and in the Invincible Armada. More seriously, no one blamed King Philip for having squandered the nation's wealth and ruined its chances for the future. Even today Spaniards speak of him as "The Wise King," identifying his ideal with that of the nation and making it their own. Looking back, they see the expression of the soul of Spain in this magnificent symphony of glory, of which King Philip was the brilliant conductor in his remote and solitary Escorial.

VIII

THE CROWN OF THORNS

The Infanta Isabella was the favorite daughter of Philip II. Victor Hugo, in *La Légende des Siècles*, presents her in *La Rose de l'Infante*, overshadowed by the disaster that befell the Armada.

> Madame, said the Duenna, with a face of gloom,
> To the young child wondering amid her dreams,
> All the world belongs to princes, except the wind.

She was born on August 12, 1566, and it had been her father's wish that she should become Queen of France. She inherited from him that zest for work which, in her old age, was to keep her toiling at her desk, clad in a nun's robe, until four o'clock in the morning. She was the soul of kindness, and played the part of a mother to her ladies-in-waiting, with whom she lived on terms of great intimacy. Her face, with intelligent eyes beneath her fair hair, contrasted vividly with the ugliness of her husband, the Archduke Albert.

She lived her life according to a strict monastic code, in a court of solemn formality in which the glorification of the Church was the dominant note. At mealtimes, Albert and Isabella dined alone, cut off from their courtiers by the magnificent dais on which they sat, and were served only on bended knee. When their carriage passed the Holy Sacrament in the street, it halted while they got out and knelt humbly together on the cobblestones. On Holy Thursday the Archduke, with his own hands, would wash the feet of a dozen poor people. He was forever making pilgrimages, carrying the relic of his patron saint on his bowed shoulders. He refused to enter Brussels without first having made his devotions at the Church of Our Lady of Hal, and he believed that his real mission was not so much to govern the country, as to bring back secretly from Germany and Holland the holy relics that had been carried off during the wars of religion. The Archduke had never been received into holy orders, but he was a cardinal and Archbishop of Seville.

Isabella, for her part, never began writing a letter without first bestowing upon it the sign of the cross, and after her husband's death she spent six hours every day at her devotions. Life at her court was lived with fasts and retreats. One of the preachers, the Italian Capuchin de Casali, was known for a sermon in which he lacerated his shoulders with a whip and thrust a crown of thorns upon his head.

The hooded penitents acted in the same way in their many processions. The young nobility, masked and cowled, ecstatically whipped one another in public in the manner of the Spaniards. Most of the court officials were Spanish and, as in Madrid, they included not only a grand major-domo, but also noblemen and women who acted as body-servants to the royal couple.

Religious worship was strict and magnificent, and the whole country was in the grip of its fanatical discipline. Dogs were no longer allowed in churches as they had been in the Middle Ages, nor were children allowed to play there. Services, which had hitherto been pretexts for festivals and parties, now became strictly religious in character.

The Jesuits, as the militant force of the counter-reformation, set up more than thirty colleges in the southern Low Countries, even in little towns with no more than 2,000 or 3,000 inhabitants. Religious orders were no longer limited to the long-established ones, such as the Franciscans or Dominicans, but increased and multiplied in the Observantine Recollects, Mendicant Minims, Barefooted Carmelites, Ursulines, Brigitines, and many others. Many nobles and burghers took their vows as members of these orders. The Barefooted Carmelite Van Ballaer celebrated his first Mass in the presence of six of his brothers, three of whom were priests and three Franciscans, while his seventh brother became a Carmelite on the same day. Money, influence and esteem, which had previously been accorded intellectuals and men of learning, now went to the monks, and there were so many of them that their demands on the national resources became a serious government problem.

In the end, the Church owned more than three-quarters of the land in some districts, and the number of priests and members of religious communities has been estimated at 60,000. In Ghent alone there were twenty convents, and those that were older, supported by the Estates General, protested against the advent of the new ones, because they feared that they would be forced to share their alms and thus suffer a decrease in income.

The government vainly attempted to check the movement, for the monks were the molders of public opinion and the government needed them for propaganda. While the Jesuits were shaping the richer classes in their own image, the more popular orders, such as the Recollects and the Capuchins, were earning their nickname "the Jesuits of the Poor." They went into the humblest hovels, teaching, caring for the sick, and even going so far as to organize the town fire-protection services.

Careful note was kept of the names of citizens who did not go to church regularly, and such persons were black-listed for all public appointments. No charity was given to those of the poor whose children lacked religious instruction, and thus the masses were radically re-Catholicized. Protestant mothers, if they needed the services of a mid-wife, were required to promise to have their children baptized as Catholics. The clergy, with the formidable weapon of excommunication at its command, made social outcasts of people who missed Mass more than two Sundays out of three.

The Protestants emigrated. According to Justus Lipsius, who was converted to Catholicism, and who held courses at Louvain that were attended by the Archduke and the Archduchess, an endless list of fugitives went northward to enrich the new United Provinces with their energy and knowledge. In 1602, Pierre Platevoet, a former citizen of Ypres, founded the first Dutch East India Company in Amsterdam. In 1615, Jacques Lemaire, a Belgian from Tournai, discovered Tierra del Fuego. Two other Belgians were among the directors of the Dutch East India Company; another, G. Usselinck, was the founder of the Dutch West India Company.

In 1624, a colony of Walloons, led by Jesse de Forest, founded New York. The Antwerp admiral, Pierre Van den Broucke, conquered Guinea and founded Batavia on the Island of Java. Jean de Laet, another Belgian, directed the affairs of the whole Dutch colonial empire, on which, as on the Spanish empire, the sun never set.

Simon Stevin, who was the inventor of the metric system and decimal fractions, left Bruges and took refuge at Leiden, as had Marnix de Sainte-Aldegonde; so, too, did Peter Minuit, who bought the island of Manhattan from the Indians for twenty-four dollars.

The same thing was going on in painting and literature; the father of the Dutch poet Joost van den Vondel was originally from Antwerp. The Protestant emigration was a drain that weakened Belgium, and resulted in major changes in the national spirit. The United Provinces, on the other hand, gained a great number of men of action, free and independent people who were to play a great part in Holland's future progress. People of this type were sadly lacking in Belgium.

This emigration explains the passivity of the Belgians, and the docile way in which they let themselves be browbeaten by the Spaniards, whereas the United Provinces, the Holland of today, were to benefit substantially from the heritage of the Low Countries for a full century.

Belgium, in the meantime, was imbued with the spirit of Spain, although there was no great mixture of blood between the two countries and the number of Belgo-Spanish marriages was small. It would be a mistake to trace the many southern types who are found in Flanders to the Spanish soldiers, for they were already noticed by travelers in the Middle Ages. The Spaniards had nothing to do with this, for their contact with the population was limited to brawls. But the Spanish religious attitude was an important formative factor in Catholic Flanders, and the key jobs that so many Spaniards in the seventeenth century held gave them great influence over the country.

All the governors of the Spanish Lowlands were chosen from the Castilian nobility; and the Belgian nobility itself imitated the Spanish manners and customs, as a century earlier it had imitated the Germans. The highest dignitaries were Spanish, such as the Infanta's chief lady-in-waiting and the grand major-domo who, at the same time, was Admiral of Aragon. Out of twenty-five ladies-in-waiting, twelve were Spanish, as were nine of the fifteen noblewomen who attended the Infanta. The confessors, chaplains, and preachers were all Spanish, and the court accounts were kept in Castilian.

The story of the famous procession of the penitents at Furnes is a good illustration of this transformation. For many centuries this town had had its traditional picturesque procession and festival with devils, giants, and cavalcades; its origins went back to a medieval mystery play. In 1636 the clergy required the first change—the devils, whose presence offended the souls of the pious, were cast out. The next step was the disappearance of the worthy giants, who were considered to be pagan. Eight years later, in 1644, the Capuchins, influenced by the style of Spain, introduced a procession of hooded penitents. In 1650, the governor of Flanders decided to turn the procession into an act of expiation to ask God's pardon for the profaning of the Holy Table as, it was alleged, two soldiers had done.

Thus the joyful procession of the Middle Ages became an exercise in piety. Those who wanted to take part in the procession had to give up all idea of fun and fantasy and walk barefoot on the cobblestones, their faces covered by hoods that prevented their recognition. They advanced through the streets bent beneath the weight of the heavy crosses that they carried on their shoulders. Despite these conditions, or perhaps because of them, many workingmen, fishermen, and burghers asked to take part in the procession. They came to choose their cross on the evening before, according to their age and stature.

The love of show that had always been a Flemish characteristic remained; it was only the sense of the show that changed. It was no longer a question of festivities, but of pilgrimages and processions that celebrated the glory of God.

The Society of Jesus was so important in Belgium that the country became a sort of Jesuit empire. It was the actual center of the society for northern Europe, and there were 1,574 Jesuits in Belgium, compared with only 2,000 in the whole of France, and 2,283 in the whole of Germany.

There were thirty Jesuit colleges in the Spanish Lowlands, and they embodied the knowledge, talent and taste for novelty of the period. Almost all of the works of literature and philosophy that appeared at this time were written by Jesuits.

Their literary production was rich enough to compare with that of the Renaissance humanists, and they had the same enthusiastic devotion to a cultural ideal which they hoped to propagate throughout the world in order to transform society. They knew everything—they were masters of history (with the Bollandists), law, philosophy, physics, and mathematics. They also produced a number of brilliant painters, such as Daniel Seghers, and talented architects such as Huyssens.

The Jesuits' activity eclipsed the universities, and it was to the Jesuits that the elite came for their education. It is wrong to blame them for the intellectual decline that was about to set in. They, in fact, delayed it, and continued fighting for disinterested thought and culture. If in the end their ideal became utilitarian, it was because their environment had, in the long run, gotten the best of them.

They were the adventurers of the faith, and they made Catholicism a living force. It was in Belgium that they wrote their most important works and exercised their greatest influence.

Belgium, however, was not to be converted to Catholicism without many difficulties. The southern part of the Spanish Lowlands had largely gone over to Calvinism at the time of their reconquest by the Spaniards. A still more serious factor was the indifferent, even unbelieving, attitude of a large part of the population that had grown weary of the excesses committed by the rival parties. It was disheartened and demoralized, no longer believing in anything, and it took a long and persevering effort of propaganda to turn Belgium into a "Bastion of the Faith."

As late as 1620, two-thirds of the inhabitants of Ghent refused to send their children to catechism classes. In 1609, the government vainly attempted to prohibit religious discussions in public, but such discussions were still carried on in the streets, and in all places where Protestants and Catholics met. The authorities, however, succeeded in converting the dissenters by isolating them and subjecting them to an incessant battering of propaganda. In the end their position was untenable. It was not long before the detection of a heretic required the organization of a complete spy system. If a heretic was innocent enough to reveal himself, he was summoned by the Bishop and an instructor was officially appointed to secure his conversion. He was confronted with arguments he could not answer, for it was difficult to maintain that almost the whole population lived in error; and he could not refuse instruction, for this made him appear to be of bad faith. In most cases he quickly recanted, at least with his lips. By 1650 the Calvinists comprised only a few unimportant communities with no major resources.

The most effective weapon in eliminating the Protestants was the proclamation that marriages celebrated by Protestant pastors were null and void. The children thus became illegitimate, and were automatically barred from all public offices or honorable careers.

Within a few years, Protestants had become so few in number that it became possible to use new methods. Heretics were regarded as sorcerers. It was no longer Protestantism for which they were prosecuted, but witchcraft; a dreadful charge, because witchcraft always carried the death penalty. Such cases were tried *in camera*. No proof was required, and the only instrument of inquiry was the torture chamber. This explains the outburst of witchcraft that flooded Belgium at this time.

Witch-hunting had another purpose. With the disappearance of the Protestants, it became necessary to find another focus for the wrath and fanaticism of the masses. After about 1600, all the edicts record the "increase in witchcraft" and, for another century, witch-hunting was rife throughout the Spanish Lowlands. Thousands of people of weak intellect were tortured for the sake of extracting false confessions, collective hallucinations were deliberately provoked, and religious people echoed the words of the Jesuit Del Rio, who denounced witches as a permanent menace, accounting for all the ills of the nation. Even children, and women of eighty, were burned to death and, at Bouchain, a single official brought 183 persons to justice in nine years. In Luxemburg alone prosecutions were estimated at 30,000, 20,000 of which ended in death sentences.

No dissension could stand up against such moral pressure. The results were tremendous, and left their mark on the Belgian population to our day. In half a century, the Spanish Lowlands had become a new country, a Spanish world shaped by a mystical faith, where mankind was transformed by the ecstasy of suffering for the greater glory of its religion.

In this country, once so free and once the cradle of Renaissance civilization, the spirit of inquiry and independent thought had disappeared. Holy images were being erected on all sides, and the countryside was covered with crosses, shrines, and calvaries, to most of which were attributed miraculous powers. The pagan fun of the Renaissance had been replaced by the novena, the procession, the jubilee, and the sermon. The country swarmed with ascetics and saints, such as St. Jean Berchmans, Jeanne Deleloe, François Taffin, and Servais Laruels.

Outside events that served the cause of Catholicism were considered national triumphs and were celebrated with public rejoicing: the conversion of a German prince, the victory of Austria over the Turks, and the successes of Spain or the Empire. Pamphlets, caricatures, and songs spread the feeling of hatred for Holland and France. The latter was represented as the great Gallican country that, unlike Spain, refused to commit itself completely to the faith, and even went so far as to conclude alliances with the Moslems and the German Protestants.

Belgium thus acquired a Catholic conscience, and the clergy and the monks took charge of it. The kings of Spain were defended by Belgians who cheerfully sacrificed themselves, accepting suffering, war, and invasion to defend them. No armed help could be sent them, but the Belgians were put under the protection of the Immaculate Conception and St. Joseph amid the fervent acclaim of the population.

Censorship was universally practiced, and no book could be printed or sold without the authority of the Church. The edicts of the Duke of Alba, prohibiting students from attending foreign schools, were applied in all their rigor. Things came to such a point that the Belgians were even forbidden to swim—a sport considered immodest and morally dangerous as it was necessary to undress to practice it.

Literature disappeared, but journalism replaced it, for those in power needed it for propaganda. The first newspapers appeared in Antwerp in 1620 with *Nieuwe Tydinghe,* which lasted until 1827, after it had become the *Courrier Véritable des Pays-Bas.*

The Jesuits and the Bollandists created the modern hagiography, but the sciences were either vegetating or becoming no more than technical systems. Martin van Velden was punished for having taught the doctrines of Copernicus (1691) at Louvain, but, for fear of ridicule, he was allowed to teach the theory of planetary rotation that had been adopted by all of Europe, provided he did not mention the earth.

It was only by taking refuge at Leiden that Simon Stevin was able to evolve his system of decimal fractions. Medicine was a sorry mixture of progress and doctrinaire ignorance. Jan Palfijn of Courtrai (1650–1730) invented the forceps, while the chemist Van Helmont (1579–

1644) and the anatomist Verheyden made other inventions and discoveries. Nevertheless, doctors still adhered to the theories of Galen, or went around during epidemics with their faces protected by leather masks decorated with eyes and a nose of crystal.

Although this totalitarian regime stifled literature and thought, it was a stimulus to the arts. Religious propaganda called for a great display of pomp and magnificence. Baroque art came to the fore with its superabundant ornamentation and its tumultuously draped statues that seemed to live in a perpetual tempest of stone.

Painting took refuge in realism, choosing insignificant subjects of no moral worth that were sufficient to give the artist the right to express himself and the means for doing so. The portrait, the still life, and scenes from the daily life of the people were a means of avoiding the prohibitions, and allowed the artist a certain freedom. This explains the ascendancy of the Flemish painters of festivity and revel who celebrated truth and the joy of reality. *Naar het leven* ("lifelike"), the motto of Brueghel the Elder, inspired David Teniers the Younger (1610–90), Frans Snyders (1574–1657), Adrien Brouwer (1605–38), and many others. There thus arose dynasties of painters who followed one another for a full half century, among them: Pieter Brueghel the Elder (1525–69); Pieter Brueghel the Younger (Hell Brueghel, 1564–1637), the painter of surrealistic diabolism; Jan Brueghel (Velvet Brueghel, 1568–1625); David Teniers the Elder (1582–1649); and David Teniers the Younger.

The weaning of the people from Protestanism called for a brilliant religion, full of display, color, life, and imagery, in which the heavens could open and angels descend to earth, and the divine and earthly worlds be united in a single triumphant universe. This required a personality of exceptional caliber: Peter Paul Rubens (1577–1640), official painter to the Archduke and master of Flemish baroque. Belgian painting was on the threshold of its second golden age.

The great Antwerp painter was no exception to the rule that many men of genius are born abroad, or have parents of different blood. Their talent seems to gain in originality by having to adapt to a new country, as though they are forced to resolve the problems posed by the traditions and the heritage of their age with greater inventive force. Before Rubens could express his full personality he had to leave the Spanish Lowlands and pass long years in Italy. It was only on his return that he discovered his full powers and his wealth of artistic originality.

He was born into a Flemish family in 1577, at Siegen in Westphalia, and did not come to Antwerp until he was ten. He began painting in the school of the "Romanists," at that time the most outstanding.

He then left for Italy, stayed in Venice and Rome, and then went to Spain. Eight years later, when he returned to Antwerp, he cast off the Italian influence, and the influence of the second-rate painting schools of the Spanish Lowlands, and produced a new style that was to revive the true traditions of Flemish art. From this time on, his work was entirely original, and the famous "Elevation of the Cross" at Antwerp, and the subsequent "Descent from the Cross" were the first fruits of his new style.

He had understood that the baroque style, which had gained the upper hand in the architecture of the Counter Reformation, called for a new type of painting—decorative, impassioned, colorful, and full of magnificence. He found it easy to express such a style without ever departing from the natural. This explains the overwhelming popularity that immediately greeted him: He was able to combine the religious attitudes of triumphant Catholicism with the Flemish love of the flesh, thus expressing in his work the totality of his age.

At Antwerp he operated a studio in which his assistants sketched pictures, under his direction, for him to finish; in this way he was able to leave more than 2,000 works behind him. He was equally happy in every form of painting, and was at once simple and sublime. He could handle mystical and religious subjects, landscapes, portraits, historical paintings, epic works, great decorative frescoes, and sensual and triumphant nudes. In some of his work he rose almost to the level of Michelangelo, and in others to that of Rembrandt. He flung on his canvases a multitude of figures bursting with vitality, in a full fire of color and cosmic movement. He had inherited the traditions of both the Flemish and the Italians, and Delacroix described him as the Homer of painting.

The twenty-four huge canvases depicting the story of Marie de Médicis, which he painted in Paris, made him a European master and a leader in every genre, surpassing Van Dyck in portraiture and Teniers in his paintings of peasant festivities. As a painter of romantic landscapes, he was to go beyond what Constable would achieve later; as a colorist, he was more dazzling than the Venetians, and some of his canvases foreshadow the luminous fairylands of Claude Lorrain and the *fêtes galantes* of Antoine Watteau (who was later to be one of his disciples).

Ageless, he was a great gentleman, diplomat, politician, and courtier, and he was almost fifty when he married a girl thirty years his junior. He was forever changing and developing, and when he died, he left behind him a world of ideas, plastic invention, and models that European painting was to feed on for half a century, and that was to last through the eighteenth and nineteenth centuries to our own time.

The key to Rubens' art lay in reconciling the styles of the Van Eycks and Michelangelo. He succeeded in combining the sense of intimacy, the realism, the instinct for atmosphere, and the intense vitality that had always been characteristic of Flemish painting, with the power, the grandeur, and the rich inventiveness of the monumental art of Italy. After his time, progress came to a stop. It was only by a complete transformation that the forward movement could be continued, and this called for a revolution that would reappraise not only the technical problems and traditions on which painting had been based since the Middle Ages, but would go beyond this and question the very idea of painting as a way of seeing the world, the existence of form, line, and the reality of the subject—all that was to be demolished by the Impressionists and abstract painters of the twentieth century.

Rubens was original in being able to develop art on such lines of magnificence that it brought architecture, painting, sculpture, and music into a single unity. Draperies fluttered around his saints, and his churches were filled with Christs, Virgins, and disconsolate Magdalenes. All of the evocative power and emotional appeal of painting were used in the service of piety; and art, transfigured by emotion and moral fervor, was left inseparable from the sensuality that is its source.

Thus Rubens combined the two opposing elements in man in a single triumphant song. Churches, palaces, and religious services became a single poem glorifying the spirit of God.

When Rubens was told that his genius was pagan, he replied that this paganism had been brought into the service of the Faith, and that the spirits it had thrown into disarray had been brought back to Christian worship. He thus re-established the sense of harmony between the public and the artist, making painting a world of sentiment and vitality, justified in an outburst of collective enthusiasm that was the triumphant expression of the Counter Reformation and the new ideals of the Spanish Lowlands.

Sir Anthony van Dyck (1599–1641), who was Rubens' favorite pupil, painted, under the master's direction and for the master's signature, a great number of works that have resulted in a confusion about their work in the early stages. He was born in Antwerp, and was no more than a high-grade apprentice when he met the demigod of Flemish painting. By the time they parted company, however, he had become a master in his own right. The trip to Italy, which he then took, made him conscious of his powers as a portraitist of genius. He had the gift of going beyond his model by transforming it into its type, and making it a symbol for all time of avarice, ambition, futility, nobility, or perfidy.

His Bologna and Genoa portraits are pictures of a decaying aristocracy. He soon set up a studio in London and became court painter. He trained a host of disciples who continued his style and taste, and thus he became the creator of English painting, nonexistent until that time. Among his masterpieces were portraits of Charles II and his family. Before he died, Flemish art had triumphed in England, just as it did in France under his Brussels pupil, Philippe de Champaigne, and throughout Europe, as it was disseminated by emigrating Belgian painters.

His compatriot Jacob Jordaens (1593–1678) was very different. He was a pure naturalist, with a sturdy plebeian temperament that rejected the aristocratic elegance of the great portrait painters. He had never left Antwerp but had remained in touch with the realistic and sensual genius of Flanders, escaping from the Italian influence in works as full of relish as "The King Drinks" and "Fecundity," in the Brussels Museum. He was a painter of revelry and unrestrained pleasures. When, at the age of fifty, he was converted to Calvinism, he managed to avoid incurring the displeasure of the intolerant and totalitarian spirit that prevailed in Belgium. He continued to paint religious pictures for Catholic Churches, alternating them with works of fleshy and alluring nudes.

Side by side with Jordaens a host of smaller masters filled the gap left by Rubens, but escaped into the cult of realism and truthfulness. Frans Snyders, whose still-life paintings show such heaps of game and victuals, was the artist who sketched most of the fruit and flowers in the paintings of Rubens and Jordaens. Jan Fyt (1611–61), another master of realism, painted at times in a manner not unlike that of Jean Baptiste Chardin.

Adrien Brouwer was a youthful genius for whom Rubens had great admiration. He passed a large part of his life in prison for his misdeeds, but in his last years, before he died at the age of thirty-two, he painted a number of wonderful romantic landscapes.

David Teniers the Younger was not only the painter of the "baboons" that incurred the contempt of Louis XIV, but also a witty artist of varied accomplishments who painted peasants and café scenes to amuse an aristocratic public. He also produced elegant conversation pieces, astonishing modern landscapes, and still-life paintings. He was associated with a number of other landscape painters, among them Jacques d'Arthois, who painted a number of pictures of the Forest of Soignes, which was a wilder place than it is today. Another was Jean Siberechts, who used a new notion of space and distance in his nature studies, making him a forerunner of Claude Lorrain and the Le Nains in his technique of atmosphere.

For many artists, landscape painting was the only means of escape enabling them to maintain their sense of truthfulness and their vitality against the monotonous background of pseudo-classicism. That trend came to the fore in sculpture, with artists such as Faydherbe and the Quellins, the Verbruggens and, at Liège, the Delcourts. François Duquesnoy, a friend of Nicolas Poussin, established himself under the name of Francesco Fiamingo (Francis the Fleming) at Rome, where he sculptured the St. Andrew in St. Peter's and, in the Church of the Madonna di Loreto, the Saint Suzanne which ranks as one of the masterpieces of the century.

The inexhaustible richness of Flemish baroque found its outlet in Belgium in the abundant decoration of confessionals and pulpits, such as those at St. Gudule in Brussels. These, in their superabundant decoration, combine the grimaces of a skeleton, the figures of Adam and Eve, the Virgin, the Devil, and a host of other figures amid banks of flowers.

The outstanding work of the period, however, is the market square in Brussels, which was rebuilt after de Villeroy's bombardment by Guillaume de Bruyn. With a team of architects working under him, he achieved a style that varied to the point of being lyrical. It is defiantly decorative, and full of a popular gaiety that has led all Europe to regard it as the symbol of the spirit of Flanders.

This square, partly medieval and partly baroque, is unique. It is the Low Countries' equivalent of St. Peter's in Rome, to the Piazza San Marco in Venice, and the Place de la Concorde in Paris. It has a rich vitality and eclecticism, that is an expression of the wealth of ideas that prevails among a people that has known how to absorb every influence and make it part of itself.

By the beginning of the eighteenth century, Belgian art was coming under French influence. A number of Flemings had been to the court of Louis XIV, including such people as Vandermeulen and the Belgian assistants of Lebrun. A large number of Belgian artists participated in the work of decorating the Chateau of Versailles, and the French classical style, which was then invading Europe with its stately elegance, came into the hands of imitators and minor masters until it dominated Belgian art. It was not until the beginning of the nineteenth century, when artists such as Navez arrived in Brussels, and people realized that Belgian painting was on the point of reawakening, that a new age was near.

While the beleaguered enclave of the Spanish Lowlands—Flanders, Brabant, Hainaut, Namur, and Luxemburg—was being turned into a Catholic fortress, a bastion of the Faith, and an advanced outpost of the Counter Reformation, the country around Liége was becoming a refuge of liberty. At the beginning of the sixteenth century, the principality had been revived by the Prince-Bishop Erard de la Marck (1505–38) who, by the Peace of St. James, achieved a happy balance between the powers of government and the rights of the inhabitants. The Emperor Charles V, whose domains encircled Liége, attempted in vain to annex it, but the Liégeois had no wish to become either Belgians or Spaniards. So strong was their dislike for Spain that the principality succeeded in resisting even the Counter-Reformation. Despite all the efforts of Philip II, the inhabitants prevented the Prince-Bishop from condemning Protestants to death or confiscating their property, with the result that the immigration of refugees and exiles from the Spanish Lowlands became a source of wealth and profit.

Liége was now larger and more populous than Lyon, and it had become a unique center of metalworking, coal mining, and weapons manufacture. Its industrialists were leaders in every field. They bottled the mineral waters of Spa, starting the first export business of this kind, and greatly stimulated the glass industry. In the meantime, the Verviers cloth industry was in full swing and, with freedom of action for both the millowners and the cloth unions, was achieving considerable prosperity. The principality's inhabitants were keen advocates of the revolution in the Spanish Lowlands, gave it full moral support, and disliked Philip II and the Duke of Alba even more than the Belgians themselves did.

The spread of anti-clericalism called for the creation of a new political party known as the Grignoux. In this party, the common people rallied behind Burgomaster Sébastien La Ruelle, known as a defender of the small man and a staunch adversary of the Bishop. He became increasingly popular, rising to power in the municipal elections of 1633. Not long after, a Belgian refugee in Liége, the Count of Warfusee, sought to obtain a pardon from the Spaniards by arranging for his murder. On April 16, 1637, the Count invited La Ruelle to a banquet in his house where sixty Spanish soldiers, disguised as servants, fell upon La Ruelle and slew him with the complicity of Warfusee's fellow conspirators. Their immediate attempt to seize control of the city that night was abortive. La Ruelle had been known as the "Father of the People," and, at the news of his death, the democrats rose, made a ring around the banqueting hall, and massacred everybody they found there. The corpse of Warfusee was hanged from a gibbet head down—just as Mussolini was to be hanged in Milan three centuries later—and the Jesuit establishments were ransacked and their rector slain as the reputed originator of the crime.

The body of La Ruelle lay in state in the Cathedral of St. Lambert, and the people filed past it in silent tribute. The extremists seized power, and the Burgomaster transformed Liége into an independent republic with its own revolutionary militia, commanded by a Prostestant officer, Bartel Roland.

Ten years later, on the day of the St. Grignoux elections, a street battle developed in which 200 people were killed. Bex and Roland again seized the Burgomaster's powers, and the people stormed the Bishop's palace, killed the Chancellor, and administered their own rough justice.

After the Peace of Westphalia, in 1648, reaction triumphed. The Bishop, with the armed support of the Bavarian army, was again able to occupy the town, and Burgomasters Roland and Hennet were beheaded. Liége, however, was not beaten. Six burgomasters were executed, one after another, but the inhabitants maintained the prosperity of the principality, and by their striving and initiative remained in the vanguard of progress.

Through the seventeenth century, the thriving industries of Liége stimulated and encouraged industry outside the principality's borders, even in the Spanish Lowlands. It was thanks to Liége that mineral coal began to replace wood charcoal, and to gain the place in industry that it occupies today. About this time, the dwindling supply of fuel for the "iron mills" had become a production bottleneck. Metalworking had developed in the Ardennes and in the land between the Sambre and the Meuse Rivers, because the forests supplied essential wood fuel for the furnaces, and the rivers and watercourses provided motive power. By 1625, Liége exported metal goods all over Europe. Wood, in consequence, became increasingly expensive and, in the quest for a cheaper fuel, experiments were made with coal, which had formerly been held in contempt. The invention of drainage pumps, powered by river water, reduced the cost of mining coal, and it was soon graduated from a mere household fuel to a universal source of heat and energy.

With coal, it became possible to start soap factories, brickyards, dye works, and a number of other industries that could not have been operated profitably with wood. With prices so low, there was coal in every house. There was a radical transformation in living conditions. Window glass was mass produced, and its use was no longer limited to Venetian glass, mirrors, and candelabra.

The busy metal industry soon benefited from the increasing division of labor. The "iron merchants" organized production in successive processes, making ingots or bars in the blast-furnaces, then sheets and plates in the rolling mills, and afterward turning out such products as nails and hardware. The industrialists had a bold eye for all forms of progress, and succeeded in reducing the costs of metal goods by introducing new production methods learned in Germany and England. It became possible to make iron kettles, which were much cheaper than copper ones and soon replaced them. With the growing number of uses for iron, men in Liége devised new techniques for the manufacture of muskets and pistols, which were then sold to all the armies of Europe.

While the principality of Liége was continuing to make progress through the middle of the seventeenth century, things were different in the other provinces of the Spanish Lowlands. Bled by warfare and invasion, their spirits were sustained by the pride of the battle for faith and soul.

Where Belgium had hitherto been a stamping ground for new political and social experiments, trading activities, industrial organization, and other pursuits, the country was now cut off by the Counter-Reformation, which turned it into a closed world in the middle of northern Europe. The best it could do was develop its domestic market and try to feed itself from its own soil. The elite of its population had emigrated to Holland, its seaward outlets had been cut off, its external trade ruined, and it had to deal with the serious problem presented by a population too dense to be adequately fed by the territory within its borders. Moreover, during the first half of the seventeenth century, it had witnessed the political and commercial collapse of Germany, which had been its main market for two centuries. The Thirty Years' War had laid waste to Germany, and its population had fallen within a few years from 20 million to only 3 or 4 million.

This was a serious state of affairs for Belgium. The country's chances of survival had always been based on the fact that its agriculture was highly developed, and that it had an effective network of communication, and a considerable reserve of population that had to be organized in order to live. It now had to find a market within its own territory, and replace the foreign merchants with the peasants of the countryside and the burghers of the cities. In undertaking this task, Belgium used all the resources that science and progress had put at the disposal of mankind. Not only was the country successful, but the population, instead of declining, actually increased.

In the end, the progress of civilization always comes back to agricultural techniques, which make it possible to feed an increasing number of people. In the slow unfolding of history, the first great advance was the appearance of the "hidden crops" that utilized the time lost between two crops to increase food production. During the sixteenth and seventeenth centuries there was a considerable increase in the cultivation of root crops, such as turnips, beetroot, and potatoes. The soil around these plants has to be kept absolutely clear of weeds, a work that requires all the labor a dense population can provide. These crops also dispense with fallow land, and, since tubers are grown underground, they resist the wind, hail, and late frosts that do so much damage to cereal crops.

Continuous cultivation fed the population without resting the earth, and led to the development of crops for the cloth industry, like flax and hemp, or oil-producing plants that improved diet. Fertilized meadows made it possible for livestock to be fed from a much smaller area. These meadows were planted with lucerne, clover, or forage crops that restored nitrate to the soil, reducing the need for fertilizer and manure.

The first chemical fertilizer used during the seventeenth and eighteenth centuries was lime. It was followed by nitrates, phosphates, and potash, until it was possible to till land that could never support enough livestock to insure a supply of natural fertilizer.

It is usual to attribute the decline of the trade in the Low Countries to the closure of the Schelde by the Dutch. This is, at least in part, an illusion. After 1600, the Schelde was not closed, and the port of Antwerp continued to exist, although it traded only with the Dutch. Moreover, the Dutch themselves were always complaining that some of the goods that formerly came to Belgium by way of the Schelde, were now sent through the French port of Calais, so that they were not carried in the Dutch transport and trading fleets.

Belgium had, of course, other ports, such as Ostend, Dunkirk, and Nieuport. Although these were blockaded by Dutch warships, the privateers who lived there were able to put to sea, and they brought back rich booty from plundered enemy vessels.

Indeed, even if the Schelde had been free and open to ships of all nations, the result would have been the same. There were no merchants left in the Spanish Lowlands, and no bankers, brokers, or exchanges. The emigration of the elite of the population had been fatal to Belgian trading activities, and the country, isolated from both France and Germany, was no longer a land of trade and commerce. Business done there was of a purely local character.

Foreign traders, who had formerly made their fortunes in the great port of Antwerp, had long since disappeared, taking their connections and business experience to the north.

While Holland was setting out on the commercial conquest of the world, Belgium was now, in the words of the historian Henri Pirenne, "expending her strength in multiplying her religious orders, her charitable foundations, her monasteries and teaching institutions, or in building glowing baroque churches, while the Dutch were building merchant fleets and setting up commercial countinghouses." The closing of the Schelde, and the reduction of the great foreign trade of former years, was to spur the Belgians to renewed energy by forcing them to reorganize.

About 1590, the Spanish Lowlands were reduced to almost the same state as France after the Hundred Years' War. The country was infested by bandits, and in many towns a quarter, or even half, of the houses had disappeared. Once order was restored, the population increased so rapidly that there were soon more than 2 million inhabitants, while there were only 1.5 million in Holland.

Between 1590 and 1650, agricultural progress restored the country's fortunes. Waterways, such as the Bruges-Ostend canal and the Ypres canal, were dug or deepened, opening the whole country to the distribution of fertilizers. For the first time in Europe cultivation became intensive, and it was soon regarded as a model of technique. The Spanish Lowlands produced great quantities of cereal for export and, by intelligent and methodical work, succeeded in getting two crops a year from the same soil. In the autumn, after the grain crop had been harvested, a turnip crop was sown. There were a number of new crops, such as flax and hops, and the arable land was increased by private companies that dried out and reclaimed the *moeren*, "marshes," between Furnes and Dunkirk.

The rural population increased rapidly. In most of the towns there was a decrease, but the villages and small townships doubled or trebled their inhabitants: the population of St. Nicolas, for example, increased from 2,000 to 5,000 between 1604 and 1662. New towns grew in importance that were to survive until our own time, places such as Armentières, Roubaix, Verviers, and Tourcoing. Mass production, with small profits on a large turnover, came into being, and new industries such as printing, papermaking, and glassmaking became increasingly important.

An increase in wealth and a better standard of living accompanied the population's growth, not only in the countryside, but in towns that had come to life again like Ghent. In the Ghent of 1600, there were only three people rich enough to have a carriage—the Bishop, the Governor, and the President of the Council of Flanders. By 1662 there were more than a hundred carriages.

At the beginning of the century Ghent's population had fallen to 31,000, but by 1690 it had risen to 52,000. This resulted in a building boom that accompanied the business boom. A large number of clockmakers, mirror makers, skilled joiners, and upholsterers came to Ghent, and the buying of patents of nobility created a new social class that had its roots in the burgher population.

The first half of the seventeenth century was an age of rebirth. The trials to which the inhabitants of the Spanish Lowlands were subjected as a result of wars did not result in any fall in the standard of living, nor in any real economic decline.

The life of the Belgians during the seventeenth century was thus a mixture of unchanging customs and scientific progress, modified by external influences. The Spanish ruff was replaced, as it was elsewhere in Europe, by the fashions of France. Material civilization, under the impulse of scientific advances, continued to make progress.

Brussels' story during this century is convincing evidence of this. During the period of the archdukes, around 1617, the Rue Neuve was surrounded by meadows in which washerwomen spread out their laundry. The lower part of the town was made up of fields and gardens, and the park, at this time famous throughout Europe, was not the narrow and formal enclosure we know today. It was a sort of Luna Park, with its woods and valleys, enclosures containing exotic animals, open spaces for games, lists for jousting, fountains, and circular riding paths —in short, everything to provide pleasant diversion. The public was allowed in until 5 P.M. in winter, and in summer from 3:30 A.M. until 9 P.M. There were bonfires, folk dances, banquets, mythological processions, and, at every crossroads, rope dancers or keepers of strange animals.

Horse racing took place in the fields of Mon Plaisir where the Castle of Laeken now stands. In winter, there was skating on the ponds of Ixelles and St. Josse Ten Noode, and toboggan runs in the park at Tervueren. In summer, high society in gilded coaches could take the air in the Allée Verte or the Drève St. Anne. On Sunday, the favorite spot was the Tivoli Garden (the name is a reminder of Italy), or the Willebroek canal. People sailed at night in gondolas on the canal, while music was played in the shadows.

The great popular diversion was still the Ommegang, which particularly attracted foreigners. Shooting with longbow or crossbow was especially popular, and even reigning sovereigns were not too proud to take part in this sport. In 1615 the Archduchess Isabella skillfully shot down the stuffed bird from his high mast, and was proclaimed Queen of the Great Fraternity of Archers. On this occasion the municipality created a fund for six poor young women, who were afterwards known as the "Maids of the Sablon" and who took their places in the Whitmonday procession in robes of blue and white.

At this time, processions wound their way amid an unprecedented display of luxury. In one there were 400 Beguines, accompanied by the entire court. The Fraternity of the Rosary had no less than 30,000 members, and the Archduke and Archduchess laid the foundations of 300 churches and chapels. Painters never tired of reproducing scenes of pilgrimages or the countless religious observances—nor of the drinking scenes and the follies of the carnival, either.

Progress developed. Streets were unsafe at night, so the commune voted a subsidy of 6,000 florins to imitate Paris in hanging oil lanterns in the streets. Under the great trees of the park, amid the aviaries, the fish ponds, and the fountains, a herd of deer was allowed to wander unmolested. Superstition, however, had not lost its hold, and the Devil was imagined to be everywhere. In the days of Maximilian-Emmanuel of Bavaria, a Beguine, after an evening walk in the park, declared that she had recognized the Devil in one of the stags. So loud were her protests that public opinion was aroused, and it became necessary to slaughter all the male beasts, sparing only the hinds. While all this took place, France was nurturing the society that produced Voltaire.

Life in Brussels was still dangerous. Streets were far from safe, and the large number of vagabonds and outlaws resulted in frequent nocturnal attacks and brawls. Brawls increased so alarmingly in taverns and elsewhere, that in the end card playing was prohibited, even in private houses.

There were still wooden houses in every district, and they were continually catching fire. This was particularly true of the house in the market place known as the She Wolf, which set what must surely have been a record. Burned down once in 1640, it caught fire again in 1690, and was rebuilt the following year with the effigy of a Phoenix on its facade bearing the inscription. "Though I was burned, yet I rise even more glorious." It was again destroyed by fire in 1695, and again rebuilt. This time the motto read, "Marvel at my third rebirth from my own ashes." The authorities finally grew tired of seeing this wooden city in flames, and they prohibited all but stone buildings.

A famous quip described Brussels as the "inn for exiled princes." One of its temporary guests was the Prince of Condé who, when he returned to Paris, took back the first windowed carriage that had ever been seen in France. Other illustrious visitors included Queen Marie de Médicis, when she was exiled by Richelieu; Gaston d'Orléans, brother of Louis XIII; the Duke of Bouillon; the Duke of Vendôme; Queen Christina of Sweden; Emmanuel of Portugal; Duke Charles IV of Lorraine; and the exiled Stuart kings of England.

Between the beginning and the end of the century there was a great change in manners and customs. Court life, which at the outset had been strict and straight-laced, was transformed under the influence of the Elector Maximilian of Bavaria, who was a great admirer of the court of Louis XIV. Soon there were as many theaters as there were in Paris. The first was the Jeu de Paume in the Fossé-aux-Loups, then the Montagne St. Elizabeth, open from 1660 until the end of the century and famous for the drinks and comfits that were served the spectators.

The great luxury of the period was the mirror. Every house, it seemed, required many mirrors and much glass, and the cost was often as great as that of the tiles and timber of the roofs.

In the houses of the great, gastronomy flourished. Iced fruit juices, or sherbets, began to be served; ice chests were made for preserving the ice cut in winter from the surface of ponds, with the evaporation so controlled as to keep the temperature around 32° F. Jam, which it had become possible to make with the increased availability of sugar, was made in increasing variety, and many sauces date from this period, such as sauce Béchamel, devised in Paris by the financier of that name. These refinements did not seep down to the burghers or the working classes, however. In most houses there was not even an oven, and cook books suggest that meat was always cooked either on the spit or in the pot. Most of the dishes we eat today, including cakes and pastry, were impossible to make in those days for lack of suitable ingredients. Sauces using spice, pepper, vinegar, and condiments formed the basis of cooking, and are still quite important.

It was not until the end of the century that the art of good cuisine was common. It reached its peak at the beginning of the nineteenth century, under the Empire. Italian cooking, which at this time was the only kind worthy of the name, was founded on a large number of entirely different dishes, rather than on quality and refinement of taste. Bread dipped in soup was still the most important element of the diet. Up to this time, the only wines drunk were those from Bordeaux and the Loire. The wines of Burgundy were either unknown or considered poor. Even in France, they were only discovered during the reign of Louis XIV.

Another innovation was the first attempt to organize transport. Early in the seventeenth century a regular service of stage-coaches and post-chaises was set up, with routes going in all directions. The large provincial cities were the first to be served, and passengers from Brussels by the "public carriages" began their journeys from inns in the neighborhood of the old grain market. It was not long before Belgium had organized services that linked it with most important foreign cities, particularly Paris. Coaches always stopped at night, and in the early days the Paris-Brussels journey took three days in summer and four days in winter. Another development was the postal service. After 1632, letters could be mailed at the Place du Sablon.

By this time, all the town houses had glazed windows, and a new method of heating, to replace the open grate and log fires of the Middle Ages, was needed. The Germans soon invented an extremely efficient closed stove. Public baths had fallen into disuse, and the baths in private houses—wooden tubs covered by a cloth canopy—were only used by invalids, because of the number of people required to serve and assist the bather. A device known as a fountain was installed in most houses. This consisted of a tank, usually copper, with a tap and a basin below. The water could be used both for drinking and for washing. In some of the princely houses, the tanks had capacities of as much as twenty-five gallons, and certain servants did nothing but carry water to keep them full.

Dining, in most houses, was a graceless affair. There was no dining room as such. A table was set up in a corridor, or an antechamber, and was removed as soon as the repast was done.

The Elector of Bavaria gave court galas and had the fashionable Italian operas of the time played in a musical academy built in 1682, in the fields around the Grand Beguinage. This academy was renamed several times, and was finally moved to the old Mint building, which had been bought by an impresario after the 1695 bombardment. The building was completely reconstructed three times, before becoming the Théâtre Royal de la Monnaie, with the classical columns that we know today. The taste for theater going was so great that a hotel, the Auberge de Coffy in the Grand Place, was turned into a theater on days when the others were closed.

In 1695, the Governor, Maximilian Emmanuel, used rain water to increase the number of public fountains, among them the Blue Fountain, nowadays also known as *le Cracheur* ("the Spitter"). Another fountain, the Milkmaid, sculptured by Marc de Vose, was surmounted by a pump intended to provide a public supply of water, like the Samaritaine in Paris.

The citizens of the Spanish Low Countries enjoyed a number of rights and freedoms that, in many cases, contrasted with the arbitrary powers exercised in other European countries. Nobody, not even a foreigner, could be arrested without a judicial warrant. When Marie de Médicis sought to exercise her royal prerogative as Queen of France by imprisoning one of her officers, the Estates of Brabant interfered at once and had him released.

The central government itself, moreover, would have had difficulty arresting anybody, for it had no police. The only police there were came under the orders of local authorities, who were Belgians, and, in practice, the real government of the country. The central government was forever coming into conflict with the provincial Estates, without whose consent no tax could be levied. Any such tax had to be granted by a unanimous vote and a single deputy could veto the whole procedure. The best the central government could do was to secure a stipulated annual tax of about 3.3 million florins.

Even so, the forms of popular liberty had to be observed, so each year the government demanded a higher grant and eventually agreed to come down to the traditional figure, and that was the end of the matter. If it became absolutely necessary to obtain the grant of a special tax, it was done by negotiation. In the event of refusal, the government used the only power it had—quartering troops in the recalcitrant city. These troops were housed by the inhabitants and their maintenance financed locally.

This was enough to keep opposition within reasonable bounds. In 1680, however, Brussels greeted the demand for an extremely small tax with the declaration that "they would let their hearts be torn from them, rather than another sou."

The populace lived almost wholly within the shelter of the city walls, for Belgium was constantly being invaded, and the Belgians endured the life of a besieged people. They passed their time building and rebuilding fortifications, and, in the country, incursions of foreign troops, with their levies of war taxes, became the normal state of things. For half a century Dutch troops were able to march freely across all northern Flanders between the Schelde and the North Sea, and to levy taxes that the inhabitants were obliged to pay. This part of the country came to be called the "land of contribution."

All the great cities except Antwerp were besieged or captured. Brussels was destroyed by the 1695 bombardment, Namur was captured and recaptured several times, Ghent was seized, and Charleroi, Ypres, Tournai, and Luxemburg were annexed. Although the great cities were not pillaged, the inhabitants were nonetheless affected by the systematic burning of the surrounding villages, which was done to bring the burghers to their knees.

The Peace of Westphalia, in 1648, freed France from any fear of Germany, and she accordingly prepared to attack the Low Countries. This made it necessary to fortify Brussels, and the defense work called for new taxes, including the "leg of mutton tax" on beer that aroused violent popular reaction. Warfare continued without respite for half a century, creating a state of tension that was constantly accentuated by the attacks that were made and repulsed, by urgent defense measures, and by the periodic spreading of false news.

Brussels was continually threatened. In 1673, Louis XIV came in person at the head of his army to examine the ramparts. In 1677, an attempt was made to blockade the city with a force of 10,000 men under the command of the Marshal of Luxemburg, but this army eventually withdrew. Seven years later another attempt was made by the Marshal of Boufflers. This failed, but not before houses had been destroyed by fire in Ixelles and Koekelberg.

Belgium's trials stemmed largely from the fact that Europe was divided in two, and the Low Countries were exactly on the geographical dividing line. On the northern side were the Protestant states—England, Holland, Westphalia, and Baltic Germany—and on the south, the Catholic world, fringing the Mediterranean. Belgium, although situated at the extreme northern end of Europe, became a second Spain. In the great rift that split Christian society, she identified herself with the southern countries and the militant Counter Reformation.

Seventeenth-century Belgian civilization was thus introverted; it stood for autonomous cities and provinces, and the other forms and institutions of the sixteenth or even fifteenth century. This framework had been made obsolete by events, and had no useful place in the world that was now taking shape. The requirements of human activity could no longer be met by city privileges, municipal government, and the concentration of trade in ports such as Antwerp and Bruges. This was the age of colonial expansion and of great states with centralized administrations. By these means, resources were increased, and the static world of the Low Countries faced the dynamic opposition of the France of Louis XIV that was to triumph through the influence of such men as Jean Baptiste Colbert and the Marquis de Louvois.

The inhabitants of the Low Countries were too firmly rooted in the past, and too busy maintaining their local privileges and the municipal systems in which they were embodied. They opposed administrative revision and the advanced forms of political action that found favor in the French Revolution.

To function as it had done in the Middle Ages, a great town or commune now had to spread its sphere of influence throughout a nation. Indeed, this was what happened in England, where the parliamentary system permitted London to dominate the whole country. The same phenomenon was largely responsible for the growth of Holland, where Amsterdam maintained a central control of the wealth of the United Provinces, which were under a common government.

In the sixteenth century, a port such as Antwerp was already an exception and an anomaly. It existed only because Antwerp had assumed an international character. In the seventeenth century the advances of science and the growing administration, coupled with an increasing centralization of culture, made the France of Louis XIV a mirror of the future that awaited great nations.

In the Low Countries this was clearly understood by men such as the Count of Bergeyck, who went over to Louis XIV, not to betray his compatriots, but to assure their future greatness. Their efforts failed in the face of resistance from the Belgian population, which would not give up established habits. They preferred to cling to their customary privileges and local rights that stifled initiative and action, and became a sort of static ideal, a stagnant form of life. The country's energy was expended for purely defensive purposes—to maintain the status quo, and to make the strongest resistance possible against invasion, the bombardment of cities, and demands for war contributions.

Only through new forms of organization could institutions formerly aimed at preserving the people's freedom of action serve the world that was to come. The earlier economic and political system of Antwerp and Flanders did not serve to unify the Low Countries, as France and England had been unified.

On the military side, too, it is striking how energetically, but ineffectively, Belgians defended their cities. They fought on the ramparts, they rebuilt with unremitting zeal houses that had been destroyed by fire, and they refused to surrender under threat of bombardment. They were, however, incapable of dealing with the root of a problem that was beyond their comprehension. What was needed was a complete reorganization of trade, industry, and administration, but Belgium's fidelity to the past did not permit it.

In 1667, Louis XIV claimed "the Queen's Rights," appeared before the walls of Tournai, and captured the city after a siege of three days. The feelings of the population were mixed. The women, in particular, found the handsome young King very attractive, especially when he rode his magnificent horse. "There goes the good-looking ruffian!" cried the Countess of Sainte-Aldegonde, a lady of the pro-Spanish nobility.

The Sun King did everything in his power to dazzle the people, making repeated state visits to the cities he had captured. In 1670, he returned to Tournai with his whole court, and the inhabitants had the privilege of seeing the "three queens"—the true queen, Marie-Thérèse, and the King's two mistresses, the Duchesse de La Vallière and the Marquise de Montespan. In 1686, he reappeared with the ambassadors who had been sent from Siam, the farthest corner of Asia, to do him homage. This policy of showmanship was successful in making the inhabitants forget the inconveniences of having been conquered, not least of which was the crushing level of taxation.

During the wars of Louis XIV, the fortress of Namur rose to European fame. It was besieged with a display of power and magnificence that astonished the whole world. The whole court of Versailles moved into the neighborhood. Among those present was Jean Racine, a historiographer of France, who was taking his duties very seriously. The Duke of Saint-Simon, the writer of the *Mémoires*, had found lodgings at Malonne; Madame de Maintenon was at Dinant; and Louis XIV himself was at Marlagne.

The capital was alive with enthusiasm. Nicolas Boileau was sharpening his quill and the military painters were busily cleaning their brushes. Many topical songs gained currency, some of them full of irony, others popular and affectionate:

> Hello Namur, with your castle grand,
> Beauty so rare on every hand,
> Delightful town I salute you now,
> I'd like you among my subjects to be,
> Surrender, Namur, surrender to me.

The unhappy factor in the siege was the rainfall that covered the brilliant uniforms of the guards and musketeers with heavy mud. The King's house, too, was swimming in mud, and this earned him many a quip from the Parisians.

The Italian comedy shows, which corresponded to our revues, poked their own form of fun at the French:

ISABELLA (to HARLEQUIN): Were you at Namur?

HARLEQUIN: Was I at Namur? My goodness, yes. Of course I was there. Look, I've got mud all over me.

ISABELLA (*sarcastically*): And what, sir, did you do in the army?

HARLEQUIN: Serve in the army! What d'you take me for? I was *commander in chief* of the wheelbarrow detachment that carted away the camp mud.

The bombardment and destruction of Brussels, on the other hand, was one of the great disasters of the century. In August, 1695, the Duke of Villeroi, Marshal of France, had orders to march on the city with a force of 70,000 men. He took up his position on the heights of Molenbeek and bombarded the city for thirty-six hours, with eighteen heavy siege cannon and twenty-five mortars. He hoped the population would revolt and force the Governor to surrender. The bombardment began on August 13, at four o'clock in the afternoon.

The effects were catastrophic. The town hall caught fire, and in it were burned tapestries, jewels, and paintings by Roger van der Weyden. The cloth hall was destroyed, as were the Maison du Roi ("King's Bread-House") in the market place, a great number of important private houses, such as those of the Aerschot, Arenberg, and de Bergeyck families, and the churches of Notre Dame, St. Nicolas, St. Anne, and that jewel of the Middle Ages, the Madeleine. The fire demolished sixteen churches and convents, and no less than 3,820 houses.

For a time, the stricken population slept in tents erected in the

Brussels park. Reconstruction, however, was undertaken with great energy. Speculation was prevented by strict price control. The work of clearing the streets of rubble was begun, but the disaster was so great that it took a full year. Public services were disorganized by the destruction of their records, but the city administration did not for a moment flag in its task.

The possibility of a rent racket was checked by fixing rents at the average level of the three previous years. Large-scale hewing of timber was organized in the Forest of Soignes, and decrees were issued fixing the prices of building materials. The energy with which reconstruction was carried out earned Europe's admiration. The city, far from being destroyed, emerged even more beautiful, since the construction of wooden buildings was prohibited. The Elector of Bavaria supervised the reconstruction and made it a masterpiece of town planning. In the marketplace the new houses of the corporations became marvels of Flemish architecture.

Damage resulting from the burning of Brussels, however, turned out to be only temporary and superficial. The 3,000 dwellings destroyed by fire would have disappeared sooner or later in ordinary fires, so that the capital loss resulting from the bombardment was thus comparatively minor. The energy of reconstruction surpassed the energy of destruction, as in 1914, after the University of Louvain was burned. The moral effect of the incident attracted immense sympathy for the victims, and Brussels' resistance was stiffened.

There is a story that the artillery on the walls ran short of cannon balls and used paving blocks from the streets as a substitute when the city was again attacked in 1708. This time the Elector of Bavaria, who had defended it in 1695, and rebuilt it in the following years, had gone over to the French. Nine successive attacks failed to gain their objective in the face of the determined resistance put up by the people of Brussels.

Namur, too, was bombarded a few years later by the Dutch, who were attempting to induce the people to revolt and force the surrender of the city. But the inhabitants, in their wrath, preferred fire to surrender, and organized bucket brigades to deal with the burning buildings. In the end, the fires were brought under control and the wooden houses were eventually rebuilt of stone. As had been the case with Brussels, the attempt to destroy the city resulted merely in sharpening its resistance, and making it more beautiful.

Throughout the century foreign troops ravaged Belgian territory. The Spaniards could no longer defend it, and the seventeenth century became known as the "century of misfortune." It would be natural to expect that depredations of this sort would have destroyed Belgium, and that their constant repetition would have made recovery impossible. Destruction wrought by armed bands, however, does not have any lasting effect upon a country whose strength lies in agriculture, as it did in the Low Countries. The Flemish countryside, as ravaged as it was, retained it productivity. The crop yields were higher than those of France, and after each war it was easy enough to restore the productive capacity of the soil.

The large number of towns, and the wealth and abundance of means of communication, made it possible to repair the damage quickly. Teniers' famous pictures of festivals show the peasants bursting with health and devouring great quantities of food against a background of war. The authorities vainly attempted to keep the duration of these festivals down to forty-eight hours, but even in the worst periods of foreign invasion they often continued for a whole week.

Moreover, the Belgian peasant was not a small landholder as he was in France. He was rather a tenant farmer or share cropper, paying for his tenure by surrendering a portion of the produce. When his farm burned down, it was incumbent upon his landlord to lend him the money needed for putting it back into working order if he wanted to collect his rent.

When there was an increase in the damage by soldiery, cultivation was limited to what was strictly necessary. Agriculture thus continued in low gear, but there was no impairment of its productive force. The result was that the losses had no lasting effect, and Belgium was able to weather the seventeenth century without even a serious decline in population.

By the end of the eighteenth century, Belgium had changed. This was not because of the wars, nor because of the poverty and lower standard of living that accompanied them. It was because the country was isolated from the main currents of European civilization.

Until the middle of the seventeenth century the country's intellectual life had been intense. The spirit of curiosity and inquiry had been kept alive by the Jesuits. Jansenism, a doctrine put forward by Cornelius Jansen, Bishop of Ypres, whose ideas spread over Europe, originated in Flanders. And the University of Louvain, the scene of passionate attacks on and defenses of the ideas of Descartes, became a great center for their propagation.

Little by little, however, things changed and the country sank into apathy. Seventeenth-century Belgium had still been carried along by mystical and religious impulses that had made it feel it was living in a state of moral and spiritual exaltation, far removed from the need for temporal power. The Belgium of the eighteenth century, on the other hand, was ossified. Habits, attitudes, and customs had become static.

The Spanish Low Countries, at the beginning of the eighteenth century, were the most astonishing example of a vitrified, stagnant country that had been seen since the days of the decline and fall of the Roman Empire. The picture is not unlike a modern novel with its robots, automatism, brain-washing, and total absence of freedom and initiative. People were born students, deputies in the provincial Estates, or even doctors of the University of Louvain. Courses and examinations were no longer anything more than a formality, for the candidate always passed and the very ideas under discussion were scrupulously unchanging. The student had nothing more to do than conform to the opinions it was obligatory to hold.

In the university courses, students were no longer taught the arguments for and against any question, nor were they taught the arguments against orthodoxy. It did not matter that they were thus unable to reply to the arguments that might be used against them since, in fact, these arguments never would be used. Preparation for examinations consisted of memorizing lists of questions and answers prepared in advance. The student who had most assiduously learned by heart what was known as the "primus" would solemnly be granted the highest honors, and later welcomed back to his native town in a triumphal procession.

The unlucky student whose memory was bad could make up for it from the contents of his purse. The dues for diplomas and doctorates amounted to 31,000 florins, and there is no case of a student who had put up this money failing his examinations. The only annoying rule was one that obliged students to take courses for a given number of years before receiving their degrees. However, this was no problem for wealthy students. Their parents entered them in the university while they were still children, and as soon as they reached the regulation age, they presented themselves for the examination, which was no more than a routine formality.

Henri Pirenne has given a picture of this conservative state of mind that will serve as an example:

"Every form of novelty seemed fraught with peril. True wisdom consisted in holding on to what one already possessed, and making the best of the situation in which one was vegetating. Every individual and every town had isolated itself—one might almost say rolled itself up into a ball—in the narrow domain of its immediate interests. And the greater the mediocrity of its interests, the more ardently it defended them. The towns of Brabant, for example, protested against the idea of entrusting a company with the work of deepening the river Demer, and giving it in return the monopoly of the navigation of the river. The Estates of Flanders refused to equip convoy vessels for the company, but since they still received an income from the convoy rights, for which they had refused to accept the responsibilities, they opposed the idea that the company should provide its own equipment."

One of the most entertaining incidents in the life of the University of Louvain, in the seventeenth century, was that surrounding the creation of a professorship of public law. In 1723, the Estates of Brabant came quite suddenly to the conclusion ("through lack of reflection," stated a contemporary) that there was no such chair at Louvain, although all other universities had one. It was necessary, therefore, that such a chair be set up, but at this point the theologians became anxious. The chief object of a faculty of public law, they said, is to study the rights of the state, and it often happens that these run counter to the rights of the Church. It would be far better if problems of this kind were not brought to the attention of students who might thereby be troubled. Still worse, these same students might be led to think for themselves and even to become conscious of heretical arguments. It was unfortunately too late to abolish the chair altogether, so the authorities waited until its occupant was dead and appointed no successor.

The Church adopted the same attitude. It had no interest in defending Christian doctrine by refuting the arguments of its opponents. It preferred to pass over their opinions in complete silence. It had a monopoly on teaching, and the students, since they were not allowed to learn anything elsewhere, lost all curiosity and came to regard their studies as a simple chore.

The University of Louvain no longer had any credit for the purchase of books. They were considered unnecessary. All that really mattered was that the professors and students be well housed. The Estates of Brabant had paid an enormous sum to build a magnificent library, which was to be destroyed by German troops in 1914. At this time, however, neither the works of Sir Isaac Newton nor those of Gottfried von Leibnitz were to be found there, for they were theologically suspect. There was no botanical garden, no dissecting room, and no laboratory. Neither the professor of Hebrew nor the professor of Greek could understand the language he was appointed to instruct; his sole function was to read and comment upon the instruction manuals.

Everything was subject to rule, even the private life of the population. Funerals and mourning, for example, were governed by law, and nobody in this period was allowed even to dress as he wished. Unduly long mourning had already been prohibited by a decree of 1696. In 1720, mourning was limited to six months, and the nephews and grandchildren of the deceased were forbidden to take part in it. For those in mourning, only their coats might be dyed black, but this license did not extend to the rest of the clothing, and any transgression was subject to a fine.

It was a frozen world in which everyone was a specialist in his own job. The son of a clockmaker had to become a clockmaker, and the son of a judge could seek no career except the bench. The year was divided into a countless succession of festivals in which no one dared refuse to participate. At Ghent, the annual kermesse ("festival") lasted a week, and it was the duty of every artisan to keep his workshop closed during this period. However, as there were seven or eight churches in the town, there were seven or eight successive festivals, and the result was that the workers starved.

The municipal offices were shared among the upper-class burghers, and, in the towns, the smaller burghers were grouped in corporations with oppressive and strict rules. In the country the lives of the tenant farmers, the share croppers, and the few small landholders were also strictly regulated and static. The corporation artisans, stubborn and fanatically conservative, opposed all new industries and processes for the sake of carrying out their routine tasks like robots, without the least change. This, they said, was a right accruing to them either through the Joyous Entry or through the city constitution.

In the monasteries, once so active and full of life, all study and research had ceased. It would, in fact, have served no purpose, for primary education was suffering from hardening of the arteries. In Flanders only three per cent of the population could read and write, while on the Dutch side of the border, every peasant "owned a little library."

It was no longer possible to require educational qualifications for bailiffs, civil servants, or officers of the court, for the posts could not have been filled. Offices, such as those of abbot or superior of a convent, and appointments to the bench, or to the local or provincial offices, had become hereditary. The holders of such offices were born for their work, and discharged it without introducing anything new from the time they took over until the time they died.

The same applied to literature. People no longer read. The number of publishers was negligible, and one of them stated in 1718 that people were hesitant about buying books for fear of being suspected of Jansenism. So dangerous was thought considered that, in 1736, the aldermen of Mons prohibited the sale of Montesquieu's *Persian Letters*.

When Jean-Baptiste Rousseau took refuge in Brussels during his exile, nobody cared that he was the greatest French poet of his time and his presence went unnoticed. Voltaire, too, passed through the city and referred to it ironically as "the abode of ignorance" and the "imagination extinguisher." The Prince de Ligne took the view that people found to be too full of wisdom should be sent to Brussels for their punishment. Only a few of the great noblemen, who stood above the general body of the nation—such men as Voltaire's friend, the Duke of Arenberg—were interested in what was going on elsewhere, and read the books they obtained from Paris.

Life went on under a regime of supervised residence that we would find inconceivable today. People were not free to move from house to house or to another town. When a peasant desired to leave his native village, it was necessary for the inhabitants to accept collective responsibility for him, in case he fell into destitution.

There was no longer any freedom, even for the workingman. It was not possible to leave one's job without obtaining permission from the public authorities, nor to take a new job without producing the previous employer's notice of termination. The only exceptions to these rules were in favor of the nomadic working population that received only starvation wages and was economically unimportant. Later, when Napoleon instituted a workbook forbidding the workman to leave his factory, and forcing him to spend his whole life under supervision, he was only re-enacting legislation that had existed everywhere before the revolution.

Life expectancy was short. The Pachéco Hospice, which then stood on the present site of St. John's Hospital on the Boulevard Botanique, was open to all women of fifty and over. At this age people were considered old, and among the working class such an age was only rarely attained. In any case, it was not a working age, for by that time infirmity had made all activity difficult.

Hospital conditions were alarming. In Brussels the sick had to lie two or more in a bed. Official reports indicate that new hospital patients, instead of being cured, nearly always became more ill than before because they picked up infections from their bedfellows. It was quite common for a new arrival to be put in the same bed with a typhoid case because there was no other bed for him, or a smallpox victim to share a bed with a scarlet-fever patient.

Space was limited, and beds were lined up end to end, the head of each against the foot of the next, so that it was impossible to go all around a bed, making adequate medical attention impossible. Anyone who died was left in bed with his living fellow patient for twenty-four hours, because the nuns who ran the hospital did not like removing corpses more than once a day. Scenes of hospital life were not unlike those seen more recently in concentration camps.

The same nuns, despite doctors' complaints, refused to hold autopsies to determine the causes of death or to recognize epidemics and nip them in the bud.

Even among people of culture, religion was interspersed with superstition. In 1754, a Londerzeel doctor, an educated man living close to Brussels, delivered to two of his patients, François van Bevere and Jeanne-Marie de Pauw, a certificate to the effect that they had been "bewitched" and stood in need, not of the attentions of medical science, but of the prayers of the Church.

Among the prejudices of the time must be listed the unanimous faith of the population. How could any people, a quarter of whom were beggars, vagabonds, and bandits left by the Church and the governing classes to grope their way in poverty and ignorance, practice any real form of religion?

In 1779, Bishop Wellens of Antwerp wrote:

"When these people are at the point of death, it often happens that the priest called to their bedside has to explain to them that God indeed exists. Their life is to be likened to a succession of sins—oaths, quarrels, blasphemy, drunkenness, obscenity, and the rest."

The Abbot de Pradt, who later became Archbishop of Mechlin, depicted the Belgians at the century's end in terms that show no trace of humor or irony:

"This is a natively moral people. It could be said of them that virtue is in their blood, and indeed that it comes to seek them rather than the reverse. They are creatures of habit, and day succeeds day in an atmosphere of undisturbed peacefulness. The good fortune of the people is its calmness, and life is lived in a straight line. Its affections have no emotion, and its pleasures no movement. Its spirit, indeed, has little brilliance; and it may justly be said that it makes greater use of its moral sense than of its intellectual faculties."

Voltaire had a wittier comment to make in the madrigal he sang to the fair Emily, Marquise du Châtelet:

> In this sad town wherein I stay,
> Ignorance, torpidity,
> And boredom hold their lasting sway,
> With unconcerned stupidity;
> A land where old obedience sits,
> Well filled with faith, devoid of wits.

Ironically he adds:

> Verses writ in gallant hand
> Can find no outlet in this land.

The Belgians, however, have long since forgiven him for his jibe.

Political life, nevertheless, continued. By the Peace of Utrecht, in 1713, the Spanish Low Countries came under the sovereignty of Austria, which brought them under the rule of the German branch of the House of Hapsburg, although this changed nothing for the Belgians. Emperor Charles VI was the legitimate heir of the kings of Spain and he became sovereign of the Low Countries. He continued to govern in the Castilian manner and re-established most of the institutions of the Spanish regime, including the State Council, Privy Council, and Finance Council. The only difference was that the Supreme Council for the Low Countries, the official organ of government, was now set up in Vienna instead of in Madrid.

However, when Austrian officials came to take charge of the administration in the Low Countries they were astonished at the Belgians' fault-finding attitude. Accustomed to the absolute government of Vienna, they understood nothing of the republican feelings of the Belgian population. In cafés, coaches, and public places, they noticed with consternation that "alike the people of the lower orders, and people of quality, civil servants, and magistrates" talked of "their august sovereign, the Emperor Charles VI, as though they were speaking only of a drummer boy."

A delegation from the Estates of Flanders and Brabant went to Vienna to see the Emperor and addressed him in somewhat haughty terms. They told him that the Treaty of the Barrier and all the acts of the administration were null and void because they had refused their legal consent. The Emperor was so astonished by their language that he made no protest. He showered fair phrases upon the delegates, although he had fully decided to ignore them, since the country was in such a state of disorder that no one could suggest an effective method of administration.

The Marquis de Prié, who was put in charge of the administration, was not an Austrian, but a Savoyard whose mother tongue was French. There was nothing of the dictator or the man of iron in him, as his earlier career had been in diplomacy, where he had earned fame for his conciliatory gifts. In private, he thought the Belgians right to vote against him. He considered Anneessens to have acted in good faith, and during the first disorders may have shown too many signs of weakness.

Emperor Charles VI had hardly taken possession of the Low Countries when he was faced with an insurrection among the Brussels guilds. The members had been stirred up by the publication of a number of ancient charters recording the rights of the inhabitants of Brussels. These had been discovered in a cellar under an old building, the Blue

Tower, which had been destroyed by the Villeroy bombardment of the capital.

Around this time the war, the state of siege, the military occupation, and the resulting poverty had brought crowds of vagabonds and unemployed into the streets of the great towns. This insubordinate element was all too ready to rise in revolt when the guilds led the way, particularly since the Marquis de Prié had no police force at his command.

In Brussels, the maintenance of order and the supervision of the ramparts was in the hands of the burghers' guard, which was violently hostile to the Austrian officials and to the authorities. In 1717, one of the sentries recognized the son of the Marquis de Prié, challenged him, and did not hesitate to shoot. By a lucky chance a corporal knocked the rifle aside and the bullet missed its mark. On another occasion, the burghers' guard stopped a carriage in which another of the Marquis' sons was riding and covered him with their rifles. The Marquis' protests were to no avail. He did not even have the power to arrest a rioter, for existing privileges reserved this right to the regular courts that consisted of Belgians.

Riots broke out in Antwerp and at Mechlin. The people of Brussels stormed the Chancellery and attempted to assassinate the first Dean who had taken the oath of allegiance. As a result, the capital had to be abandoned to the insurgents until troops arrived and restored order.

The Marquis de Prié was obliged to find somebody of whom he could make an example, for the affair had become a question of principle: the guilds had claimed the right to resist the government and disobey its regulations. Fifty guild deans were allowed to escape, and only a few subsidiary troublemakers were arrested, among them Frans Anneessens, Dean of the guild of stone-cutters, masons, sculptors, and slate-workers. He was brought before a court composed of Belgians, and condemned to death. Anneessens had, in fact, acted imprudently, for he had spoken in public approving the actions of the looters and incendiaries, and threatening the government to answer them "with powder and shot."

His execution produced great public demonstrations. The executioner wept and asked the condemned man's forgiveness, and the clergy had all the church bells rung.

The Marquis de Prié was nevertheless accused of undue weakness, and was himself ordered prosecuted for betrayal of his trust, but death saved him just in time. The Emperor replaced him with his own sister, the Archduchess Elizabeth, an old maid of forty-five. She was learned to the point of pedantry, had a speaking knowledge of Latin, and never went out unless accompanied by a Jesuit. Her two manias were piety and etiquette. She kept the aristocracy in check, forbade great ladies of the court to sit in her presence, and would not allow them to go visiting in a coach-and-six.

On Holy Thursday, she herself washed the feet of the poor, but she refused to touch a man and insisted accordingly that the poor should all be females. Even at table, she did not allow herself to be served by male servants—only ladies of the nobility were allowed to approach her. She took her meals alone, not even inviting princely visitors to dine with her. On the other hand, she never missed a pilgrimage or a procession, and in due time she made the court "yet another convent."

The comic event of the "reign" of Marie Elizabeth was the burning of her residence, the old Coudenberg Palace, caused in the middle of the night by the carelessness of the cooks, who were making jam. She was rescued just in time by a stout pikeman of the guard who carried her off in his arms. This was indeed a disagreeable situation for an old maid who had earnestly desired never to be approached by a man. The story goes that she had her rescuer punished for lèse majesté.

When Charles VI died in 1740, his successor was his daughter, the Empress Maria-Theresa, who was to become enormously popular in Belgium.

Marie Elizabeth had by now been replaced as governor by the easy-going Charles of Lorraine, a great lover of carillon clocks and pretty women, who delighted the Belgians by his idiot-king manner. Work and solitude were equally intolerable to him, and he was accordingly at home to everybody. His kindly familiarity endeared him to the Belgian nobility, who were at that time, in common with the rest of Europe, opening their minds to the new French ideas. Among them was one great writer, the Prince de Ligne. Charles of Lorraine cared little for spiritual matters. Hunting was a sufficient outlet, and it was said that, in 1780, he killed the last stag in the Forest of Soignes. It is certain that on December 23, 1762, his bag consisted of forty-one boar, sixty-three hind, nineteen stags, six roebuck, and a wolf.

This is no doubt what the Prince de Ligne admired when he spoke of the charm of the drinking, eating, hunting libertine court that Charles of Lorraine held at the Chateau at Tervuren. He was a weak governor, but his regime was distinguished because absolutely nothing happened, with the result that his contemporaries looked back on this period as a golden age. In 1775, while he was still alive, the Estates of Brabant erected a statue to him.

The only invasion during the eighteenth century was that of Fontenoy, where the famous words were spoken: "Gentlemen of England, pray be the first to shoot." The hero of this war was the Manikin Pis.

In 1742, the English, who had landed at Ostend to help the Belgians, had carried off the little statue that Duquesnoy, full of irony, had sculptured in 1619, to decorate one of the Brussels fountains. The English claimed that they were preventing the French from getting the statue, but it was successfully taken from them at Grammont. The French soldiers were so pleased with the statue that they sent it to Paris as a trophy. The people of Brussels took the matter up with Louis XV, who graciously consented to deal with the matter in person, and the Manikin was courteously restored to its accustomed place. By way of reparation, the King presented it with a French court uniform in gold brocade. The cross of Louis XV and a three-cornered hat is still in its large collection of uniforms.

About the middle of the eighteenth century, Brussels still had only about 50,000 inhabitants, or less than the city of Liége. Its center remained the magnificent market place which, with the Théâtre de la Monnaie, built by Maximilian Emmanuel, gave it the air of a capital city.

The Rue Neuve was then called the Longue Rue Neuve. It was a rich residential road, and its church, Notre-Dame du Finistère, as well as the neighboring church in the Fossé-aux-Loups, was very well attended. The monks who served the latter church bestowed the name of their saint on a sugary biscuit they manufactured. This pastry, half cake and half confectionery, is now known in Brussels as *pain à la Grecque,* but this is a corruption of the original name *wolvengracht,* the Dutch for Fossé-aux-Loups.

High society still took the air in the Allée Verte. Coudenberg Palace had not been rebuilt, but a new residential neighborhood was springing up around the Place de Bavière. In the town itself, a number of rights and customs had survived from the Middle Ages. Borgendael, with the thirty houses around it, formed an enclave enjoying legal independence and the right of asylum. Bankrupts could not be prosecuted there, and any of the crafts might be practiced without the craftsman's enrolling himself in one of the corporations.

Parish church bells rang every hour of the day, and the baker, when his bread came from the oven, blew a trumpet call to advise his clients that they might now come and buy. The dockers of the canal port, like the porters of the Paris market, had the exclusive right to carry packages and, like their French counterparts, they protected themselves, not with a big hat, but with a sack or cape thrown over their shoulders. This led to their being nicknamed the *capons du rivage.*

As in the previous century, women went to morning mass in the hooded Brabançonne mantle, a garment that continued to exist up until the nineteenth century under the name of *faille.* In the evenings men met in the neighboring taverns to play a friendly game of cards until curfew. A fair example of the life of the rich in this period is shown by the important burgher and high official, President Nény.

While sitting in an armchair upholstered in flowered silk, he could contemplate on the red walls of his office a picture showing Jupiter transformed into a swan, a portrait of the Empress Maria-Theresa, and prints of the works of Rubens and Van Dyck. He also had various scientific instruments, such as thermometers and barometers, and a glass case containing small sculptures and various knick-knacks.

His kitchen was more interesting, for it contained twenty-nine saucepans of red and yellow copper. In his stables were four carriages, indispensable as a means of transport, and six horses. Two of the carriages were berlins, one with brougham seating and the other vis-à-vis.

His country house near Vilvorde was on the banks of the canal where he could watch the barges go by. His household crockery was of Luxemburg faïence, and in his garden, in the fashion of the time, was a little temple with plaster statues and a hermitage. Because the master of the house was fond of good eating, he persuaded friends to send him game, choice fruits, and vegetables out of season. From the Abbey of St. Hubert he received "the honey of young bees, more delicate than that of the old."

He did his work, quill in hand, almost entirely with documents and files, for by now paperwork had replaced man to man dealings. The pattern of his life was the same as that of the eighteenth-century French. Everything now came from Paris—fashion, art, architecture, or ideas. The new architecture invading Belgium produced public buildings in neoclassical style with Greek façades with Doric or Corinthian columns.

Most Belgian artists entered the schools of France and made their careers there. It was to Paris that a musician such as André Grétry of Liége went in quest of glory. Under Louis XV a whole crowd of Belgians took part in the work of Versailles, just as they did under Louis XIV, so that it is quite fair to say that the Palace of Versailles is partly Belgian. The Low Countries themselves were now dotted with churches, statues, and mansions in the style of Louis XV. There was no longer any Belgian school, or any Flemish art.

In literature, the only writer of any importance from the Low Countries was the Prince de Ligne, a great European nobleman who was as much at home in Vienna as in Paris or Brussels. Although intellectual life was stagnating, interest in public affairs was lively and even violent. The government came in for pitiless criticism, and the French minister in Brussels was astonished to note it. "The freedom of speech so much talked about in England," he stated, "could not be carried any further than it is here."

The country was republican, and legislation protecting individual liberties was so effective that any foreigner automatically enjoyed the benefit of the same rights as those possessed by a Belgian citizen. He could neither be arrested nor deported without due process, and the courts always refused to hear such cases.

At one time the publicist Linguet, who was later to die on the scaffold in Paris, took refuge in Brussels carrying a number of important political papers that the French government did not want published. In vain the French government asked the court of Vienna to seize the dangerous documents. The Comte de Nény was obliged to refuse. "It was undoubtedly," he added, "his knowledge of our constitution, and his confidence in it, which led him to choose this city for his domicile."

It was this country, with its extraordinary trend toward republicanism and freedom, that the Emperor Joseph II was to attempt to convert into a land of absolutism.

IX

THE AGE OF REVOLUTION
1778–1830

In 1753, Brussels received a new Austrian minister—the Count of Cobenzl, a brilliant and cultivated man with a great enthusiasm for the arts and a great admiration for Rubens. He collected paintings and engravings, subsidized painters and sculptors, and corresponded with intellectuals in every country. He also set up libraries that were open to the public, among them the famous Burgundy library, whose magnificent manuscripts had lain until then forgotten in cellars. His aim was to secure publication of the works of major Belgian writers and, as an encouragement to letters in general, he founded the Belgian Academy.

From the outset his attitude was openly anticlerical. At this time the bishops sought to prohibit Jansenist works. Since ecclesiastical censorship, under episcopal direction, was all-powerful and independent of government control, he kept the bishops in check by subordinating it to state censorship; the first care of the censor was to allow the works of the French philosophers to find their way into Belgium.

Before long he was at odds with the Church. On September 20, 1773, at 7:00 A.M., Cobenzl had the Jesuit colleges throughout Belgium closed and replaced by new institutions known as the Theresian Colleges. In these, the study of the sciences and the history of human development was substituted for the study of Latin. The same spirit had governed his action in founding the Belgian Academy. It was designed to cast out "ingrained and ignorant prejudices," and its membership, which was subject to governmental appointment, excluded the Bollandists as a matter of principle, and admitted only those priests who supported the new ideas. It quickly set to work organizing contests and competitions to foster "progress and enlightenment." The Jesuits were soon accusing it of being a society of Deists and Voltairians.

Cobenzl's economic reforms, however, were most important. Paradoxically, Belgium was a country cut off from its neighbors, although it occupied a central position in Europe on territory that formed the obvious road between Germany, England, and France. Its production potential was considerable; it had its own metal and textile industries, and was the only country in Europe with surplus grain available for export. Nevertheless, customs barriers erected around it by Holland and France condemned it to economic suffocation and, even within the enclave of the Low Countries, the tax of the sixtieth part imposed by the principality of Liége cut Belgian territory in two.

The Austrian government, however, decided to restore the former prosperity of the country by attracting into its territory the Atlantic-bound traffic from Germany that had used the route during the sixteenth century, but that more recently had been using the waterways and ports of Holland. The underlying idea was the same as the one that later led to the first railways being built by independent Belgium. The essence of the problem was to create convenient and fast channels of communication to replace the long, slow-moving canals and rivers of Holland and the Rhineland. The solution lay in building paved roads, planned to provide direct and easy travel, and to lure traffic into Belgian territory.

The program was started quickly and the Belgian network of roads and major highways increased from about 37 miles in 1715 to nearly 620 miles in 1789. These included the great highway between Aachen and Ostend that, for the period, was the equivalent of a direct railway route.

In order to secure the greatest return from the investment in new highways, a more modern type of vehicle was designed. This was the heavy stage-coach that was distinguished from older vehicles by its greater carrying capacity, and by a degree of comfort at that time practically unequalled. It was a box coach, mounted on springs, and pulled by four or five horses. A special feature was that some of the horses were free harnessed—outside the shafts—and their pull was therefore more flexible and more rapid.

In the body of the stage there were several compartments. The coupé, a compartment of three seats, was in the front and situated high up, offering a good view of the road. The central section was less luxurious, and only travelers sitting by the windows were able to see the countryside, while the others sat face-to-face on benches. Behind was the roundhouse, containing cheaper seats for travelers of more modest means. Others managed as best they could on the roof among the luggage. Many rapid journeys were made by the stage-coach service, with its experienced postilions and its many posthouses and inns where travelers might take their meals. For those who could not face the fatigue and discomfort of a road journey, there were the horse-drawn canalboats. In this land of canals, they provided a comfortable and convenient means of travel. Passengers between Brussels, Antwerp, Ghent, Bruges, and Tournai could make their journey in comfort, playing a game of cards, reading, and taking their meals on board. With this new means of transportation, Belgium became a much-traveled country and Voltaire declared that "the little country of the Belgians" was the only one that could match France in possessing a road network worthy of Rome.

Much the same progress occurred in industry. Belgian metalwork had been kept in check by the high costs of production. Manufacturers still depended on expensive charcoal for the manufacture of good-quality iron. However, in 1770, Jean-Philippe de Limbourg, a master founder of Liége, discovered how to replace charcoal by coke and thus found the means of expansion that was later to take place in England.

So far, however, collieries could not be mined at a depth greater than about 600 feet, because there was no way of removing water. Then, in 1725, the first steam engine to pump water was put into operation by Viscount Desandrouin, an important industrialist whose name indicates that his patents of nobility were recent. His Newcomen pump, named for the inventor, Thomas Newcomen, was to remain in service until 1834.

The new equipment made it possible to work deeper and richer seams, extracting coal that brought fabulous profits. An enormous number of new companies were registered, and the capital engaged was, for the period, very large indeed. A new coalfield was found near Charleroi, and collieries were also sunk in the Herve country.

Coal borings were made as far afield as Flanders and Brabant, at Ninove, Louvain, Nivelles, Gavere, and at the other end of the country at Dinant and Bouvignes. Belgian industry began to take its modern form of large-scale mechanical development, heavy investments, and great returns. The coal that was mined increased from 400 tons in 1762 to 21,000 tons in 1785.

The population was increasingly rapidly. In thirty years the number of inhabitants in Brussels increased by a half, and in Mons by a third, while in many country districts the figures doubled. Total population reached the hitherto unsurpassed figure of 2.5 million for the Low Countries proper and, if the principality of Liége is included, 3 million.

Modern commercial practices were taking root at the same time.

Chambers of commerce were set up in Bruges and Ghent in 1729; in Ghent a commercial academy was established in 1781, and each region began specializing in branches of manufacture that are still a part of their activities today. Textiles were produced in Flanders and Verviers, and collieries were located in Hainaut and around Liége, together with the industries dependent upon them, such as metalworks, weapon factories, and glassworks.

The first steps were taken in town planning. This was a new art, popularized in Europe by Louis XIV and Louis XV of France. In every town the aim was to create shady walks and large central squares from which streets and tree-lined avenues would radiate. The architectural plan of all Belgian cities has remained, and still remains, in the pattern that was created then and that is now the nucleus of bigger agglomerations.

At Antwerp the center was the Meir, at Ghent the Kouter (Place d'Armes), at Namur the Rue de Fer, and at Liége the Carré and the Place St. Lambert—the palace of the prince-bishops, the façade of which was reconstructed after a fire.

The main market squares were rearranged in Tournai and Mons, and Brussels acquired the aspect of a capital city. Around the Place Royale and Rue Ducale an aristocratic residential district was built by the architects Guimard and Montoyer, including the magnificent group comprising the present government buildings.

The efforts of Cobenzl, and the spirit that animated the Austrian administration would have been less effective had it not been for other European developments during the same period. It was the end of the long economic stagnation of the seventeenth century and the beginning of a new age. In England the industrial revolution was beginning; Germany was reawakening; the wonderful age of French philosophy and enlightenment was illuminating men's minds; and southern Europe was aware of ideas that were shaping European society. Little by little, people were beginning to recognize that no problem is insoluble, and that there is no scourge from which humanity cannot free itself. Under the influence of the new philosophy, it was possible to look forward to a time when epidemic, famine, pauperism, recurrent warfare, and rebellion would disappear, and science would take its place as a new form of religion. All the fundamental notions of the modern world date from this period. Everybody was obsessed with the idea of progress, the old framework burst its bonds, and science, which had been no more than a dream, led the way to an almost infinite expansion in the scope of human endeavor. At the same time, England was in the early stages of that great industrial revolution that was to show the peoples of the world the vast resources now at the command of men and nations, in the development of the machine age.

Throughout history, industrial and commercial systems have generally flourished by having both raw materials and markets. Many nations have secured a monopoly in wealth and development by these means. The Roman Empire itself had been only a system of exchange in which the city of Rome served as middleman between the East and the West, and, because it controlled the Mediterranean with its fleet, provided the livelihood of all the seaboard countries. Never before, however, had there arisen so vast a market as that which opened during the eighteenth century. It stretched from England to America, and southward to the Indian Ocean, and still had half the world in which to thrive and expand.

In 1785, the English had driven out the French and become mistress of India. Their next move was to destroy the Hindu textile industry in order to have a full monopoly over this enormous country's production of raw materials. Thus, England thought, she would be able to manufacture cotton piece goods to sell throughout the world, and turn India into a mass market that would absorb her manufactured products.

So great was the demand, however, that fears soon began to arise as to whether the cotton produced by these plantations would be sufficient. The English then had the idea of buying the entire American cotton crop, and later of encouraging American colonists, who had just won their independence, to start new plantations with English financial help.

Piece goods of Indian cotton were so cheap that there was virtually no limit to the opportunities for export sale; the only limiting factor was the availability of English labor. Between 1783 and 1787, the factory payroll increased from 80,000 to 350,000 workers, and the value of Indian textile material imported increased from £355,000 to £1 million.

Production became the order of the day. The first step was to recruit peasant labor, and scouts were sent into the countryside to bring women and children into the cities. Even so, however, there was not enough human labor, and before long animals, waterfalls, and rivers were being used as sources of power. Finally industry turned to the only source of power still untapped—coal and the steam engine.

Feverish attempts were made to discover all the patents that had been taken out in the past century and then lain forgotten in the files. Handsome sums were paid to inventors, and they were encouraged by promises of prizes and shares in the profits. Contests were promoted with big prizes offered to bring new inventions to light. Dyeing machinery, which had been prohibited around 1755, was now exhumed, and laws that had slowed down production to protect the worker against the machine and maintain the employment level were quickly repealed. By 1789, wide use was being made of mechanical equipment that replaced hundreds of workingmen, including the famous spinning jenny and the Compton-Kennedy, each of which had a thousand spindles. The Watt steam engine, that had been patented in 1769 but had so far not been used, was now generally employed.

Collieries opened on every side. Demand was constantly increasing, and anybody who owned coal-bearing ground and had neglected to develop it now set to work to sink a pit. The streams and canals of Lancashire enabled this new coal field to be developed, and waterways were dug everywhere so that the coal could be brought easily to the factories. A nation that had hitherto been entirely agricultural was becoming a great industrial country and leading the world into the age of coal and iron. As early as 1787 locomotives made their appearance; and Wilkinson, the first maker of blast-furnace iron, laid more than twenty miles of rails himself. It was England's greater industrial and financial potential that gave her the upper hand in the conflict against France and Napoleon. Belgium, like England, was beginning to industrialize, and during the nineteenth century was to become one of the great economic powers of the world.

In the meantime, the new ideas that had taken root in Europe were preparing her for revolution. Characteristic of the period 1776–90 was the series of insurrections that broke out in different countries: the American Revolution of 1776; revolutions in Holland, Sweden, Ireland, and Geneva; the Brabant revolution; the Liége revolution in 1789; and, subsequently, the French Revolution. These upheavals came one after another with virtually no interruption.

England alone escaped the revolutionary contagion. This was because the whole of her strength and energy was absorbed between 1780 and 1815 in her industrial expansion. In the Low Countries, however, the moment soon came when the ill-considered reforms of Emperor Joseph II were to shake the somnolent country out of its long sleep.

Joseph II came to the imperial throne in 1780. He was the son of Empress Maria-Theresa and the brother of Marie Antoinette, the new Queen of France. He already had fifteen years experience in the government of the Austrian states. This bustling and authoritarian sovereign came to the Low Countries in 1781. He had decided to make an incognito visit to his provinces and to decide for himself what measures and reforms should be introduced. He made his way through Belgium, clad in a suit of coarse cloth and accompanied only by a single aide-de-camp, giving his name as Count Falkenstein. He went about in an open carriage or a post-chaise, making quick visits to barracks, schools, and factories, claiming that he had taken everything in at a glance.

To everybody's consternation he refused to attend the receptions and ceremonies prepared in his honor; he lodged in a democratic manner in local inns, inspected and observed, had brief chats with businessmen, industrialists, and civil servants, and, despite his considerable courtesy, was noted as showing "a certain coolness towards ecclesiastics." He returned to Vienna convinced that reform was desired by the Low Countries and determined to introduce it. The new emperor was a large man with piercing eyes and abrupt gestures, who struck everybody by his appearance of authority. He sought, as he said in his speech at Luxemburg, to govern the Low Countries "from his armchair."

He was, in fact, a reformer of that particular type later called by the Germans "activist." The name refers to one of the two possible lines of attack on institutions and procedures that are unreasonable in themselves and which make the task of administration difficult. One technique is a step-by-step advance, easing a way around obstacles and looking to time and the natural development of opinion—supported by adroit propaganda—to change the old customs and substitute progressive and intelligent measures. The other technique is a bold frontal attack, shattering all obstacles and relying on the *fait accompli* and energy of the attack to intimidate opponents, enfeeble their resistance, and resign them to the new state of things.

Joseph II, as an activist, thought it useless to temporize. He meant, he said, "to root out the silly old prejudices" and "destroy all pigheadedness." It was but a short step from the language of Joseph II to that of the French revolutionary leaders; for he, like Robespierre, was out to be "pitilessly kind." He considered that "all men are brothers and it is their duty to be useful to one another." As a democrat wearing a crown, he thought it useless to consult the people. "I need no consent from you to do good," he wrote to the Estates of Brabant, and "my duty is to save you, even if it be in spite of yourselves." It was his belief that rank, birth, and even education were of no importance; that rich and poor had the same right. It mattered nothing to him if men in power were nobles or commoners, well or badly dressed, "in boots, combed or not combed." Even the most eminent authorities could not shake him. "Your remonstrances no doubt proceed from a delirium," he wrote coolly to the Archbishop of Mechlin.

However, unlike modern dictators, he did not understand how formidable a weapon propaganda can be in the hands of a government that uses it skillfully. Even the strong cannot dispense with it as the final factor of success, that meticulous psychological solvent in which all opposition will disappear.

It was in vain that the Emperor's advisers adjured him to come to terms with the Church. With its support, he might have introduced a great variety of political reforms, but he preferred instead to throw down the gauntlet and make a direct attack on the clergy. In a country where priests and monks had great influence, he proceeded to issue a number of decrees afflicting the faithful, irritating believers, and setting in motion the forces of religious fanaticism without providing the government with any real support.

On March 17, 1783, he abolished, with a stroke of the pen, all the contemplative orders and establishments, declaring them to be "completely useless to religion, the state, or their neighbors." Four months later the Hermits of the Woods and Plains were prohibited "on account of the inconveniences resulting from them." On September 26, 1784, marriage was declared to be a civil contract and removed from Church control. A year later, sermons were brought under censorship, and this was extended also to episcopal charges.

After this came a flood of new decrees. Individual religious fraternities were abolished and replaced by a single brotherhood, of the "Active Love of the Fellow Man," on April 8, 1786. Pilgrimages and jubilees were prohibited and processions—to be held without music or banners —reduced to two a year. A census was taken of Church property with a view to eventual confiscation. On June 16, Church appointments were brought under government control.

Four months later, a decisive measure was enacted suppressing the older ecclesiastical seminaries. Training for the priesthood was to be confined to two general seminaries directed by the German Stoeger. They were put under state control, so that future priests would be no more than civil servants.

In the meantime the clergy was maddened by the censorship of their sermons and took steps to organize anti-government opinion. The various sects laid aside their mutual dislikes to show a united front against a government that was determined to give the Belgians no breathing space. Joseph II hastily enacted a measure that was to convert the Low Countries into a political desert.

On January 1, 1787, he anticipated the French Revolution by introducing a reform even more radical than those made by the Constituent Assembly. He abolished with one blow all the privileges, traditions, and constitutions he had solemnly sworn to observe, such as the Joyous Entry, and issued two edicts destroying the whole traditional political organization of the Low Countries.

The independent provinces, that had been self-governing through the provincial Estates, were now superseded by districts similar to the future departments of the French Republic, administered by *intendants,* "commissioners," appointed (and subject to recall) by the Emperor. There were nine of these districts, just as there are now nine Belgian provinces, each of which was named after its chief town—the district of Brussels, the district of Antwerp, and so on. The districts were divided into areas, each of which was administered by a subcommissioner in the same way as is done now. The administration of justice was to be brought under a system similar to the Napoleonic system. There were sixty-four courts of the first instance and two courts of appeal, known as the Sovereign Councils of Brussels and Luxemburg. Above these was a Supreme Court of Appeals. All judges, of course, were appointed by the government.

There was no provision for any transitional period, so that hundreds of thousands of office-holders who judged, administered, governed, and controlled the country, were thrown on the streets overnight, without notice and without indemnity. Most of these offices were lucrative and had either been purchased by their holders, or were their main means of livelihood.

Joseph II had already alienated the clergy, the peasantry, the small burghers in the corporations, and the nobility, who had just been deprived by decree of their feudal rights. He now proceeded to alienate everybody in any public position. The new decrees had repercussions in every branch of the nation's life, extending into commerce, industry, finance, rural life, health, police, justice, the arts, charity, the army, the tax system, education, and religion. The Emperor's supporters, who had been ready enough to acclaim a modernization of the administration, were suddenly reduced to silence and swept aside in the storm created by the many threatened interests. The first protest came from the Hainaut Council on January 12, and the next from the Estates of Brabant on January 29. Both referred to the Joyous Entry, and threatened to suspend the collection of taxes.

There now appeared on the scene a leading Brussels lawyer, Van der Noot, a man of thundering voice and sallow complexion, who had never been outside his native town. He was as ignorant of the rest of the world as he was knowledgeable about the ideas and privileges of his fellow citizens. He molded and inflamed popular opinion to the point of revolt, forcing the government to retrace its steps. The suspension of tax collecting had been ordered for June 1, 1787; on May 30 the two governors, Albert and Marie Christine, were accordingly obliged to defer enforcement of the edicts of the new regime.

Joseph II, meanwhile, knew nothing about what was going on. He was on a visit to Russia and was with the Empress Catherine II at Kherson, in the Ukraine, when he heard of his government's capitulation. Confusion and indignation made him wild with rage and his blood "turned to poison in his veins."

As a result of the mobilization against Turkey, Austrian forces in Belgium had been reduced to 22,000 men, many of whom were natives of the Low Countries, and they were carried away by the agitation. Municipal guards, consisting of armed volunteers, were formed everywhere, and passed in review in uniform, bearing their banners, before the local magistrates. In every hat was the new revolutionary cockade of red, yellow, and black, the combined colors of Brabant and Hainaut. On September 21, 1787, the authorities, totally helpless, had to repeal the hated edicts.

Although Joseph II gave way on political measures, he blundered in insisting on enforcement of the measures he had taken against the clergy in 1781 and 1786. The bishops, who had hitherto remained faithful to the Emperor, at once joined the opposition and used the immense wealth of the Church to subsidize a "patriotic committee," set up to organize resistance. Van der Noot shared the leadership of this body with a new leader, the liberal François Vonck, a Flemish lawyer whose ideas were even more advanced. The Vonckists were not anticlerical; for such a shade of opinion was almost unknown in Belgium. They were, to a large extent, supported by the clergy, and subsidized by such leading prelates as the Abbey of Tongerloo.

There was a great contrast between the two men. Van der Noot, with his broad shoulders, his head cocked to one side, his pock-marked face, and his protruding eyes, was no more than a conceited mischief-maker with a gift of gab. Vonck, thin and frail, possessed a fund of energy and realism.

The Vonckists had organized a secret society, *Pro Aris et Focis* ("For Altar and Home"), that had cells all over the Low Countries and was preparing an armed insurrection. Agitation throughout all of Europe was soon to make it impossible to maintain order in Belgium.

In France the government was foundering under a financial crisis, and was compelled to summon the Estates General. In Brussels the government had, at the end of 1787, reopened the two ecclesiastical seminaries in order to ensure the obedience of the clergy; and the Estates of Brabant had been content to vote the necessary taxes and disperse. At this very moment the Paris parliament declared the ordinances of the French government to be illegal; and the councils of justice of the chief Belgian provinces, inspired by this example, proclaimed that the measures taken by the government of the Low Countries were "contrary to the fundamental laws of the country." Joseph II now decided to use force. To break the Estates' resistance he trained his guns on the Brussels market place, suppressed the Estates of Brabant and of Hainaut, and annulled the Joyous Entry on June 18, 1789.

These measures had no effect, because the French Revolution broke out. The news of the taking of the Bastille on July 14, 1789, led to spontaneous riots in Tirlemont, Tournai, Louvain, and Diest; on August 18, the outbreak of the Liége revolution made the Belgian revolt inevitable.

Volunteers recruited by Vonck now began to leave the country and to assemble in Breda, Holland, where Van der Noot and Vonck had set up their insurrection committee. Vonck put his little army under the command of a retired Flemish officer, Colonel Van der Meersch, who proclaimed the dethronement of Joseph II and proceeded to march into Belgium. The force got as far as Turnhout and secretly occupied the houses surrounding the market place. Two Austrian battalions, consisting for the most part of Belgian soldiers, advanced unknowingly into the square. They were greeted by a withering volley of fire from the Vonckist troops, took panic, and were put to flight.

Six hundred volunteers from Flemish Zeeland marched on Ghent, where the Austrian garrison consisted of only 300 men. The city opened its gates, and organized opposition became impossible. The government's soldiers deserted or went over to the Belgians, and the peasantry felled trees across the main roads to bar their retreat. The few thousand occupation troops still in the Low Countries were seized by panic, and the Austrian government considered itself lucky to be able to evacuate its remaining troops to Luxemburg.

Now that the Low Countries were liberated, however, there was strife between the Vonckists, who represented liberal opinion, and the Statists, or partisans of the provincial Estates, who sought, under the leadership of the ever-vocal Van der Noot, a return to a medieval form of government.

Van der Noot returned to Brussels on December 18, 1789, with a bodyguard of the Archduke's pikemen, riding with his entourage in court carriages. He at once attended a thanksgiving service in St. Gudule and then proceeded to the theater, where he was crowned with honors and acclaimed as Father of the Country.

Some form of constitution was required and, with great enthusiasm, the new constitution of the United States of America was adopted. The Constitution of the States of United Belgium, dated January 11, 1790, contained whole phrases and paragraphs taken verbatim from the American Declaration of Independence of July 4, 1776. The Belgian Parliament, like that of America, was now to be called the Congress, and Van Eupen was appointed Secretary of State.

The Belgian provinces—Brabant, Flanders, Hainaut, and the rest

—were to have the same sovereign rights as the American states, or the cantons of Switzerland. It is, however, a mistake to blame Van der Noot and his friends for not having given Belgium a stable form of government, or for failing to organize an effective administration. The form of government they set up was the same as the one that had, for two centuries, successfully governed the neighboring United Provinces; as it had been fully successful there, it is not fair to say that this constitution was inapplicable or unworkable. The constitution provided that the various Belgian provinces should act as a single unit for three defined purposes: national defense, foreign policy, and coinage.

All powers held in common were put into the hands of the provincial delegations, as was the case in Holland and had been the case in the former Estates General of Belgium, and the paralyzing veto was abolished. The assembly was to be sovereign without any limitation on its powers or any requirement that the provinces be consulted in advance on every vote. The only stipulation was that its decisions required a three-fifths majority, or fifty-six votes out of ninety. The Statists were now able to rely, as were the Jacobins in France, on the common people in the towns that had been whipped to fanaticism by the clergy. They had control, and only the army, commanded by Van der Meersch, was outside their influence. They accordingly began by proclaiming their opponents "enemies of the country."

In vain, the freer spirits of the country—the intellectuals, the leading burghers, the industrialists, and all the advocates of the new ideas —sought to rally around Vonck. They were brushed aside before they could properly understand what was happening. Blue, which they had adopted as their color, was designated as the color of sedition. The Archbishop of Mechlin, in his Lenten Charge of February 17, declared them "enemies of religion and of the state." Equally vain was their attempt to gain support from the people, for the masses were firm Catholics and would not follow them.

The Statists were openly prepared to deal with them in a "day of insurrection," and the monks, led by the Recollects and Capuchins, encouraged the people of the great cities to put the Vonckists to death. In Brussels, the crowd and its monastic leaders went around marking the houses of the "enemies of the people" by scrawling the words "to the tumbril" on them, and pillaging while the Vonckists were unable to raise a finger against them.

On the pretext of an alleged plot to assassinate the Father of the Country and his partisans, the Statists assembled thousands of peasantry armed with pitchforks and rifles in Brussels, under the leadership of priests riding on horseback. In the churches the Capuchins openly preached that it was an act pleasing to God to kill a Vonckist. A *levée en masse* among the peasantry was organized under the leadership of armed monks who demanded a crusade, while wearing swords and crossbelts beneath their cowls, as they shouted for blood. The capital was forcibly occupied by 20,000 of them, and the October riots in Paris sparked the same excesses in Brussels.

A youth named Van Krieken, accused of having laughed at a priest in a passing procession, was lynched by the crowd. His head was impaled on a pike and carried through the streets, as had been the head of the Princesse de Lamballe in Paris on October 6, 1790. The Belgian government took no countermeasures apart from declaring the incident "illegal" and "regrettable."

Joseph II died on February 20, 1790. In his last days, desperate, he accepted all the conditions imposed by the insurgents while pleading with the Pope to intervene. He was succeeded by his brother Leopold, who offered the Belgians the full restoration of their independence and promised to respect all their privileges. The Statists refused this offer because they feared they would be playing into the hands of the Vonckists. The Austrians then decided to reoccupy the Low Countries under an agreement with the Russians, reached at Reichenbach on July 27, 1790. A small army of 30,000 men had no difficulty in mopping up the Congress troops and, on December 2, 1790, they entered Brussels. The States of United Belgium had disappeared, not because they had been unable to create a strong state, but because they had not succeeded in uniting it in the mystical enthusiasm that became the heritage of the French Revolution.

While these events were in progress in the Low Countries, a decisive blow was in preparation at Liége. In the second half of the eighteenth century, Prince-Bishop Velbrueck, who had come into power in 1772, adopted a new policy that relied on the most liberal and advanced elements in the principality. At this time the economic development of the country was at its peak. Liége was a city of 83,000 inhabitants, an enormous population for the period, and considerably larger than that of Brussels.

Verviers was less populous. It dated only from 1651, and was a completely new city, without corporations or privileges, where the predominant influence was freedom of work and of competition. A deluge of new inventions, new ideas, and new technical progress had put the factories, workshops, and collieries of the principality in the first rank of the civilization of the time. Liége had become famous throughout Europe because of its pumps for clearing flooded colliery galleries, colliery lifts that made it possible to mine at levels hitherto inaccessible, and test benches for weapons. Since a third of its coal production was exported to Holland, it was independent of the Low Countries.

In Liége industrial progress was now the watchword, filling the people with vitality. The absence of corporate regulations that led to the growth of a big industrial proletariat, had also eliminated the restrictive conditions of the Middle Ages and the Renaissance. It was a triumph for individualism and the new doctrine of the rights of man.

In this field, Liége was considerably more advanced than France herself. By 1780 a revolutionary spirit was spreading through all classes, rich or poor. The Liége printers were defying censorship and flooding Europe with newspapers and pamphlets. The seventeenth-century struggles to defend privilege and local autonomy were forgotten. The strife now was for the rights of man, and the workers, unlike those in France, took a direct part in political life.

Velbrueck had been succeeded as Prince-Bishop in 1784 by Hoensbroeck, in the course of a lawsuit in which he was opposed by the café keeper Levoz, concession holder for the Spa games. Unfortunately for Velbrueck, it set the people aflame, in the name of what were then called "The Rights of Citizens," and he was replaced.

Liége gave a delighted welcome to French revolutionaries like young Mirabeau, who visited there on his way back from Berlin. Events in France were followed with passionate interest and, by the time the news came of the fall of the Bastille, the population was organized into a single party that vindicated the sovereignty of the people and was ready to follow the example of the Paris insurgents.

On August 15, 1789, a congress, consisting for the most part of workingmen, was called at Polleur near Verviers. On August 18, two leaders with advanced views, Fabry and de Chestret, led the party that stormed the Liége town hall. They notified the magistrates that the people had withdrawn their authority, removed them from office, and themselves took over the work of burgomasters. They then marched at the head of the crowd in quest of the Prince-Bishop, who had taken refuge in his chateau at Seraing. They brought him back to Liége in triumph at night and, by torchlight, amid the shouting of the crowd, they forced him to recognize the revolution.

A week later the Prince-Bishop, terrified and at his wits' end, took flight. On his table he left a paper declaring that he was going away for reasons of health. In the meantime, in a meadow at Polleur, the metalworkers of Franchimont had formed a constituent assembly and had voted a Declaration of the Rights of Man similar to the one proclaimed in Paris. The Revolution had been brought about by the alliance between the liberal burghers and the workers' proletariat. The people who came to power were not the small burghers, but were the colliers, the iron founders, the armorers, and the weavers. The Estates of the principality could not avoid recognizing an accomplished fact;

Joseph II, dumbfounded, bitterly treated the Revolution as a "farce" and proposed to "laugh it off."

The Third Estate now went to extremes and, once more taking the lead over France, not only abolished all feudal rights, but also the proportional tax on incomes. Riots became a permanent feature, and the revolutionaries, trying to avoid an Austrian occupation, came to terms with the King of Prussia, who agreed to send his troops into the city in the name of the Empire. The ostensible purpose of this agreement was to keep order, but in reality it was aimed at preventing Joseph II from coming into the city. When the Prussian troops withdrew a few months later, another revolution broke out. The people of Liége ordered the dethronement of the Prince-Bishop and enacted universal suffrage.

After the Reichenbach Convention, Liége was deserted by the Prussians, and for a time reaction set in. The Prince-Bishop proceeded to prosecute the revolutionaries, but the repercussions did not become severe until after Neerwinden, when a certain Doctor Chapuis of Verviers was sent to the scaffold because, as Mayor, he had committed what the Bishop held to be sacrilege in performing civil marriages.

As early as 1790, Liége revolutionaries were migrating in large numbers to Paris. There they organized a legion of Liége troops who played a decisive part in the French intervention in Belgium and the subsequent annexation of the Low Countries.

The time for the unification of the Low Countries was now at hand. Hitherto, the Belgians and the people of Liége had had a hearty dislike for one another. Moreover, the Brabant revolution itself had been a reactionary and traditionalist affair, so that the rift separating Liége from the rest of the Belgian provinces had been widened. When, however, both revolutions collapsed in the face of Austrian repression, the people of Liége, and those of Belgium, were at last able to unite. France had become their only hope, and they sent her a joint appeal. Although they had been kept apart by different ideals and different national traditions, they were now joined together in defense of the same ideal.

One of the first acts of the French revolutionaries had been to declare peace with all the world. There was no intention of annexing, or even disturbing, the Low Countries, and the revulsion in French public opinion was to a large extent the work of the Belgians themselves. As early as 1791, the Vonckist emigrants, who had taken refuge in Lille to escape the Austrian troops, and the Liége soldiery who had found their way into France, were forming themselves into armed bands, with an increasing tendency to support revolutionary ideas. They took root so quickly that their leaders, Vonck and Van der Meersch, preferred to withdraw and abandon their troops.

When the Austrian government succeeded in having these bands kept away from the frontiers of the Low Countries, Belgian democrats and the Liége volunteers met again in Paris. There they formed the Committee of United Belgians and Liégeois, the first foreshadowing of Belgium as we know it. The date of their fusion, Jaunary 20, 1792, may be taken as modern Belgium's birthday.

In a manifesto of April, 1792, they adopted a new Belgian Constitution, with a referendum, an appeal to the people, and provision for an assembly to be elected by universal suffrage of all citizens of full age. Above all, they clamored for a war of Belgian liberation.

Their anti-Austrian propaganda, and their speeches in the legislative assembly, helped influence French opinion. Just as the annexation of the Low Countries, in the days of Louis XIV, had been difficult because the population did not desire a French occupation, it now appeared easy and tempting, because the Belgians were asking for it and the action to be undertaken was a war of liberation.

Three Belgian army corps were massed at Lille, on the northern frontier, and at the same time, a Liége legion was formed at Givet. With the help of these troops, the battle of Jemappes, November 6, 1792, secured the liberation of Belgium, and was in a large measure a Belgian victory. It was the Belgians, under the command of the Walloon Dumonceau, who decided the issue on the left wing, by capturing the fort of Quaregnon and forcing the Austrian army to retreat.

In Mons, Brussels, Flanders, and more particularly, Liége, the victors were hailed as liberators, even by people who had formerly been Statists. At Namur, the friends of France had organized a Society of Friends of Liberty and Equality, with membership that included the majority of the population. The "Marseillaise" was sung, and when it was learned that Rouget de Lisle was one of the French officers besieging the citadel, he was sought out and agreed to write "couplets for the Belgians" to the tune of the "Marseillaise." Public enthusiasm rose to a delirious peak.

In most of the Low Countries, and particularly in the Dutch-speaking regions, the former Statists still thought only of restoring their old privileges, and this brought the French Commander Charles Dumouriez into a conflict from which there was no escape. He organized elections to enable the Belgians to govern themselves, but a reactionary majority got control of the administration almost everywhere and set to work to persecute the democrats and the friends of France. To prevent them from being wiped out, it became necessary to organize new elections, in which the candidates were almost forced upon the electors. The elections were scarcely free except in Hainaut, part of the Namur country, and in particular in Liége—that is to say in the country that was in the future to be Wallonia.

Political difficulties were acute, and there was no government in the Low Countries just at the time when a general state of war was bringing France up against the whole of Europe. The Belgians had not succeeded in organizing themselves, or in achieving unity, and the convention accordingly began a campaign of intimidation and agitation for unification with France. This unification was forced by the people of Liége, who were, as always, at the head of the movement, and enthusiastically voted their own annexation to the French Republic on June 20, 1793. The Jacobins of the principality, under the orders of the painter Defrance, went so far as to demolish St. Lambert's Cathedral, stone by stone, since it was considered a symbol of the *ancien régime*.

After seven months of insurmountable difficulty, the French armies were beaten at Neerwinden, and the Low Countries were again occupied by the Austrians. By now, however, Austria was thoroughly disgusted with Belgium, and the Austrian generals asked for the territory to be evacuated. By June 26, 1794, it was reconquered without difficulty by the French armies, after the battle of Fleurus.

The fourteen months during which Belgium was governed by the Austrians were those of Robespierre's ascendancy in France, when he was making the guillotine a permanent fixture of the landscape. This was to have important consequences. The first stroke of good luck befalling the Low Countries was that they thus escaped the Terror, at its peak between the battles of Neerwinden and Fleurus. The first French occupation had been marked neither by executions nor by reprisals, and the guillotine was still practically unknown in Belgium. Aristocrats and priests were not sent to the scaffold, and revolutionary upheavals did not dig the same bloody ditch between classes as they had done in France.

Even when the Low Countries had been reconquered by French armies, there was neither emigration nor confiscation of the property of the former governing classes. In 1794 there was a headlong flight, but confidence soon returned and almost everybody came back to the country, apart from a few high dignitaries who preferred to continue their careers in the service of Austria. In Brabant there were only 300 emigrants in all, among them General Beaulieu, who was later to be one of the famous adversaries of Napoleon. The governing classes thus succeeded in keeping their fortunes and influence intact throughout the Revolution.

At the same time, Belgium was not cut in two, as was France, by anti-clericalism and the religious persecution that created a definite rift between the Catholic Church and a large part of the population. In

Belgium, when Church property was put up for sale, the people who bought it were not the peasantry, but the nobles and burghers and other persons of long-standing privilege, who were the only people possessing the necessary capital. This was, in fact, the origin of the fortunes of a number of present-day families. In France, purchasers of national property were to constitute a great anti-clerical party, bound together by a community of interest and hostility to the power of the Church. Nothing of this kind happened in Belgium. Life was not dominated by the continual fear of revenge, and the story of the Low Countries throughout the nineteenth century does not reflect the atmosphere of civil war and class hatred that forced France to make her way from revolution to revolution.

There ensued a period of poverty and arbitrary government, due to the state of siege and the military occupation by the Republican armies. On October 1, 1795, the country was definitely annexed to France. This brought Belgium back under a proper legal system and gave the inhabitants the same laws and the same rights as French citizens.

The annexation swept Belgium as a positive tidal wave. Laws were published to ensure everybody's cooperation with the government, and the concept of the public weal and community interest now took precedence over individual rights and privileges. All citizens were equal under a regime based on freedom in every field—freedom of trade, freedom of thought, freedom to work, a civil code, the abolition of feudal rights, the proclamation of the equality of all before the tax collector, the abolition of internal tolls and duties, privileges, tithes, and hereditary powers. Justice was now meted out by juries, municipal governments were elected, the corps of notaries was established, stamp taxes and registration taxes were introduced, population registers were kept, divorce was authorized, and education was made compulsory. Reforms swept away the *ancien régime* and brought together, under the same laws, the principality of Liége and the remainder of the Low Countries.

The people of Liége themselves provided the proof that this fusion would have been impossible without a revolutionary dictatorship. The Jacobins of Franchimont and Polleur were indignant at finding themselves united, not only with the reactionary Flemings, but also with the burghers of the city of Liége. They therefore demanded the right to join with Spa, Stavelot, and Aachen in forming an administrative unit to be known as the "mineral waters district" that would have united in one group all the thermal springs of the region. Protests of the same sort would no doubt have been raised in every town and village if the Belgians had been consulted.

The reforms, in fact, became permanent because they were structural and pointed less to the creation of a new political system than to a new state of society. It was no longer a question of fragmentary and partial measures that could always be discussed and amended. The framework and basic organization of society was being transformed and a new world was being born. "There is a greater difference between the France of today and the France of 1788," said Dumouriez in 1793, "than that of the Gauls at the time of Julius Caesar."

There was still one obstacle with which the new state had to deal. This was the power of the clergy, who had now lost their fortunes and their landed property, but still wielded strong influence over the masses.

This circumstance was not peculiar to Belgium. Similar conditions prevailed in quite a number of the French provinces, such as Brittany, the Vendée, and Languedoc. The problems were the same, and in the first elections held by the Directory in 1795, they came to the surface. In Belgium, as in France, the majority of the voters were for the moderates, and they elected a majority favorable to the anti-revolutionaries.

It was to avoid a counter-revolution that the Directory organized the coup d'état of Fructidor. This was the signal for a large-scale anti-religious campaign. The clergy were required to take an oath of hatred for royalty, and the Belgian priests who refused to take it had their churches closed. About thirty of them were prosecuted and condemned to deportation to Guiana.

New elections showed a big swing to the left, and Liège even elected a "Communist," General Fion, a partisan of Babeuf. Flanders and Brabant, however, remained stubbornly faithful to the Church. The population followed only the "recusant" priests who had not taken the oath. This was the period of the "blind Masses," celebrated clandestinely in houses with closed shutters, situated in big squares and open places. The Masses were celebrated at an hour that had been fixed in advance, and the people were given word of them without the knowledge of the authorities and could be present without actually seeing the service. The period came to be known in Flanders as the *Gesloten Tyd*, "Time of Closure." Even the University of Louvain had to close its doors.

It was not the anti-religious measures that led to the so-called Peasant War. This episode, a kind of Belgian Vendée, was occasioned by the dislike of the rural inhabitants for military service. As in western France in 1792, the very idea of conscription infuriated the peasant population. The Directory, threatened by trouble abroad, was forced to order mobilization and, as the orders were issued, the peasantry rose in revolt under the leadership of the clergy in the hope of escaping service. The insurrection was the work of bands with no common organization and it amounted to no more than a flare-up. It spent itself vainly in the Hageland under Rolliers, in Kempen under Corbeels, and in the Ardennes it was rather significantly nicknamed the "war of cudgels."

Belgium suffered cruelly during this period, but France, whose life she was sharing, was suffering just as much from poverty, banditry, and economic stagnation. France and Belgium suffered together the consequences of the state of emergency, the war against Europe and the financial disorganization. Both were a prey to the so-called "chauffeurs," who painted their faces with soot and burned or tortured peasants in an effort to extort money from them. In France there were 77,000 conscripts, and three-quarters of them deserted or went into hiding. In 1794, the French textile industry's output, previously amounting to 2.6 million pieces, fell to only 800,000. Everywhere there was poverty, fear, and political denunciation.

Belgium, on the other hand, got off comparatively lightly. The condition that prevailed in France did not, in Belgium's case, last so long, nor was she split by civil war. Accordingly, Belgium emerged from the Revolution morally intact. She had lived through the events of these years without understanding them, without taking any real part in them, and even without rebellion. When, for example, crosses were torn from the churches, the only reprisal taken by the more pious souls was to organize teams equipped with mirrors that they flashed from afar in the eyes of the steeplejacks in the hope of dazzling them into losing their footing and falling to their death.

The fact was that the governing classes had been careful not to take sides. The great landowners, the nobility, and the burghers had been thinking only of defending their own interests by collaborating with the French administrators; and the French, among them Bouteville, had managed in the end to bring them around to supporting the new regime. The Revolution had actually given them a new means of fortune building, and they had done well out of it. Rents and revenues that formerly had gone to support the monasteries now accrued to the nobles who had bought up the land at depressed prices. The confiscation of Church property had put enormous resources at the disposal of industrialists who were thus able to find the capital needed to equip and modernize their factories. Moreover, there was an abundance of labor, local dues and tolls had been abolished, and communications were open to the Rhineland, southern Holland, and more particularly, the French Republic, so that the export market was almost unlimited. The industrialists had formerly been producing for 3 million customers; they were now producing for 30 million.

What was happening in Belgium at this point was the counterpart of what had happened in England a quarter of a century earlier, after the enormous Indian and American markets had been conquered. On the one hand was a young and growing industry that never lacked markets; on the other were undreamed of export outlets. This was a rare and profitable combination, and the benefit of the suppression of the French internal duties accrued almost entirely to Belgium, now the most advanced industrial region in the Republic. The population of the Low Countries began to increase rapidly. In the department of the Schelde, which corresponded to eastern Flanders, the number of inhabitants rose from 560,000 to 615,000; in the Lys, or western Flanders, from 459,000 to 519,000; and in the city of Liége, excluding the suburbs, from 38,000 to 48,000. Brussels, the former capital, had suffered from the exodus of administrations and civil servants, but the population nevertheless rose from 66,000 in the year 1800 to 75,000 twelve years later. This increase in population reflected the rapid growth in the country's wealth. It had no counterpart in France where the only department to show an increase from 125 to 200 inhabitants per square kilometer was the north, which had close economic links with Belgium.

After the coup d'état of 18 Brumaire, the advent of the Consulate restored order, brought civil strife to an end, and succeeded in rallying all classes to the support of France. The Catholic masses in Belgium were satisfied with the Concordat of 1802 and Napoleon's agreement with the Pope, and they rallied enthusiastically to the new regime.

Belgium was not only the most populous, but also the most advanced region in the new Empire. Its agriculture was the most developed, its industry the most up-to-date, and its spirit of initiative and enterprise the most active. Belgium took the lead, and the boom that now occurred tied its economic structure to France and produced a fabulous degree of expansion. Even the blockade of the Continent had no other effect than to serve Belgium's interests by giving her the European as well as the French market.

As had been the case in England twenty years earlier, there was an intense demand for patents, and the almost unlimited increase in opportunities for production and sale set the industrialists in urgent quest of new inventions and processes. Belgium had been transformed by mechanization; coal had replaced charcoal in metallurgical practice, and up-to-date techniques in the treatment of pig-iron made it possible for steel to be used instead of iron. Belgian industry led Europe—at the end of the Empire it had eighty-nine blast furnaces, a figure not reached in France until the days of Napoleon III, half a century later.

A single spinning machine could do the work of a hundred men and save its owner tens of thousands of francs each day. Profits rose enormously and all available capital sought its outlet in industry. After

1807, steam engines appeared everywhere, and the new system of pumping flooded mine galleries enabled coal to be won from ever-increasing depths.

In 1798, Liévin Bauwens, a Ghent tanner, set out to steal from England the secret of the Spinning Jenny, the new spindle machine that could not be exported on pain of death. He set himself up in England with teams of workmen who secretly learned how the machine was operated. Masking his activities by pretending to form a colonial-produce business, he succeeded in buying the machines under the counter, took them apart, and sent the pieces to Belgium in bales of coffee and cases of sugar.*

Bauwens was discovered by the English police. He fled, leaped onto a ship, and eluded his pursuers who had mobilized an entire fleet to arrest him. There was a dramatic pursuit on the high seas, but it was only his effigy that was hanged in public in London. He then set up in Ghent the first mechanical spinning-mill on the continent. "My wish is," he had said, when as a young man he had returned from a trip to London, "to sacrifice my fortune to my country by giving it those machines that made England so great." He was, in fact, to ruin himself in doing so, but as early as 1810 he had achieved the dream of his life, and soon the huge Ghent spinning-mills were employing 10,000 workmen.

A counterpart to Bauwens was the English mechanic William Cockerill, who entered the service of industrialists in Verviers-les-Biolley in 1799. He brought them the new machinery for spinning and preparing wool, and transformed the woolen industry.

It was to Verviers that Napoleon sent young French industrialists for training. Cockerill's son flooded France and all of Europe with his machinery: carding machinery, pressing and stamping machinery, and many other types. This was a time when many patents were obtained, and it became possible to organize the chemical industry and the illuminating gas industry.

In the meantime, the Belgians were increasingly inclined to support the imperial government from which they drew their prosperity. Reforms were no longer contested. The speed and efficiency of the administration gained the people's admiration. For the first time, prefects made a practice of posting the administrative acts, so that the public spirit might be associated with the functioning of the new institutions, and the least important citizen be convinced that he was collaborating for the common good. Everything was now clear-cut and

---

* The Archduke Albert had brought sacred relics from Germany in barrels of cheese. The comparison paints a clear picture of the difference between the two centuries.

efficient, from the civil code to the judicial institutions and the metric system. Teaching was done in lycées that served as models for all of Europe. Vaccination had been made compulsory, and the terrible scourge of smallpox that formerly had killed five out of every twelve children disappeared. Grain was stored and famine avoided.

The price of bread, that for centuries had differed widely from province to province, and could double between one year and the next, became uniform, and the standard of living was stabilized. This was perhaps the most outstanding event since the beginning of civilization, for it permitted the enormous growth in Europe's population between the nineteenth and the twentieth centuries.

The Belgians were the main beneficiaries of the French annexation. They were enriched by France's revolutionary adventure, which made it possible for the Belgians to earn fantastic profits. Belgian goods could now be distributed to the farthest corners of the Empire, using the rivers and waterways that, through the Schelde, the Meuse, and the Rhine, linked Belgium with France and joined the network of canals that the Empire continued to develop.

Wheat from France flowed into Belgium, assuring food for the working masses, so that the peasant population could be employed in the factories. Industrialists could be sure of a docile and well disciplined labor force, for imperial regulations paralleled those of England, prohibiting strikes, requiring workers to carry workbooks, and making them completely dependent on their employers.

The ceaseless warfare that was to ruin France brought Belgium big orders for army supplies. Indeed, Belgium got the greater part of these orders because of her labor supply and better industrial capacity. It might even be said that it was not so much France that had annexed Belgium in 1795, but Belgium that had annexed France for purposes of economic exploitation.

It is perhaps an illusion to think of the conflict between England and the Empire as a simple fight for the independence of the Low Countries. There was, in fact, little point in Napoleon's remark that Antwerp was "a pistol trained on the heart of England." The same thing had, in earlier years, been said of Calais, and later of Dunkirk. Moreover, the port of Antwerp, blockaded by the English fleet, was filled with shipping that was completely paralyzed and was serving no useful purpose for the Empire.

No port, however great, could put Great Britain in peril. The conflict between England and France was fought on a vaster scale, involving the conquest of the world's markets. It was in the Mediterranean, rather than in Belgium, that revolutionary France, the occupying power in Italy and the ally of Spain and the Spanish fleet, could throw its shadow over Egypt and as far as India.

During negotiations for the Treaty of Amiens in 1802, England had not asked that the port of Antwerp be neutralized or closed, as she had earlier in the cases of Dunkirk and Mardyck. It was the problem of Malta—which France refused to evacuate—and the occupation of Naples, that were later to lead to the rupture of the peace.

It was not for the sake of Antwerp that Napoleon was to fight for twelve years with "perfidious Albion." The differences between them were deeper and more important: The real objectives were the control of the Baltic, the Mediterranean, and Spain and its colonial empire. The conflict was essentially economic, and it was the English working-man, even more than the English sailor, who was eventually to overcome the French soldiers.

A single example provides a striking illustration. If a contemporary had been asked to state what he considered the most important event between 1800 and 1810, he would have been given the choice of a number of events. These might have been taken at random from many different fields, such as:

- The creation of the French Empire and the rise of Napoleon, in the course of which France conquered all Europe.
- The battle of Austerlitz on December 2, 1805, a masterpiece of intelligence and planning that ensured France's alliance with Austria and Russia, and thus extended her influence as far as the Black Sea and the Pacific.
- The battle of Trafalgar on October 21, 1805, that gave England undisputed command of the sea.
- The invention by Fulton of a steamship that could sail up rivers.
- The perfection, by the Frenchman Christophe de Dombasle, of a two-wheel plough that replaced the older swing plough.
- The general adoption of beet cultivation, and the substitution of beet sugar for cane sugar.

There can be little doubt that the contemporary would have said that the battles of Austerlitz and Trafalgar and, in particular, the creation of the French Empire, were the important landmarks of the period. In fact, however, the peace of Vienna, dictated after Austerlitz, lasted only two years; the effects of Trafalgar would have been of short duration if subsequent events had not forced France to give up the quest for sea power. The Empire of Napoleon was doomed to disappear twelve years after it had been created. In all three cases the episodes in question were only superficial.

On the other hand, the steamship was to make it possible for colonial produce to be carried very cheaply, and this transformed the whole life of the human race. The universal adoption of the de Dombasle wheel plough was to put a final end to famine by enormously increasing the yield of agricultural land. The use of beet sugar brought jam and fruit preserves into general use, reduced the price of sugar within three generations from fifteen francs to seven and a half francs per kilogram, and considerably improved the general standard of living. Parallel to this, owing to improved cultivation, the price of bread fell after 1830 to thirty or forty centimes per kilogram, and salt became cheap enough to be used to preserve the pork that became a staple of the diet of the poorer classes throughout the year.

The result of all this, and the real importance of the period, was a continual improvement in the standard of living, in new inventions, and economic transformations. These were much more important than military and political triumphs which appeal more to the imagination but never last. Whatever contemporaries might have thought, the key events of the Anglo-French war were not military ones. The brilliant victories of Napoleon and Nelson played only a secondary part, compared with the deep-seated economic changes that were readjusting the balance of power between the two nations.

For a period of fifteen years Napoleon won victory after victory, beating down his opponents one after another, marching his armies from Madrid to Vienna and to Moscow, and forcing England to sit by while he organized Europe as he wanted. This succession of triumphs, however, weakened France much more than they strengthened her. She got from them no lasting increase in her strength, while the economic power of England grew continuously despite the defeats she suffered.

In this matter figures speak for themselves. It was England's exports of cotton goods that provided her with increasing wealth: they rose from 1 million pounds in 1785 to 2 million pounds in 1792, and 5.5 million pounds in 1806. Between 1788 and 1804, English production of pig-iron, the key product on which her metal industry was based, rose from 68,000 to 250,000 tons. Despite the state of war, the value of English imports of American cotton increased from the 1791 figure of £189,316 to £17 million in 1800, and no less than £127 million in 1820. The transformation of these imported textiles, and the subsequent export of the products, gave England a constant influx of capital and economic resources that enabled her to resist France. In 1783, the English cotton industry employed only 80,000 workers. By 1830 the number had risen to 830,000. It is easy to imagine the scale of the annual accrual of capital that must have resulted from such an export trade.

War expenditure represented only a small part of the enormous profits being earned; even on the military side, the victory was virtually won in advance. After Austerlitz, when Napoleon thought that victory was his, England's reply was to double her real wealth. She inundated Europe and the rest of the world with her manufactured goods and raw materials and she increased her financial and economic strength, enabling her to pay larger and larger armies, and find more and more allies. The result was that the military defeats she had suffered lost all importance to her.

France, in the meantime, was unable to do without English goods, so that to a large extent she herself was financing the budget of her enemy. It would have cost her many million francs to build a fleet capable of defeating England at sea, and French resources made it impossible to finance a program on the scale required. It was forty years before France was able to catch up with the economic arrears resulting from the Napoleonic era. Not until 1830 was French industry able to equip itself with steam engines, in the same way English industry had done, and to build up the country's external trade to the pre-1789 level of 1 billion francs.

It is true that mankind owed its liberation to revolutionary and imperial reforms, but those who were responsible for France's economic destiny were not up to the job of organizing the country's material progress. The time was to come when the resources of the French Empire would be exhausted, when the burden of war taxation would lead the people to revolt, and when the pressure of economic forces would lead to Napoleon's political downfall. He would no longer be able to count even on the support of the Belgian population.

In 1805, Belgium completely rallied to the French Empire. All classes of the population supported France for fear of losing the profits of the industrial boom that had begun about 1800. Opposition had ceased to exist; Napoleon's reconciliation with the Pope had won over the Catholic masses and gained him the support of the bishops. The liberals also supported him, as did the wealthy classes who were busily becoming wealthier, and the result was that Belgian opinion was unanimous in its support of the Empire.

This support was to be rudely shattered by the resurgence of religious strife. When Napoleon broke with the Pope, about 1809, there was a reawakening of Catholic opposition and a religious war broke out between the Belgian bishops and the Empire. The same thing was happening in France; the leaders of the movement in Belgium, Monseigneur Hirn, Bishop of Tournai, and Monseigneur de Broglie, Bishop of Ghent, were themselves French prelates. Opposition to the Empire was not specifically Belgian, but it became particularly acute in Belgium because of the enormous influence of the Church on the Flemish population. An additional factor was Belgian hostility to compulsory military service, which had hitherto been unknown.

Even in central and southern France a large proportion of the conscripts in this period were deserting and, like the Vicar of Ars, concealing themselves in the woods. It is easy, then, to imagine the reaction of the Belgian population. It reached its peak with the increase in the Belgian contingent from 110,000 conscripts in 1810 to 160,000 three years later. The total contingent, including the national guard, thus amounted to 260,000 men, or double the twentieth-century scale of enrollments, at present between 100,000 and 120,000.

The imperial regime was becoming a dictatorship. Dislike for the Empire and its system of supervision and police action turned into positive hostility toward France under the influence of arbitrary arrests, such as that of the Mayor of Antwerp. After the military collapse in 1813, only Liége was still supporting the French regime. The allies were able to occupy the country without any opposition. The interval, begun with the French conquest twenty years earlier, now ended as rapidly as it had begun.

It is true that the citizens of Namur covered de Grouchy's retreat after Waterloo, donning their old uniforms and manning their old guns to open fire against the allies. Such events were rare, however; the French regime had been too short for the new generation it had formed to reach manhood.

The collapse was crushing. Once over the Rhine, the allies found no opposition. Fortresses once considered impregnable, such as Namur and Luxemburg, fell without resistance. The citadel of Namur no longer had any cannon; the same was true of other fortresses, since they had been disarmed and their equipment taken to the Rhine to defend what was believed to be a natural frontier. Nevertheless, the twenty years of the French annexation had made it posisble for the Belgium of the future to be born. It had made a unit of a people that had previously thought only in terms of the province and the village.

France had created a new social class in Belgium made up of the city burghers, the big capitalists, the nobles, and the landed proprietors. Napoleon had put power in their hands, and they were the ones who were to be responsible for directing Belgium's affairs and providing all the country's leaders throughout the nineteenth century. They were, in fact, an elite, open-minded and hard working, ready and willing to absorb the best elements from the middle class, the rural elite, and the intellectuals. They thus provided the unifying and guiding element in Belgium until the twentieth century, despite the rise of socialism and democratic thought. After 1830, they made possible the creation of an independent Belgium. They enabled the country to overcome its difficulties and to develop continuously until our own times. Such men, in their boards of directors and local and central government assemblies, provided the country with leaders used to handling business affairs—as well as civil servants, intellectuals, and other people of note. This class was to be the backbone of the nation.

Belgium's capacity to finance the astonishing industrial expansion after 1800 was due to this concentration of national wealth in the hands of a few tens of thousands of families. After 1815, all that was necessary was for the Belgians to become conscious of their intrinsic unity. This was to result from the "Dutch challenge."

For the Belgians, life under Napoleon was a mixture of the present and the past. It was the Empire that ordered the destruction of the old ramparts in Brussels and their replacement by the wide boulevards of today. Squares and streets were renamed—the Rue Royale, for example, became the Rue Imperiale. Brussels was given a new coat of arms, consisting of a crenelated turret surmounted by an eagle; charity workshops were organized as part of the struggle against poverty; and an attempt was made to incorporate suburban communes into the city to create Greater Brussels.

The city fire brigade was 150 strong, with headquarters in the town hall, but most of its material was strategically housed at a number of points in the outer city. In the spire of the Église de la Chapelle, a night-watchman kept a permanent fire-spotting watch, blowing his trumpet every half-hour to indicate that all was well. A regular postal service was organized, and the city acquired no less than four letter boxes in different parts of the town. The chief collection each day was at 10:30 A.M., and mail was delivered by a squad of twelve postmen, a figure that in those days was considered enormous. Brussels was linked by stagecoach to points throughout Europe, and every day there was a departure for Louvain, Mechlin, Turnhout, Diest, Mons, and other centers. The city had 120 cabs and carriages for hire, and the municipal guard that discharged the functions of the police was 150 strong. Cafés and public resorts were still regulated, but their closing hours were later than had formerly been the case. Closing time was announced by a bell that rang at midnight during the summer and at 11:30 P.M. in the winter.

Throughout the country young people were learning French ways through the propagation of French civilization in the imperial lycées. In Brussels, there was now a stock exchange and many industries. The city's population had, of course, declined when it ceased to be the capital of the Lowlands and became merely the chief town of a department, since many civil servants had departed, but the population increased again, and by the end of the Empire amounted to 75,000 inhabitants.

On the occasion of every French victory, the population was required by order to illuminate their houses. This happened so often that the people ceased to use lanterns, which blackened and spoiled too quickly, and took to using candles fixed in bottles placed behind their windowpanes. The effect, with all the windows illuminated, particularly where the houses were old, was to create a positive fairyland. Local traditions continued and there were many festivals. The great ommegang of Antwerp still staged its procession, carrying a whale forty-three feet long and sixteen feet high, with the mechanism and the men who operated it concealed. The whale squirted sudden jets of water at spectators as it passed through the streets. In the procession, too, were many chariots depicting mythological subjects, and the famous twenty-five-foot giant who shook his head as he walked, had a place of his own in the folklore of Antwerp. He was reputed to have been painted by Rubens.

In the time of Napoleon popular legends were still a living force. One of them claimed that the name of Antwerp did not mean "on the wharf" but rather "the thrown hand," from the Dutch *hand werpen*. As the story went, a giant, who had exercised his tyrannous activity on the Schelde boatmen, had lost his hand and had it thrown into the river by the hero Brabo, whose name, of course, was the origin of Brabant.

About 1810, however, the feature that impressed most observers was the division of the population into old and young. The elders still wore the dress of the old regime, with the tail coat of the eighteenth century, breeches, stockings, and buckled shoes. They wore, of course, a peruke, or had their hair powdered and bound behind by a ribbon. On rainy days they donned boots and a cape, and some of them still wore a three-cornered hat. The young, on the other hand, were dressed in the modern fashions that had come from Paris. They wore trousers and the long coat that was to become the frock coat, and their hair was cut short under the round hat that was the ancestor of the top hat. Priests, for the most part, had not yet adopted the soutane, which was not worn regularly until the nineteenth century. Indeed, they wore the breeches and black stockings of the eighteenth century.

For the working class, the standard of living was extremely low. Wages were based, as they had been during the eighteenth century, on the price of bread, the normal wage being sufficient to buy a daily supply of between two and seven pounds of black bread, which was considered sufficient to feed a household. Bread was eaten with a little bacon fat or grease and a few vegetables. As soon as the worker rose in the social scale, his wages rose rapidly. There was no longer a proportion between the wages of a worker and those of a technician or foreman. A high civil servant of those days was paid fifty times as much as a clerk; today he is paid only four times as much. In addition, his working day was shorter and his holidays were longer.

Workers were the victims of the industrial expansion that took place under the Empire. They lived in great poverty and, in 1809, the workers of Ghent were prohibited from organizing a friendly society to provide against the risk of unemployment because it was considered necessary that they should remain wholly at the mercy of their employers.

Although the industrial prosperity would no doubt have covered an increase in wages, a single set of circumstances kept the worker in a state of subjection: Any vacancy in the factories could easily be filled from the influx of workers from the country. It was, therefore, impracticable for wage earners to unite to demand an increase in wages and they had only one other resource open to them. The demand for labor was increasing and, with children engaged in the factories from six or seven years of age on, the highest earnings went to the families with the most children. Moreover, it was only the few years after their birth that children cost their parents anything, and these are the years in which the cost is least. The bigger the family, therefore, the higher the earnings, and the wage earner, instead of asking for better wages, concentrated on having as many children as he could.

Unfortunately, the worker was also increasing the amount of labor available and creating conditions in which wages could not rise. The workers did not blame the employers for this state of affairs. They considered it the result of the free interplay of economic forces, and as a result they resigned themselves passively to their situation.

An example can be found in the experience of Liévin Bauwens, who was an important industrialist in Ghent at this period. He required a large labor force that he recruited from the Flemish countryside. He began offering high wages, paying, in this period when a carpenter was receiving not quite two francs a day, between five and eight francs for workers in his cotton spinning mills. In 1810, however, there was a shortage of cotton, and wages fell by half. The working class, who had left the country to take jobs in the new factories, were reduced to unemployment and famine; and soon there was yet another catastrophe—the beginnings of a Dutch regime.

In the new kingdom of the Netherlands, Brussels again rose to the status of a capital city. A great change came over it, and the population rapidly rose from 75,000 to 100,000 inhabitants, thus at last exceeding that of Liège.

Instead of the old ramparts, there were great boulevards planted with trees. The city, no longer hemmed in by its walls, began to spread over the neighboring countryside. It took the unusual form of a city divided into an upper town, inhabited by the wealthy, and a lower town. In this period the Place de Brouckère and the new Théâtre de la Monnaie were built, and the first royal palace and the botanical gardens were also laid out.

A great event was the installation of gas street lights. The lamps were lit for the first time on August 1, 1819, and fed from a gasworks in the Rue Saint-Roch. Brussels was thus the first city on the continent of Europe to use this form of street lighting. Nevertheless, although the city had taken this lead among European capitals, its life still resembled that of a French provincial town, lived on lines that were soon afterward described by Balzac.

Among the middle classes the young people were given only a single suit each year. They wore it for the first time at Easter, and then kept it for Sundays and holidays; after the following Easter they put it into everyday wear.

There were not many amusements. Women spent most of their time at home, making lace or doing needlework, for it was not considered proper for them to go out. They were careful, of course, to do their work so far as possible sitting in the ground-floor window, so that young folk passing in the street might see them and they themselves might lose nothing of the spectacle of outside life. They went out only for a family walk in the afternoon, and to Mass on Sunday morning, but it was not thought seemly to bow or smile to persons they did not know, and even when they acknowledged an acquaintance they did not think it proper to stop.

Dinners and receptions were rare and occurred almost always on birthdays, weddings, baptisms, and the days of patron saints. At other times there were visits between neighbors, when cronies drank their tea and played Pope Joan or Lotto. These gossip parties ended early—about eight o'clock—and the ladies went home to supper.

Women had two different styles of dress, according to their class. Rich women wore a long, elegant gown, with a shawl covering their shoulders and ending in a point in the middle of the back, and on their heads silk hats. In summer the shawl was silk or lace and in winter it was woolen, often cashmere, with fringes. Workingwomen or servants wore a short, sleeveless jacket, with a hood that served as a hat. Their frock of cotton or wool was known as the *faille*, and remained fashionable until the middle of the nineteenth century. It was a universal garment, worn even by elegant women in the mornings when they went to market or to Mass or were doing their housework. For visiting, the silk bonnet, with ribbons under the chin, and the shawl were quite indispensable.

Men's fashions were considered behind those of the French. Persons in official positions still wore the ceremonial dress of the First Empire, with an austerely cut coat, breeches, and white stockings. Women, on the other hand, were careful to avoid "Parisian extravagances," but luxury found its outlet in the infinite variety of shades and types of material made possible by the progress of the textile industry. Every new shade was given a new and whimsical name. There were, for example, the "frightened mouse" (grey), the "lovesick toad" (light green), the "astonished toad," and the "spider contemplating a crime." The materials produced had names such as poplin (still in use), and zinzoline, stokolmie, and bazarinkoff, which appear to have some connection with Sweden and Russia.

By now, men were wearing the new hat, the *gibus*, or top hat, that had made its first appearance in England about 1800. It was worn by all social classes, even by tramps and beggars. In 1815 it had become the standard headgear of coachmen and servants, who were abandoning the three-cornered hat. Later it was adopted by their superiors. No other type of hat was now worn. King Charles X wore the top hat in France, as did Louis Philippe. In Belgium, the revolution of 1830 was fought in top hats. Throughout the nineteenth century, all of Belgium's ministers and statesmen, from Frère-Orban to Malou and Beernaert, wore the top hat.

On the other hand, only old men sported beards. All the young men shaved, and the great majority of the congress and the provisional government of 1830 consisted of clean-shaven men. Before long, however, fashion produced its compromise in the form of side whiskers.

In 1815, after the collapse of the Napoleonic Empire, the victorious allies decided to create a new state, the Kingdom of the Netherlands, to be a buffer state against France. The Belgians had not been consulted. Their lot was to consist in "amalgamation" with the Dutch to form a single nation. All possible measures had been taken to guarantee that the inhabitants of the south would have conditions of "perfect equality" with their northern neighbors. There were to be two capitals, Brussels and The Hague, and the Estates General were to sit in each alternately. No discrimination was to be made between the two peoples, and there was to be an equal number of Belgian and Dutch deputies, so that no part of the country would have a chance of oppressing the other.

Moreover, in view of the religious difference that had been one of the great causes of separation during the sixteenth century, the constitution was to guarantee freedom of worship, and the stipends and emoluments of the Catholic priests and bishops were to be borne out of public funds.

There was, indeed, one catastrophe from which Belgium was saved by her union with Holland. During the preceding twenty years, the Belgian provinces had set up powerful metal and textile industries, the earnings of which were essential for the country to survive. All the markets for their produce lay in France and there was no knowing what would become of them, now that they were separated from the French market. Union with Holland produced an alternative solution that came almost as a miracle, since wealthy Dutch colonies represented an outlet for Belgium equivalent to that which England had had in India.

The creation of the Kingdom of the Netherlands should therefore have been welcomed in Belgium with universal satisfaction, but this was not the case. To the Belgians it was a source of disappointment, and there was a constant stream of complaints. There were 3 million Belgians, compared with only 2 million Dutch, and the equality of representation in the Estates General was looked upon as an injustice. More important was the fact that the Belgian governing class was comparatively small in number and, in the Flemish countryside in particular, hardly anybody could read or write. The result was that Belgium could produce few people fitted for the more important jobs, and Belgo-Dutch relationships were at once poisoned by the disproportion in the numbers of civil servants coming from the two regions. The Belgians felt they were being discriminated against and they complained bitterly of the new regime.

The Kingdom of the Netherlands thus started on the wrong foot, and the Belgians, finding themselves treated as second-class citizens, grew more and more bitter. As always, the idea of amalgamation with people of a different race and religion quickly led them to oppose the union and become increasingly conscious of their national existence. Shortly afterward, the diplomat La Moussaye summarized the position by saying: "The Belgian hates the Dutchman and the Dutchman despises the Belgian and considers himself greatly the superior."

As early as 1819, a large number of songs and ditties appeared in Belgium that showed the state of opinion:

> I am not a Dutchman
> And I don't want to be.

and then again:

> Yes, I am a Belgian,
> And that's what I think's grand.
> And I am proud, upon my word,
> Of the name of my Fatherland.

The Belgians and the Dutch, far from being united by their common citizenship, reacted in exactly opposite ways. The governing body of the new Kingdom hung on to the illusion that fusion would occur by degrees, as a result of living together. Instead, there grew up a collective antagonism, fed by a multitude of vexations. As this grew more and more acute, it united Belgians and Belgian opinion in a single bloc, and in the end made the Kingdom of the Netherlands unworkable.

The founder of the new state, King William I, had been born at The Hague in 1772, and was forty-three years old when he came to the throne of the new kingdom. He was the son of William V, and a descendant of William the Silent, Prince of Orange, who organized the revolution in the Low Countries against Philip II during the sixteenth century. In reality he was more than a Dutchman—he was a Prussian. His mother was Fredericka von Hohenzollern, a Prussian princess, and he had married the daughter of Frederick William II of Prussia. He had grown up an admirer of Frederick the Great and hated the English parliamentary system.

He had had a long military career. He had fought at Landrecies and later at Fleurus against the French revolutionary armies, had attempted to land with the English in the Helder in 1799, and had fought against the French at Jena. In spite of all this, he was primarily an economist, and his mind was completely taken up with administrative and financial problems.

"For him, everything is material, positive and mathematical," said a contemporary. He hated display and was interested only in figures. He said of himself that had he not been king, he would have wished to be the best businessman in the Netherlands. In fact, he ended by abdicating, and finished his life indulging in financial speculation in Berlin.

He wanted to govern his kingdom like an industrial or commercial firm, without consulting the inhabitants or considering their wishes. His one thought was to increase their material prosperity, and his belief was that a wealthy people would necessarily be a happy people. A Marxist before the days of Marx, he believed that Belgo-Dutch antagonism arose solely from their different standards of living and education. He believed that when the two peoples reached the same level of culture they would find it easy to understand one another.

He thought himself infallible and took the advice of no one. To his government he appointed ministers of indifferent caliber who found that the best way of flattering him was to leave minor errors in their reports so that he might have the pleasure of correcting them. A more serious aspect of his character was the fact that he did not like the Belgians and found it difficult to understand them.

"I should much rather have my Holland by itself," he said in 1825. "Then I should be a hundred times happier."

The clue to his faults was the idea that he had a mandate from Europe to assure the fusion of the Belgians and the Dutch, and he imagined that, if quarrels and insurrections arose, he could always appeal to the great powers to reduce his opponents to reason.

On the other hand, William, conservative and even backward as he was in politics, was a bold innovator in other fields. He wanted to turn Belgium into a great commercial and industrial country that would rival England and gain as much wealth by conquering the markets of the world.

The structure of the Kingdom of the Netherlands, as he saw it, was based on a close alliance between Dutch trade and Belgian industry. Holland, with her colonial empire, had contributed a big market, and with her fleet she had an outlet that Belgian industry did not possess. Belgium for her part, with her cheap labor, her reserves of coal, and the progress she had made in mechanization, had a great industrial potential. The two countries together formed a powerful economic system, and the two parts, being complementary, would each contribute its own aptitudes and resources.

William's work in the financial field was particularly remarkable. Starting from zero, he created a credit system intended to finance new industries and thus insured the rhythm of investment necessary for Belgium's progress. To assure industry of a supply of fresh capital and the necessary outlets, he gave the export trade first priority, sacrificing the internal market and with it the working population's wage level and standard of living.

Allowing for the difference in period and situation, he achieved in the Netherlands results very similar to those accomplished in the Congo by King Leopold II. There are, in fact, striking resemblances between the two sovereigns. William, like Leopold, despised popularity and did not cater to public opinion. He lived in a narrow world of businessmen, big industrialists, and bankers. All his undertakings were surrounded by an atmosphere of secrecy that prevented the country from understanding them and exposed him to attacks and campaigns of denigration. Both sovereigns were primarily financiers and interested in letters and the arts only to a minor degree. Both were authoritarian, both subject to fits of anger, and both, in spite of themselves, went beyond their resources and capacities.

Each man built on a huge scale, and in neither case did anyone understand the meaning and magnificence of their work at first, because the public believed them both to be self-seeking. In both cases the misunderstanding arose through the sovereign's own withdrawal and insistence on working without any control. They were both expressions of a century in which financiers and businessmen were the real adventurers; and both were to be vindicated by posterity for the same reasons.

William, from the moment of his accession, had shown how little importance he attached to public ceremonies and display, and also his contempt for the public acclamation that greets manifestations of prestige. His enthronement took place in Brussels on September 21, 1815, in the Place Royale, and those present noticed that the crown put on his head was made only of gold-painted wood with colored glass stones, and that the heraldic lions on the King's cloak were made of copper. This seemed to many to presage a reign that would not last, and this contempt for appearances was certainly destined to play its part during the short period in which the Kingdom of the Netherlands was to exist.

Religious problems at once became politically important. The Belgians were divided into Catholics and liberals, and the latter had many points in common with the Dutch Protestants, for both were anxious about the excessive powers of the Church and between them constituted a majority in the Estates General. It was this fact that enabled the young state to begin to function.

The Belgian Catholics, led by their bishops, had looked with suspicion at the accession of a Protestant sovereign. Guarantees given them by the Fundamental Law seemed to them to be dangerous. The wording of Article 193 was as follows: "No form of worship may be prevented unless it disturb the peace and public order." The text was inoffensive in itself, but some Catholics interpreted it as meaning that processions and other ceremonies might be prohibited.

This was indeed the thesis of the Bishop of Ghent, Monseigneur de Broglie, in his "Doctrinal Judgment," in which he rejected the Fundamental Law and forbade civil servants to take the oath. "To swear conformity to a law," he said, "which puts into the hands of government the power to interfere with the exercise of public worship, when it has been the occasion for a disturbance, is to submit the exercise of our holy religion to dependence upon the wishes of its enemies and the malice of ill-disposed persons." In taking this line, Monseigneur de Broglie was giving William an advantage, for Ghent's Belgian liberals were disturbed by his uncompromising explosion and rallied to the King's side. The King thus obtained the government majority he needed. He could count on the Dutch, and the Belgians were divided, with the Catholics standing alone against the liberals.

The King then set about his general reorganization of industry, and the work he accomplished was indeed revolutionary. In ten years, Belgium was transfigured and the nation joined England at the head of world progress. After 1820, the use of gas for lighting purposes spread through the cities, providing a new use for coal. With the Newcomen steam pumps and Davy safety lamps the yield from the collieries increased, and coal production reached 2.5 million tons annually. New mines now came into production and, just before 1830, no less than thirty-three new concessions were granted in Hainaut and the Namur district. Belgian industry was using 185 high-pressure steam engines, some of which developed as much as 80 horse-power. The traffic in the port of Antwerp doubled in 10 years, and the number of ships using the port rose from 585 to 1,028. The Belgian textile industry, expanding to supply world markets, became a strong competitor of the English industry. Ghent had 80 mills with 283,000 spindles; the Cockerill factories manufactured the most up-to-date machinery in Europe; and Verviers was exporting its woolen cloth as far afield as Timbuktu.

The long-standing weakness of the Belgian economy had been a lack of credit organization, and even this disappeared under William's influence. In 1822 he created the Société Générale, an industrial bank with a capital of 50 million gold francs; its influence was to dominate the whole of the nineteenth century. With the new prosperity, the Belgian population increased rapidly. It now amounted to 3.9 million inhabitants, compared with 2.3 million in Holland, and the rate of increase was double the rate prevailing in France during this period. "If we think only of the material interests at stake," wrote Henri Pirenne, "the revolution of 1830 appears inexplicable."

This formidable expansion, far from consolidating the new Kingdom of the Netherlands, was to throw it out of balance by giving the Belgians an undue importance. Only the people of the south benefited from the new wealth. They grew apart from the general body politic and the mistakes King William made quickly worsened the situation.

Between 1822 and 1825, William made two mistakes: he decided to make Dutch the administrative language throughout Belgium, and he attempted to take control of education and the seminaries in order to bring clerical resistance to an end. Under the threat of William's influence, the clergy set up a private form of education in opposition to the official education. It was organized by parish priests in the country and by the teaching brotherhoods, with the result that the state schools lacked pupils. The government's reaction was to ban the teaching congregations, and to re-enact all the measures of persecution introduced by Joseph II and Napoleon. This time, however, it had to deal with an active and resourceful clergy, resolutely backed by the masses, and claiming that it was fighting in the cause of liberty.

Before long, Bishop Van Bommel exclaimed: "Let us all shake hands, Protestants, Catholics, and liberals. Let us all with equal zeal take up the cause of unlimited freedom, the only plank in the platform of safety."

At the same time, a new generation was coming to the fore, not only in Belgium, but throughout Europe. This was the time when Belgian liberalism, under French influence, was changing in character. The old liberals of the Empire period were now overridden by an enthusiastic generation of revolution-minded youth, obsessed with the idea of the rights of man and liberation of the people. New newspapers began to appear, such as the *Courrier des Pays-Bas* in Brussels, and the *Mathieu Landsberg* in Liége, in which liberal and Catholic positions were reconciled. Young people wanted jobs, and they wanted an elective parliamentary regime that would give them the right to speak and to act, and even to seize power. At the same time, the Catholics were influenced by the ideas of the French Catholic liberal Félicité Robert de Lamennais, and they adopted, as he had done, the principles of liberty. Agreement between Catholics and liberals, seemingly impossible, became a fact.

The new body formed was known as the Union of Oppositions and behind its common program against an authoritarian government was the magic word "liberty." A certain de Potter, writing in the *Courrier des Pays-Bas*, on November 8, 1828, had given them their battle cry: "So far, we have been hunting out the Jesuits. Our target now is the legislators. Pursue them, mock them, put them to shame!" Throughout the country, the leaders circulated a huge petition that, with the support of the clergy and the Flemish masses, received 40,000 signatures by November, 1828.

If this opposition had been national in character, it would at once have raised the Dutch against itself. Its members, however, limited their aims to general reforms, such as ministerial responsibility and equal access of everyone to the administration, thus turning the government's own principles against it. "You allowed young people to be brought up in liberal thought," wrote Jottrand in the *Courrier des Pays-Bas* on October 31, 1828. "The generation you have raised cannot now be governed at your own sweet will."

Tension was increased by unemployment and the resulting agitation of the workers. In 1829, a new petition contained 300,000 signatures, an enormous figure that can only be explained by the fact that priests had caused the mass of illiterate peasants to sign.

At the beginning of 1830 William was forced to take back all the unpopular measures he had enacted during the preceding five years. These included his laws concerning education, those imposing the Dutch language on the administration, and certain fiscal measures that were causing the cost of living to rise. But at the same time he redoubled the press prosecutions, had de Potter thrown into prison and later sent into the exile that made him a sort of national hero.

The problem, in reality, was that of two generations opposed to each other, for the high birth rate of the period of the Empire was now flooding the country with young people who were anxious to play a part in what was going on. In a country where the population is stable, it is almost impossible to shake the power of the mature generation, those who hold jobs and are masters of the situation. When the population is increasing, however, society is likely to be thrown out of balance by the number of energetic young people coming forward to play a part in events. They are inevitably bound together by a feeling of common problems and, having nothing to lose, they seek allies on every hand to begin a revolutionary enterprise. Joining the younger generation in Belgium about 1828 were many lawyers, writers, journalists, and intellectuals, exasperated by the King's absolute rule and aware that they could never reach the top unless the whole system was changed.

The Orangist governor of Liége, Sandberg, analyzed the position with rare lucidity in a report he submitted to William:

"The sponsors of the revolution are neither the nobles nor the priests," he wrote. "They are the young lawyers, the young folk from the lower classes, the people who want to rise in life, the malcontents of every sort. The movement, although it is not French, has a strong affinity with events in France—hatred of privilege, local linguistic claims, trial by jury, ministerial responsibility, access to jobs—these are their watchwords." They were so young that Alexandre Gendebien, who in 1828 was thirty-eight, seemed a patriarch, as did Firmin Rogier, who was thirty-seven. Paul Devaux, editor of an important newspaper, was only twenty-seven; Sylvain Van de Weyer was twenty-six; Charles Rogier twenty-five; Renard de Tournay twenty-four; Jean-Baptiste Nothomb twenty-three; and Chazal twenty.

Supporting them was a crowd of adventurers who had not been able to find their place in society. They included ex-officers, such as Van der Meere, Pletinck, Van der Smissen, and some professional revolutionaries, but for the most part they were lawyers or connected with the law.

The leaders, great as were their talents and desire to get to the top, would have been powerless had they not been able to enlist the support of an army of malcontents who were ready to bring the struggle down to street level. This group included the hungry workers who had been ready enough to endure poverty and starvation wages, but who were now driven past endurance by the unemployment arising from increased mechanization and the conversion of industry. They were willing to take the initiative in riots and disturbances.

It was the working class that had borne the brunt of the country's industrial expansion and its plight was wretched indeed. In 1830, a Brussels laborer's wage was fifty centimes a day. This seemed normal to everybody; and, on September 18, 1830, when the workers of Brussels rose in revolt to demand an increase of twenty-five centimes a day, it was Levae, the revolutionary, who exclaimed to de Potter: "There is some force in the background urging the workers to put forward claims that are either impossible or ridiculous." Most observers agree that the wage of a Belgian worker was lower by half than that of an English worker, who was himself badly off.

Wages had been frozen in 1820. In 1822, new taxes on flour milling and slaughtering resulted in a rapid increase in the prices of bread and meat. The receipts from these taxes were earmarked as a subsidy for industry in order to facilitate its expansion, amounting, in fact, to a concealed cut in wages.

Strikes and workers' associations were banned, and specialists among the workers, who were traditionally well paid in Belgium, were unable to unite to obtain adjustments in their wage scales as the cost of living rose. The wage of a Verviers weaver, for example, showed no increase between 1820 and 1827. It amounted to 1.48 francs a day, while his wife earned 42 centimes and his son 52 centimes.

Now, in 1829, the index of food prices rose from 64.2 to 97.3, and in 1830 it rose another ten per cent. The index of agricultural prices went from 65 in 1824 to 122 in 1830, and the price of wheat from 5.43 to 10.93 florins. The purchasing power of the masses was rapidly waning, and the unusually long winter of 1829-30 placed another severe strain on their resources. Conditions were like those that had prevailed in France in the great winter of 1788. Here was the classic economic cataclysm that is the forerunner of every revolution.

The industrial crisis had reached such a point that the employers were even suspected of encouraging the workers to break the machinery in order to have an excuse for stopping their wage payments. At the beginning of 1830 there was a sharp increase in bankruptcy. The Cockerill firm had to ask for government aid, the wheat harvest was below requirements, and the difficulty in making ends meet foreshadowed yet another rise in the cost of living.

In this atmosphere, the working class of the big towns was seized by panic and, backed by political agitation, was ready to explode. The revolution in 1830, therefore, sprang from a double revolutionary current. In the first place, it was a political revolution led by young men of the middle class who wanted reform and were pressing for a parliamentary regime. Secondly, there was the revolt of the proletariat, organized by hungry workers who were at first only the cat's paw of liberal leaders—who were later unable to hold them in check.

The young intellectuals were not interested in the problems of industrial expansion and cared little for the lot of the people. Nonetheless, they egged on the hungry masses, and the movement that began only as agitation for reform was turned into a revolution.

The government was in no position to contain a real revolt, and the part played by the masess led to its sudden fall. In the industrial towns, hungry workers were ready to break up machinery and erect barricades in the streets as a protest against high prices and low wages.

The Dutch army was largely made up of Belgians and was not very reliable. Moreover, Belgium was feeling the effect of an enormous increase in its population, that was like a bomb inside the Kingdom of the Netherlands. Not only did it produce the mass of hungry workers in the street, that represented an angry and unstable group in the big cities, but the increasing number of inhabitants in the Belgian south was creating a growing pressure that disrupted the Belgo-Dutch system. By the early part of 1830, the opposition was demanding full ministerial accountability, equal access to all employment, freedom of education, and freedom of the press. What these words concealed, however, was the conquest by the Belgians of the Kingdom of the Netherlands.

This took the form of a revolutionary ebullience that spread little by little into the provinces of southern Holland that had been conquered by the Calvinists during the seventeenth century. The Catholic populations at Bois-le-Duc, Berg-op-Zoom, and from Breda to the Rhine discovered their affinity with the Belgians and began to side with them morally. The union of the two countries was thus working for the benefit of the south that was absorbing and submerging the north. Still more, action was soon taken by a number of Dutch deputies to create a pro-Belgian majority in the Estates General. With the agitation in its early stages, the Paris revolution of July, 1830 lit the powder trail, creating a wave of enthusiasm throughout Europe. In Germany, the poet Heinrich Heine sang of it as of the coming of spring. In Italy, the head of the revolutionary government in Bologna compared it with the creation of the world, "a six-day job." Nobody in Brussels wanted independence, or even separation from Holland. The Belgian revolutionary groups who were keeping up the agitation in the big towns were, however, in close contact with the revolutionary clubs in Paris. A month later, the revolution broke out in Belgium and the country was dragged into it without wishing it and without foreseeing it.

In 1830, William was in his fifty-ninth year and Brussels staged a great festival in his honor, including fireworks and theatrical performances. The fireworks were canceled for fear of incidents, but there seemed no reason for stopping the performance of Daniel Auber's opera *La Muette de Portici* that was to be given at the Théâtre de la Monnaie on August 23.

This opera deals with the fisherman Masianello, a rebel against Philip IV of Spain in one of the revolutions that marked the mid-seventeenth century. One of his arias is the famous "Amour Sacré de la Patrie." The opera was given a rousing reception by an audience consisting of high society and the middle class. The streets of the capital were filled with unemployed workers who formed groups, out of curiosity, around the theater exit, and who were not slow to organize a procession. Some of the youngsters proposed a demonstration outside the offices of the newspapers that favored the King. Wiser heads decided to go home, but the firebrands took control of the situation and began burning private homes, such as that of the unpopular minister Van Maanen. They also ransacked grocery stores and shops that sold firearms.

The next day the confusion and absence of any responsible authority were plain for all to see. The burgomaster of the capital was away in the country. The little garrison of Brussels, with too much to do and no orders, was unable to deal with the situation; in principle, its duty to intervene arose only if a state of siege had been proclaimed. It hastened back to the barracks and the bands of rioters wandered where they wanted through the city. Shopkeepers, anxious about their store windows, and the bourgeois, who did not want their houses burned down, issued an appeal for volunteers to serve under the popular d'Hoogvorst in an administrative commission and civil guard.

Since there was no sign of the lawfully constituted authorities, this new commission ruled the city. As news of these events spread, committees of prominent local citizens were organized in Liége, Verviers, Huy, Louvain, and Namur, civil guards were formed, and delegates were sent to The Hague to demand a remedy for the people's grievances.

Contemporaries looked on these events as a dangerous proletarian outbreak and a threat to property and the peace. The young revolutionary intellectuals were concerned. They understood too late that the agitation they had sponsored in the country had turned into anarchy, and that these disturbances would be a pretext for William to send his troops into action and call himself the savior of the middle class.

Alexandre Gendebien treated the *Muette de Portici* incident as a schoolboy's prank, Lebeau considered it a misfortune, and Charles Rogier refused to come to Brussels. Rogier, in fact, only accepted the leadership of the Liége volunteers at pistol point, pale-faced and in consternation. There can be little doubt that the outbreak was proletarian in character and similar to disturbances that were occurring throughout Europe because of unemployment and poverty. At Aachen, Duesseldorf, and in the Rhineland problems were the same.

Everywhere people were singing the "Marseillaise." Everywhere the French tricolor was hoisted side by side with the red flag that, since the French Revolution, had become the proletariat's symbol. At Verviers, the municipal pawnshop was stormed and the management forced to restore to the workers, free of charge, all they had pawned for sums of less than ten florins. The houses of tax-collectors who collected the unpopular taxes on bread and meat, were pitilessly ransacked.

At Brussels, the proletariat held their meetings in Rue Haute cafés, laying plans to destroy the machinery of suburban factories, as their English counterparts had been doing around Manchester. One evening, three armed bands went out in three different directions, destroyed the Wilson, Rey, and Bosdevex-Bal factories, and ransacked more than twenty country houses and twenty-seven shops. Damage amounted to more than 1 million florins.

The insurrection was not against the Dutch, but against the middle class, and the fears it aroused are easily understandable. But once order had been restored, the middle class found itself master of the city and used this position to press for the reforms it desired. Having itself stepped outside the law, its only support came from the people. The bourgeois feared both the popular revolt they had just suppressed, and the King of Holland whose powers they had usurped.

William himself was delighted with these events. For some months he had been hoping for disturbances, so that he might suppress them and re-establish his authority. Moreover, he believed he had a European mandate and remarked jocularly: "The gentlemen of Brussels know the treaties as well as we do, and they will have no wish to let themselves be beaten into submission by the allied powers."

In fact, all he wanted to do was to let the revolution burn itself out. He contented himself with sending his eldest son, the Prince of Orange, who was very popular among the Belgians, to reoccupy Brussels peacefully with a force of 6,000 men.

If the Prince of Orange had simply marched into the city with his troops, he would at once have settled the situation. Instead, he was frightened by a delegation of local notables who assured him that barricades would be set up at every street corner. They begged him to come alone to appraise the situation. Fearing the consequences of any blood-letting, he decided to go to the town hall; there he was surrounded by an armed mob and, much alarmed, withdrew with a promise to plead the cause of the rebels to his father. The illegal government of Brussels thus became legitimate, and, after September 1, 1830, more and more volunteers began to pour in from all over the country.

William did not like hasty decisions. "Night is the best counselor," he used to say. In the face of this astonishing news, his only reply to a Brussels delegation demanding administrative separation was that he would call the Estates General and consult them in order to recon-cile, if possible, all conflicting interests.

He knew well enough that the local notables who had seized power would be unable to maintain their authority, and that Belgium would soon be sinking into a state of anarchy. European revolutionaries were converging from all sides on the capital, and all the country's own adventurers and professional agitators were joining forces with them. The departure of the Belgian deputies for the Estates General on September 13, 1830, left the field clear for the hotheads, and new leaders came to the front: Charles Rogier, who had come from Liége with 300 armed volunteers, most of them traveling by stagecoach; a former hotelkeeper, Plentinck; Niellon, a French officer who had re-signed his commission to manage a puppet theater; the Spaniard Don Juan van Halen; and others, including Gendebien, Felix de Mérode, Sylvain van de Weyer, Ducpétiaux, and Lesbroussart. All the provinces of France were represented, the French contingent including the Alsatian Larivière, Dr. Grégoire from Charleville, and the Lyon actor Jenneval, who became the author of the "Brabançonne." There were also Poles, Germans, and revolutionaries from every country. This was the army of European revolution that appeared wherever trouble was brewing. They were expert in forming clubs of agitators and preparing to overthrow the government.

Life, however, went on. While Brussels was in the insurgent's power, William was very busy at The Hague marrying off his daughter Mari-anne. Skilled in temporizing, he had decided to accept the idea of administrative separation in order to gain time. It was necessary to organize elections in the two new regions of the country, prepare new electoral registers and, especially, ask the consent of the guarantor powers. The King, therefore, set aside the petitions of the moderate elements in Belgium who had sent one deputation after another to him.

He knew that his troops were at the gates of Brussels. The dis-turbances were occurring in only two of the nine Belgian provinces, and in only four big cities. The rest of the country—all of Flanders and half of Wallonia—was firmly held by the Orangists. In the capital itself, everyone of any importance was either supporting the King or keeping clear of the conflict. Banks were refusing to open their tills to the insurgent authorities, and hungry, penniless volunteers were leaving the city daily. William was reserving his entry into the city until such time as the wealthier classes called for his help. Then his soldiers would be hailed as liberators.

If the insurgents had possessed any money in September, 1830, there would never have been a revolution, but their leaders, without funds to feed their troops, realized that they had to seize the public treasury. The only way to force the banks and the civil servants to hand over state funds was to form a provisional government. This forced the revolutionaries to claim not only reforms, but actual independence. The civil guard opposed this step and the Liége volunteers began leaving Brussels. The extremists, led by Charles Rogier, now prepared to act, not against the Dutch authorities, but against the middle class and the moderates, who represented armed strength. To secure their downfall he started a violent campaign of agitation and, for the first time, used the name of Belgium. The rising at once became a national one. The "Brabançonne" was heard on September 12, and other patriotic songs—"La Marseillaise des Belges," "La Bruxelloise," "La Liberté Belge"—came out in great profusion. It was now the middle class that could be accused of "treason." In the meantime, anti-Dutch propaganda made it possible to appeal to the masses without letting the revolt become a purely working-class affair.

On September 20, the revolutionary party seized the town hall and disarmed the civil guard. This created a state of anarchy, for there was no outstanding citizen who would accept leadership of the city. The French minister in Brussels wrote to his government that Belgium was calling for the King's intervention and that the end of the disturbances was at hand. Dutch agents, who appear to have favored the agitation, were delighted; and Prince Frederick, who followed events closely through his spies, announced that he would march into the city the following day.

This was the cue for the headlong flight of all the revolutionary leaders. Not only did conservatives, such as Félix de Mérode and Van der Smissen, leave the city, but so did the more radical leaders, such as Niellon and Chazal, while Rogier himself hid in a farm in the Forest of Soignes. Others crossed the French border and took refuge at Valenciennes. At the same time the Estates General voted in favor of administrative separation by the enormous majority of eighty-one votes against nineteen, the Dutch having supported the Belgians in the motion. The Belgians, therefore, had won their case and the revolution no longer had any meaning.

On the morning of September 23, Dutch columns entered the city with their bands playing the overture to *La Muette de Portici*, the musical theme for this page of history. They were the only troops the King could spare without compromising his border security; should they be beaten, it would no longer be possible to contain the revolt. But defeat of any sort seemed absurd. D'Hoogvorst alone remained in the city in order to secure an honorable capitulation at the last moment.

The Dutch had no difficulty in forcing the Schaerbeek Gate, and charged down the Rue Royale. Snipers hidden on the rooftops opened fire, but they were unable to stop the advance. If the Dutch could reach the royal palace, they would be masters of the upper town and would have the rest of the capital in their power.

When they reached the park, however, their officers made a tactical error. They ordered their troops to take cover under the big trees of the park to re-form and continue the attack. They did not realize that they were encircled. The Place Royale could only be reached from the park by a single gate. The troops would have to cross an open esplanade that the insurgents were raking with their fire. As soon as the insurgents realized that the attackers had halted, their combat troops literally sprang up from the earth. New supporters poured in from all over through the other city gates, and the revolutionary leaders who had taken flight returned hastily to organize the defense. Confusion in the city was such that when the disheartened Dutch decided to retreat nobody noticed their departure. It was not until scouts, surprised by the silence in the park, ventured warily in to see what was afoot, that they realized that the revolution had triumphed and that William had lost Belgium.

This collapse of Holland's best troops before a handful of insurgents seems difficult to explain. The fact is that they did not come into Brussels to fight and, as soon as their commanding officers saw that they were not greeted with cheers, their only thought was to negotiate the end of struggle. Prince Frederick had no thought of engaging in an open battle that might well compromise the popularity of his dynasty.

In the morning, in announcing the entry of his troops, Prince Frederick wrote as follows:

"These officers and these soldiers are your fellow citizens, your friends, and your brothers. They do not bring you punishment or vengeance, but only order and rest. A generous pardon will cover the faults and irregular acts that have been produced by the circumstances of the time."

It was by design that he left the Porte de Hal free, so that foreign volunteers who were not covered by the amnesty might be able to leave the city. Moreover, he refused to bring his artillery into action.

He was astonished at the resistance that developed. On September 22, he issued another proclamation:

"I came under the King's orders to bring you news of peace." He proposed to occupy the city jointly with the national troops and civil guard. If he had been able to communicate with the Belgian leaders, an agreement would undoubtedly have been reached. He found, however, nobody with whom he could negotiate. Anarchy prevailed among the insurgents and there were no longer any recognized authorities. The Prince's emissaries even had trouble finding D'Hoogvorst, who had written the Prince before he entered the city that there were no longer any leaders and that there was no real authority with whom he could negotiate. D'Hoogvorst agreed to meet the Prince and discussions began. Agreement had almost been reached on September 24, on a mutually honorable end to hostilities when Rogier, who had returned from the Forest of Soignes, realized that the Dutch did not wish to attack and broke off the negotiations. Rogier seized power and restored order among the insurgents. He appointed the Spaniard Don Juan van Halen Commander-in-chief. He was a man who owed everything to him and who could do nothing but obey his orders.

He ended the powerlessness of the Belgian combatants, who had been fighting in great disorder. He brought the country to life, sent his emissaries everywhere, and invited the Dutch soldiery to desert. Indeed, he was the real leader and organizer of the revolution. He seized state funds, secured advances from the Société Générale, took possession of the ministries and public services, discharged the Dutch civil servants, and finally brought back from exile the most popular man in Belgium, Louis de Potter, an act that brought him the unanimous support of all the insurgents. Finally, by issuing appeals to all the provinces, he transformed the resistance of Brussels into a national effort. The provisional government consisted of Gendebien, D'Hoogvorst, Jolly, Van der Linden, Coppin, Van de Weyer, and Félix de Mérode. It rallied around Rogier for the sake of maintaining order. The Dutch retreat became a rout, because the Belgian soldiers deserted and went over to the revolutionaries with their weapons.

The bands of insurgents, reinforced by countless volunteers from all sides, now had only to march straight ahead to occupy the whole of Belgium. The litter left by the routed armies reached all the way to Antwerp, where the Dutch Commander Chassé agreed to evacuate the town, and concluded an armistice. The provisional government, however, had no authority over its troops, who proceeded to violate the terms of the armistice by attacking the Dutch. Chassé replied by ordering the bombardment of Antwerp, which burned for several hours, and Belgium was swept by a wave of indignation.

The Orangists, who supported the King and who probably represented the majority of the country, were accused of moral complicity in this crime. Flanders itself came out in support of the provisional government, which soon had control of the whole country except for the citadels of Antwerp, Maastricht, and Luxemburg.

The fortresses were to decide the independence of Belgium. The Brussels insurrection would have served no useful purpose if William had been able to retain the citadels built since 1815, a forbidding network that encircled and dominated the entire country. Insurgent Belgium was thus cut off from France, and it would have been easy for the Dutch to stage a victorious return. The garrisons, however, were composed mainly of reservists who were there to work off their temporary recall to the colors and whose main thought was of going home. Moreover, soldiers of Belgian origin had been posted there, rather than elsewhere, and it was no part of their plan to let themselves be killed in a fight with their fellow countrymen. All of these strong points capitulated without resistance under the double pressure of desertion by Belgian soldiers and the threat that their food supplies would be cut off by the insurgent population.

The course of events at Namur was characteristic. This was an almost impregnable fortress, firmly held by the Dutch. The officer in command of the city, which was then completely encircled by its wall, immediately declared a state of siege and held the inhabitants prisoners within the ramparts under the shadow of his guns.

By some mistake, the garrison troops opened fire on the crowd without warning. The people revolted, raised barricades, and put themselves under the command of ex-soldiers of the Napoleonic armies. They at once attacked the gates of the city wall to allow the volunteers outside to join the city's inhabitants. The Iron Gate held out for a whole day. Suddenly, however, news circulated that the Dutch troops had no more funds and had eaten nothing for twenty-four hours. By an extraordinary mischance, all the food depots were in the town itself, in the barracks, and General van Geen was obliged to ask for 7,000 loaves of bread and a supply of flour to be delivered to the garrison in exchange for which he would withdraw his troops into the citadel.

The Belgians accepted the offer and evacuation began at once. When it was completed, the armed insurgents made difficulties about the delivery of the food. Van Geen threatened to bombard the city if the promised bread was not delivered, but actually he was in a quandary. He knew that when his troops had eaten the food allowed them, the blockade would continue and it would be necessary to yield. While he was thinking it over, his hungry soldiers began deserting. The Dutch Commander eventually decided to surrender so that he could at least withdraw such troops as remained to him. The latter, however, wandered off in the course of their march, and by the time he reached Louvain he had only sixty-six officers and fifty or sixty men. Much the same was happening throughout Belgium.

The warriors who had fought during the September rising in Brussels must not be thought of as Belgian patriots in the modern sense. Their insurrection had been in the name of liberal and humane ideals that were a direct reflection of the French Revolution, and for them it seemed right and proper to die in the cause of liberty. Belgium was born from quite a new sentiment: hatred for the Dutch.

This hatred came to the surface in the beginning of September and mid-October, 1830, and it was so violent that all observers were astonished. The presence of Dutch troops constituted a threat that converted a simple desire for freedom—which could have been satisfied within the framework of the Kingdom of the Netherlands—into a Belgian national revolt. It made the masses forget their poverty, diverted the workers from the social revolution they claimed, and imbued everyone with a common feeling of patriotism.

Letters written by the combatants show clearly enough how these feelings grew. One of the most striking was a hasty message to his parents written by Isidore Gillain of Namur, the son of a brewer, at the beginning of the September rising. In it we look in vain for any reference to Belgium or the fatherland, and find only the ideal of liberty expressed in terms that reflect the contagion of the spirit that had animated the volunteers of the French Revolution:

"I have decided to die, rather than give way to these Dutch cowards. . . . Many brave men among us have died in defense of their freedom. But, in return, we have killed these swine who want to bind us in their chains. This evening, perhaps, we shall be masters of the town. I will not let my courage flag, and, if die I must, console yourself with the thought that your son died for freedom.

Good-bye, I am off to the fight.

If I am all right, I will write again on Sunday or Monday.

Good-bye, don't grieve for me.

Courage! We shall win.

My kisses to all.

Isidore GILLAIN."

After the September victory and the creation of a provisional government, there was a general rush for vacant jobs and positions. The Dutch civil servants had to be replaced, and tens of thousands of Belgiums were appointed without great regard to their competence or qualifications. Once more a revolution was putting itself on a firm basis by giving a huge body of newly promoted officials and their families an interest in maintaining the new regime.

Within a few days even the least aggressive petitioners were being appointed to high positions. A young man named Van Praet, who had played no part whatever in the revolution, but was the brother-in-law of Devaux, one of the leaders, wrote to Rogier to ask him for a job:

"I am in some difficulty about this for two reasons," he explained. "In the first place, I have no special request to make, and secondly, I do not know what is available."

Charles Rogier was inundated with requests from people he did not know, from boyhood friends he had forgotten, and from people who described themselves as "friends of the public welfare," who were anxious to help by receiving a good salary.

Van Praet, who had previously held a small job as a filing clerk at Bruges, was appointed secretary of the legation in London. There he met the minister, Count of Aerschot, and was invited to all the gala dinners—at one he sat between the Duke of Richmond and the Duke of Devonshire. The famous Lord Brougham, who was to put Cannes and the Côte d'Azur on the map of fashion, would stand aside when Van Praet passed into the dining room. All Belgians took part in the same giddy ascent in the social scale. For those who were young and ambitious there were abundant positions and promotions.

Van Praet's position came to nothing; he had to return to Belgium with his tail between his legs. On the way back he met a congressional delegation that was going to England to visit Prince Leopold of Saxe-Coburg. He told the delegates he could speak English and knew everybody in London and took upon himself the responsibility of accompanying the delegation. This time he used his opportunity well. He won the Prince's favor, was engaged as his secretary, and so began his ascent. He later became a minister and played an important part in politics until the time of Leopold II.

When the provisional government had filled up the gaps in the administration, it hastily set to work to carry out the program of the Union of Opposition. It did this by publishing a long series of decrees that embodied every conceivable form of liberty. These included freedom of assocation, and abolition of the state police and of theatrical censorship. At the same time, it organized elections, and its campaign was so violent against the Orangists that no candidate from this camp presented himself at the polls.

A single slate ran for Congress on November 3, 1830. There were 46,000 voters, but only 30,000 voted to elect the deputies who were to give Belgium its constitution. There were no opposition candidates, but more than a third of the voters abstained. These were the Orangists, who would have preferred to maintain the Belgo-Dutch economic link, and the industrial prosperity resulting from it, in a federal state that respected Belgian autonomy. They attempted to take part in the local elections that came afterward, but those who were elected were subsequently disqualified and the matter was not mentioned again.

The Belgian national congress met on November 10, and from this moment events moved swiftly. On November 18, the congress proclaimed the independence of Belgium; on November 24, it voted the perpetual exclusion of all members of the Nassau family. On February 7, it passed the new Belgian constitution; and all Belgium had to do now was to choose a king.

One important task still remained, however. This was to secure European recognition for the new state.

How could Belgium gain recognition by the great powers? It could not be done by force, for the insurgents had only an undisciplined army, without leaders and without real military value. On three sides of the new state, the strongholds of potential invasion—Flemish Zeeland, Antwerp, Maastricht, and Luxemburg—were firmly held by the encircling Prussians and Dutch. Seldom had the country been more sorely threatened and more impotent in the face of threats. Without France, Belgian independence would not have lasted more than a few weeks.

The Prussians had mobilized at once and wanted nothing more than to march into Belgium. The Russians concentrated an invasion army in Poland, the Austrians considered the Belgian revolution a danger to the order of things in Europe, and the English were indignant on seeing the Kingdom of the Netherlands disappear. Still more serious was the fact that the Vatican, morally the greatest power of the period, spoke in favor of the restoration of William I and took sides against the Belgian revolution.

The Belgian priesthood, in supporting the insurrection, had done so in spite of the Pope's attitude. Pope Pius VIII and his secretary of state were allied with the Austrian statesman, Metternich, and partisans of the legitimate monarchies. They had no sympathy for insurgents whose ideas they condemned. The agreement between the Catholics and the liberals seemed scandalous, and they disapproved of the principles of the new constitution. The stamping out of the revolution by the great powers, and the restoration to power of William, would have had their support if it had been undertaken.

Moreover, it cannot be said that the recognition of Belgium's independence was the result of the political sense and diplomatic skill of the Brussels leaders. Indeed, for six months they seemed to be living in a dream and to have lost all touch with reality. The speeches, the declarations, and the threats the Belgian deputies hurled at Europe are enough to convince the modern reader that he is reading a story of madmen.

Gendebien and the other leaders of the French party openly defied France. Lebeau, once so moderate in his views, proudly declared: "The conference of London must recognize that it is not concerned with the question of frontiers." Gendebien proclaimed that he would refuse to accept the basis of separation, "even with the Russians at the gate of Louvain and the Dutch at the gate of Schaerbeek." When Sebastiani, although he favored the Belgians, said to Gendebien: "If Saxe-Coburg sets foot in Belgium, we shall open fire at him with our guns." Gendebien replied: "Fine! We shall ask the English to reply to your guns." When the French ministers asked him not to endanger the peace of Europe, he cried out: "Let the French government go to the devil!"

In the end, the French and the English were discouraged and agreed that nothing could be done about the government and the congress of Belgium. Sebastiani said with a sigh: "The Belgians have no ideas except mad ones. They had better take care, or other people may think in the same way."

"Everyone agrees in saying the Belgians are mad," cried the English minister Viscount Palmerston. "It is a waste of effort arguing with them." "More than ever, this country wants war," moaned General Belliard, the French representative in Brussels. "It wants war against the confederation, war against Holland, and war against anybody else it can find."

It was even worse when it came to choosing a king. The more radical spirits in Belgium favored the candidacy of one of Napoleon's relatives, Prince Auguste de Leuchtenberg, son of Eugène de Beauharnais; the moderates supported the election of the Duke of Nemours, one of the sons of Louis Philippe. Nobody knew these two candidates, and neither of them had officially come forward.

The Prince de Leuchtenberg was still a minor, serving as an officer in the Bavarian army, and was quietly posted for garrison duties at Eichstadt, where he did not even read the Belgian newspapers. The Duke of Nemours was a youngster of sixteen years uninterested in politics.

How then was Belgium to gain European recognition? It was the consequence of an extremely simple situation that had nothing to do with the Belgians, but that had an irresistible influence on the powers meeting in London. Nobody, as things stood, wanted a war. France did not want one because her King Louis Philippe knew he would be risking his throne. Prussia did not want one because she would be beaten if she were not supported by England and Russia, and in this case would lose the Rhineland. Austria did not want one because she was at peace (as was the King of Prussia), and knew that a war would be a jump into the unknown.

The English, however, were particularly afraid of a general war, because they knew it would be disastrous for their interests. They would have liked to see the restoration of the Kingdom of the Netherlands that they had created in 1815, but they knew that in a general conflict, whoever might be the final victor, either France or Russia would gain the leadership of Europe. If the coalition were victorious, Russia would be powerful enough to seize Constantinople and the eastern Mediterranean and thus to threaten English hegemony in India. If France were victorious, she would annex the left bank of the Rhine and would then be in a position to resume her struggle against England.

The Belgian incident, therefore, could only be brought to an end by a compromise, and there were only two possible solutions to ensure peace. These were:

1. The status quo, consisting of the recognition of Belgian independence, and the giving of Limbourg and Luxemburg to Holland as compensation. This was the easier solution, since everybody would keep what he had, and it would give some measure of satisfaction to Prussia, while Belgian independence was in itself a victory, or at least an advantage for France and for England.

2. Partition, which would be inevitable if no compromise could be reached, and which would be the only way of avoiding war. It would have involved giving Brussels and Ghent to the Dutch, Liége and Luxemburg to the Prussians, and the rest of Wallonia to France. Everybody would thus get something, there would no longer be any point in fighting a war, and the balance of Europe would be maintained.

It is as well to take stock of this situation before giving Talleyrand, Louis Philippe, or Palmerston any credit for the independence of Belgium. All these statesmen were in reality only seeking a means of keeping the balance of power in Europe to preserve the peace. Belgium was just a pawn in the game.

Belgian opinion was but scantily informed of the realities of diplomacy. The easy victory of September, 1830, had gone to the country's head and there was opposition to the idea of giving up Maastricht and Luxemburg. Many of the insurgents would have preferred a general war and they even believed they would be able to drag France into it with them.

Their contacts with France existed only through the clubs, and they did not realize that the great powers had agreed to avoid a general war. Still less did they understand that if they persisted, they would get, not war, but the partition of their country, since this was the only solution that would satisfy everybody.

Between November, 1830, and June, 1831, the congress in Brussels wasted a great deal of time trying to prevent the inevitable. The real game was being played elsewhere, and the Belgians, by their evasive delays, succeeded only in giving the King of Holland the time he needed to reorganize his army. It was only at the last moment, when Dutch mobilization was almost complete, that the Belgian moderates, influenced by Lebeau, took fright. They proceeded at once to Prince Leopold of Saxe-Coburg's election to the throne of Belgium. The Prince was English by marriage, a friend of the Czar, and acceptable to France, so that he was, in fact, the European candidate.

They also persuaded the congress to ratify the Treaty of Eighteen Articles that recognized Belgian independence and even promised the country part of Limbourg. Leopold I was able to take his place on the throne of Belgium, and he made his ceremonial entry into Brussels on July 21, 1830.

At this moment, the King of Holland, William I, reappeared on the scene. He believed that his hour had come, and launched his army against Belgium without any idea of an annexation, but simply to improve his own frontiers. He had had time enough to reorganize his forces, and the Dutch, maddened by the hatred the Belgians felt for them, were out to give "these rioters" a lesson. Within ten days, between August 2 and August 12, the Belgian army was cut in two and Leopold I, after his defeat at Louvain, was almost taken prisoner. The new King had only time enough to call France to his aid, and the arrival of the French army saved Belgium just in time. William had waited too long before he struck; he would no doubt have settled everything to his own advantage if he had acted two months earlier.

There was a serious crisis, where the partition solution almost won the day. The Belgians eventually had to accept the much more severe Treaty of Twenty-four Articles, and, a year later, another French army had to come, besiege, and capture the citadel of Antwerp. Belgium remained in a state of war with Holland for nine years, which enabled her to retain temporary possession of Limbourg and Luxemburg. Leopold I, after almost losing his throne within a few weeks of his accession, was in the meantime able to apply himself to organizing the young state.

X

LEOPOLD I AND BELGIAN INDEPENDENCE

King Leopold I was the eighth child of a small German princely family, the family of Saxe-Coburg-Gotha, or more precisely, Saxe-Coburg-Saalfeld. He was born in Thuringia in 1790, and his only possible future lay in a rich marriage. Heaven had, however, endowed him with one special gift. He was one of the best-looking men of his time, and even Napoleon at St. Helena described him as the prince whose appearance had most dazzled him. Men and women were equally impressed, for his personality had a kind of radiance, and his expression dignity, moderation, and energy.

Like all the German princes of his time, he had seen his family swept away by the French invasions. He flattered Napoleon and later entered service in Russia, where he fought in the ranks of the coalition. His sister Julie had married the Grand Duke Constantine, brother of the Czar, and he thus moved in the very highest ranks of European society.

His good looks did the rest. He came with the Czar to the court of England and won the heart of the heiress presumptive to the crown, Princess Charlotte. Hers was a capricious and impassioned character which, however, he successfully dominated, persuading her to break off her engagement to the Prince of Orange. This was the same prince whom Leopold was to supplant in Belgium, and who was to come within an ace of taking him prisoner at Louvain.

This marriage made Leopold the future prince consort of England. It was the first act in the dramatic cycle of the Coburg dynasty, which, surprisingly enough, has not yet tempted the skill of any dramatist or novelist. It is a story that would certainly serve as a rich canvas fraught with tragic themes, disasters and portraits of men and women of exceptional caliber.

Leopold had been married scarcely a year when his wife died in childbirth; the child died too, and Leopold's fortunes collapsed. But his character was too strong and his ambitions too tenacious for him to be unduly cast down. Very shortly afterward, his widowed sister, Princess von Meiningen, married the Duke of Kent. Leopold, who had become British by marriage and had remained at Kensington Palace, became the "favorite uncle" of their young daughter who, as Queen Victoria, kept up a life-long correspondence with him and married his elder brother's son.

He was offered the throne of Greece, which he accepted too hastily and later refused, in February, 1830. However, his connections with most of the royal houses of Europe put him in an extremely strong position and resulted in the offer of the throne of Belgium.

He was shrewd enough to wait until the offer became pressing before he accepted it. His hesitation was not on account of the constitution under which he would have to reign. This document, indeed, seemed ridiculous to him, and he was amused at the idea that he would have to respect the "sovereignty of the people." He was, however, a practical man, and counted on his own experience and skill to get the better of written texts. He decided, therefore, to adapt himself to each situation as it arose and make the best of it.

He was now forty-one years of age and still attractive. He was adept at rejecting proposals while still appearing to see eye-to-eye with those who made them, in accepting proposals without committing himself, and in convincing people that he shared their views.

The ten-day campaign and the Louvain disaster discredited all the Belgian leaders. Deputies, ministers, and generals were in disgrace, or even suspected of treachery. This was a chance for the newly enthroned King, since he was the only leader still uncompromised, and his hands were therefore free. He was able to set up a "nationalist monarchy" based, despite the constitution, on his own diplomatic prestige and on the mandate he had by implication received to organize the nation's defense.

The constitution was essentially republican. The monarchy had been written into it as a symbol and an ornament, simply for the purpose of winning European sympathy for the young state; and it had been conceived in such a manner that the monarch had no real powers. Although it provided that the king should choose his ministers, promulgate the laws, and declare peace or war, it also stipulated that he should be independent and inviolable, so that he became on paper a sort of supreme and irremovable civil servant who could take no action without the agreement of his parliament and the country. The basic article read: "All powers come from the nation." This was even more radical than the French constitution of 1790, which watered it down by saying, "All powers come essentially from the nation."

Moreover, although the monarchy was made hereditary and perpetual, there were precise provisions by which the king's mandate became conditional. On his death the succession of his heir was not automatic. It was to be preceded by an interregnum, with all authority vested in parliament until the new sovereign had taken the oath before the combined chambers and so obtained his constitutional powers. At the end of each reign, Belgium reverted for a short time to republicanism.

However, there was one important article in the constitution that had not been fully appreciated, and which enabled Leopold to reestablish his authority: the article providing that the sovereign should be head of the army. Congress had decided that the king should be in supreme command in peace or in war because it feared the intrigues of generals with a taste for conspiracy and a tendency to interfere in politics.

Directly after his accession Leopold assumed the role of generalissimo and thus exercised real power. While his political acts were governed by the advice of his ministers and precluded any exercise of his personal will, his prerogatives as head of the army were a direct mandate from the country and gave him the power to make effective decisions. It soon became a tradition to appoint a general to be minister of war. He could have little power against a soldier king under whom he had served before his appointment and under whom he would again be serving when he left office. Such a minister could scarcely take an attitude opposed to that of his supreme chief; and the king would naturally be consulted and have his say on all questions connected with military appointments. It was to him that officers and men took the oath of loyalty and he alone commanded their allegiance. He reviewed the troops, lived with them, and rewarded them in such a way that they soon became a royal party that took its stand against the political groups in the country.

The same applied, to a large extent, to diplomacy. Leopold was in direct touch with the sovereigns and ministers of Europe; his letters, his personal contacts, and his influence made him his country's first ambassador and the real minister of foreign affairs. It was in his name that diplomats and ambassadors were accredited to foreign courts.

They were his representatives, took account of his opinion, and, before long, considered him as their real chief.

The King thus had under his orders two important sections of the administration that played a major part in the country's political life. It was from these two areas also that his son, Leopold II, was to recruit the officers and civil servants needed for the Congo, by virtue of his right to have them enter his personal service.

Leopold I relied on the army and the foreign service to build up his political resources. His ministers had to deal with him as an active force, but they were constitutionally obliged to "cover the crown" and maintain the fiction of the independence of the monarch. This made it impossible for them, when disagreements arose, to consult parliament or even to make their complaints public. The King, on the other hand, was responsible to no one and did not have to explain what he did. He could delay signing orders that displeased him, he could postpone appointments of which he disapproved, and he was soon to become an active political force.

By September, 1831, he was devoting his time to the reorganization of the army. He always wore an army uniform, making it a rule never to appear in public except dressed as a lieutenant general. This practice was continued by his successors. At this time, such events as the creation of the Order of Leopold, or even the mere appointment of a civil servant, were apt to cause a storm, for the least of the King's acts was highly suspect in a "republican parliament" and fierce opposition was easily roused. The King, nevertheless, succeeded in making the country accept him as head of the army and as the means of wiping away all trace of the 1831 humiliation.

"He was the guardian of the national honor; and it was this, as much as his own personal honor, that determined the way in which he acted," says Pirenne.

It was the King, on his own initiative, who entrusted the reorganization of the army to General Evain. In April, 1833, the Chambers refused to give him the credits required for the army, and he accordingly dissolved them. A year later, in August, 1834, he removed from office the ministers who disagreed with General Evain, and thus gave the constitution a new interpretation that created a precedent.

But all this was minor compared to the part he played in diplomacy. He was a son-in-law of the King of France, uncle of the Queen of England, a relative of the Czar and of the English prince consort, and soon, also, of the King of Portugal. He was close to all the European heads of state. He maintained his influence by an enormous correspondence with kings and prime ministers, and no Belgian government was able to function without him. If a serious external problem arose, he was the only person who could deal with it effectively. He had, in fact, established what amounted to a dictatorship.

As he grew older, his effective powers were consolidated by precedent, which gave him new rights at every turn. These included the right to remove ministers from office, to dissolve the Chambers, to defer indefinitely the signature of orders that displeased him, and many others. The threat of delaying his signature was often used as a means of bringing pressure upon his ministers.

In order to free himself from subjection to a civil list, he proceeded to build up an immense fortune by lucky speculation made possible by his many sources of information. It was this same fortune that was later to enable Leopold II to finance the exploration of the Congo.

The King's marriage, like the rest of his life, was successful. Paris and London had agreed that he should marry a French princess—not to guarantee the neutrality of Belgium, but to maintain the Franco-British balance.

Queen Louise Marie, daughter of King Louis Philippe, was a saintly lady whose refined and generous nature is brought out in her letters and diaries. "Happiness as well as grief may make one sad," she wrote, "and tears have sometimes the value of prayer." Her sweetness and beauty gave the monarchy a sentimental popular appeal by which it was firmly consolidated.

Leopold I died on December 10, 1865; on his deathbed he acknowledged that he had lived under a lucky star. The eighth son of a German princeling, he had lived a life of fabulous adventure. His only tragedy had been the death of his first wife. He did not know that his son-in-law would be shot, that his daughter would go mad, that one of his grandsons would die as a child, another before his accession to the throne, or that the third, after surviving a war, would perish, his head smashed on a rock. One of his granddaughters, the Queen of Saxony, was to run off with her lover in the course of adventures that were to scandalize all of Europe. Another granddaughter was to marry the heir of the Bourbons, still another the heir of the Bonapartes, the head of whom had been his worst enemy, and his great-granddaughter was to become the dethroned Queen of Italy. Through the veins of his descendants was to flow the blood of the Hohenzollerns, the Hapsburgs, the Bourbons, the Orléans, and the Princes of Savoy and Wittelsbach.

There is something Shakespearean in the history of the man and his family. It is a drama played out among sudden deaths, abdications, exiles, romantic escapades, reverses of fortune, and major warfare. The tale develops against a magnificent and tragic background, providing inspiration for poets, and a haunting memory for the imaginations of the future.

The first effect of the 1830 revolution was to plunge the country into a serious economic and social crisis from 1830 to 1835. Belgian industry was paralyzed by the loss of the Dutch markets and the end of direct relations with Germany, which depended on free communication by water across the estuaries of the Schelde and the Rhine.

At Ghent, for example, there was now a permanent army of 30,000 unemployed, and only four of the city's eighty factories retained a semblance of activity. Between 1830 and 1836, the number of cotton spindles fell from 209,000 to 139,000. Activity in the collieries and the metalworking mills declined at the same time, and the Orangists had no trouble supporting their argument that the separation of the two countries had been a disaster.

Misery and poverty were to be the lot of the Belgians for a number of years, but did not compromise their independence. On the contrary, misfortune was a cement that unified the nation, giving the people the sense of a common destiny and a common outlet for their energy. Their patriotism was stimulated by the difficult circumstances.

It was the crisis that made the Belgians decide to unite more closely to overcome it. Their problem was the restoration of commerce with Germany. To resolve it, they took up an idea that the Liége metallurgists had had in 1829—to link Antwerp with the Rhine by building an international railway that by-passed Dutch territory in the south. This new means of transportation was a substitute for the waterways the Dutch had closed.

The new railway restored Belgium's faith in the future. The lines from Antwerp and Brussels led, on the one hand, to Bruges, and, on the other, to Liége and Cologne. Railway development of this period played much the same part as did the great New Deal undertakings in the administration of Franklin D. Roosevelt. There was a great body of unemployed to provide the necessary labor, and the orders for material kept the metallurgical industry busy for a long period.

Confidence returned to the business world, credit reappeared, and there was an increase in the number of banks and businesses. Between 1830 and 1839 the number of corporations increased ten-fold, from 15 to 151, and the Société Générale came into its own. Traffic in the port of Antwerp reached, and later exceeded, its 1829 level, and foreign observers realized that Belgium was to become one of the great industrial nations of Europe. The French minister so informed his government, in a report that was to prove prophetic. Belgium's advance, however, was beset with many difficulties. The linen industry crisis, for example, began in 1835 and reached its climax between 1840 and 1845. The young nation had to find its own salvation; its leaders succeeded by means of an economic revolution that enabled an agricultural country to industrialize by using its large reserve of cheap labor.

All observers were impressed by the dynamic qualities of nineteenth-century Belgium. It seemed a motley country, made up of peoples of different races and languages and divided into Liberals and Catholics. However, it was like a living entity that was going to develop a tremendous organizational power. This ensemble of urban population and large towns surrounded by intensively cultivated countryside that formed suburbs, coincided with the economic transformation of Europe.

Belgium developed an economic system in which material prosperity, external expansion, and the conquest of foreign markets became the nation's principal objectives. Its political life was based on individualism, the autonomy of the communes, respect for the parliamentary system, and the art of compromise.

Belgium's change to a liberal and constitutional state on the English pattern determined its role in the nineteenth century. Belgium became a kind of continental England. Its political life, like that of England, was based on alternation of power between two great parties, one more conservative and the other the more advanced, but both of which shared the same middle-class ideals and represented the same social classes. Separated from France, which was still faithful to revolutionary ideals and the struggle for justice, Belgium continued the work of industrial and commercial organization that had been started by William I, in the days of the Kingdom of the Netherlands.

Despite the strong linguistic ties between Belgium and France, there was a deep cleavage between the two countries. France was still the country of the Ideal and the Absolute. Throughout the nineteenth century she clung to a sentimental, passionate policy that led her from revolution to revolution and from crisis to crisis, felling in turn, Charles X, Louis Philippe, and the Second Empire. Belgium steered clear of revolution and disturbance and concentrated on industrial expansion.

Disposing of machinery and methods of mass production that enabled her to bring her mining and metallurgical resources into play, Belgium was able to exercise her initiative and spirit of enterprise freely. Economic interest re-established within the country a certain moral unity that could not be achieved by political means, and it became apparent that the parliamentary system was the best adapted to this situation. Whereas in France the parliament had created cleavages because the country was beset by strife and political passion, in Belgium it was a source of strength and balance.

Belgium also resembled England in the weak political power of its government. It had no police force and could offer no resistance against an insurrection except by proclaiming a state of siege. Public order was dependent on the burgomasters of the great towns, which were practically independent, so that they held power under the constant threat of revolt.

Absolute government was impossible because of opposition by an important section of opinion. All problems had to be settled by compromise or by negotiation between the government and the interested parties. This made any abuse of power impossible. This apparent weakness assured the calm of the country and enabled its institutions to function regularly with no risk of revolution.

Over a period of 120 years, between 1830 and 1950, no Belgian government was overthrown by force. During the same period there were at least four successive revolutions in France and three in Germany. In England and in the United States there were none. In these countries, the same factors that prevailed in Belgium produced the same results.

Belgium had the highest population density in Europe. Few of its towns were more than three miles from a railway, and its countryside was little more than a great suburb. Community of interest had cemented its national union, and party strife, although intense at times, was only superficial, and did not impede the country's economic expansion.

The nation's strength and political equilibrium were based on republican tradition. Her material progress advanced unchecked.

The fortunes of medieval Belgium had been woven in wool; those of the Low Countries of the Renaissance period had sprung from agriculture and trade; and the nineteenth century was the age of iron and steel. There was a great expansion in metal production, particularly in the Liége region with its abundance of coal, where a large labor force had specialized for two centuries in the manufacture of armaments. The "Walloon method" of production had been invented at Liége as early as the sixteenth century. It consisted of a first stage that produced a high-grade cast iron, and a second that purified the product with a blast of air that oxidized it. Almost all kinds of ore could be used and the result was a considerable drop in price.

Before long, John Cockerill, with the help of Mushet, an English specialist, set up the first coke-operated blast furnace at Seraing. The furnace was sixty-six feet high and the blast of air and burning gas that activated reduction produced temperatures up to 2000°C. The progress of reduction could be watched through a blue-glass window, and the furnace produced ten tons of metal daily. Large-scale production brought down the price of iron and there was a corresponding drop in the price of machinery. Seraing could now produce industrial engines of 180 horsepower. In 1825, Seraing fitted a naval sloop, the *Atlas*, with a 240-horsepower engine that gave it a higher speed than any ship then in existence. It was the end of sailing ships.

This scale of manufacture required capital in amounts no bank was able to supply. William I, however, advanced the money from state funds. He said in public to John Cockerill: "Don't be afraid to go on with your great work. Remember that the King of the Netherlands always has funds to be used in the service of industry."

A new process now came into use. This was puddling, an English invention dating from 1784, that converted iron into steel by a stirring process that burned out carbon and reduced it to the required concentration.

On the eve of the 1830 revolution, Cockerill had proposed that the government construct a railway to provide a direct link between Antwerp and Liége. The revolution, in fact, owed part of its origin to the agitation produced around this idea, for in May, 1830, a railway line linking the Grand Hornu colliery with the Mons canal at Condé contributed to the disturbances. The wagonmen thrown out of work incited the workers to attack the colliery and the house of the manager, Degorge. The "Degorge pillage" is still a legend in Belgium.

After the revolution railways became a necessity. Cockerill proposed to make Belgium economically independent by building a railway that would link her with Germany, through Liége and Verviers. This would be part of a cruciform railway system, with branches to Brussels, Antwerp and Ghent. This project would have been impossible if it had not been for the existence of the great metalworks at Seraing. But at the same time, the enormous orders for rails, locomotives, trucks, cranes, tanks, and other equipment made Seraing's fortune. They called for an immense tonnage of iron and were the basis for the works' continuous expansion.

On May 5, 1835, the first Belgian train left Brussels for Mechlin. Its builder, the British engineer George Stephenson, was hidden in the crowd in a third-class carriage.

Before long Cockerill had two blast furnaces, two collieries, eighty-one forges, fifteen puddling furnaces, and a great number of metallurgical workshops in operation. An alarming description of this industrial complex is given by Victor Hugo, who was on a visit to Belgium:

> When once you have passed the place called Petite Flémalle, the entire valley seems to be studded with the craters of erupting volcanoes. Some you may see from beyond the wood, disgorging great eddies of scarlet vapor, and starred with a thousand sparks. Others delineate the doleful black outline of the villages on a red background. Further on, you may see their flames through the gaps in a group of buildings. It is as though an enemy host had just marched across the country, and twenty sacked townships were shown you at a single glance, through this sinister night,

in every aspect and every phase of fire, with its flame, its glow, and its smoke.

All you have been looking at, however, are the blast furnaces of Mr. Cockerill.

From this workmen's chaos comes a violent and fierce din. Something of the supernatural seems to have been borrowed from the sad solemnity of the midnight hour. Here are the wheels, the saws, the boilers, the rolling mills, the cylinders, the beams, and all those monsters of copper, brass, and sheet-iron that we call machines, and to which steam has given a frightful and appalling life. You may hear them roar and whistle, rattle and creak, sniff, bark, and scream as they tear the bronze, twist the iron, and mash the granite. At times, in the midst of the smoke-blackened workers who harass them in the fiery arena of the mill, they will roar like hydras or dragons, tormented by demons in the nether hell.

Nevertheless, the only thing that insured the expansion of the metal industry was the fall in the price of steel and the parallel increase in the number of uses for it. Another invention was put through its first trials at Seraing. This was the Bessemer process, in which steel is smelted in converters equipped with bellows, producing it twenty times more quickly than before. Later, the Martin process was used in bulk production; and the Thomas process removed the phosphorus that until then had made many ores unusable and converted it into agricultural fertilizer.

Not long afterward, methods were devised for using blast-furnace gases, which burned in tall flames that could be seen from afar like "funeral pyres of lost energy." They were now harnessed to drive 10,000 horsepower engines in the factories.

There was a host of new inventions. In the rolling or blooming mills, a single worker could control all the movements of a mass of steel, weighing a full ten tons, trimming it, balancing it, and bringing it forward untouched by human hands. At Liége, Charleroi, and the Borinage, the metalworking mills developed unchecked.

Soon after 1880, Belgian factories were built all over the world. One factory was built in China and another in Spain, and the industrial might of Russia began with the construction of the Dniéprovienne at Ekaterinoslav, the Donetz basin collieries, and the iron-ore mines of Krivoi Rog. A little later, a new leader, Adolph Greiner, set up steel mills in Austria, Italy, and as far afield as Persia.

The expansion of the metal industries led to prosperity for other branches of industry, and each new step forward brought profit to the country as a whole. Everything was now made of iron—ships, dynamos, bridges, household equipment, reinforced concrete buildings, tools, watches, and precision instruments. Modern Belgium was built on iron and crossed the nineteenth and twentieth centuries on a bridge of steel. Around the year 1880, when the Seraing mills built the three steamships that were to enable the British explorer and journalist Henry Stanley to sail up the Congo River, their very names were a symbol of the time: Belgique, Espérance ("Hope"), and En Avant ("Forward").

Throughout the nineteenth century, the political life of Belgium was a long struggle between two great forces: the Catholics and the Liberals.

Belgian Catholicism, far from declining, was making considerable progress around 1840. Between 1839 and 1846, the total membership of religious orders increased from 4,791 to nearly 12,000, and the people as a whole numbered no more unbelievers than formerly. In 1842, the Church secured the passage of a compromise education act that put practically the whole of the country's education into its hands. It now had control of almost all the rural primary schools, and in the whole nation, including both urban and rural districts, it operated half the primary schools and the majority of the secondary schools. The state paid the salaries of the religious schoolmasters; it had no resources with which to develop public instruction in competition with the clergy.

The Liberals, who were the leaders of political opinion in most of the great towns, began to organize against this situation. Their action was destined to be successful because it was necessary. Representative of modern ideas, they were the only party in Belgium capable of putting through the reforms that all of the European countries were now adopting. These included free trade, centralized government, credit organization, public education, and a reduction of the cost of living.

As early as 1846, the Liberal movement had enough strength behind it to stage a decisive demonstration. On June 14, a congress of 384 delegates from all parts of the country met in the Brussels town hall to draft a statement of party doctrine. There were, as it turned out, two groups of opinion. The first consisted of the more progressive elements, who wanted to secure a full democracy by the extension of voting rights. On the other hand, the doctrinaire Liberals, led by Rogier and Frère-Orban, wanted to organize a declericalized modern state that would assure the liberty of the individual without any direct appeal to the people. The latter group won the day. In the election of 1847, the trend of opinion in their favor was overwhelming, and the first all-Liberal government came into power. Its Prime Minister was Rogier, but the effective leader was Frère-Orban.

Frère-Orban was a lawyer of modest beginnings who had made his mark early in life by his energy and clear thinking. He had married a Liége heiress of the powerful industrial Orban dynasty and this had assured his fortune. The story goes that his young bride's family had long been set against the match because they considered the young lawyer nothing but a social climber. One evening, however, he calmly walked into the Orban box at the theater, bowed respectfully to the parents, walked up to the girl, and took her in his arms in full view of the astonished audience. The Orban family were caught short and had to put the best face they could on the matter by quickly announcing the engagement.

Whether the story is true or false, it conveys a true picture of Frère-Orban's energetic and authoritarian character. He was an incisive speaker who would never retreat from an obstacle and who preferred to seek out the opposition in order to annihilate it. He gained in prestige from his good looks and his commanding presence; and he found a way of uniting behind him the important industrialists, who had formerly supported William I and were now becoming the leaders of the country, and the hot-headed young people who were the motive force of the Liberal party.

As head of the government, he was at once faced with the 1848 revolutionary movement. The February insurrection in Paris had overthrown Louis Philippe, and the shadow of revolution was again falling across the whole of Europe. In Belgium, however, it proved possible to maintain political calm by extending the suffrage, raising the number of voters from 59,000 to 79,000.

In vain, the French insurgents attempted to stage a march on Brussels. A band of armed revolutionaries, accompanied by Belgian emigrants, was checked without difficulty at the village of Risquons-Tout, near Lille. A train that attempted to force the frontier was surrounded by Belgian troops and captured at Quiévrain with all its passengers.

The doctrinaire Liberals had not needed to introduce political reforms to calm the revolutionary agitation. Frère-Orban, however, decided to bring his economic program into action immediately. He was a believer in free trade, and accordingly reduced tariffs and declared that grain should be imported free of duty. For the Liberals, the first priority was to bring down the cost of living to enable Belgium to produce goods cheaply through a low wage level and export its products to the whole world. One step in this direction was the cancellation of the octroi duties levied by the cities. In the city of Liége, for example, these duties took ten per cent of the workers' income. They were reimbursed by the state, raising the standard of living of the people and promoting internal trade.

Frère-Orban also sought to create a solid financial organization that would enable the state to maintain credit and give aid to individuals. This was the purpose of the creation of the National Bank in 1850. It was not long before the National Bank in Belgium was playing the same role as an economic stimulus as was the Bank of England across the Channel.

Economic liberty was not enough for the Liberals, however. They

wanted freedom of education too, and Frère-Orban was naturally led
on to attack the "state-within-the-state," which, in his view, was a fair
description of the Catholic Church in this period. He was attacking
the position of a body that had a virtual monopoly of all education
and complete domination over the people in the rural areas. On February 14, 1850, in the face of the bishops' protests, he set up ten atheneums, or high schools, and fifty teachers' training colleges in the big
cities. The religious instruction in these schools was to be given by
priests, but the bishops refused to make the necessary appointments
and the new educational system fell under the Church's interdict.

Frère-Orban had been moving too quickly, and the measures he
enacted upset not only established habits, but also a number of vested
interests. Moreover, he had sought to finance his reforms by imposing
a succession tax. This was very small—only one per cent of the inheritance value—but his opponents dubbed it a monstrous spoliation, and
he was accused of "taxing the tears of family mourning." This was one
of the factors that led to the fall of the Liberal government and the
rise to power of a ministry of conciliation and consolidation, led by
the moderate-minded de Brouckère.

So ended the first phase of Liberal organization, and for some years
governments of conciliation and national union stayed in office. They
found support among the majorities of the center, while Frère-Orban,
energetic and authoritarian as ever, led the Liberal opposition.

No matter how the ministers in power opposed Frère-Orban politically, they had no alternative but to continue carrying out his program, lowering tariffs and concluding a great number of commercial
treaties, which had the effect of creating a free-trade regime. So strong
was the personality of the Liberal leader, and so irresistible the development of the time, that these interim governments were in effect preparing the ground for the return of the Liberals to power.

It was not long indeed before Frère-Orban was back in the government as a result of the agitation that developed when the Catholics
carelessly allowed a trial of strength to develop in Brussels. This occurred in 1857, when a center-party government, led by the Catholic
Unionist Pierre de Decker, a man well known for the moderation
of his views, made the mistake of bringing forward a bill, known as
the Convents Bill, dealing with charitable gifts and foundations.

This was considered by the left wing to be an act of provocation. The
Liberals, who had the big towns behind them and the support of the
burgomasters, accused the government of trying to revive the "dead
hand," the system of property escaping taxes through unchanging ownership that had been a bone of contention in many countries in a
more distant past. They staged a protest march in the streets of Brus-

sels, and began a riot that, with the police taking no effective action, proved a success. De Decker was forced to acknowledge that he could no longer maintain order and therefore had to resign. This was followed by municipal, and later by parliamentary, elections, in which the Liberals put themselves forward against the Catholics as defenders of liberty and legality. As a result of the elections, they returned to office and remained there for thirteen years, covering the end of the reign of Leopold I and the beginning of that of Leopold II.

About 1840, Victor Hugo came to Belgium and the impressions noted in his letters give a lively picture of the country in this period. He shows us a Belgium that, at the same time, is both ancient and modern, backward and tremendously progressive. Its contradictions impressed him the more because he was looking at them with fresh eyes and was full of curiosity about this country that, in spite of himself, he found fascinating.

Wherever he went there was a survival of ancient traditions inherited from a distant past. At Tirlemont, for example, Hugo was present at a "Charivari of the Horns" organized by the young people for a widower who was remarrying. He admired the old wooden houses of Ypres, still standing alongside their brick neighbors. He noticed the enormous number of priests and monks, the Trappists digging in the fields, and the countless religious orders in white robes, gray soutanes, or black-frocks who swarmed in every street.

He was amused by the inscriptions that parish priests put on the doors of their churches: "No dogs in the house of God." But to his astonishment, he found the churches closed to the faithful all afternoon, whereas in France the houses of God were open all day. Inside the churches, vergers were always ready to receive tips, and would extort money from tourists by hiding pictures and statues behind curtains that could be removed only for a suitable consideration. Sometimes, indeed, the showing of art treasures would be refused, as for example in the Mechlin Cathedral, where the "Last Judgment" had been covered with a curtain on the pretext that it was not decent.

Victor Hugo found much fun in the many exhibitions of exaggerated modesty among the inhabitants. At Ostend, where the restaurants served neither fish nor oysters, but only veal, he admired the bathing beauties, whom the waves undressed on the sandy beach:

> Men and women bathe together, the men in pants and the women in a bathing wrap. The wrap is a simple chemise of light woolen material that comes down to the ankle, but which, when wet, clings to the figure and is often lifted up by the waves. There was one young woman who looked very well in this fashion, perhaps indeed too well. At moments she had all the looks of an antique bronze statue with her pleated tunic.

Girdled in the foam of the sea, this lovely creature might have stepped out of the mythology of old.

Hugo made the tour of the Belgian art towns and was astonished at the picturesque spectacle he found there. Wherever he went, he climbed to the top of the cathedral or the belfry to get a bird's-eye view of the whole town, with its public buildings, its market squares, its streets, and its seething crowds. From the top of the cathedral at Antwerp, he could see as far as Flushing in one direction, in the others as far as Ghent, Mechlin, and even to the towers of Breda. He contemplated Brussels from the heights of St. Gudule in a storm, and was startled into admiration of the market place, which he thought to be Spanish. At Bruges, he was particularly impressed by the beauty of the women, who seemed to him to be of a southern type, and were described in a guidebook as "the Circassians of Belgium." At Ghent, he climbed the towers of St. Bavo and contemplated the countless bridges across the city's four rivers. At Mechlin, he visited the cathedral carillon, but he was grieved that all the churches were daubed with white or yellow inside.

Throughout the country, he noticed that the population was astonishingly dense—one of the most concentrated in Europe. "In this country, there is a town every six leagues, just as in France there is one every sixty leagues." The Belgian cities, as Hugo saw them, contained none of the modern public buildings. In this period there was neither the law court building, nor the present royal palace at Brussels. One might see the river Senne winding its way across the meadows, and on the horizon were green hillsides, known as Lacken, Ixelles, Auderghem, Schaerbeek, Etterbeek, Molenbeek, and others. The towns themselves were a world of the Middle Ages, with a confusion of lanes, old gables, tiled roofs, turrets, and battlements.

Wallonia seemed to Victor Hugo as foreign and exotic as Flanders. He wondered at the shop signs and inscriptions, among which he noted, at Namur, "Crucifix-Piret, haberdasher." "Here," he cried, "is Catholic Flanders with a vengeance; no such name as Crucifix could exist in the France of Voltaire." Hugo confused Wallonia with Flanders, and even believed that Flemish was spoken there. Another of his mistakes was thinking that most of the Belgian public buildings were Spanish. He echoed Boileau in calling Ghent "the proud Spaniard," and described Bruges as "half-German, half-Spanish." Mons, he thought, bore the marks of the meeting of Flanders and Spain. He believed the baroque style, the scrolls and gables, were the result of Spanish influence, whereas in reality they were of Italian, or purely Flemish origin. He even wrote his impressions in verse:

> O noble Flanders, where the torpid north,
> Warms in Castilian suns. . . .

It was Hugo who created the legend of "Spanish Belgium," with the women whose brown skins told of their southern blood. So strong was his conviction, that even in Franche-Comté he saw Spanish styles in buildings that, in fact, showed only the Flemish influence: "And then Besançon, that old Spanish town."

At Namur he saw a shop sign "Menendez-Woden, watchmaker." This produced from him the exclamation: "Here is a Castile name linked by a hyphen with a Flemish name. Is not this, indeed, the Spanish domination of the Low Countries, signed, sealed, and delivered in a proper name?"

Outside these old towns, with their sleepy and backward provincial ways, Hugo was astonished to find the most modern country on the continent, a country of large-scale industry and glowing blast furnaces. He was carried away by the unheard-of speed of the trains, and began to understand that a new world was being born, that the century of speed was dawning, and that perhaps poetry, too, would have new worlds opened to it. He wrote:

Yesterday, I went from Antwerp to Brussels and back. I left at 4:10 P.M. and got back at 8:15, having in the interval spent an hour and a quarter in Brussels, and covered twenty-three French leagues.

The speed is extraordinary. The wayside flowers are no longer flowers, but just blotches or rather stripes of red or white. There are no more points but only stripes, and the corn looks like great heads of yellow hair, and the grass like long green tresses. Towns, trees, and steeples dance in a mad mixture on the far horizon. From time to time a form, a shadow, an upright specter appears and disappears in a flash beside the door. This is the guard who, as custom requires, is armed in military fashion when on duty. In the carriage, people say to one another: Only three leagues more, we shall be there in ten minutes. In the evening, as I was returning, night was falling. I was in the first coach, with the locomotive just in front with its dreadful noise, and its flames throwing out great red lights that tinted the trees and hills as the wheels whirled madly around.

As we went, we met and passed the Brussels-bound train. There is nothing in the world so terrifying as these two speeds side by side, seeming to the passengers to multiply each other. From one train you can see nothing in the other; you can see neither carriages, nor men, nor women, but just light or dark forms as in a whirlpool. From this whirlpool there arose cries and laughter and shouts; and on each side there were six wagons, and more than a thousand people were being carried, some northward, some southward, as though on the wings of a storm.

By the time I got back, the night had fallen. Our locomotive passed close by me in the dark on its way back to its stable. The illusion was complete. One could hear it groaning in its whirlpool of flame and smoke, like a weary horse."

The approach to Liége struck Victor Hugo with astonishment. Belgium, fiery and infernal, appeared to him at Seraing, as he beheld a blast furnace for the first time:

> Here beside the road is a terrifying candlestick, eighty feet high, flaming across the countryside and throwing its sinister light on rock, forest, and fell. Further on, as you enter this valley, buried in the shadows, there is a mighty pair of jaws, filled with embers, that open and shut themselves abruptly. . . ."

The mills were lighting up.

The same contrast between the extremely modern and the unchanging customs and traditions impressed not only Victor Hugo, but every traveler who came to Belgium. Local customs were maintained everywhere. At Christmas, the children, dressed up as the Three Magi, would sing before every doorway with a star of red paper lit by a lantern. There would be morning aubades for the new year, and serenades for newly engaged couples; and Hugo himself had seen the horns of widowers who married again. Many traditional festivals would be held, like the St. Thomas, when children would employ a thousand ruses to take their mother prisoner in one place and their father in another, making their liberation conditional on promises of chocolate and cakes.

Everybody lived in his own little district. Neighbors would meet neighbors in the cafés in the evening, and even the street had a family character, for it was there that life was lived. It was here that people worked, took their pleasures, were born and died, and celebrated marriages almost always between neighbors.

The Brussels of 1840 was made up of two distinct cities. One of them was a world that was fast disappearing, the lower town where the river Senne rolled by, its heavy, oily water filled with dead dogs. It meandered around the curves and islets, beneath old houses with their balconies and their corbels. Here and there it would be stopped by a little dam and made to turn a mill or receive the evil-smelling waters of tanneries, breweries, and factories. And in the middle of the town stood the wonderful market place, where tourists flocked because the romantic age had made the past fashionable. The English writer Motley was to write soon after:

> I haunt this square, because it is my theater and my stage. Here so many tragedies, so many scenes of violence, so many comedies have been played out, all long familiar to me. When I say that I know nobody in Brussels, I may be wrong. I know nobody who lives there today, but the dead of this square are my old familiar friends.

It was here that Egmont and Hoorn met their deaths. Here fell the heads of the rebels and the tyrants of four centuries. Here passed all the princes in their Joyous Entries to the city. Here came Charles the Bold, Maximilian, Charles V, Philip II, Louis XV, Joseph II, Napoleon; and, above all, through five centuries of history, here were Roger van der Weyden, Rubens, Van Dyck, Jordaens, David, Delacroix, and Wagner.

The modern city with its residential districts was very different from old Brussels. The city was full of greenery and open places, for an eighth part of the surface was covered by gardens. The outskirts of the town were still untouched. At Anderlecht, for example, nothing had changed since Erasmus lived there in 1521. It was still a land of running water, of meadows, and of pretty farms planted with alders and rows of poplars.

The city was already covering too wide an area for the number of its inhabitants, and this is a characteristic that has survived into our own times. Life was so concentrated into single streets and small districts that it was quite a business to get from one district to another. The people of Brussels, indeed, were so disinclined to leave their own neighborhoods that there was no system of public transportation before 1835.

The first bus service dates from 1836. Its starting point was the railway terminus in the Allée Verte, and its coaches had attractive names, such as the Comet, the Lizard, the Progress, the Tug, the Bruxelloise, and the White Ladies. Road transport between different towns made its appearance about 1840.

The mail service was also slow in developing. Up to 1831, Brussels had only seven letter boxes, and in that year the establishment of a new one in the Rue des Sablons was on every tongue. The mail was collected twice each day, at 5 A.M. and again at 2 P.M.

Letters were not yet sent in envelopes. Each letter was carefully folded and sealed simply with wax. The weight of a letter was of no importance, for the rates charged were calculated only by distance. The postage would have to be paid, not by the sender, but by the addressee. He had the right to refuse it, and would examine it carefully before deciding from the handwriting who had been the sender and whether it was worth the money.

Brussels was now within thirty-six hours' journey from Paris by stagecoach, and the fare included meals for passengers at Péronne and Senlis. There were more than 150 departures each week, but seats had to be booked a week in advance and there were three different classes, each of which paid a different fare.

Each stagecoach was driven by postillions, and it had a conductor whose job was much the same as that of a ship's captain. He was in supreme command, could issue what orders he liked, and had the job of maintaining discipline and dealing with all incidents. It was he who gave the order to go, crying "Light up! light up!" The stage would travel about eight miles, and then the horses—there were between four and eight for each coach—would be changed at a posting stable, and the former ones would be led back at a walk to the previous post. The journey would be delayed by many stops, and in winter the passengers would be frozen with cold, as there was no system of heating, and would have to cover themselves with greatcoats and hooded mantles. When the coach had to climb a hill, the passengers would often alight and proceed up the hill on foot, not so much to spare the horses as to warm themselves.

Distances, however, were growing shorter. It was now five hours' journey from Brussels to Antwerp, six to Ghent or Mons, twelve to Lille or Liége (sixty-eight miles away), and fourteen to Ostend—an average speed of about five miles per hour—and it must be remembered that the stages carried a heavy baggage load. Travelers could, if they wished, go by the mail carriages that covered the distances much more quickly, but cost a great deal more. The railways slowly replaced the stagecoaches, among which were the famous Van Gent coaches. There was no railway service to Paris before 1840, and the Belgian railway network developed only gradually during its first half-century. Between 1830 and 1835, the number of stagecoach services between Brussels and Paris increased fivefold, a clear indication of the close relations that were being built up between independent Belgium and France. It was only around 1850 that railroad competition came into play, and the stagecoach traffic was reduced by half. The last coaches maintained service between the smaller towns, specializing in carrying freight, as some of the companies, such as the Messageries Van Gent, have continued to do until our own times.

The glittering scene of prosperity among the governing classes had a darker, tragic, background of poverty among the lower orders. The industrial working class at this time was only about one-tenth of the population of the country, but the enormous effort of industrial creation, from which modern Belgium was to emerge, was made almost entirely at their expense.

The Belgium of 1830, born of a proletarian uprising, was soon to find itself in tragic circumstances. In the name of the national interest, the governing classes reduced the lower orders to poverty and want; in refusing workers the right to strike, they were condemning them to a half-century of forced labor. The small wages that were paid were no more than ration tickets.

The real drama of nineteenth-century Belgium was not the strife of the political parties, but the grinding down of the lower classes in order to leave scope for the organization of the country. Their lot grew progressively worse for thirty years, and Karl Marx, who was living in Belgium at this time, based on their example his theory of the "predestined pauperization" of the working class in the midst of the general prosperity of the country.

The cost of living was rising continuously, but, between 1835 and 1850, wages in Flanders fell to three-quarters of the 1830 level. This was an indirect, but nevertheless inevitable, consequence of the separation of the country from Holland.

Children would go to work in the collieries at the age of nine. The diet of the lower classes consisted of black bread and potatoes, and it was only drink, which was becoming more and more widespread, that made their life endurable. Between 1833 and 1844, for example, the Verviers district reported a 46 per cent increase in the consumption of hard liquor.

The working-class districts in the big cities, such as the Batavia district in Ghent, were real human hells. Housing and sanitary conditions were such that the mortality rate was frightful, offsetting the excessive birth rate.

Industry worked a fifteen-hour day, the worker reporting at 5 A.M. and working until 8 P.M. in summer, and 10 P.M. in winter. In the heavy industries that needed stronger labor, 46 per cent of the applicants for jobs were turned down on grounds of debility, and the proportion was 36 per cent for artisans and 26 per cent for the workers of Liége as a whole. The ranks of the female workers were thinned out by their working conditions; the employers in Flanders, however, insisted that it was impossible to do without them, for the quality of yarn depended, they said, on the composition of female saliva, for which there was no mechanical substitute.

The workers, beset by poverty and fatigue, could play no part in politics, and 85 per cent of them were illiterate. One can only admire their resigned attitude and the religious sentiments that made them so docile. They did not protest the increasing number of accidents from unprotected machinery, but contented themselves with organizing prayer meetings and carrying their offerings to the churches. There is bitter irony in the fact that these unlucky people had been sent to the barricades in 1830 as a protest against the high cost of living, and that they paid for this gesture with generations of suffering.

Doctors of this period describe the workers in Flanders as if they belonged to a different race. Dr. Mareska of Ghent wrote:

They were all pale, wan, and sallow. Their lips, the insides of their mouths, their gums, and the insides of their eyelids were discolored. Their voices were feeble, and their eyes dull and expressionless. Their faces and

extremities were puffed with fluid, or excessively thin. All their movements and muscular contractions were slow and painful, and their
physical inertia was associated with a very high degree of moral inertia.
Thin and discolored muscles could be traced beneath their skin, through
which the shape of all their bones could be seen. In a great number of
cases, organic misery went beyond this extreme degree of anemia. The
symptoms were of a special kind, known at the time under the general
description of Flemish sickness or famine fever.

The fact was that the workers were victims of a tragic degree of
undernourishment. The Heymans-Mareska report of 1842, resulting
from a medical inquiry into the workers' diet, was definite on this
score:

> The food contains none of the essential elements, no animal substances,
> and no fats. The consequence of this is that the stature of the cotton
> worker is smaller than that of the normal man throughout his life, and
> particularly during puberty. His weight, compared with that of a nor-
> mally developed man, is smaller by about five kilograms. Phthisis and
> laryngitis are about twice as frequent as among workers in other industries.
> The workers are predisposed to these maladies by their poverty, bad food,
> the bad air of the closed life of the workshop, and also by want of
> exercise in the fresh air.

The industrial workers were not the only ones to suffer in this way,
but also the peasants. During the great crisis of 1846, the newspapers
would tell daily of cases of death from starvation. In January 1847,
at Aeltere, a whole household of four people was found dead from
hunger. At Wynghene, cases became so frequent that the local police-
man was given the job of calling at all houses each day to see if the
inhabitants were still alive.

Life was so much like a concentration camp that those who did not
die of hunger were carried off by typhus and other diseases.

These were the times when people were singing in the streets ditties
set to old tunes against the Rogier–Frère-Orban ministry:

> In the silver moonlight,
> Rogier, friend so kind,
> Flanders still must importune
> Because she bears in mind
> Winter is a-coming,
> Hungry, cold, unshod.
> Loosen up your purse-strings
> For the love of God!

The governing classes were completely indifferent to the spectacle.
Briavoinne, who waxed enthusiastic about the progress of Belgian
industry, attached very little importance to the standard of living of

the working classes. He states simply that in the metalworking industries their wages were smaller than those of the English workers, poor though the latter were, and also that they were badly nourished and less robust. "They produce less and they are not so good in standing up to the fire," he wrote.

Weavers found it difficult to earn seventy centimes daily, and lacemakers earned less than a franc. Only specialized workers could earn as much as a franc and a half to three francs. Children had to work thirteen or fourteen hours daily—if they did not, their parents would die of hunger. There was no schooling, for it would have been impossible to go to school, and 80 to 90 per cent of the people were illiterate. In Flanders, there was one pauper for every four inhabitants, compared with one in six in the rest of the country.

There are a number of contemporary accounts of the way of life among the metalworkers in the Cockerill mills at Seraing, where the workers had the benefit of a welfare organization and were better treated than elsewhere. About the year 1870, when the position of the working classes had already improved, the food of these workers was made up solely of bread, lard, and potatoes. There was no beer and no meat, and the diet did not change on holidays. The one saving grace was that the fall in the price of sugar had made it possible for them to add a little syrup or apple jam to their diet. The wives of the workers were able to maintain their homes only by going out daily to do housework, or by taking in work to do at home, such as knitting, mending, washing, or ironing for rich clients. The great majority of them, however, had not been able to get the necessary training. On Sundays, instead of resting, the women would have to do their own washing and housework. It took half a century for the wages of specialized workers, who were comparatively better paid, to rise from two francs daily in 1850, to four francs in 1900, and five francs in 1914. People have always been astonished that the revolutionary wave of 1848, which stretched from Paris across the whole of Europe, created no disorder of any kind in Belgium. It has been said that this was due to the reasonable outlook of the workers and the solid foundations of the young kingdom.

Such an explanation is no more than bitter mockery. The Belgian working classes had been reduced to complete impotence, and it would have been utterly impossible for them to create trouble. Wages were just enough to enable each member of the family to have one kilogram of black bread each day. It was impossible to save money, and a strike would have entailed death by starvation at the end of a few days. The masses, moreover, were passive and inert. In 1830, it had taken the agitation organized by the young members of the middle classes to start them on the road to revolt. By now, the Belgian middle classes were firmly wedded to one or the other of the two great political parties, and the republican spirit no longer existed.

The Paris of this period had an educated working class that read the newspapers and pamphlets, thought things over, and discussed them. In Belgium, on the other hand, nobody could read and all discussion was either impossible or prohibited. The least attempt at political propaganda was repressed with a ferocity that, in our own time, could be found only in the Soviet Union. In 1846, the mere demand for "work and bread" was enough to send four agitators before the Assize courts. In 1848, there was a strike of cotton spinners, all of them practicing Catholics who used to go to Mass with their families each morning. The leader was sentenced to five years imprisonment, and thirty-three others were given sentences of up to two years imprisonment. In 1857, another strike brought twenty-seven convictions, and several of the convicted men were given two-year sentences. In 1859, there were seventy sentences passed in connection with yet another strike. Writers of newspaper articles, if their tone was considered violent, would be visited with immediate imprisonment, and a little later a fanatically uncompromising writer, named Defuisseaux, was given twenty-seven years imprisonment.

The workers, for their part, had no real feeling that they were being oppressed, and often were on the same side as the employers. In 1834, when John Cockerill bought out the state's share of his business and became sole owner, he walked to his office through a shouting lane of enthusiastic workers. The people cheered joyfully, repeating the slogan on the banners: "All this is ours and only ours."

The easy way in which public opinion adjusted itself to the injustices of the capitalist system resulted from the enormous risks that had to be taken by the men who created industrial enterprises. There was never any certainty that the capital laid out would earn its keep, and the factories of the period had to be started without any knowledge as to whether the market would absorb what they produced. The middle classes bought only annuities and fixed-interest bonds, and refused altogether to risk capital in the newly created companies. People who set up factories nearly always went bankrupt unless they were supported by the banks. It was often necessary for factories to choose sites in the country, since no labor was available in the cities. The working force consisted of the neighboring peasantry, who came to work in the factories for small wages. Their arrival would often bring wages down, and this was the only way new industries survived.

A fall in world prices or in domestic prices had to be met by cuts in production costs, which in practice meant cuts in wages. It was only by these means that it was possible to finance industrial enterprises and keep them going. The dominant force was imperious necessity rather than any question of pity or charity.

Since it was impossible to find capital from outside sources, the industrialists of the period had to set up their own factories by using their savings or their personal fortunes. This, as a rule, left them with no reserves, and if it became necessary to write off a loss, make good a mistake, renew the machinery, or adjust the business to price changes, the only way this could be done was by a downward pressure on a wage-level that was already low. It was the standard of living of the working classes that acted as the safety valve for the losses and contingencies inevitably accompanying the expansion of industry.

The same phenomenon characterized the first five-year plans in the U.S.S.R. In such conditions, protests on humanitarian grounds are of no avail since the conditions prevailing are indispensable to the creation of large-scale industry. The inhuman side of the development is offset in everyone's eyes by the fact that a new factory "gives work" and thus allows thousands of workers, who would otherwise have been unemployed, to earn livelihoods.

Leopold I, as he grew older, was always an amused observer of this bourgeois world, so different from the world of princely courts of the Europe of the First Empire in which he had grown up. He had seen many countries and many men, but his own people, as he watched them with eyes forever full of surprised curiosity, were beyond his understanding.

He himself had been born into a society where money counted for little, and he had several times passed from wealth to poverty, and from hardship to fortune. He did not disguise his astonishment at the attitude of his subjects toward money and business. "Any decline in their income is to them the equivalent of suffering," he remarked.

At first he had thought of the Belgians as anarchists and had been uneasy about the future of his throne. Later, however, he gained confidence when he discovered that in reality they were extremely prudent and conservative.

At the time of his accession, he thought of the constitution that put a severe limit on his powers as advanced and dangerous. "Gentlemen," he said bitterly, "you treated the monarchy roughly, when it was not there to defend itself." He had, however, succeeded in securing for himself the better part of his prerogatives, and had accordingly ceased to attach great importance to legal texts. It went over his head when Frère-Orban said to his colleagues: "Let us show the King that we are not his ministers, but those of the nation." He was quite content to continue exercising the real powers.

As he grew older, he became more and more surly and misanthropic. He was now a widower, preferred solitude, and was unwilling to enter into conversation with anyone. He did not correspond with his ministers, or even with his secretary Van Praet, except by short notes that he scribbled with an impatient hand.

Leopold was, in fact, disappointed by the new age. He had once been the arbiter of Europe and the counsellor of kings, but the accession of Napoleon III in France, and the increasing strength of Bismarck's Prussia, had diminished his influence.

The Emperor of the French would doubtless have liked nothing better than to annex Belgium, as his uncle, the first Napoleon, had done. He was furious with what he called "the intrigues" of the Saxe-Coburgs, and particularly with the attacks against him in the Belgian newspapers, which the Brussels government was prevented by the constitution from suppressing.

Napoleon III's irritation on this count is not unlike that of Louis XV, who was so enraged by the insults in the Dutch gazettes that he refused to believe his ambassadors when they explained that the same gazettes were just as violent in their attacks on the ministers of the United Provinces themselves. "In this country," they explained, "nobody is punished for disliking the government."

Leopold I died before the decisive crisis of Sadowa in 1866. At this moment, the existence of Belgium was indeed imperiled, and it needed all the energy of Frère-Orban to defend it in the face of the intrigues and ambitions of Europe. Leopold, however, lived long enough to see great changes, both in the period and in his country.

In the bourgeois world of the Second Empire, on the eve of the triumph of Bismarck's Germany and the resulting transformation in the European balance, observers looked upon Belgium as a kind of Switzerland. Its aristocracy, in common with the English, was forever making room for newcomers and granting new patents of nobility. The new nobility multiplied, and the old families were swamped by the rise of the bourgeois.

The court balls ranked as among the most brilliant in Europe. There was a special ballroom, the Blue Drawing Room, reserved for members of the high aristocracy, the princes and dukes whose ancestors dated from the old regime. All the world of industry and commerce, and even the small bourgeoisie, however, would receive their invitations to the balls.

The army still wore the uniforms of the First Empire. The regiment of Guides wore red breeches and green tunics with loops, and plumed helmets; and the lancers, with their long lances, would be wearing their shining Polish shakos as they charged. No officer might marry without a permit from his colonel, and his wife was required to have a dowry of not less than 50,000 gold francs.

It was, however, the civic guard, an institution peculiar to Belgium, that had the job of keeping order. It was made up of bourgeois elements who elected their own leaders and, until 1914, its status was as high as that of the army. Its officers, indeed, had precedence over the regular officers of the army itself, to the great indignation of the cavalry and the smart regiments.

On the railways there were four classes, and a good bourgeois family could not with decency go as low as the second class, since it would be discredited by mixing with clerks and small shopkeepers. A member of the nobility could go into only a few professions. He could go into the church, he could enter the state service as an officer or as a judge, or he could become a lawyer or an engineer. These latter professions were sources of fabulous incomes about the middle of the nineteenth century, and their members were apt to become eminent personalities. The smaller bourgeoisie was a middle class that was continuously rising. Its salons were in the cafés, like the Café of the Thousand Columns in Brussels, where business and politics were discussed. On Sundays they would all go out to the suburban taverns and eat onion fritters, chicken waterzoie, cramique, and many other Belgian specialties.

For a full half century, Brussels itself was a huge builders' yard. The city authorities gave every encouragement to new building and awarded prizes for the best façades. In many cases they made agreements with the inhabitants of a definite district to reconstruct it. New roads were built with funds obtained from loans and state subsidies that enabled the city to buy the land from the owners. Often, too, part of the money would be put up by the inhabitants themselves, who had a more highly developed sense of business than was usual in other countries. Sometimes they would form syndicates among themselves to buy up houses that would have to be demolished in order to make a new road. They themselves would be the first beneficiaries, since the presence of the road would increase the value of their own property enormously. The same thing was happening in other cities. Liége, Antwerp, and Ghent doubled or trebled in size in a few years, following city-development plans arranged on modern lines.

In Brussels, the building of the huge law-court building was begun in 1866. Its architect, J. Poelaert, went mad before he died. This enormous building, a mixture of every conceivable style, covers sixty-five acres, with buildings on fifty acres. The central Salle des Pas Perdus covers more than three-quarters of an acre, and above it is a cupola and dome nearly 500 feet high. There are 245 halls and chambers, including twenty-seven audience chambers. The architect himself had intended to emphasize the pseudo-Egyptian character of the building by crowning it, not with a dome, but with a pyramid. It was his successor, Benoit, who put on the dome and the gilded royal crown that are the summit of the building as we know it.

The river Senne wound its way around pleasant islets in the heart of the city. However, each year it overflowed its banks, and the evil-smelling mud that filled the streets and most of the cellars of the lower town made Brussels one of the most unhealthy cities in Europe. Epidemics took a terrifying toll. As recently as 1866, the death toll from cholera was 3,467. But the population, which supported the artists and admirers of the good old times, opposed any improvement in hygienic conditions that would spoil the picturesque character of the town. Burgomaster Anspach, however, described the river as a "man-eater," and energetically pushed his plan to have the river put underground for a mile of its course through the city. The work was undertaken by an English company that first, however, had photographs taken and reproduced for art lovers, showing all the picturesque but unhygienic districts that were to disappear. The old houses, with their balconies fringing the stream, were mercilessly pulled down and the work continued through underground water-pockets and shifting sands.

In the same period, there was a transformation in the artistic and intellectual life of the country. Until the Second Empire, there had been little intellectual life in Belgium, and few events of intellectual interest. Exhibitions of pictures were held only once every two or three years. There was little interest in music, and the Théâtre de la Monnaie almost went into bankruptcy in 1840, despite government subsidies. The taste for music at the popular level led to the formation of many choral societies and amateur orchestras, paving the way for the generation of musicians that was to come.

There was soon a happy change for the better, however, due to the influence of refugees whom the vicissitudes of politics drove into exile from France and Germany, and who found their way to Brussels. In 1852, after the advent of the Second Empire, more than 7,000 exiles entered Belgium. Karl Marx lived there, and it was in Brussels that Edgar Quinet married the daughter of an immigrant. Others who were living in Brussels included Marceline Desbordes-Valmore, Théophile Gautier, and Gérard de Nerval. In 1844, the English novelist Charlotte Brontë came to Brussels to study French in the Hégar School, and Brussels was the city that she depicted in her novel *Villette*.

Among the immigrants were politicians whose influence was to be important, including Ledru-Rollin, Proudhon, Louis Blanc, Considérant, General Lamoricière, and the Pole, Lelewel. The poets Verlaine and Rimbaud came to Brussels in 1870; Baudelaire had been there before them. The most important influence in the reawakening of public opinion, however, was the lectures given by Emile Deschanel, father of the future president of the French Republic. He started a series of lecture-discussions, in which a great number of French writers and politicians took part. Among them were Challemel-Lacour, Madier du Montjau, and Bancel. About this time, too, Victor Hugo was turning his own house into a center of intense literary activity.

Under the influence of the ferment of ideas that resulted from these new contacts, a certain interest in literature and art manifested itself. The first Belgian writers, Pirmez and Decoster, made their appearance. Although a number of writers were attracted to Paris, as was the case with Camille Lemonnier, a more propitious atmosphere was being generated in Belgium itself and, about 1880, there grew up the movement known as "Young Belgium." The plastic arts, however, were a traditional form of expression for the Belgians, and here the change was even more striking. The young painters at the beginning of the nineteenth century had been under the influence of their period, and particularly the influence of the French painter David and the neo-classical school. It was in Brussels that David took refuge when he was exiled from France, in 1816, for having voted in favor of the execution of Louis XVI, and where he was to live in exile for the rest of his life. His chief pupil was born in Charleroi. This was François Joseph Navez (1787–1869), who was to be the chief influence in the rebirth of Belgian painting.

Navez was the first to understand the primitives and restore their prestige. His studio in Brussels was frequented by all the young painters of his time, and its influence on the formation of their ideas was considerable. In the field of portrait painting, Navez left a number of masterpieces, in particular a portrait of the Hemptinne family (1816) that is now in the Brussels Museum.

It was against Navez that the new school of Belgian romanticism revolted. The school was limited to painting, and its main aim was to cease imitating David and the old masters and to make a fresh start with Rubens, whose work was being copied in its grandiloquence by painters such as Wiertz and Wappers. This was nicknamed "operatic romanticism," because the artists would paint on large surfaces, not unlike the backdrop of a theater, and the figures would be posed theatrically. There was a small-scale romanticism also, a school of anecdotal work and genre scenes in period costume, in which painters such as Madou gained distinction.

It was from these influences that there emerged painters such as Henri Leys (1815–69), who imitated the German and Flemish primitive. His nephew, Henri de Braeckeleer (1840–88), was to share with the well-known painter Jan Stobbaerts the distinction of being one of the restorers of Belgian art. He was from Antwerp, and came to be known as a "lighting magician." He began by imitating Rubens, and later developed a style composed of hachures and sparklings of light, forerunning impressionism and pointillism, and making him one of the predecessors of Van Gogh. Other painters to become famous included the Stevens brothers: Joseph (1816–92) revived the style of Snyders and Fyt, and Alfred (1829–1906) made his career in Paris as a painter of pretty women.

By the time of the Second Empire, Belgium was again a country of painters, and Belgian artists were making their mark in Europe as they had in the great periods of the country's history. The Belgian, Félicien Rops, friend of Baudelaire and Théophile Gautier, was rising to eminence in Paris, while in Brussels, painters such as Eugène Smits, Charles de Groux, Louis Verwee, Louis Artan, and Hippolyte Boulanger (1837–74), were paving the way for the impressionism of James Ensor.

About 1850, the standard of living of the working class in Belgium had materially improved. Wages were still low, but the peasantry and the workers were now able to wear wool in winter. White bread was replacing black or brown, even for the poor. Meat, almost unknown among the lower classes in 1800, now came to the poor man's table once a week, and to that of the average worker twice.

The workers were moving into houses with glass windows, built during the eighteenth century for the burghers and nobles, and the wood-shuttered peasant cottages were disappearing. The slums of the day were the fine bourgeois houses of the preceding century. The rich were moving out into new districts where new houses were being built.

At the same time, the backward industries were catching up to the others. The glassworks expanded enormously because of the growing demand for window glass, and the glass-fronted cupboard was now increasingly common in bourgeois houses and was about to become so in those of the working class. Between 1828 and 1850, throughout western Europe, there was a fourfold increase in the production of sheet glass and, by the end of the century, production had grown tenfold. The production of pig iron was doubled, and there was to be a threefold increase within thirty years. At the same time, prices were falling, and raw materials and manufactured products were coming within the reach of every purse. Iron fell to a quarter of its former price. A ton of steel, selling for eighty gold dollars before the introduction of the Bessemer process, could soon be bought for twenty gold dollars.

Apparel for the working class also fell in price. Woolen cloth that cost sixteen gold francs per meter in 1816, could be bought for 1.45 gold francs in 1833. Sugar, selling three centuries earlier at levels equivalent to several hundred kilograms of bread, fell from five gold francs a kilogram in 1800 to sixty centimes towards the end of the century, or the price of about two kilograms of bread.

The last Belgian famine occurred in 1845. It was not the result of a shortage of grain, but of a disease of the potato, the staple item in the working class diet. The time of shortages was, however, now coming to an end, and, instead of famines, the future was to be marked by economic crises on the modern pattern.

In the country districts, the peasantry ate meat only on Sundays. During the week they were content to make their main meals of lard, cabbage, and potatoes, and they took their butter to market in the cities. In backward regions, such as the Ardennes, the diet consisted almost wholly of potatoes. The men of this period suffered from stomach disorders on account of the unduly heavy and indigestible diet, and women of forty often looked as though they were sixty. The working class wore only corduroy trousers, that resisted wear, but the women, in many cases, still wore the peasant costumes of olden times.

Up to about 1900, wages were still very low. At Grand Halleux, in the Luxemburg province, a young nine-year-old cowherd earned only ten francs per year, but he got a tip on Sundays, or on the occasion of each cattle sale. He was hired only from April 1 to November 11, and, until his discharge at St. Martin's, he was fed and dressed by the employer. The clothes customarily handed out to him are an indication of what country costume was like at that time. They consisted of a cap, a cloth vest worn with a blue cloth smock, a pair of cloth trousers, and a pair of work shoes. The smock did duty as a shirt, and the arms were covered only with cloth sleeves.

An agricultural laborer was paid sixty centimes per day plus food, and his working day ran from 7 A.M. until nightfall. These figures date from the middle of the nineteenth century. There was a progressive rise to a franc a day, and around 1900, the rate had reached 1.5 francs, in 1910, it was two francs, and in 1914, three francs. It is clear from these figures that the standard of living was rising fast. From now on, the old feudal idea of considering it an honor to serve the employer was to progressively disappear. Farm labor was getting scarcer, for the workers were making their way toward the factories. They disliked the humiliating character of serfdom in the country and preferred the proletarian life in the city.

While the bourgeois world was reaching its apogee, the Liberal party, which itself represented this social class through the qualified-voter system, remained solidly in power. Frère-Orban returned to the head of the government after an absence of five years, and made full use of the country-wide reaction to the Convents Bill and the mistakes made by the De Decker ministry by taking up an attitude that was frankly anti-clerical.

In his first ministry (1847–52), Frère-Orban had centered his policy on economic problems. These comprised banking and credit, the buying out of the Schelde toll rights and the city duties (or *octrois*), the promotion of free trade, and the fall in the price of grain. His policy with regard to the Church, on the other hand, had been comparatively moderate. The project of setting up a system of state education had been no more than sketched, so that the sensibilities of the Catholic masses should not be offended.

Now that he was sure of the country's support, he and the Liberal party began to act with a firmness and a capacity for decision that enabled it to execute its program fully. Frère-Orban himself would have no compromise. Though he was an apostle of liberty in every form, he became increasingly authoritarian and aggressive. Societies of freemasons and free-thinkers were being formed everywhere. A succession of new laws was enacted, and these were to become the weapons of the fight: a law against attacks from the pulpit; laws setting up state control over the administration of parish property; laws regarding charitable foundations; laws doing away with the priests' right to refuse burial to unbelievers, or to require that they be buried in a special place. In village cemeteries, the space reserved for unbelievers had been known as the "dog's ditch."

This was the beginning of a long period of guerilla warfare between the liberal bourgeois and the working class. The latter were still deeply attached to the Roman Catholic faith, but they had no voting rights. The Liberal government was opposed to any extension of the franchise and preferred to rely on the enlightened leadership of the upper middle classes. Frère-Orban himself considered that the people were incapable of understanding their true interests and should be led forcibly into the paths of progress.

The Catholics reacted to the threat, as they had in the days of William I, by calling on the masses to support them. This was a period of considerable external danger, and the ambitions of the Second Empire had obliged the Liberals to rearm the country. The Catholic demagogues were thus able to find a campaign platform in anti-militarism.

In 1859, the problem of the Antwerp fortifications, resulting from the growing tension between France and Belgium, had brought most of the Antwerp electorate into the field against Frère-Orban. The continued development of the city was threatened by the militarized zones in which all building was forbidden and the forts by which the city was encircled. The Catholics were quick to seize the electoral advantage that this created for them. Instead of appealing primarily to the body of qualified voters, they had the idea of creating more agitation by organizing mass meetings.

In this they followed the example of England, where the advocates of free trade had secured success by this method. An intensive campaign broke out against the Liberals, who were accused of having betrayed the interests of the city. The Liberals were overwhelmed by the avalanche of criticism, and in the end had to support the movement that had been unleashed against them. However, this did not prevent their being swept out of power in the elections of 1863, in which the whole of the Catholic slate was elected. The Catholic party now began to reorganize on a new footing. The leadership of the movement was in the hands of young and dynamic chiefs, such as Victor Jacobs and Charles Woeste. They drew encouragement and aid from such French Catholics as Montalembert, who took part in the Mechlin Congress of 1863. Their strength came from the masses, and they did not take long to recover their drive. They drew up a popular program, the chief planks in their platform being the reduction of taxation and military expenditure. Their systematic propaganda led national opinion, while the Liberals were divided among themselves through the continued bickering between the progressive and the doctrinaire factions.

The internal political picture of Belgium was thus undergoing a transformation just at the moment when the reign of Leopold I was coming to an end and a new sovereign, Leopold II, was on the point of acceding to the throne.

XI

LEOPOLD II AND THE CONGO

Leopold I died on December 10, 1865. His son, Leopold II, took his oath before the assembled Chambers and acceded to the throne. The young sovereign, who was later to be so authoritarian, began his reign in an impressively modest vein. He was conciliatory with everyone, and constantly repeated: "I cannot act with the same authority as the late king." He listened to his advisers and enchanted his ministers and the parliamentarians by his hard work, his zeal, and his smiling amiability. He was nevertheless a genius of wilful and imperious disposition.

He understood at an early age that, in the industrial era then in its early stages, the chief problem was raw materials and markets. One of the keys to England's low production rates was the possession of colonies, from which she obtained her cotton, jute, oil-yielding materials, rubber, and other raw materials.

Leopold thus became a man with one fixed idea—"Belgium must have a colony." He repeated this to everybody, and even had it engraved on one of the stones of the Acropolis that he brought back from Greece for Frère-Orban. Even this did not convince the elder statesmen, for the new monarch was as yet only thirty years of age, inexperienced, and lacking in prestige. To give himself a more impressive presence, he grew a full beard.

As a man, he stood out to an astonishing degree. His personality was somewhat disconcerting to his contemporaries, for he jarred upon the Belgium of his period. He was tall, very thin, and flat-chested; in his youth, indeed, his poor health had led to fears that he might be tubercular. He limped and often had to lean upon his stick. He spoke extremely slowly and he impressed those with whom he talked by giving each word strength and majesty. In his old age, he spoke of himself in the third person, even when he was talking to his intimate friends. He did not say "Give me that book," but "Give that book to the King," or "I hope you will carry out the King's wishes." To his servants he would say, for example, "The King is not pleased." The things he said, whether true or false, were often severe. On one occasion, he asked a young nobleman who had been presented to him, "What do you do?" When the young man replied, "Nothing," his answer was, "I do not congratulate you on that."

He had a sarcastic wit and did not hesitate to amuse himself at other people's expense. An example of this occurred at an important dinner in the Brussels Palace, when he saw his brother, the Count of Flanders, in animated conversation with the lady next to him, telling her scandalous stories about the other people present. Since everybody was talking at once, the other diners could not hear what he was saying; but after the meal, when the general conversation had lapsed, the Count of Flanders was prevented by his deafness from perceiving the silence around him, and his voice could still be heard telling his tales. The lady who was receiving his confidences was obviously frightened, and tried in vain to make him stop. Leopold carefully abstained from giving the signal to rise and waited quietly until his brother had finished. When the latter realized at last that everyone was listening to him, Leopold gave the signal for the end of dinner with a smile.

There are, of course, a number of far-fetched stories of his wit. It is said, for example, that the Dean of Ostend, into whose parish the King came each year, approached Leopold in order to draw his attention respectfully to the scandalous life that he was said to lead. "But how did you know all this, Dean?" asked the King.

"Sire, I have been told these things by persons who can be trusted."

"Well," said the King, "it seems I have more Christian charity than you. Do you realize that people have told me exactly the same thing about you, but I didn't believe them?"

Leopold II was original in that he was a great admirer—and almost the only one during his period—of Louis XV and also of Louis XI. Perhaps this was because they both had the same taste for secrecy that he had, and also the same caustic wit—or, perhaps, the same contempt for humanity and public opinion.

It would be wrong to suppose, however, that Leopold II was incapable of affection and deep grief. He had a son, the Duke of Hainaut, whose death at the age of eight was the great tragedy of his life. Many years later one of his ministers said to him, "The King has been fortunate!" He replied, "Fortunate? I? I lost my son!" He blamed his Queen, Marie Henriette, who had been born Archduchess of Austria, for the fact that all the rest of his children were girls. He treated them harshly, both during his lifetime and in his will. As he grew old, he became misanthropic and lonely. This has given him, in the eyes of history, a peculiar grandeur, but it also contributed to making him unpopular in Belgium.

When he wished, he was perfectly able to charm the people with whom he was talking, to persuade financiers and the most convinced opponents of his projects that they were perfectly viable, and to bring the most eminent men into his service. When, however, he found that any of his followers were not as docile as he required, he had no hesitation in breaking them.

With his qualities and his faults, both of which may have contributed to his success, he was one of the most remarkable figures of the nineteenth century. He succeeded, not only because of his personality and his strong character, but also because of his way of making the most original and daring of his plans seem to be the expression of the age in which he lived. He was very quick to understand—well ahead of Belgian opinion—the importance of international relations, and he realized that matters of consequence were settled not only in Europe, but overseas as well.

The traffic in vegetables was revolutionized by the use of produce from every continent: wheat from Canada and Argentina, groundnuts and oil-yielding crops from tropical countries, coffee from Brazil, sugar from Cuba, fruit from the Antilles, and, later, rubber from America, Africa, and the Dutch East Indies. Belgium's share in the world pool of raw materials was to come from the Congo. This territory was to play a great part in Belgian expansion after 1920, and to facilitate its revival and economic well-being after the war of 1939–45. Belgium owed it to the work and tenacity of Leopold II.

The King was himself a financier. He had inherited from his father a fortune of 20 million gold francs, equivalent to about 500 million francs or 10 million dollars in 1958. He increased this by good investment and speculation, and made it an instrument of his power and greatness. He was deeply involved with the root of the great conflict of the nineteenth century, the substitution of the new strength of capitalism for the old divisive policies symbolized by frontiers and the age-old rivalry of nations.

Unlike William II or Franz Joseph, Leopold II was one of those modern sovereigns for whom military force was replaced by financial combinations. During the second part of the nineteenth century, capitalism was closely bound up with colonial development. Only the cheap raw materials from tropical countries enabled capitalism to maintain its progress and to overcome successive crises. This gave the King the idea of a colonial empire and, first, he sought to create it either in Asia or in Latin America.

Africa was still a virgin continent. Europe and Asia were struggling for possession of it, the former with missionaries and explorers who were finding their way up the great rivers—the Senegal, the Niger, and the Congo—from the Atlantic Ocean, and the latter through the slave-trading sultans from the Indian Ocean, who represented the influence of Islam and the Arab world. The final result of this conflict was not so much the possession, however temporary, of raw materials and consequent financial profits, as it was the lasting conquest of human souls and human populations. If it is true that Africa is still open to Europe at the present time, and if it represents the best chance of Europe's future because the white population can still be assimilated, this is due much less to explorers, like Stanley and Savorgnan de Brazza, than to the farsighted policy of leaders like Leopold II.

The occupation of the Congo, therefore, was no mere egoistical exercise intended to serve the interests of a single country or of a single man. It was rather an episode in the long rivalry in Africa between the influences of Europe and those of Asia. This had been in progress since the fourteenth century, when the Portuguese were beginning the colonization of the western coast of the Dark Continent, while the Asiatics were busy on the eastern coast with Zanzibar, on the Indian Ocean, Egypt, and North Africa.

This rivalry has continued to our own times. The immigrant populations of Asiatic origin, whether Arab or Hindu, are far more numerous in the twentieth century than the European colonists. Without the Belgians, who drove back the Asiatics by snatching the Congo from the sultanates of the Indian Ocean, the Arabs would today be in possession of Central Africa. From this vantage point, it would have been possible for them to prevent the European nations from acquiring control of the territories stretching across the African continent from the Cape to Algiers.

With the perspective of time, it is clear to us today that this work that determined the future of Europe in its relation to Asia was the major event in the latter part of the nineteenth century. The Congo was the most extraordinary example of the creation of an empire, by the work of a single man, that history has ever known.

Between 1870 and 1905, while Belgian interest was mainly taken up with party strife, the establishment of an empire in Africa was the main objective for Leopold II of his reign. He had begun by acting as patron of a scientific exploration society, known as the International African Association, and he accepted the office of president. When a king plays the part of president, he enjoys a certain advantage over his competitors. Another trump in his hand was Belgian neutrality. When Leopold called the International Geographical Conference of Brussels in 1876, the name sounded inoffensive enough, but the King was sure that it would enable him to establish the seat of the Association in Brussels, since a neutral country alone could provide the necessary guarantees that the work would retain its humanitarian and moral character. The King was the only person with sufficient funds to finance the projects that he undertook, and he had the command of personnel through his position as head of the Belgian army. It was thus that he was able to recruit a galaxy of officers, among whom were Captain Crespel and Lieutenant Cambier, to begin the systematic exploration of Africa. In the diplomatic field, in the meantime, he had men such as E. Banning and A. Lambermont to deal with the European negotiations.

As early as 1877, the Belgian section of the International Association, and its planning committee, were the only sections that had positive results to show. Leopold II learned that the English explorer Stanley had discovered the upper course of the Congo, followed it from the Great Lakes to the estuary, and disclosed the existence of about 11,000 miles of navigable waterways. He brought the explorer into his service at once, and the diplomatic battle began. While Stanley signed treaties, in the name of the Association, with the native chiefs and gained the right to occupy the disputed territory, Leopold II was persuading Europe to recognize his sovereignty. The first opposition came from England, which was supporting the logical claims of Portugal to the estuary waters that Portuguese explorers had used since the fifteenth century.

The intervention of England roused the jealousies of Germany and France. On August 23, 1884, France, in exchange for a pre-emptive right, recognized the rights of the International Association to the Congo. A day before this, on August 22, the United States had taken a decisive step by recognizing the Association as a sovereign state. On November 8, Germany decided to do the same in order to keep the English out. The Belgian government knew nothing about this, because the King had carried out all his negotiations in secret. When the Berlin Conference was held to discuss the division of Central Africa, in 1885, the Belgian government had to be brought up to date, but it was quite willing to support what it considered to be a mere whim of the King. The Belgian diplomats, including Lambermont, had orders to follow the King's command, since the ministers were interested only in internal policy.

Leopold II succeeded in making the Germans fear that he would hand over the rights to France; the English that he would sell out to Germany; and the French that he might possibly withdraw altogether, making it necessary to consider the whole question afresh. He thus had no difficulty in obtaining recognition for the new independent state of the Congo. Everyone believed that the King of the Belgians would never be able to maintain his position in these distant territories, and that sooner or later he would have to give them up to a friendly power.

The officers of Leopold II, however, were now occupying the whole of the Congo basin, and all that was necessary to extend the frontiers was to play off the jealousies and rivalries of the other powers against one another. On February 26, 1885, Leopold finally received from Europe the title he had sought, and the president of a simple scientific association became a chief of state. The fiction of the International Association now disappeared, and the organization of the Congo began.

King Leopold had to increase his financial resources and, for this purpose, he initiated a scheme of state trading. The necessary corollary to the scheme was, of course, forced native labor, with corporal punishment being inflicted on the natives. Cardinal Lavigerie gave the King the support of the Church and its missionaries, loans were floated, and options sold on the Belgian market to provide funds on an ever-increasing scale for the new enterprise.

Organization, however, was not enough. The Congo also had to be defended against those who had long been its real masters—the slave-trading sultans from the Zanzibar coast, the Sudan, and the Abyssinian borders, who made systematic raids with their armed bands for a long time after the arrival of the white man.

In 1889, Leopold II had to call another antislavery conference in Brussels in order to bring the other nations to his aid. After 1892, the fight began in earnest, and it had many ups and downs. In the first instance, it was a campaign against the black Sultan Gongo-Lutété, who was eventually forced into submission by Lieutenant Dahnis. The Arab sultans soon formed a coalition and succeeded in mobilizing a force of 100,000 men. They took Hodister's Belgian force by surprise and defeated it at Riba-Riba in May, 1882.

The subordinates of Leopold II recruited black troops and began a new offensive. By a succession of concentric operations, they succeeded in driving back their opponents on all sides. The Sultan of Udjidji, on Lake Tanganyika, had a number of well-trained troops armed with European weapons, and with these he attempted to resume the fight. He was finally defeated at Kabambaré and the conquest of the Congo was complete.

The Belgians were about to occupy the Sudan and to open the way to Egypt and Abyssinia, when they were stopped in 1897, by the general revolt of their black Batélélé troops. This was a serious matter, comparable to the revolt of the Sepoys in India, and the four-year campaign of repression lasted from 1897 to 1901. The Batélélés were trained soldiers, armed with European weapons, so that they were formidable opponents.

Leopold II, in financial difficulties, now found himself on the verge of bankruptcy. Belgium had once refused to take over responsibility for the Congo, but Parliament now gave the King a donation of 25 million gold francs, enabling him to re-establish his position. From then on, he refused to make any concession to Belgium. He was creating a sort of financial monarchy, founded on state monopolies, forced labor, and the absence of commercial freedom. This was particularly irritating to the other powers.

King Leopold was now able to say of the Congo, even with more justice than Louis XV said of France, "*L'Etat, c'est moi.*" He was an absolute dictator. In his hands he held the executive, the legislative, and the judicial powers that are usually kept separate. To these he added the total ownership of the soil and the human beings who worked it, which gave him financial powers that have seldom been at the command of other monarchs. He let it be known among his entourage that he had become the greatest landowner in the world, with domains stretching over 1.25 million square miles, or eighty times the area of Belgium. For him, political power and financial power were as solidly merged as they would have been if Louis XIV had, at the same time, been a Rockefeller. He created a type of state capitalism that even Napoleon or Peter the Great had never been able to conceive. In each region of the Congo, official organizations known as "national committees" held 50 per cent of the shares of all companies having concessions to develop local resources. The King and the state, interested in their profits, supported them with all the weight of their great authority. The inevitable result was the exploitation of the native peoples who had no defense against the forced deliveries of rubber and ivory, or the regime of forced labor that tore them from their villages to put them into construction sites and far-off camps where they died by the thousands.

It was not long before these conditions, however necessary they may have been to finance the early stages of the Congo's development, came under the fire of world opinion because of the number of abuses, and could not continue much longer. In 1903, the British government took the part of the black population against the King, and its official protest forced Leopold to agree to an international committee of inquiry being sent to the Congo.

There was now a risk that the Congo might fall under the influence of the great powers. Interference, based on more or less humanitarian pretexts, could only be prevented if the colony were taken over by Belgium. The Anglo-French Colonial Agreement of 1902, and the rapid growth of Germany, made it appear that the only way to save the Congo was to annex it to Belgium. Leopold II attempted vainly to delay this transfer, which was not to take place until 1908. He considered it an injustice and laid the blame bitterly at the door of the Belgian parliament.

He had, however, given his country a royal gift. He was depriving himself of his powers as an absolute monarch, but in return, with his work duly accomplished, he was able to take his place in history, where alone, beyond the superficial vicissitudes and contemporary reproaches of an epoch, subsist the deep-seated intentions and universal value of human effort.

While Leopold was concentrating upon his work in Africa, considerable changes were going on in the internal politics of Belgium. Belgium was thirty-five years behind France, and more than a half-century behind England in the advancement of the working class, but this improvement was now in progress and the workers were taking their place in modern society and making themselves felt, not only in Parliament, but throughout the economic life of the country. This was the bloodless revolution that, without any display of violence, characterized the end of the nineteenth century.

To understand it, we must retrace our steps a few decades. At the moment of Leopold's accession, in 1865, Frère-Orban was still head of the government. The power of the Liberals was waning, and the violence of party strife seemed to be at its peak. In 1870, the Catholics went to the polls to attack the cabinet's "military follies" that had raised the total strength of the army to 120,000 men. In all the big towns, progressive candidates opposed the doctrinaire Liberals. At a single stroke the parliamentary majority went to the Catholics.

The first cabinet that took power was a militant one under Baron d'Anethan, but this was soon replaced by the more moderate Malou-de Theux government which survived, with some difficulty, from 1871 to 1879. This tenure of office was marked by a long period of inactivity. When its leader was asked what he had been doing during the eight-year period, his only reply was: "We went on living."

The inactivity ended in 1879, when the Liberals were again successful and Frère-Orban returned to power. He had been able to win his victory only by reconciling the progressive and doctrinaire factions, but the two halves of the Liberal party had only one common element in their program: anticlericalism. Frère-Orban was able to maintain agreement between them, and carry on with the government, only by initiating a political struggle against the church. This was inevitable because of the internal cleavage within the party, but it was to result in Frère-Orban losing his power for good.

He proceeded to have an education bill voted, an act that did not seem likely to plunge the country into civil war. It required that every village have a free public school. This conformed to Frère-Orban's principles, but it was clear that the clergy, who depended for their support on the great masses of the people, would not allow the new law to pass without a struggle.

The Liberals were also violating the unwritten law that says that a minority government can continue to exist only if it avoids coming into conflict with the majority of the country, which only tolerates it. Perhaps the Liberals might have won the day after all by skill and moderation, bringing the country along with them and reassuring it with adroit propaganda.

Party unity, however, demanded an aggressive program and made it necessary to present the new law as a declaration of war against the church. Even the balloting seemed like a battle. In the senate the bill passed by only one vote cast by a Liberal senator from Bruges, who had himself been elected by a mere ten-vote majority, and who had himself brought from his deathbed to cast the deciding vote. He died the following day. The Catholics considered his death as a punishment from heaven, but the Liberals replied that the true miracle was his having lived long enough to enable the bill to be passed.

The opposition at once began to organize. The bishops decided to erect a free Catholic school opposite each state school. To raise the necessary funds they circulated a subscription list that galvanized the country and, within a few months, raised a total of no less than 40 million gold francs. The struggle, thus engaged, soon passed far beyond the bourgeois electorate, and the success of Catholic education became a plebiscite. The official schools soon emptied; 30 per cent of the pupils left, and 20 per cent of the teachers gave up their jobs and went over to the "private" schools. Frère-Orban resorted to reprisals. Poor people, whose children did not attend the official schools, were threatened with the loss of their allowances and public servants in like circumstances were dismissed.

The cost of the new education policy, with its consequent increase in the number of official schools, called for increases in taxation, to the great indignation of the bourgeois electors. The budget deficit was the last straw that caused the government's fall. Graux, the minister of finance, was obliged to raise an additional 25 million gold francs by taxation (dubbed by Catholics the "Graux taxes") and to increase the public debt by 105 million gold francs. The real paradox of the situation was that a law intended to give everyone the free choice of his children's school seemed, in effect, to be leading to the ostracism of the Catholics because of the many measures of government persecution.

The masses, although they did not vote, expressed their opinion even more effectively by sending their children to the "free" schools and subscribing to the cost of their upkeep. Within two years, no less than 200,000 children, or two-thirds of the total number of pupils, went into the free schools. In the same period, 1,340 teachers deserted the state schools and took service in the Catholic schools.

The discontent that was spreading throughout the country resulted, of course, in widening the split between the Liberals who were actually in power. In the 1884 election, in which the main slogan was "Down with the taxes!", the progressive Liberals put forward independent lists of candidates in almost all the constituencies. The downfall of the government was inevitable, and the Catholics obtained a majority of thirty-six seats. Frère-Orban left the government for good. This was the end of the last phase of the experiment in Liberal organization.

The next event was the coming of socialism. The Catholic victory in 1884 was regarded by contemporaries as a mere episode in their struggle with the Liberals, who were expected to stage a comeback later. But two years later an unexpected landslide upset all forecasts, and the political balance in Belgium was completely reversed when suffrage was extended to the working class and the peasantry. This made it possible for the Catholic party to remain in office for twenty years.

In 1880, the workers' booklet, a relic of the Napoleonic period, was still required. Any worker wishing to leave the service of his employer had to obtain the latter's permission to seek work elsewhere. The worker who lost his job, even for the most innocent of causes, was reduced to begging. Frère-Orban had given workers the right to strike, but this meant nothing, since inciting workers to leave their work was still a prohibited act.

Pregnant women and children under sixteen were still required to do exacting work at night, on pain of losing their jobs altogether. There were no safety measures and nothing to prevent unhealthy working conditions. These were particularly bad in the glass industry, where ten years of normal working life usually resulted in death by tuberculosis or permanent crippling. The standard of living did not meet even the most urgent requirements. Savings banks received practically no deposits, for saving was utterly impossible. Employers, on the other hand, accused the workers of being improvident and met suggestions of wage increases by saying: "What's the use? They would only spend it!"

When foreign competition, particularly from Germany, began to threaten the economy, the leaders of Belgian industry replied by lowering wages still further. The most important reduction occurred in 1880, and the workers were unable to do anything about it. A weaver's wages had now fallen to only eighty centimes per day, and some of the girls in the spinning mills earned only thirty centimes per day, the price of a kilogram of bread.

Auby, who made an enquiry into conditions, remarks that most working-class families could barely stretched the wages they received "to feed themselves as though they were prisoners, even in cases where the woman contributed her modest portion of work to the family community." He asks how it is possible for the workers to solve this problem. "Clearly," he writes, "it can only be done through expedients which the worker alone knows. It means reducing the daily ration of food; eating rye bread instead of wheat bread; eating less meat or none at all, and the same applies to butter; being satisfied with a little grease for all seasoning; reducing the family home to one or two rooms where father, mother, boys, and girls sleep side by side; saving on dress, on laundry, and on cleanliness; doing without every form of amusement, and indeed resigning themselves to privations of the most painful kind."

The excessive poverty of the Belgian worker, on the other hand, was in sharp and unexplained contrast with the progress and general wealth of the country. Stimulated by free trade, traffic in the port of Antwerp had increased sixfold between 1860 and 1880. Coal production had increased from 9.5 million tons in 1860, to 18 million tons in 1883; and the exports of that year amounted to 1.33 billion gold francs, compared with only 200 million gold francs in 1850.

The total volume of trade, which had amounted to only 100 million francs in 1831, was to increase by 1911 to 7 billion francs. The national wealth, at this time amounting to 50 billion gold francs, made Belgium the richest country in Europe, indeed, in the world, in terms of wealth per person. But neither the workers nor the peasantry had derived any benefit from this. The peasant class was ruined by the competition of Russian and American grain. The farmers came to the cities looking for jobs as workmen, and, in so doing, they forced wages to even lower levels. When Frère-Orban gave the workers cheap season-ticket facilities, he helped to drive wages down even faster.

There was a constant decrease in the rural population. It had constituted half the total population in 1846, but by 1880 it was no more than a quarter, or about the same proportion as in the United States

in the twentieth century. This continuous drift of population toward
the towns made labor cheap, and all attempts to secure higher wages
failed. Far from rebelling against this state of affairs, the working class
accepted its lot. "No complaint from the side of labor," was the comment made about 1880 by an official Liberal observer, Eudore Pirmez.

The public regarded the situation as normal. The Catholic leader
Charles Woeste warned his party against the possible disappearance of
pauperism, which, he said, would put an end to charity, one of the
noblest of the Christian virtues. The Liberal chief, Frère-Orban, based
his argument on different premises, refusing to take any action and
declaring that "any regulation of labor is no more than a form of
servitude."

Any resistance by the working class seemed hopeless. The first organized strike took place in 1857 among the textile workers in Ghent. It
was quickly broken, as were the sporadic strike movements of 1860.

The year 1864, however, saw the creation of the Workers' International, and it was after this that socialism made its appearance in Belgium. One result of the rivalry between the Liberals and the Catholics
had been an improvement in education, and this made it possible for
a popular elite to emerge. Schools organized by the communes and
"reading societies," such as were formed among the Ghent weavers,
revealed the rising intellectual level of the workers and the development of their collective conscience. Soon the first socialist pamphlet was
issued, the "Catechism of the People" by Defuisseaux, which sold
260,000 copies. There was a gradual weakening of the antagonism between the revolutionary spirit of the Walloons and the passivity of the
Flemish, which made it possible to form a single nationwide socialist
party.

It was at Ghent that the poverty of the working classes led to the
first attempt at popular organization. As early as 1877, a workers congress was held in the city to form a Flemish socialist party. The energetic
leader, Edward Anseele, gave it its original form, that of a workers' cooperative for the baking of bread. It was established in 1873, and given
the name Vooruit ("Forward"). The cooperatives soon branched out
into the manufacture of clothing and pharmaceutical products for the
working class and reduced selling prices so much that the number of
master bakers fell from 274 in 1879, to only 11 in 1905.

The old spirit of revolt was still alive; it had marked the history of
Ghent through the ages; it again came to the surface in the creation
of the first workers' union, in 1857; the first workers' newspaper—
Werkverbond—in 1859; Belgium's first strikes; the creation of the

Willemsfond for the furtherance of the Flemish movement; and the campaign for making the language of the university Dutch.

There still remained the task of creating a socialist movement in Wallonia and overcoming the obstacles created by the differences in language and cultural background. The organizers realized that the coordinated action of the working classes would depend on their financial resources and set to work to create a socialist world within the capitalist society. They created selling and manufacturing cooperatives, set up factories and companies, and, by dint of this practical and essentially Belgian approach, were able to found a new workers' party in 1885.

At this time, under the influence of a sudden crisis, the wage level again began to fall. Between 1883 and 1885, the total exports from Belgium fell by 10 per cent and unemployment began to increase. But the working class, by and large, was now conscious of its strength and of its aspirations, and the progressive faction in the Liberal Party, under the leadership of Paul Janson, was openly advocating universal suffrage.

The socialist revolution took exactly the same form as the early phases of the 1830 revolution. Through an insignificant incident—an anarchist meeting at Liége—a spontaneous explosion took place. Those who had been at the meeting, including a number of foreigners, staged a demonstration in the streets, and the meeting turned into a nocturnal riot. Unemployment was rife in the city and the crowd of demonstrators grew rapidly and began breaking shop windows, without the police being given a chance to intervene. The following day, a strike broke out in the entire district, and work came to a stop in the rolling mills, the glassworks, and the collieries of the industrial region. The strikes soon spread from Liége to Charleroi and the Mons district, later reaching Ghent and the rest of Flanders. The flame spread over the entire country, without any definite leaders or strike orders, or even any clear-cut reason for the strike itself. The working class demonstrated in the streets, attacked the factories and country houses of the rich, and triumphantly set fire to them without meeting any effective resistance.

The police were powerless. It became necessary to call out the troops and proclaim a state of emergency. Orders were given to open fire on the mob—this was done at Reulx—and the civic guard was called out. Eventually order was restored and an attempt was made to inquire into what had happened. A major trial was organized for the rioters who had been arrested, but it could not be proved that there had been any organized conspiracy, since no plot and no leaders could be discovered. The working class had risen spontaneously. A new force, long growing underground, had now come into the open and the country was astonished to find itself cut in two.

The bourgeois regime had many ways of defending itself. Any authority that was attacked by the rioters could meet force with force. It was organized, which the rioters were not, and the energy with which it could act depended directly on the extent to which it was threatened.

As soon as the Socialists succeeded in getting control of the situation, they were careful to give no pretext for a repression. At this stage, they concentrated solely on obtaining by legal means the universal suffrage that existed already in France, England, Germany, and most of the other nations of Europe, so that those who opposed it seemed to be defending the wrong cause.

No government could hold out long against the pressure of a pacific and organized mass that, by refusing to commit acts of violence, gave the authorities no pretext for crushing it. This tactic, applied with great intelligence by the Socialist Party, assured the triumph of the working class.

The movement began with a series of "black meetings," not unlike those that had been held during the wars of religion. The men would meet in the open country to evade the prohibitions of the authorities, and the workers would gather around speakers who hid in the shadows, remaining invisible so that no one could give them away and have them discharged from the factories where they worked. Later, when the working class had shown its strength, the authorities had no alternative but to tolerate processions that wound their way through the streets, followed by ever-growing crowds. In 1887, there was a concentration of 13,000 miners in Brussels and people were greatly impressed by their organized and well-disciplined ranks. In 1890, a procession of 80,000 men paraded quietly through the streets of the capital and similar demonstrations were held in other parts of the country. These crowds had no voting rights and could therefore have no direct influence on the elections, but the peaceful demonstration of their strength made the government's position impossible. There was no way of refusing voting rights to these men who were demonstrating both their strength and their political maturity, particularly since the ideal they sought was democratic and parliamentary.

The leaders of the socialist movement had perfected a system that was more effective than any act of violence in intimidating the ruling bourgeois class and overcoming its resistance. They took the country in hand with their propaganda and growing agitation. Then, when things had come to a boil, they brought their supporters down into the street and organized peaceful processions in which increasing numbers of their adherents took part, giving the demonstrators increasing confidence in themselves while avoiding any disorders.

The funds required for the campaign were collected from the profits of the workers' cooperatives and the industrial ventures into which the Socialist Party had entered. These consisted of bakeries, spinning mills, printing-plants, and shops that monopolized the working-class business. The decisive weapon, however, was fear. The governing class could never be sure that the masses would not escape from the control of their leaders, or that a shot or some other incident would not touch off the fuse that would plunge the country into the horrors of civil war. These tactics were applied very intelligently by the Socialists. Step by step universal suffrage was achieved, and with it the ascendancy of the working class.

From this time onward, the country was moving toward a revision of the constitution. In 1890, the Socialist Party, with the help of the progressive Liberal Paul Janson, had secured the introduction of a reform bill. This was supported by great working-class demonstrations and, under the pressure of the demonstrators, the first reading of the Bill in the Chamber was passed by a unanimous vote on November 17, 1890. Most of those who voted for it imagined that it was an empty gesture.

The bill then went into committee, where it came up against the opposition of the parliamentary groups and attempts were made to torpedo it. This was the mistake that made its success certain. It gave the Socialist Party the excuse it needed for bringing its supporters out into the streets, and a general-strike order was issued, to be put into effect the day on which the Chamber would finally reject the bill.

Tension was mounting and, in the overheated atmosphere, the governing class began to lose its grip on the situation. Before any effective action could be taken, a spontaneous strike broke out in the collieries. The firmness of the miners' political aspirations and the orderliness of their behavior had a contagious effect, and the entire working class supported them. Everyone now understood that the political system was dealing with a force that could not easily be frustrated. In a state of panic, the Chamber decided the bill must be given a quick passage before the spark ignited the powder.

This required a revision of the constitution, and the two Chambers met as a constituent assembly. The great majority were Catholic and secretly hostile to the extension of the suffrage. No party, however, had the two-thirds majority that would have been necessary to pass a constitutional amendment. However, a solution had to be found, for the assembly was debating with the threat of revolt hanging over it. The deputies knew that if they did not pass a bill that would satisfy the working class, the country would hold them responsible for the consequences.

An extension of the suffrage was agreed upon in principle, but no agreement was reached on the formula by which it should be brought about. The electorate at that time consisted of 137,000 voters. The Liberals wished to extend the number to 400,000 and the Catholics to 600,000; the Socialists, on the other hand, were demanding an electorate of at least 1.3 million.

With the parties apparently powerless to solve the dispute, the working class resumed its agitation, and this time the masses were ready to resort to violence. A compromise clearly had to be found. The decision that was reached gave the vote to all men of twenty-five years of age and over, but extra votes were given to fathers of families, taxpayers, and holders of university degrees. The result was that there would be 850,000 people with one vote each, and a further 520,000 privileged voters who would among them have 1.24 million votes.

This system favored the petty bourgeoisie and the Catholic peasantry. In the elections that followed, the Catholics secured 104 seats and the Liberals only fourteen. Liberalism was now definitely wiped out and socialism was taking its place. There were thirty-four Socialist deputies in the chamber and, by the same methods as before, the party was sure of being able to secure further extensions of voting rights and eventually a system of universal suffrage.

The Socialist victory had stemmed from the same basic laws that have ensured the triumph of the oppressed throughout the pages of history. The first of these was the renunciation of violence. The working class in France and in Germany during the nineteenth century was wasting its strength in armed insurrections that the bourgeoisie was able to put down without difficulty and that brought no appreciable benefit. The workers of Belgium, on the other hand, never resorted to force.

Next, the Socialists attempted to gain the support of a part of the property owners by convincing them that their cause was just. Thus they would succeed in securing the support of the progressive elements of the bourgeoisie, divide the ranks of the governing class, and insure universal suffrage.

They understood that any appeal to force would be playing the game of the ruling classes. It would give them the pretext of accusing the workers of being anarchists and disturbers of the peace, thus disposing of the situation by repression instead of by discussion. Insurrection is not an effective method of overcoming a class that is sure of itself and that holds the reins of power. A more effective policy is to undermine its resistance and to prevent it from presenting a united front against its opponents. This is the secret of all revolutions, from the struggle of Christianity against the Roman Empire, to the French Revolution.

Inside the working class itself, the Socialists were able to convince the masses that hatred was a negative and sterile weapon. It was not by hate and verbal abuse of the bosses that the conditions that they embodied would be eliminated, but by the creation of a feeling of solidarity among the masses that would give them the energy and enthusiasm needed to make their organization a reality. Edward Anseele had the idea of sending a free gift of 10,000 loaves of bread from a cooperative bakery in Flanders to the strikers in Wallonia. By such actions, working-class unity was created throughout the country. Its strength was to become the more irresistible as the doctrine of the first Socialist leaders rose above mere individual interest. "The cause we are defending is not only the cause of the workers," said César de Paepe, founder of the Socialist Party, "it is the cause of humanity itself."

A movement conducted in this spirit was bound to succeed because, in the end, it convinced and swept along even its opponents. Another factor in its favor was its lack of money, which implied a total disinterest on the part of the propagandists and enabled them to act with greater intensity and effectiveness. The shortage of financial resources created a feeling of fervor and enthusiasm that was felt even by the lukewarm and the hesitant. Workers whose wages were not enough to keep their own families went without the necessities of life so that they might help the party.

In 1892, the Socialist newspapers considered it a godsend that they were allowed a party subsidy of 1,200 francs. Their editorial staff worked for nothing, as did the leaders of the trade unions and the party militants. The total receipts of the party amounted to only 1.8 million francs a year.

The violence of the repressive action taken against them only stimulated their enthusiasm. In 1886, five demonstrators were killed and twelve others seriously wounded when troops opened fire. The soldiers had been ordered "not to worry about the law," so that all resistance could be smashed by a policy of terror. A few days later, seven more workers were killed. In 1893, a woman was killed at Jolimont, and five men died soon after. The civic guard opened fire on six miners in the streets of Mons who were attempting to stage a peaceful demonstration; they died of their wounds. In 1902, three more workers were shot down in Brussels during a general strike. (In the same way, in 1950, the shootings at Grâce-Berleur, and the death of the demonstrators, resulted in the abdication of Leopold III.)

In the end, these methods forced the government to give way. The victims were always on the same side, and a general uprising by the working class was a possibility that could not be excluded. The moral pressure was such that no one could hold out indefinitely against it.

Eventually, even the police were doubtful about opening fire upon the crowd, and in the last analysis it was this sentiment that assured the victory of the Socialists.

However, the success of the workers' movement did not force the Catholic party out of office. Instead, it kept them there for thirty years, for they were the only party with sufficient influence upon the rural population to be able to stand in the way of revolution and reassure the more peaceful voters. The Liberals could no longer rely on any but the bourgeois elements in the great towns. Moreover, they were divided among themselves. The progressive section allied itself with the Socialists, and the doctrinaire group lost all political influence. According to the ordinary laws of party politics, the election of 1884 should have tilted the balance once more in favor of the Liberals. The surprise was that it resulted quite definitely in favor of the Catholics.

The revolutionary success of socialism had sprung from the fact that its doctrines had been always based on consideration of the general public interest; this had earned it a great deal of sympathy and undercover support from all classes of the population. After their victory, the violent speeches of the Socialists in the Chamber, their obstructive tactics, and their exaggerations alarmed the more moderate elements who began to fear the introduction of universal suffrage. The right-wing leaders, therefore, limited their concessions to the workers to granting minor demands; this weakened the Socialists by progressively taking away their platform. At the same time, the right-wing politicians congratulated themselves on protecting the electors against anarchy and the "red flood."

The Catholic Party appeared as the defender of public order. In each election, as the Socialist agitation increased, so, too, did the number of Catholic deputies. In 1896, there were so many that the benches in the Chamber where they sat, decorously attired in their frock coats, came to be known as the "black forest." The introduction of proportional representation resulted only in stabilizing the position. In 1900, thirty-one Liberals and thirty-three Socialists were returned to the Chamber, as opposed to eighty-five Catholics. The position between the parties was frozen.

The Socialists realized that they could not secure an electoral victory and decided to resort once more to a general strike. However, during the preceding fifteen years, they had succeeded in passing social legislation that had given considerable satisfaction to the working class, so that now most of the workers could see no reason for rising in revolt. Wages had risen considerably, the trade unions were playing a continuous part in economic life, and the revolutionary spirit was fading. The Catholics, for their part, had not been idle. Under the influence of Pope Leo XIII and leaders such as Canon de Potter and Godefroid Kurth, they had created a Catholic workers' party and set up Catholic trade unions. The masses, therefore, were divided.

The general strike of 1902 had been badly planned and executed, and less than half the workers took part. The Socialist leaders put an end to it themselves. They had, in fact, been defeated, and they had also blunted the edge of the chief weapon of the working class, which was primarily moral and psychological. Success was possible only if based on a deep-seated revolt of public opinion, and Socialism had now revealed its basic weakness. The factor that had previously insured the Socialists' success was not the threat of a tidal wave of revolt, but rather the general feeling that their cause was just, which even their opponents felt and which weakened their resistance. The party leaders understood the lesson and returned swiftly to wisdom. It had been necessary to end the strike because of the shortage of money, so they now set about re-establishing their financial strength through the cooperatives, the companies, and the factories, which represented their real strength. Thus, little by little, they introduced an organized socialist system inside the capitalist regime.

Experience was to show the wisdom of these tactics. In the ensuing elections, the Catholics began to lose votes regularly.

The political situation of the country stabilized just at the time when Leopold II handed over the Congo to Belgium and succeeded in securing the passage of a bill providing for compulsory military service. The country's wealth and prosperity now seemed to have reached a peak.

Only 1,000 ships had entered the port of Antwerp in 1830, but now the figure had risen to over 7,000 each year. The population of the large cities had grown to an astonishing degree. Belgium now had seven or eight cities with 50,000 inhabitants each. Ixelles, only one of the suburbs of Brussels, had a population of 80,000 and paid more taxes than the provinces of Limburg and Luxemburg together, or than most of the large cities of France. The population of the capital was almost 900,000; of Antwerp, 400,000; of Liége, 250,000; and of Ghent, 200,000. In each of the cities the burgomaster was a real potentate with more powers than a minister. Each town council had complete control over its budget, its civil servants, and its taxes.

The Belgium of 1830 had a population of only 4 million, and its national capital was estimated at 11 billion gold francs. The population was now 7.5 million and national capital was estimated at 51 billion gold francs, which meant 6,700 gold francs per person.

The railway network was the densest in the world. In France, there were 6 miles of railway track per 62 square miles; in England, there were 8; and in Belgium, 18. There were 6,200 miles of roads; coal production had risen from 9 million tons in the middle of the nineteenth century, to 18 million in 1880, and 23.5 million twenty years later.

External trade was now near 5 billion gold francs. Belgium exported a third of her production, a higher proportion than England. Out of 7 million inhabitants, 3 million were employed in industry, and the peasant population represented only 23 per cent of the total, a lower figure than in the United States of the twentieth century. Trunk telephone lines between the different towns had been in existence for twenty years. It was a team of Belgian engineers that was to build the Metro in Paris. The Belgium of this period, with its "tentacle towns," and its countryside with the houses packed closely together beside the roadway, looked like a single continuous city.

When Leopold II died in December, 1909, the Congo adventure had helped to create basic changes in the country's attitude. This huge territory had played the same part for Belgium as the India of the eighteenth century had played for England, and contact with it had transformed the attitudes of many Belgians. The development of the Congo, however, had only been possible because the way had been prepared for it by the previous expansion of Belgian capitalistic enterprise all over the world.

The Congo adventure was in its early stages in 1886, when Cockerill formed the *Dnièprovienne*, and with it started the company's first metallurgical and mining ventures in southern Russia. Katanga and Kasai were still undeveloped when Belgian capital was building new railways in South America and China.

Leopold II had used his influence and his resources in the interest of Belgian ventures all over the world. As soon as a national firm was in difficulties, he intervened to save it, often with his own money. This was the case, for example, with the Peking-Hankow railway. It was on the verge of having to give up its concession at the last minute for lack of a few hundred thousand gold francs needed for bribery. The situation was, however, saved by the King, who made an advance from his personal funds.

It was the King's support that enabled Belgium to acquire a financial empire of 3,800 miles of railway track (equivalent to the radius of the earth) in South America, 1,900 miles in China, and a monopoly of public services and electrical supply in seventy-six large foreign cities, including thirty-seven cities in Russia and twenty-five in Spain, Egypt, France, Italy, and Greece. Belgian investment throughout the world exceeded 15 billion gold francs, and included fifty-six big firms in Germany, sixty-eight in Spain, and seventy in France.

In the Congo itself, the Belgians turned the desert into an El Dorado. When the King, no longer able to support the cost of the colony, turned it over to Belgium, contemporary opinion did not regard this as a good business deal, but rather as a bold and risky operation. The outlook appeared very different from what it is today—the wealth of the Congo was apparently exhausted. All the resources that had made it possible to make money out of the Congo in the early stages—ivory, rubber, and natural produce—had become unusable; no one suspected that its soil would yield uranium, gold, diamonds, and the thousand and one treasures that were to make its fortune in later years.

When Jadot agreed to finance the Compagnie du Kasai, he said to Leopold: "This is a fine lottery ticket I'm buying." Belgium herself was to take a lottery ticket in the Congo as a whole, and, by hard work and bold action, she was triumphantly to change its face. The grandeur of Leopold's work in the Congo is of a piece with the work of the Belgian leaders of his period who were seeking means to spread the influence of Belgium to every country. Empain was building railways, tramways, and power stations; Jadot and Francqui oriented the expansion of Belgium toward China; and Ernest Solvay invented a new process for the production of soda and held patents controlling the chemical industry the world over.

It was this elite that created modern Belgium. They did not come from the nobility or the traditional upper middle class, as one might have supposed. All the industrial and financial leaders, who actually ran Belgium at the end of the nineteenth and the beginning of the twentieth centuries, were of lower middle class origin. As in the United States, they were self-made men—sons of teachers, small shopkeepers, lawyers, notaries, and country doctors. Many of them had known poverty in their youth, and in some cases—such as Francqui, Thys, Theunis, and Bemelmans—they had to take service in the army in order to make a living. Others began in modest jobs, and not one of them had an influential or wealthy family to support him. In Belgium, there were no "dynasties" of millionaires and industrial chiefs that were to be found in other countries.

It might almost be said to be a tradition in this country that the son of a man who is the head of a big business has no chance of making a success there himself. He usually finds it better to seek his fortune elsewhere. For example, Maurice Despret, the future president of the Banque de Bruxelles, was the son of a director of the Société Générale, but he could not enter his father's company and had to begin in another bank. It often happened, also, that a minor clerk with no family or fortune, would rise to the highest of positions. This was the case with Baron Bayens, who entered the Société Générale as an assistant clerk about 1865, and died its governor, in 1914. René Tilmont entered the Banque Nationale as an assistant clerk in 1898, rose to director in 1924, and later became vice-governor.

Edward Empain (1852–1929) was the son of a village schoolmaster. For lack of money, he was not able to go to the university or be given an officer's commission in the army. He nevertheless became a tramway and electricity magnate. Gevaert, the founder of the great Antwerp photographic-paper manufacturing firm, began life as a small local portrait photographer. Jean Jadot (1862–1932) was a young railway engineer, and Ernest Solvay, the future soda king, was the son of a colonial produce merchant and never succeeded in getting his engineering degree. The financier Emile Francqui (1863–1935) was the son of an impoverished solicitor whose death left him without means, so that he had to enroll in the army as a volunteer. Albert Thys (1849–1915) was the son of a country doctor; he also was obliged to enroll in the army at the age of sixteen.

The expansion of the Belgian coal mining industry during the nineteenth century was the work of Evence Copée (1851–1925), a simple mining engineer from Mons who, at the age of twenty-four, was the inventor of the first coke oven. The financier Alfred Loewenstein (1877–1928) was the son of an unsuccessful foreign-exchange broker, and had to leave his education unfinished to take up work on the exchange at the age of twenty. André Dumont (1847–1920) was the son of a geologist; he became a mining engineer, and then spent a long time vegetating as a lecturer at Louvain before he discovered the immense Campine coal-mining basin in the province of Limbourg.

The merit of all these men was that their youths had been difficult and that they had had to make their own way. They were thus symbols of a Belgium whose chief stimulus had been adversity and who had made its fortune by hard work and a ceaseless struggle against obstacles to become what it is today.

Belgium was now taking her place in the mainstream of civilization. It was not only the captains of industry who were triumphing, but also painters, musicians, and writers. Since the days of the Second Empire, the foundations for the art of a James Ensor had been laid by such men as Eugène Smits, Charles de Groux, Félicien Rops, Alfred Verwée, Louis Artan, and Hippolyte Boulenger (1837–74). From this time onward, Belgian painting became a major influence. Its Impressionism was no longer derived from the Impressionism of the French schools of the same period, but from Belgian masters.

This new art was born from the brush of landscape painters like Jean Stobbaerts, who painted animals in the dazzling light of the outdoors, and Willem Vogels (1836–96), who was a painter of fog, storm, and snow, and made bad weather a subject for his art. This was the period of the great school of French Impressionism that was producing masters such as Manet, Degas, Monet, Sisley, and Pissaro. It was the time, too, of a young Belgian painter, Henri Evenepoel (1872–99), who set himself up in France and died there at the early age of twenty-seven. During his short career, he succeeded in bringing the expression of direct sensation to the point of genius.

James Ensor had already made his appearance. He was the greatest and most universal of the nineteenth-century Belgian painters, and the only one whose work reflects the geniuses of the past and is of a stature fit to be placed beside their work.

He was born in Ostend, in 1860, of an English father and a Flemish mother. His first phase was the so-called "dark period" (1869–83), in which he sought to throw a figure or a still-life into astonishingly strong relief, so that the subject would transcend the limitations of the medium and haunt the imagination of the beholder. Later, he discovered light, and allowed it to invade and almost devour his pictures, until it almost seemed to become a substitute for painting. In 1883, he painted the "Oyster Eater" (now in the Antwerp Museum), a canvas that is both material and spiritual in its appeal. This period is marked by a number of still-lifes, all transformed into festivals of color. Still later came the period of masquerades and carnival scenes, in which the painter gave full reign to his feeling for the burlesque and the tragic. His humor, unbridled imagination, and sense of satire are apparent even in his skeletons, and his paintings, smiling or macabre, are rich in color and pictorial invention. This period reached its peak in 1888, with his "Christ Entering Brussels." Ensor takes his place beside Bosch and Brueghel, with canvases that are increasingly a triumph of poetry and nonconformity, and in painting that is pure emotion, color, and fantasy. This was the prelude that was to lead through the luminous enchantment of Impressionism, that marked it and gave it its reason for existence, into the bold art forms of the twentieth century that were to produce Fauvism and Surrealism.

It was James Ensor who, by divorcing himself from all contemporary influences, placed Belgian painting in the forefront of European art.

While Ensor was overshadowing the painters of his generation, the great sculptor Constantin Meunier (1831–1905) had become the artist of the workers, carving the epic of human suffering in the image of their life and toil. His stevedores and miners ("The Labor Monuments"), created a new vision of humanity, and he erased the memory of the academic sculptors of the past who had filled Belgium with their elegant, but unoriginal, works. Such men included Simonis, Fraikin, Dillens, and Vinçotte. Others of later date included Jef Lambeaux, Rombaut, and Victor Rousseau.

Twentieth-century painting began with the school at Laethem-Saint-

Martin, near Ghent. There the chief painters of the period assembled around the sculptor Georges Minne. The school deliberately created a fashion for spiritualization, releasing art from brutal realism to give it, by subtle deformations, an internal significance.

From this school came landscape painters such as Valérius de Saedeleer and Albyn van den Abeele, who conceived "the sensual world as the sign and symbol of a more moving reality." They were seeking to express "the invisible through the commonplace." They were closely linked to symbolic poets such as Maurice Maeterlinck and Emile Verhaeren, and also with young Flemish poets such as Karel van de Woestijne, whose work had much in common with theirs.

Some of the painters of the period kept themselves clear of the schools. These included the naturalized Dutchman, Jacob Smits; Eugene Laermans (1864–1940) of Brussels, the painter of stylized and mutinous crowds; Leon Frédéric; and Rik Wouters (1882–1916). Artists of such caliber increased their influence, and it was they who developed an expressionism that reached its peak with Constant Permeke, born in Antwerp in 1886. He was one of the most powerful geniuses of Flanders, with an art that was both elementary and lyrical. His career continued into the twentieth century.

Permeke's direct painting, in which realism is converted into an expression of the world, has an astonishingly vital plastic strength that raises it above its medium. It is opposed to the Surrealist vision of Fritz van den Berghe and Paul Delvaux. These painters revived the sense of mystery and the magic of surprise in art, and, in the face of traditional Flemish genius, they embodied the spirit of the new century, their influence lasting to our day.

In music, it was the turn of the Walloons to triumph. They formed, by tradition, a school of their own that had developed continuously since the days of Grétry. Musicians from Liége emigrated and made their careers in Paris. More intimate as musicians than the Flemish, and, perhaps, the French, they brought a sensitivity to their work that was entirely their own. This was the case, at the end of the nineteenth century, with César Franck, composer of the *Béatitudes*. He was born in Liége, but spent almost his entire life in France. Others, such as Peter Benoît (1834–1901), François-Auguste Gevaert (1828–1908), Edgar Tinel (1854–1902), and Henri Vieuxtemps remained in Belgium, while performers like Eugene Ysaye became famous throughout the world. Another musician, Adolphe Sax of Dinant, influenced modern jazz by inventing and popularizing the saxophone.

In this period, Belgian literature in French was being reborn. In the middle of the nineteenth century intellectual life was still static, but the arrival in Brussels of French exiles from the Second Empire opened a window to the outside world. A literary and artistic elite was created and new life breathed into Belgian writing.

A group of young writers under the leadership of Max Waller (Maurice Warlomont, 1860–89) made their rallying point a literary review, *Le Jeune Belgique* (1880-97). Its aim was to re-create the literature of the nation in works telling of local life, legends, and folklore that would give artists new themes of inspiration. It was in this spirit that Charles de Coster had sought to portray the soul of the sixteenth-century Low Countries under the Spanish oppression, in his *Legend of Eulenspiegl.* Another contemporary writer, Octave Pirmez (1832–83), had the same ideal.

Even in the early days of *Le Jeune Belgique,* however, there was a double tendency. The movement included not only the "writers of the soil," who stayed in their native country and wrote of its towns and provinces, but also writers whose careers developed in Paris and whose work was indistinguishable from the French literature of their period.

Already, Camille Lemonnier (1841–1913), a disciple of Emile Zola, had risen to high standing in the French Naturalist school *(Un Mâle).* After him, two great writers had a major success in the Symbolist movement: Maurice Maeterlinck, with world-famous works such as *The Blue Bird* and *The Life of the Bees,* and Emile Verhaeren, with forceful poetry such as *Les Forces Tumultueuses* and *Les Villes Tentaculaires.* Along with them were other symbolist poets like Georges Rodenbach *(Bruges la Morte)* and Charles van Lerberghe *(La Chanson d'Eve),* and, especially, a great number of novelists "of the soil" who remained entirely Belgian, writing simply of a Belgian town or district. Georges Eekhoud (1854-1927) wrote of Antwerp *(La Nouvelle Carthage);* Hubert Stiernet of the Hesbaye country; Georges Virrès of Kempen; Maurice des Ombiaux of the Entre-Sambre-et-Meuse region; Georges Garnir of the Ardennes; and Bonjean of the region of Fagnes. Around 1900, Henri Davignon was writing of Flanders and Furnes *(Un Pénitent de Furnes),* and Henri Carton de Wiart wrote of Liége *(La Cité Ardente).*

Belgian playwrights were also earning fame in Paris. Among them were Fonson, Crommelynck *(Le Cocu Magnifique),* and Francis de Croisset. Many essayists and historians, too, were beginning to spread Belgian thought throughout the world.

This period saw the first signs, on an as yet small scale, of a great literary renaissance that was about to take place. This renaissance was to be an outstanding feature of the first half of the twentieth century, and Belgium was to contribute some of her most original and most influential writers to French literature.

XII

ALBERT I AND THE FIRST
WORLD WAR

Leopold II was succeeded by Albert I, who came to the throne on December 23, 1909. The country over which he was to rule had become the fourth greatest industrial power in the world. The progress of Belgium can only be compared with that of the United States of America. America's wealth, however, had been founded on the production of cheap raw materials and high labor costs; the scarcity of labor made it necessary to develop machinery and mass-production methods. Belgium's prosperity, on the other hand, was based on low wages, a low cost of living, and the concentration of population in a small area, which eliminated many transportation costs.

Within twenty years, the standard of living of the working class had risen considerably. The wages of miners, for example, had risen from 920 gold francs to 1,580 gold francs; and savings-bank deposits had increased from 453 million gold francs to 1 billion. It was said that this transformation had "given the workers a country of their own"; it had, indeed, reconciled them with the wealthier classes. Without an appreciation of these conditions, it would be impossible to understand the national unity of 1914 and the spontaneous resistance of the people against invasion.

By 1914, the Belgian worker had become one of the rulers of the country, controlling its economic life through cooperatives and trade unions. The Socialist Party was now a power in the land. Since the first cooperative bakery had been founded in 1880 in Ghent by Edward Anseele, 200 new production and sales cooperatives had been set up in different parts of the country. They united the working class into a hard core in the capitalist system. In the meantime, another form of organization, "the *mutuelles*," or "friendly societies," spread social insurance to its 380,000 subscribing members. Profits poured into the party till, enabling the party to continue the education of the working class.

The worker now had at his command organizations that provided every necessity of life. In his shops he could buy Socialist bread, Socialist milk, and Socialist clothing; through the network of the "People's Houses" he could organize his leisure, outings, journeys, youth camps, newspapers, and books. The Catholic Party copied this form of organization in its "Christian Democracy." Its social work and welfare personnel was still considerably less than that of the Socialists, but it had the upper hand in the country districts where the *Boerenbond* ("Peasants' Union") was able to amass a working capital of 13 million gold francs by 1914. On the eve of the First World War, the Catholic organizations and trade unions had more than 100,000 members.

Wallonia was dominated by the Socialists, while Flanders was held by the Christian Democrats and the *Boerenbond*. A new force had, however, come to the fore. This was the Flemish Movement, founded in the middle of the nineteenth century under the influence of the Liberal Willems and the Catholic David. Until the revision of the constitution, it was weak and unimportant, but with the enactment of universal suffrage it very quickly became a power in the land.

The masses who could not speak French now had the right to vote. The Catholic Party, which derived the greater part of its support from Flanders, hastened to enact a series of language laws that made the Flemish fatherland a reality.

As early as 1886, bank notes were printed in both languages. In 1897, the Civil Guard received its orders in Dutch, and from now on Belgium became more Flemish each year. The Dutch language was used more and more in education, administration, and public life. The local dialects of West Flanders, Antwerp, and Limburg were gradually unified, and the language of the Low Countries became increasingly important as a literary medium.

Belgian unity was now being transformed into a kind of moral federation of two nations. North of the line between Lille and Maastricht, which passes south of Brussels, the French language minorities in the big cities were diminishing and disappearing. Flemish youth was becoming nationalistic and putting in its claim for autonomy or administrative separation. Similar claims came from part of Wallonia, and the Socialist leader, Jules Destrée, in a famous letter to King Albert, summed up the situation by saying "Sire, there are no such people as Belgians."

Along with the ideas and doctrines of the Socialists, the Liberal ideal

still survived in the big cities, and Catholic sentiment held the field
in the country districts. To this was added the opposition between the
Flemish and the Walloons. With the question of education still at the
center of the political scene, the country was divided, not only by party
strife but also by a clash between opposed ideologies, increasing the
danger that the nation might suffer profound disorganization. It was,
however, this very division that gave the nation its unity and its
strength. A century earlier, in 1820, Belgium's political life had consisted of the opposition between two great groups: the Catholic and
the Liberals. In 1910, there were six or seven groups, the members of
which were scattered all over the country and living side by side. The
people, as a whole, were united rather than divided by this diversity
of opinions and backgrounds. A Flemish Catholic in Ghent would feel
more affinity with a Walloon Catholic than he would with a Flemish
Liberal or Socialist; and a Walloon Socialist would have closer bonds
with an Antwerp Socialist, whose language he could not understand,
than with many of the Catholics in his own part of the country.

These different concepts, that created local opposition, were a source
of unity on the national level. Belgium could not be divided into two
blocs, since each would contain large minorities that would have to
be abandoned to their opponents. National unity sprang less from
the power of the state or the national economic life than it did from
the acute consciousness of the opposed individual views. Nationality,
as it now took shape, may be defined as "a common fashion for all
Belgians of regarding the things that keep them apart."

Conditions were indeed much the same as in Switzerland, where,
for example, the canton of Vaud, which is Protestant and French-
speaking, is spiritually closer to the Protestant but German-speaking
canton of Basle than to the French-speaking but Catholic canton of
Geneva. In other words, it was the existence of differences that helped
to create unity. This was the moral situation in Belgium on the eve
of the end of the long peace and the beginning of the First World War.

Albert had ascended the throne in 1909, scarcely two years before
Agadir, and five years before the beginning of the war. He was to die
during the year that followed Adolph Hitler's rise to power. Albert's
reign coincided with a period of greatness and prosperity such as Belgium had never known before. His reign was marked by a new conception of the monarchy in which the king was no longer the supreme
arbiter, but rather the nation's fellow-worker, gaining his moral strength
and his real powers from the nature of his functions.

His mother, one of the younger daughters of the Hohenzollern family, was a woman of high principles and had raised him to be upright

and conscientious. He had had an austere boyhood and never even had a fire in his bedroom until after his marriage. He married Elizabeth, a princess of the Wittelsbach family, whose father had studied medicine so that he might care for the poor. Elizabeth herself was a musician, an artist, and a woman of great culture. Albert inaugurated a type of monarchy in which the king's power was based on his personal influence and activity, and on his contacts with the least of his subjects. His queen made her entourage a center of the country's artistic and cultural life.

Apart from the greatness of heart and nobility of spirit that were the King's chief characteristics, the dominant feature of his career was the good luck that never deserted him. It played a great part in his accession to the throne. He was not born to be king, and it was only a succession of three deaths that brought him to the throne: the Count of Hainaut, only son of Leopold II; Albert's own brother, the Count of Flanders; and the latter's elder son, Prince Baudouin.

He was lucky, too, in his marriage. He was allowed to make a love match, and Queen Elizabeth, daughter of a branch of the House of Bavaria, had had an education unusual for members of reigning families. From this she had emerged as a princess who was passionately interested in art and who loved the company of intellectuals, and whose simplicity and modesty won all hearts and contributed greatly to the popularity of the monarchy.

There was yet a third piece of luck: all the problems that arose became trumps in Albert's hand and solutions came easily. He was successor to an unpopular sovereign and this at once put him in a good light before the nation. The war, which was soon to follow, made him the symbol of his country and its idol. Despite reverses in the early stages, the territory of Belgium was never completely overrun, and the King was never forced to leave it. He withdrew beyond the line of the river Yser, and remained in direct contact with his government and his ministers. He never, therefore, had to make his decisions single-handedly or bring his personal responsibility into play, but was able to remain above political parties to the end.

There was only one serious problem at the time, and even this was solved in the sacred name of national union. The Socialists did not accept the monarchy and were putting forward a republican program, but war and invasion put an end to their activity and the King was freed from political strife. The only complaint that was later to be made against him was that he accepted universal suffrage in 1918. This reproach, however, came from the extreme right and the King's attitude served to bring left-wing supporters to his side, thus appeasing those whose hostility had been the only dangerous threat to the monarchy.

It may be said of him that his good fortune never left him until his last moment, when he died as the result of an accident, falling from a high rock at Marche-les-Dames. However, if he had not died at that time, it is probable that, six years later, he would have had to face defeat and exile at the age of sixty-five, and would have had to deal with problems insoluble for the head of any state. His premature death may therefore have been his last and final stroke of luck.

His qualities, both as a king and as a human being, were so exceptional that he well deserved his good fortune and his happiness. King though he was, he nevertheless remained a man, and he was able to realize the true ideal of a modern sovereign which is to serve, rather than be served. He granted unceremonious audience to everyone who wished to speak with him, and he cut through the isolation of court protocol by attitudes and gestures that went straight to the heart. He made such a gesture on hearing of the death of Marshal Foch, when he left for Paris the same evening to pay his last respects. In 1914, his popularity took on a mystic form that, in the eyes of his subjects and of the rest of the world, it was to keep for the remainder of his life. He became the embodiment of his country and of its heroic resistance to the trials that destiny had laid on King and country together.

Physically he was a giant, and he could take Queen Elizabeth in his arms and carry her without undue effort to the top of the palace staircase. It is nevertheless a curious fact that this man, whose calmness and confidence were to become legendary, was secretly disturbed and anxious, with a tendency to take a pessimistic view of events. On the Yser front during the 1914 war, public opinion credited him with blind confidence in the final victory but, in actual fact, he came to the conclusion several times that defeat was certain. His outward serenity is even more laudable, as it sustained the morale of his troops and his people. His disillusion stemmed from his being too close to the discussions of the Allied statesmen and their weaknesses. His courage did not come from ignorance and illusion, but from nobility of spirit and a sense of duty that he wished to fulfil to the bitter end.

When Albert came to the throne in 1909, the leader of the Socialist Party was Emile Vandervelde; the Liberal Party was led by the eloquent and witty Paul Hymans; and the Catholic Party by Charles Woeste, a converted Protestant who controlled the entire party organization and placed his main confidence in its militant elements. At this time the working class, particularly the older people, was still largely illiterate, and political propaganda had to be disseminated through colorful illustrated posters. The left-wing parties covered the walls with gaudy pictures of rubicund and Pantagruelian priests seated at table before monstrous plates of succulent food, or of gaunt Jesuits with crafty eyes pulling down the walls, while prelates in mitre and vestment brandished their crosses.

The Catholic Party replied by representing the Socialists as bandits with lighted torches, storming the walls of the city and setting fire to it; or they gave them the aspect and the costume of ruffians and hoodlums from the Paris slums. To judge by the Catholic propaganda, a school without God could produce nothing but murderers and robbers. This was the time when France was passing through the terror of the "motor bandits," whom the gendarms could not capture, who eluded all pursuit, and who, when they were finally run to earth, would rather kill themselves than surrender, after a long siege. With this in mind, the militant Catholics made a habit of pasting up little posters bearing only the words, "If Bonnot, Carouy, and Garnier had been Belgian voters, which list would have had their vote?"

Amidst this deluge of colorful and astute propaganda, the good Belgian people went tranquilly to the polls. The candidates were nominated by the local party associations, who made their lists as they wished. The voter's job was merely to ratify the party's choice, and the candidates at the top of the list were certain of election. All an aspiring parliamentarian had to do, therefore, was to make certain, a few months in advance when the lists were being drawn up, that his friends were active members of the local association. This was the policy adopted by young deputies who now began their political life by replacing the former Catholic chiefs. Among them were Henri Carton de Wart and Jules Renkin; and, on the Socialist side, Emile Vandervelde, idol of the militant Socialists and president of the Workers' International, who had a brilliant team of future ministers around him. Among these were Jules Destrée, artist and poet, who had gone into politics because, he said, he was "mad about justice," and Edward Anseele, the organizer of the party's economic machine. The Liberals, who were still the representatives of the higher bourgeoisie in the cities, were grouped around Paul Hymans. They comprised an elite of intellectuals and men of distinction, including burgomaster Adolph Max of Brussels, the lawyer Paul Emile Janson, the future prime minister Albert Devèze, and financiers like Emile Francqui, who were to play so important a part in postwar Belgium.

Life in those days was very different from what it was to become after 1918. The street scenes had an originality that distinguished Belgium from other countries. The drugstore windows were still decorated with great globes of red and green, but they had no modern posters advertising specialty products. The food shops were overflowing, and this was one of the more striking characteristics of Belgian life. In no other country were there such heaps of things to eat, and each shop display looked like a still-life painting by one of the Flemish masters. The windows of the cigar and tobacco shops were like a fairyland. The trade was free and unrestricted—there were no official tobacco bureaus, as there were in France. The tobacconists offered costly cigarettes and cigars with jewel-like bands in boxes with sparkling labels from every country in the world.

The city of Brussels had continued growing, and by now it was an anachronism. The authority of the burgomaster stopped a few hundred meters from the town hall and, within these strict confines, there was neither a railway station nor a cemetery. The nineteen burgomasters of the communes around the capital had infinitely greater powers, and much more money, than the capital city itself. A commune such as Ixelles, measured in terms of its population and its wealth, was fully on a par with Brussels. The communal budget was often as large as that of a ministry and the receipts sometimes exceeded those of several provinces, such as Limburg and Luxemburg, put together.

Poverty, however, lived side by side with luxury, and Brussels was still a "city of blind alleys" where most of the inhabitants lived in evil-smelling courts and alleyways. Access to their dwellings lay through noble gateways and imposing façades that led into the courtyards of the former houses of the nobility. Here lived the teeming population of the poor. The death rate was high. In the streets of the bourgeois quarter, one inhabitant in every hundred died each year, while in the working-class districts the proportion was one in every twenty-eight. The average life of a rich man at the beginning of the twentieth century was about fifty-four years, and that of a worker only eighteen years.

The struggle of the working class against the bourgeois world expressed this state of things. About 1910, however, the Catholics began to prepare to fight the Socialists on their own terms by organizing, within their ranks, the Christian Democratic movement.

Albert had just ascended the throne when a new political battle broke out. The Socialists and the Liberals had formed a coalition in the hopes of coming to power. The tactical mistakes of the Catholic minister Schollaert, who had introduced an unduly radical education act, had solidified the opposition against him, and Albert gave Charles de Broqueville, the youngest of the Catholic leaders, the job of forming a transition government that would have the organization of the new election as its main task. The Socialist-Liberal combine expected victory at the polls, for the Catholic majority had been dwindling; in the 1908 elections, it amounted to only six votes in the chamber. The electorate was, however, alarmed by the violent language of the more advanced left-wing politicians and the Catholics, far from being driven out of office, were returned to Parliament with a majority of eighteen votes.

The Socialist Party, on the other hand, had managed to build up its fighting funds and was now in a position to organize a prolonged general strike that would ruin the property-owning classes and force them to grant universal suffrage. The Catholics had stubbornly refused to countenance the idea of equal voting rights for all, which by now prevailed in all the great countries of Europe. Justice, and the moral strength of the country, was on the side of their opponents. The Catholics again refused to introduce the necessary constitutional revision and the general strike began on April 14, 1913. The order and discipline prevailing among the strikers was extremely impressive. To many people it appeared less a revolutionary gesture than a demonstration in defense of legality, and the Catholics created the impression of wanting to risk the future of the country.

The government, having allowed the struggle to begin on these terms, found itself caught in a trap. They knew that, as the financial reserves supporting the strike were used up, the movement would fall into the hands of the more violent elements, and that the troops that would have to be mobilized to keep order would refuse to open fire on the strikers, and might even go over to their side. Charles de Broqueville was intelligent enough to understand this and skilful enough to convince his own party. The Christian Democrats did not consider the Socialists to be wholly their enemies, since they were fighting with them for the same cause. Thus, while 370,000 strikers paralyzed the country's industry and were threatening a march on Brussels, political developments were foreshadowing the cooperation between the left-wing Catholics and the Socialists that was to mark the twenty years between the two wars.

On April 22, 1913, the chamber, after resisting for a week, accepted the principle of a constitutional revision. This vote enabled the Socialist Party to assume power. Count de Broqueville still had time to pass a more conciliatory education act through Parliament in May, 1914; this satisfied the left-wing and sanctioned the principle of compulsory education. Only a few months later, the country was swept into the gathering storm and once more the story of Belgium became indissolubly linked with the history of Europe.

The German empire, lying just beyond the Belgian frontier, had been growing continuously in wealth and power. Its economic strength affected all the neighboring countries, and, whether they realized it or not, they were unable to avoid coming within its sphere of influence. Links of increasing importance were forged between Antwerp, and indeed the whole of Belgium, and Germany. Export firms were growing in importance and many German traders were coming into the country, so that people were beginning to discuss Zollverein, or Belgian-German customs union.

The shadow had fallen not only across Belgium, but also upon the Congo. As early as 1911, France had handed over some of her African territory to Germany and thus accepted, not only the encirclement of the Congo, but also the possibility of its coming under German control. After Agadir, the French agreed not to use their right of pre-emption over the Belgian Congo without German consent, and this right was tacitly given to the Germans. This was admitted by the French Prime Minister, Joseph Caillaux, when he told the Chamber that the matter of possessions in Africa could not be considered to have been finally settled.

It is a curious fact that, as the peril grew greater and more apparent, Belgian opinion did not side with France. In 1904, Leopold II had rather naïvely told Chancellor Von Bülow that the Belgians "had more confidence in Germany than in France," and in the Belgian Chambers deputies declared that it was not possible to stop Germany in "her search for a place in the sun." Just before the war, the French military attaché in Brussels wrote to his government that, if Belgium should be forced to choose her own allies, it "was scarcely probable that she would decide in favor of France." Belgian opinion was to have a rude awakening. On August 2, 1914, the German Ambassador in Brussels, Von Below, handed to the Belgian government a twenty-four-hour ultimatum demanding the right of transit for the German armies. The psychological shock resulting from this was felt throughout Belgium. There was unanimous indignation and the country rallied firmly around the King. Albert had the ability to find the words that were needed to galvanize the nation, and this country of different languages and cultures, where nationalism did not exist, was transformed in every way as moral and patriotic forces came into play. The Church, under the direction of Cardinal Mercier, took the lead.

Belgium now appeared to herself and to all the world as a victim of the right, a martyr nation that had sacrificed herself for a just cause. The first use of the phrase "iron curtain," which has since become so famous, was made by Queen Elizabeth when, thinking of her German relations, she declared: "An iron curtain has fallen between the Germans and myself."

Chancellor Bethmann-Hollweg had referred to Germany's treaty obligation as a "scrap of paper," and the German ambassador in Brussels had said "the Belgians will line up to see us pass." All this contributed to making Belgium a symbol for the world, but the country was nevertheless to be crushed by the precise, well-balanced machinery of the Germany military plan. Despite the Belgian victory at Haelen on August 12, 1914, the German armies reached the French frontier according to schedule.

Acts of individual heroism could do nothing against the organized force of modern warfare, waged with such overwhelming resources. The five Belgian divisions went down before the fifty divisions of the German army, and, on August 20, the Germans entered Brussels and crossed into France four days later to begin their march on Paris. The biggest problem for the Germans was transporting the enormous body of invasion troops, their supplies, and matériel, in conformity with a minutely fixed timetable. Each unit was advancing through unfamiliar country and the memories of 1870 had made the francs-tireurs an obsession. They knew they were in a country where the population was the densest in Europe and they constantly feared an attack from the rear, or an uprising that would take them by surprise. This led the German High Command to give stern orders to the troops, and to seek to ensure their security through terror.

A city like Brussels had more inhabitants than all the German divisions together. Panic broke out whenever the Germans fired on their own troops by mistake, or when they had to deal with detachments of enemies hidden in the woods. This led to Saxon units burning the town of Dinant and shooting 700 civilians, including thirty-nine children between six months and fifteen years of age. At Louvain, where the German soldiers had opened fire on their own men by mistake, they set fire to the famous university library; incidents of the same kind occurred at Andenne, Tamines, and Francorchamps.

But the victims of these atrocities did not die in vain, and their sacrifice was more important for their country than that of the soldiers who fell at the front. They helped to make the violation of Belgian neutrality a symbol of outraged justice, forcing every country in the world to treat the conflict as a moral problem. There can be no doubt that this saved Belgian independence, which would have disappeared if the country had given free passage to the German armies. Still more certainly, it saved the Belgian Congo.

The little Belgian army was at first driven back on Antwerp, where it kept several German divisions busy during the Battle of the Marne. When it became evident that the fortifications could not stand up to the German 420 field howitzers, the King and the army escaped to the line of the Yser, where they dug in on this last shred of national soil. There they succeeded in resisting the German assault, thanks to the floods that once again protected this country of marsh and canal.

Almost the whole of Belgium, however, had been conquered and was to remain under enemy occupation for four years. This little state with its tiny territory had, on a moral level, become a world power. All the world was interested in its destiny. Crowds in every country were indignant at the tales of enemy atrocities. The figures of Albert and Elizabeth, in their refuge at Le Panne, had become part of the legend of the time, and their resistance put heart into the Belgians and gave them a blind faith in final victory. The Dutch border was protected by electrified barbed wire, but, during the four years of war, more than 40,000 young men crossed it, in peril of their lives, to make their way to join the Yser army.

Meanwhile, occupied Belgium had gained an immense prestige in the world, and people of every country joined to provide it with food. Despite the Allied blockade, an international organization under the chairmanship of Herbert Hoover, in the name of the United States, and the Marquis of Villalobar, in the name of Spain, secured permission from the Germans to protect the population against famine by providing the necessities that they lacked. This brought out the enormous difference between a country accustomed to self-government through communal autonomy and a people accustomed to a centralized administration. In Belgium, where the burgomaster of each town held power, a new government was created on the initiative of the communes, the provinces, and the economic leaders; it was this government that took over the administration of the country. The state, as such, appeared to have lost its usefulness. Through the initiative of individuals, a different method of government was found, when the necessity arose, that expressed the consciousness of their solidarity and their mutual interest.

A national committee was formed under the leadership of the great industrialist Ernest Solvay and the financier Emile Francqui. The committee undertook to feed the country and to restore its economic life, in cooperation with the American Aid Committee. The self-appointed leaders got in touch with the Germans, who were only too happy to deal with an authority capable of saving the country from anarchy. They coordinated the activities of the provinces and the communes and united the country against the invader by reconstituting the state and the government from the bottom up, in the name of the boards of directors of businesses, the labor unions, the burgomasters, and the local authorities.

The resistance against the invading Germans was expressed by the burgomasters of the big cities (some of whom, like Adolph Max at Brussels, were deported); by university rectors and professors like Pirenne and Frédéricq; by political party committees; and by the Catholic Church under the leadership of Cardinal Mercier. The latter,

Archbishop of Mechlin and Primate of Belgium, issued pastoral letters, such as the one entitled "Patriotism and Endurance," to be read in all the churches in the country. In these he praised the spirit of sacrifice and the high moral values uniting all Belgians, the love of justice, and loyalty to the King and the soldiers at the front. By proclaiming the fact that the occupation was both illegal and temporary, he sustained the morale of the country.

There were only a few Flemish "activists" who agreed to collaborate with the enemy. An enormous espionage network was organized for the benefit of the Allies, to facilitate the escape of young people, and to keep the nation active and aware of its task. Many newspapers were secretly printed and published, including the *Libre Belgique* and the *Flambeau*. In vain, the Germans deported 120,000 workers and stripped the country of its machinery and raw materials. The resistance only grew in a feeling of collective exaltation. Trials borne in common proved a stimulus rather than a discouragement, and the Belgian nation seemed to be reborn in the worship of the King fighting on the Yser with his army, the government outside its borders at Sainte-Adresse near Le Havre, and the new mystic symbolism that they represented.

The Belgian army, however, was not satisfied simply to resist on the Yser front, where it had lost a quarter of its men during the battles of 1914. It also took part in all the battles that were to follow, when the youth of Germany was destroyed at Langemark and Ypres. For four years, the Belgians mounted guard on the Yser until, at last, they took part in the final victorious advance to the Scheldc. In thc Congo, Belgian troops were aiding the British to conquer Germany's African colonies, and, after General Tombeur had secured the capitulation of Tabora, they kept Ruanda and Urundi.

As the war continued, it exceeded by far the framework of Belgium; the real happenings were now being played out on a world scale. In 1917, in the speech announcing the entry of the American people into the war, President Wilson defined this change by saying that the aim of America was not vengeance or the assertion of its material strength, but the triumph of justice—that war was terrible, but that justice was more important than peace. He further said that America was fighting for democracy and for the rights and freedom of small nations so that the universal rule of justice would ensure the peace and security of all nations, and the world would at last be free.

For the first time in history a president was justifying a declaration of war, not because of any national interest or injury the nation had suffered, but on grounds of the moral solidarity of the world, and the pity that everyone felt at the spectacle of women and children being slaughtered.

When the German spring offensive of 1918 had been checked, the empires of central Europe crumbled. When the armistice was signed at Rethondes, on November 11, 1918, the Belgian army, now made up of 200,000 men, had played a glorious part in an unremitting offensive. The final line of battle passed in front of Ghent, Tournai, Valenciennes, Sedan, and Metz.

Albert, with the Queen and the royal princes beside him, re-entered Brussels in triumph on November 22, amid scenes of wild delight. A few days after the armistice, the King and the representatives of the Belgian political parties held a meeting in the Chateau of Lophem in Flanders. It was no longer possible to delay the reforms that had been promised to the Socialists as long ago as 1913. A new figure came to the fore as head of a government of national unity. This was the lawyer Delacroix, whose government was given the task of securing the constitutional amendments by the election of a parliament that would also be a constituent assembly. All Belgians aged 21 and over were to take part in electing the assembly. Another task assigned to the government was the creation of a Flemish university at Ghent.

Universal suffrage had come into effect without recourse to legal forms. The country's recovery, however, was to be made possible only by a union of all parties, for the destruction to be repaired was on a very large scale.

The number of houses that had been totally destroyed was around 100,000, or the equivalent of a town of half a million inhabitants. In the country, the number of cattle had been halved, and a quarter million acres of cultivable land had disappeared. In industry, the destruction wrought had been such that a less hardworking country would have judged it irreparable. Of the 2,500 coke ovens, more than 1,500 were out of use, and so were 46 of the 57 blast furnaces. All that had been spared was the human labor force, for military and civil losses were less than 50,000 men. The labor force in Belgium had fallen by only 2 per cent of the able-bodied men, as compared with 16 per cent (one man in seven) in France.

At a time when production capacity depended more on the availability of labor than on any other factor, Belgium had been only slightly damaged. France, on the other hand, despite the moral uplift resulting from her victory, was soon to show how sadly her energy and means of action had been impaired.

Early in 1919, preliminary negotiations were held in Paris with a view to the eventual drafting of the Treaty of Versailles. In these discussions Belgium was given exceptional advantages. These included priority for reparations; an immediate payment on account of 2.5 billion gold francs; the annexation of Eupen and Malmédy; and a customs union with the Grand Duchy of Luxemburg.

The nation's claim against Holland, on the other hand, did not have the same success. The Dutch succeeded in evading all the demands, and delayed the solution of the problem of communications between Antwerp, Liége, and the Rhine across Dutch territory indefinitely.

Another people might well have wasted time and energy on useless recrimination. Belgium, however, faced the facts and took action at once. This practical spirit was the secret of Belgium's success. Parliament decided on the construction of Belgium's own canal to link Antwerp with Liége, despite the almost overwhelming technical difficulties that appeared to lie in the way. Such a canal would enable Liége traffic to reach the sea without the assistance of Belgium's neighbors.

The same spirit was to be seen in the political parties. Their attitude was no longer founded on political passions and sentimental slogans, but rather on the realities of life. In the elections of 1919, the first held on a basis of universal suffrage, the Socialists won a great victory and the Catholics lost their majority in the Chambers. The Socialist cooperatives, the foundation of the party's strength, now had a million members. The friendly societies had 400,000 members, and the trade unions and the "Houses of the People" had 700,000. The Socialists now constituted one-third of the town councils in the great cities and controlled the active life of the country.

Opposed to the Socialists were the Catholics, grouped in four independent sections. The first of these were the Christian Workers, with a membership now amounting to half a million. The others consisted of the Federation of the Middle Classes, composed of petty bourgeois and town shopkeepers; the Federation of Associations and Clubs, representing the conservative elements; and, finally, the powerful body of peasantry that belonged to the *Boerenbond* and the agricultural organizations. The system brought together banks, trade unions, professional bodies, youth organizations, cooperatives, and friendly societies. It served to maintain the influence of the Catholic party in all social classes and made it the defender of the material and moral interests of the population.

The part played in Parliament by the Liberals was now secondary. Political reality in Belgium was based on the great bodies of Catholic and Socialist opinion, and it was through these that the parliamentary machine was able to operate without difficulty. All problems were first debated inside the parties. It was here that the conflicting interests— peasant and industrial worker, intellectual and bourgeois, Flemish and Walloon—were sorted out, so that proposals came to Parliament three-quarters ready for passage, and the function of the parliamentary machine was mainly to record them. This system facilitated the functioning of the institutions of government, and ministers had to govern in agreement with the country as a whole, which meant settling important problems by compromise, without damage to national unity. The problem of education, a divisive factor for so many generations, now appeared to be finally settled. The solution reached had been the solution of freedom, and the important concern for all parties, between 1920 and 1930, was the material development of the country.

The problem of getting Belgium back to work was not so much a question of repairing war damage as it was a problem of adapting the country to the modern world by rebuilding it on new foundations. Agriculture became the key factor in reconstruction. It was reorganized by discontinuing the growing of grain and concentrating on livestock breeding, raising export crops, and cultivating truck-gardens with high yields. It was not long before Belgium was exporting annually 500,000 Belgian francs in fruit and flowers, and increasing the intensive cultivation of early crops. The production of endives alone rose from 5,500 tons in 1913 to 45,100 tons in 1927. Belgium became one of the biggest exporters of eggs in Europe, and was soon able to meet all the local requirements for milk, butter, and meat. In 20,000 hothouses, the country undertook the cultivation of table grapes and was soon producing 5,500 tons annually. Total agricultural production increased fourfold. It employed a labor force of 600,000 workers, and became profitable through the large-scale use of transport.

In industry, while many workers in England were unemployed, Belgian production reached 40 billion francs in a single year, considerably more than the total of wartime destruction. The industries that were particularly prosperous were the new ones, such as artificial silk, glass-making, and chemical industries. The Congo was at the beginning of an upswing that was not to be checked, while the mother country scored its economic success by ceaseless rationalization and the vertical concentration of industry, coupled with the reduction of net costs.

The working class knew that its standard of living depended on the export trade, which was in turn a function of industrial production costs. The spirit of creation and rivalry carried the working class along in spite of itself. The Belgian workers were among the first in Europe to have their wages based on a sliding scale, so that they were automatically adjusted to the cost of living. There was also, however, an agreement for wage reductions when export markets contracted; and the workers themselves proposed to employers the measures of economic adjustment that would enable industry to stand up to competition.

Expansion in the Congo aided expansion in Belgium. The former tropical cultures—rubber and ivory—were abandoned in favor of mine production, particularly copper in Lower Katanga, but also cobalt, uranium, tin, and gold. There was an expansion in cotton- and coffee-growing before the war boom of 1930–40.

The annual traffic in the port of Antwerp now amounted to 23 million tons. The length of docks in the port increased from fourteen to thirty-one miles, and the building of huge new locks, such as the one at Kruisschans, made it possible for the dock area to extend over an area of 1,500 acres. A two-way tunnel was built under the Schelde, and the Albert and Terneuzen canals made seaports out of inland cities. In the port of Ghent alone, 9 million tons of merchandise were loaded annually into ocean-going ships.

At the same time, there were deep-seated changes in the habits and the way of life of the country, and in the relations among men. This was a result of the abundance of new inventions and the consequent raising of the standard of living, which had improved the world over since the beginning of the century. The first indication of this improvement in the postwar period was the change in dress. Fashions became increasingly uniform. Around 1900, there were still special dresses for housemaids, working women, and peasant women, whereas dresses for the bourgeoisie and women of high society were cut on a different pattern. After 1920, the housemaid began wearing the same silk stockings as her mistress and went to the movies, just as did her mistress. Luxury goods, such as bicycles, motorcycles, cameras, and, later, radios, became commonplace possessions at all levels of society. The felt hat of the clerk, the small shopkeeper, and the millionaire became to all intents and purposes identical, and the factory girl could have a permanent wave as easily as the wife of a minister. This was the first time in history that such a phenomenon had occurred, and it marked the beginning of a new age.

Another leveling factor was education. The plumber's son could now sit for, and pass, the same examinations, and obtain the same degrees, as the son of the lord of the manor. But the astonishing thing was that the son of the millionaire ever succeeded in graduating, for previously ignorance had been one of the privileges of the wealthy classes. Now, however, they were forced to apply themselves to their studies like everyone else. The leveling process was equally noticeable in the life of the aristocracy and the great families. Sons of these families now made their careers in offices, or went into banking, the export trade, shopkeeping, or the liberal professions. A half-century earlier, any such careers would have been thought dishonorable.

At the same time, there was a continuous rise, not only in money wages, but also in purchasing power. In 1900, the average worker could earn the price of half a kilowatt of electricity by an hour's work;

by 1938 he was earning the price of three kilowatts, so that his purchasing power had risen sixfold. In 1900, an inner tube for a bicycle tire cost 200 gold francs, the equivalent of the earnings of six days' work; but, by 1938, the same price would buy the whole bicycle.

This upward movement had actually begun in the early days of the nineteenth century, but it had been checked and made less noticeable by recurrent economic crises. Later, about the middle of the twentieth century, a new phenomenon appeared: This was the fall in the price of basic foodstuffs, notably bread, whose price became so negligible that it no longer played any real part in the worker's budget. One might hope that, by 1975 or 1980, it will be almost free. Between 1938 and 1948, the food intake of the average Belgian in the poorer classes rose from 2,700 calories daily to 3,000 calories; in India, by comparison, the increase was only from 1,800 to 2,000 calories. At this rate, the food intake in Belgium reached saturation, and from now on spending tended to go into luxury foods, more expensive clothing, and other products.

It had now become impossible for an industrial country to live on a narrow market, and industry began to burst the national barriers. Between 1920 and 1940, Belgium had to give up a number of industries that required a mass market, such as automobile manufacture and aircraft construction. Even for the metallurgical industry expansion was checked because lack of markets precluded installing and operating continuous automatic rolling mills with high production and low costs, similar to those in great Britain, Germany, and France.

At the same time, the country was becoming increasingly unified. It was beginning to form a single social class with common interests, and the demands of the time resulted in the evolution of but one policy, dictated by the needs of expansion. Belgium could no longer develop, as she had been doing in 1900, by meeting world competition by cutting wages. Customs barriers were being erected on all sides and new industrial problems required the collaboration of all parties. The result is that today there are no longer distinct policies for the defense of the interests of the working class or the ruling class, but one single policy that is national and international at the same time.

Between 1918 and 1958, a few simple elements dominated the internal life of Belgium. The three great political parties—the Catholics, the Liberals and the Socialists—competed for power. The electoral votes, however, usually made it impossible for any one party to secure an absolute majority in Parliament. It was, therefore, necessary for the parties to govern by coalition. They were, for the most part, right-wing majorities consisting of Catholics and Liberals, or left-wing majorities consisting of Liberals and Socialists, or Socialists in alliance with the left wing of the Catholic Party.

The working-class party that had come to the fore with universal suffrage and the advanced ideas that were gaining ground all over Europe, benefited first from the revolutionary impetus that was to be found everywhere. In seven years, between 1918 and 1926, the country was dominated by the growing power of socialism. With strikes, elections, and mass demonstrations, it seemed that the Socialists were on the road to gaining control of the government by the ordinary procedures of parliamentary institutions. Their advance, however, was progressively checked by the results of inflation, financial deficits, and the disequilibrium resulting from war damage that necessitated loans, credits, and other aid from the capitalist world.

In 1925, the elections gave the Socialists their largest postwar majority, but still returned a compact group of Christian Democrats to the Chamber. The Poullet-Vandervelde government came into power. It was committed to a socialist program, which made it appear that, for the first time, the working-class masses were going to govern the country. Socialism had, however, retained its revolutionary character and did not yet display the skill in planning that was now needed for organizing the country's economic life. Moreover, the actual mechanism of economic crises, inflation and deflation, and the new financial techniques of full employment and credit injection, were as yet unknown.

The Poullet-Vandervelde government came up against the results of inflation and currency devaluation. It fell as the result of a financial crisis, during which it had to accept the collaboration of the big bankers in order to stabilize the currency, a necessity for the working class. It was forced to agree to a series of capitalist reforms, including the transfer of the state railways to private capital. It was thus paralyzed by its necessity to abandon the basic principles of socialism. Power then passed into the hands of a Catholic-Liberal coalition, that retained it consistently for eight years.

There was now a change in the main center of interest in Belgian political life. Between 1927 and 1932, its chief feature was the renewed importance of the Flemish movement. In the early postwar period, this movement had been weakened by the fact that its more extreme elements had collaborated with the enemy. By this time, however, it had regained all its power and bite; it was based on deep-seated feelings among the Flemish. At each election, more Flemish nationalists were returned to the chambers. Processions of demonstrators would fill the streets, chanting their battle cry: "Is the gull on the wing? Storm at sea!" It became necessary to enact a large number of linguistic reforms; laws on the use of the languages in the administration, Flemish and Walloon units in the army, and, especially, the full-scale Dutch organization of the University of Ghent, a necessary step because of the intellectual progress made by the educated Flemings.

Although Belgian internal politics reflected the immediate preoccupations of the country, they were also influenced by events elsewhere in Europe. The world-wide economic crisis of 1929 marks the transition from old-fashioned capitalism to economic planning. There were changes, too, in Belgian socialism, and new leaders such as the theoretician Henri de Man, author of *Au Delà du Marxisme* (Beyond Marxism), and Paul-Henri Spaak began their careers. They were very different from the doctrinaires, such as Emile Vandervelde, of the earlier period.

This was the beginning of the second phase of the internal political life of the postwar period. In the Catholic Party a new team came on the scene with Paul van Zeeland, who assumed the same place in Belgium that was held by Roosevelt, in the United States, and Keynes, in Great Britain. He personified a new type of man that had emerged from the growing importance of economic science in the modern world—that of a technician who, in fact, directed the great nations and the destinies of their peoples.

Van Zeeland had been born at Soignies, on November 11, 1893, and at the age of thirty-three had become a director of the Banque Nationale. He was a minister at forty-one and became head of the government on March 26, 1935 at the age of forty-two. During his period in office, his main work was not so much the devaluation of the Belgian franc and the reconstitution of the country's economic position after a serious financial crisis, as the fundamental reconstruction of the Belgian economic system. This involved a reorganization of credit, state control of the economic structure, and the banking and industrial systems that are the base of all modern societies. Among his colleagues were the most brilliant men of the period, including Henri de Man and Paul-Henri Spaak, a member of the distinguished Janson family, who made his debut in the new government of national unity. Spaak was to play an important part in political life before the war, become Prime Minister, and represent Belgium in the exiled wartime government in London as Minister of Foreign Affairs. After the war, he was to become one of the leading figures of the new Europe.

It was Paul van Zeeland's work of organization and reform that was largely responsible for bringing Belgium out of the old system of uncontrolled capitalism and into the new equilibrium that enabled her to come through the war and the postwar period unscathed. Paul van Zeeland, however, who had kept himself apart from party strife and put himself on too high a level, had time to carry through only the chief reforms in his program. It became necessary for him to withdraw in face of the wave of demagogy symbolized by the coming of Rexism. This movement was led by an extraordinary individual, Léon Degrelle, who, after a meteoric rise, became the equivalent of the

Fascist and National Socialist leaders who were appearing at this time all over Europe.

Degrelle made his first appearance about 1931. He had been born at Bouillon, on June 15, 1906. His father was a member of the Luxemburg provincial council, so that the family was already in politics. In 1925, Degrelle enrolled in law school at Louvain, but was never able to pass any examination at the first attempt and eventually failed three times in his final examination, before he abandoned his studies altogether. He had discovered, however, that he was a talented agitator, and it was this which was to bring him to the fore. He took advantage of the financial scandals, of which there were many in this period, invented the name "banksters," and organized the Rex movement, taken from *Christus Rex*. He left the Catholic Party, went into opposition against it, and eventually put forward his own candidates in all constituencies. In the 1936 election, to everyone's surprise, his candidates secured nearly 400,000 votes, gained a quarter of the seats held by the Catholic Party, and returned twenty-three deputies to Parliament.

Mussolini had sent Degrelle a clandestine subsidy of 20 million francs for propaganda purposes. When Degrelle was accused, however, of aspiring to a dictatorship, he replied by sending out millions of photographs of himself, smiling and relaxed with his wife and family around him, with the caption: "Does he look so terrible?" All his adventures, both before the war and during the occupation, had the same explosive and spectacular character. In the end, he joined the German army and formed a Belgian anticommunist legion. When the system collapsed, he succeeded in finding a plane that carried him by night to Spain where he went into hiding.

Rexism was no more than a storm in a teacup, but it disorganized all of Belgium's political life and made it impossible to form a government majority. The Catholics could not win enough seats to form a coalition with the Liberals and, with a quarter of the Chamber consisting of Communist, Rexist, and Flemish nationalist demagogues, the parliamentary machine could no longer operate.

This marked the beginning of the third phase in Belgium's prewar political scene. Rexism gained renewed strength in Flanders, and the appearance of a number of Fascist movements, offshoots of German National Socialism, exercised a growing pressure on the unity of the country. It became impossible to maintain the Franco-Belgian alliance, and the country was drawn inexorably into the developing world conflagration for which the Munich Conference and the Ribbentrop-Molotov pact paved the way. At this time, Albert I had been dead for several years; after the end of his reign, the young Leopold III ascended the throne.

XIII

LEOPOLD III AND THE
ATOMIC AGE

Albert died accidentally, in 1934, at the age of fifty-nine. He had always had a passion for heights and open spaces, and had always been a keen mountaineer. Moreover, he was aware of the fact that one of his Hohenzollern-Sigmaringen ancestors had given up all his earthly possessions to take refuge in the mountains, where he had become a hermit. He was alone at dusk when he climbed one of the rocky peaks at Marche-les-Dames, near Namur. There he lost his foothold and was found with his head smashed at the foot of a rustic statue of Christ, known as the *Vieux Bon Dieu*. There he died on February 17.

His unexpected death was one of a series of disasters that followed one another between 1934 and 1940: sudden death and internal change, the broken Franco-Belgian alliance, and the advance of Fascist ideas under the influence of the totalitarian countries. From this time onward, life was going to take on a noisy and spectacular aspect.

The reign of Leopold III opened with yet another tragedy. In the course of a drive on the Swiss roads, at Küssnacht near Lucerne, the King was involved in an accident and Queen Astrid was killed. Not many years before, Princess Astrid's arrival in Belgium had been compared with the coming of Hans Christian Andersen's Snow Queen. She had arrived from Sweden in a snow-white boat, and the marriage had thrown a romantic aura around the future sovereign. Leopold III ascended the throne of a country that was developing rapidly, and in which Flanders was becoming increasingly conscious of its individual national origin.

In 1846, Belgium's population had consisted of only 1.8 million Walloons and a compact mass of 2.5 million Flemings. In 1900, however, the French-speaking population showed a major increase to 2.6 million, compared with the 2.8 million who spoke Dutch. Despite the fact that the birth rate was higher in Flanders, the gap had decreased from 650,000 to only 250,000. There was now a rapid reversal of the trend. By 1944, the population of Flanders amounted to 4.2 million, representing half the population; against this, there were only 2.9 million Walloons. The balancing factor was the bilingual population of the Brussels district, amounting to 1.3 million.

The Catholic Party had had to reorganize and adapt itself to the linguistic division. It was now known as the Catholic bloc, and consisted of a federation of Walloon and Flemish groups. Both the Social Catholic Party, which was French-speaking, and its Flemish equivalent, the KVV, were divided into separate sections for industrial workers, bourgeoisie, rural people, and the middle classes, forming, in all, eight distinct groups. The established party, however, had no difficulty in adapting itself to this situation and, as 1939 drew near, it even succeeded in getting the better of Rexism.

But the strength of the Flemish movement was still growing. The French minorities in Flanders emigrated to Brussels, creating some difficulty for the party, because it hastened the division of Belgium into three separate regions: Flanders, Wallonia, and the Brussels district. The latter two had sufficient seats in the chamber to outvote the Flemings, since the combined influence of 3 million Walloons and 1.25 million inhabitants of Brussels was just sufficient to outvote 4 million Flemings.

Flanders, nevertheless, was becoming a separate entity. It had its own susceptibilities, a strong desire to manage its own affairs, and a particular desire to wipe out the memory of the unhappy days when it had been dominated by the chosen few who spoke French. There now arose a generation of financiers and industrialists like Gevaert, who made it one of their conditions that business in Flanders should be done in Dutch, and refused to do business with those who were unwilling to accept this stipulation. There was a strong movement supporting the demand that businesses with their headquarters in Flanders be under Flemish ownership. There was, for example, great public indignation at the fact that the Limburg collieries, discovered and developed by the Walloons, were not under Flemish financial control. Part of the "national" wealth, it was claimed, was going "abroad."

Flanders thus became not only a nation, but a complete intellectual and spiritual world of its own that grew and developed and discovered itself in its art and literature. The literature of Flanders had its beginnings in the thirteenth century—well in advance of the literature of Holland—with writers such as the popular encyclopedist Maerlant and the storyteller Willem, author of *Roman de Renart*. Willem's *Roman de Renart* was far superior to the French version of the same legend. Later, in the fourteenth century, Flemish literature produced such mystic writers as Ruysbroeck the Admirable, who became famous throughout Europe; the nun Hadewych, a mystic poetess; a century later, Anna Byns, another Catholic poetess and apostle of the counterreformation, who was to oppose the Rabelaisian Calvinist Marnix de Saint-Aldegonde. After this, Flemish literature suffered from the general decline of the Low Countries. It sank into a long period of mediocrity from which it was raised only at the beginning of the nineteenth century by the popular novelist, Henri Conscience. It was not until the middle of the century that a great poet was born: Guido Gezelle. He was an obscure country priest in western Flanders, whose acute sensitivity, human emotion, and intense love of nature made of him a great poet.

Having something of his own to say, Gezelle proceeded to say it, casting aside the academic and stilted language of his period and forging a means of expression of his own. The patois of western Flanders was still direct and full of vitality, and Gezelle proceeded to transform it by bringing in a great number of words that were either original or neologistic. The spirit of Flanders was traditionally composed of two elements: a zest for reality and a capacity for mystic withdrawal. Gezelle was an intense incarnation of the latter and, though his poetic world was somewhat small, he succeeded in expressing the emotions of a soul in communion with nature, into which it plunges passionately and finds God.

> Pure and wild is the loveliness of flowers,
> Children of innocence and truth.

> Not a leaf is stirring
> Until, at last, in the watery depths,
> The gathering blue o'erwhelms the green-streaked image.

Among the successors of Guido Gezelle was Albrecht Rodenbach, but it was not until the end of the nineteenth century that another great poet, Karel van de Woestijne, came into prominence, only a few years after the birth of the movement known as *Van Nu en Straks* ("Today and Tomorrow") in 1893. He was a perfect contrast to Guido Gezelle. Woestijne's poetic work is an autobiography in which he faces the world and defies it. He was imbued with the consciousness of sin that is characteristic of modern man, but he had none of the resignation and humility of the Christian priest to whom nature is only the expression of the soul of God. He was rebellious and hypersensitive

—now lyrical, philosophical, or epic; and he felt himself to be the center of a complex modern universe for the whole of which he wanted to find expression. This Fleming, passionately imbued with the life and spirit of his own countrymen, was essentially a great individualist who sometimes extolled and sometimes execrated womanhood:

> VENUS. Caress my brows, Adonis, stroke my hands.
> Touch me, Adonis, I am all afire.
> See on the moist turf my waiting body quiver,
> With summer glory in my breasts forever.
> Adonis, my flanks are each a burning brand,
> Let your hands feel the heat of my desire.
>
> ADONIS. O Woman, Woman, are you Death?

Karel van de Woestijne's work is marked by some of the same characteristics as that of his contemporaries, such as Stefan George and Rainer Maria Rilke, but he dominated the literature of his time with the strangeness and the power of his personality. He was the most brilliant figure in the *Van Nu en Straks* movement, which was to prove a forum for several important writers of prose. The first of these was the critic August Vermeylen (1872–1945), who brought Flemish literature out of its provincialism and gave it a universal audience. The storyteller Cyriel Buysse (1859–93) was known as the Flemish Maupassant and wrote from the point of view of the peasant, describing his country's nature in work that was both epic and a social indictment. Later came the novelist Stijn Streuvels, who wrote *The Flax Field* (1871). He was a nephew of Guido Gezelle and had an influence on prose comparable to his uncle's influence on poetry. Last came Herman Teirlinck, a novelist and playwright born in 1879, whose irony often makes one think of Anatole France, and who gave life to the theater and the literature of his period.

Among these major literary craftsmen were two popular novelists, Felix Timmermans (1886–1947) and Ernest Claes (born 1885). Their work was sometimes ironic, sometimes Rabelaisian (as, for example, in Timmerman's *Pallieter* and Claes's *De Witte*), and though their style and craftsmanship were by no means sure, they nevertheless achieved European fame. Except for one writer who was more universal (Elsschot, born 1882), all the writers who began before 1914 wrote in a regional vein, and their work is therefore of limited value. It treats only of the life of the Flemish people in their villages and small towns.

In 1920, it was the turn of the revolutionary generation—subject to the new influences of the period—whose theater was Europe. The most advanced of this group was Paul van Ostayen (1896–1928), who wrote

Music Hall (1916) and was both a disciple and a forerunner of the Dadaists. His contemporaries of more moderate scope included Raymond Herreman (born 1896), Richard Minne (1891), Maurice Roelants (1895), Philip de Pillecyn (1891), Frans Smits (1891), Gerard Walschap (1893), and Maurice Gilliams (1900). All of them were similar in character, for, in a world becoming increasingly universal, the artist could no longer live within the confines of local, or even national, culture. This growing internationalism became even more striking in later poets such as Bert Decorte (1915) and Herwig Hensen (1917), and writers of prose such as L. P. Boon (1912) and Johan Daisne (1912), who was a disciple of Kafka.

Belgian literature in the French language was developing on quite different lines. It was in direct touch with Paris, and the work of the Belgian authors was no longer separate from French letters in general.

In the history of literature, the "regional" phases have always been preparatory stages. When the literature of a country is being re-created after a period of comparative silence and inactivity, its rebirth usually goes through three phases. At first, the writers are apt to limit their work to singing the praises of the life and customs of their own land. In the second stage, they paint a more general picture of humanity and tackle problems on a higher level, integrating them into the main current of literary activity of their period. Finally, the third phase produces artists with a more universal message, whose work goes beyond national frontiers to rise above nationality and language.

In the nineteenth century, during the period of *Jeune Belgique*, the French-language literature of Belgium was still to some extent a prisoner of the regional formula. By 1920, however, it had broken through this narrow framework, and there was no longer a separate literature for Belgium and France, but a single movement in which all writers in the French language were finding their place. The writers of Belgium were now no more than French authors, but they were more original in their work because they were lucky enough to have a double cultural background and to be the product of a country that was politically and spiritually foreign. This gave them an intellectual environment richer in basic influences and sources of inspiration.

This was the period when Paris, as well as Brussels, saw the ascendancy of writers such as Charles Plisnier, who won the Prix Goncourt with *Mariages* and *Faux Passeports*; Francis Waldner, another Prix Goncourt winner; André Baillon (*En Sabots* and *Histoire d'une Marie*); Robert Poulet (*Les Ténèbres*); Georges Simenon, whose reputation became world-wide; and others such as Frans Hellens, Marie Gevers, Alexis Curvers, and Françoise Mallet-Joris.

Belgian poets now included such names as Henri Michaux, Odilon-Jean Perier and Marcel Thiry. In the world of the theater, among many others were Suzanne Lilar and Michel de Ghelderode. In criticism, history, and essays there were Eugène Baie (*Le Siècle des Gueux*), Robert Vivier, Georges Sion, and Henri and Jacques Pirenne.

But Belgian literature was not confined to only French and Flemish writers. In the southern part of the country there was a rich dialect literature in the Walloon and Picard languages. This literature had already achieved fame during the Middle Ages and in the period just before the Renaissance. In those days, the poets of Wallonia and the Artois had earned fame as far as Paris, like the Hainaut poet Conon de Béthune. Liége was now the center of this literature, and all its writers wrote in Walloon. They included Jean d'Outremeuse among others who found readers in all parts of Europe. Since the fifteenth century, however, the progress of French language and literature had driven the local languages into the background, and the artistic and intellectual stagnation in Belgium during the seventh century had resulted in their rapid decline.

They did not come to the surface again until the nineteenth century, but then produced major poets such as Defrêcheux, Joseph Vrindts, and Henri Simon. The latter wrote some fine verse, including his description of the death of a great tree which had dominated the entire countryside:

Slipping beneath it, you felt that you were entering a church.

The woodmen, however, felled the tree; and, in the distance, the peasants felt their hearts grow heavy, for they could no longer see it in its place on their familiar horizon:

Where the giant had stood was but a hole in the sky.

The dialect literatures played an essential part in the development of French letters as a whole. They were necessary because they were a source of enrichment and originality, freshness and vitality. They had remained close to Latin, and they were in direct touch with the popular spirit, so that they rejuvenated the language with many expressions and phrases that were more original, and, indeed, more French, than the slang and the artificial language of the cities.

Today, however, Belgian literature and French literature have become world-wide in character. They are no longer simple expressions of a country, but rather of something wider. The authors now constitute a single complex that may be called the French cultural domain. This domain is no more than a spiritual influence, but it extends to everyone the world over who uses the French language from Liége to Beirut, from Saigon to Quebec, from Haiti to Geneva and Paris. It is an immense force, not only because of the wide area of French culture, but also because of the large number of people exposed to it. There are only 48 million Frenchmen and French-speaking Belgians, but there are 4 or 5 million French Canadians, 1 million inhabitants of French Switzerland and the Val d'Aoste, 3 million Haitians and Antilleans, and at least 10 million people in the French Union in Africa and Asia. All these people have accepted French as their language, and they represent a group of some 70 million people spread over the whole surface of the earth.

These people are to be found at the crossroads of all the great cultures, at the gateways of continents and the points at which civilizations meet. From Canada their influence spreads over the North American continent; from Lebanon, Vietnam, and India, they encircle the huge continent of Asia. From French Switzerland, in constant touch with Germany and Italy, their influence spreads into central Europe; from Algeria and Dakar into Africa; from Haiti into Central America; and from Belgium and Luxemburg into northern Europe.

Today culture goes beyond language. It has to be an expression of the whole of human civilization, for there are no longer any privileged civilizations, but only centers of more intense vitality and cultural systems that are richer in creation and recreation, more fecund in art and invention. When all who speak the French language become conscious of their spiritual solidarity and unite in a purely spiritual federation, they will represent an immensely powerful force in world civilization. This is because they will have been the first to create an unmaterialistic empire, with neither fatherland nor frontiers, that will enable a Canadian to be at home as easily in Port-au-Prince or in Beirut as in Geneva, Brussels, or Paris.

On the political front, the decade 1934–44 was more charged with great events and richer in sudden drama than had been the case for many centuries of European history. The world was developing rapidly and events kept the same tempo. When Leopold III came to the throne, the Franco-Belgian alliance was virtually at an end. Reparations from Germany, which had created a unity of spirit and interest between Belgium and France, were no longer being claimed. The elections of 1932 had earlier shown that a large part of the people of Flanders were in revolt against the Franco-Belgian military pact.

The great crash of 1929 had played the part of a social revolution and its results had transformed the face of Belgium as radically as had the rise of neighboring dictatorships. The Rexists were in the ascendancy; the Socialists were in retreat before the Communists; and in Flanders the situation was in the hands of the Flemish nationalists, who formed a number of groups, from the Germanophile *Verdinasos* to the political autonomists of the VNV (*Vlaams Nationaal Verbond,* or "Flemish National Union"). This was the prelude to the Second World War.

The events that led to the war of 1939 can only be understood against the background of the general movement of civilization. During the first part of the twentieth century, a new fact had come to the surface of human history. This was unemployment and the alternation of boom and slump that could and did plunge millions of people into poverty and despair, striking at the very roots of society. The German inflation of 1923, and the great world crash of 1929, were revolutions in themselves. From these sprang the violent popular movements and the resurgence of demagogic doctrines that gave rise to dictatorships in various parts of Europe. These were events that, in Belgium, were favorable to the Rexists and the Flemish extremists.

Another vital force was the immense power that modern techniques had put into the hands of propagandists. Through the radio and large-circulation newspapers political leaders could now come into direct contact with the crowd, a factor that favored ideology and the spread of new doctrines. These forces played a new and important part in the preparatory stage of the 1939 war. They were, perhaps, more important than the military events that followed them.

The war of 1914 had not only carried the Allies to victory "on waves of petroleum," it had also created many new weapons and increased technical progress. The forces of civilization were making it possible to revolutionize warfare. Within a few years, Germany was building armored divisions and developing the use of aircraft in association with new weapons, thus producing effects that could not be foreseen by the adversary, which created a decisive advantage for a potential aggressor. The first half of the twentieth century had also witnessed the decline of both France and England, which coincided with the rebirth of Germany and the expansion of Germany's industrial potential.

The decline of England became apparent in 1920 in unemployment and the loss of world markets; in France, it was already in progress at the beginning of the twentieth century, but its consequences were not seriously felt until after the First World War. This decline, at a time when rapid progress in armament manufacture, and the growing importance of technology and industrial potential, were putting stability and security out of reach, was one of the decisive causes of the 1939 conflict. The national wealth of France had been estimated in 1903 at 250 billion gold francs, and by 1914 it had increased to 300 billion gold francs; but by 1938, on the other hand, it had fallen to 131 billion gold francs. The increase in the national income had fallen from three per cent a year, around 1850, to one per cent a year, between 1900 and 1914, and, after 1920, it had stabilized. French industrial expansion came to a halt, in contrast with the continued industrial expansion in Germany.

It took the United States five years to produce the 10 million tons of munitions that were to make it possible to defeat the Third Reich. In the same period, French industry could not have produced more than 1 million tons at most. There was thus a gap in Europe. The balance of power had become an illusion and governments and peoples were faced with a dramatic problem of conscience.

After 1936, the German reoccupation of the Rhineland and Belgium's consequent return to neutrality marked the end of the long period of postwar peace. From now on, Europe was under the shadow of the growing strength of National Socialism and the Third Reich. This was the situation confronting Leopold III when, on the death of his father King Albert, he came to the throne of a country that was deeply troubled and uneasy.

The dominant feature in the character of Leopold III was his courage. He set a high value on his duties and responsibilities and never shirked them. It was he who took the initiative in 1936 with an official declaration announcing Belgium's return to neutrality. But France and Belgium were subject to the same perils and caught in the web of the same destiny. It was not long before Hitler's aggression had re-established the solidarity of the two countries.

In September, 1939, the Belgians were not immediately pulled into the war; they succeeded in preserving their neutrality for the moment, but no one had any illusion that this would last more than a few months. The Pierlot government took advantage of the interval to import large quantities of grain and raw materials, and even succeeded in importing enough food to enable the country to be self-sufficient.

The twenty years between wars had resulted in a complete transformation of Belgian agriculture. The intensive growing of early fruits and vegetables and export products had been substituted for grain and basic food products. All that was needed was to reintroduce the latter to enable Belgium to meet her internal requirements. A good use was thus made of the short eight months' delay. Then came May 10, 1940, and disaster was at hand.

There had been no declaration of war when German aircraft flew in at dawn and destroyed all Belgian aviation on the ground. Parachute troops dropped from the sky, stormed the bridges over the Albert canal, and seized the strongest and most modern of the forts, like that of Eben-Emael. The Belgian army was at its full strength of 650,000 men, but it was defeated even more rapidly than in 1914. The campaign lasted

only eighteen days, and 9,000 men perished in the course of an unbroken retreat. Not until the eve of capitulation was an attempt made
to stand firm, but by then the Belgian army was already disorganized
and in confusion after the shock of the overwhelming mass of the
enemy and its vastly superior matériel.

Once again the facts had shown how impossible it is for a small nation
to defend itself unless it has united its forces in advance with those
of a coalition of stronger powers. The break-through of the German
tanks at Sedan marked the destruction of the Franco-British armies and
forced the surrender of the Belgian army, which had joined forces with
them. The Belgian army's resistance could not have lasted more than
a few hours more when Leopold signed the capitulation of May 28,
1940, in which he stood by his troops and became a prisoner with them.

This disaster tolled the knell for the small nations, but it also produced
a serious constitutional problem. No minister had been willing to coun-
tersign the capitulation and the Pierlot government, which believed
in carrying on the struggle to the death, took refuge in France and
later in England. After the armistice of June, 1940, the British Common-
wealth was the last remaining champion of the coalition and carried
on the war singlehanded against the powerful Nazi empire that dominated Europe.

Defeated Belgium, as in 1914, passed through four years of occupation. This time, however, the atmosphere had changed, and the single-
minded national attitude of the First World War no longer prevailed.
The Germans destroyed the autonomy of the communes that had
made the spontaneous and organized resistance of 1914-18 possible,
and set up in its place big centralized units like Greater Brussels. There
was no longer a national committee to run the country and organize
its food supplies.

The Flemish extremists, the Rexists, and all the others who were
later to be known as *inciviques*, "bad citizens," turned the occupation
into a civil war. Amid the executions of the patriots, the maquis, and
the deportations into Germany, there was intense propaganda for the
New Order. The Rexists and the Flemish nationalists took over the
newspapers and collaborated with the occupying power by calling for
a community of ideas and ideals.

The Flemish nationalists and the supporters of Léon Degrelle formed
a Flemish legion and a Walloon legion that were sent to the Russian
front, but their efforts did not break the morale or the resistance of
the population and, by the time of the country's liberation in September, 1944, half a million workers had been deported and the death
camps were filled with members of the resistance. Belgium, however,
emerged from her trials stronger and more united. Despite the occupa-

tion, or perhaps because of it, the nation's vigor had remained intact, and it was able to set to work with renewed energy.

Belgium's recovery, following directly after the liberation in September, 1944, astonished the world. It was an extraordinary example of collective energy and initiative. While all Europe was still plunged in the threefold horror of war, famine, and chaos, it took Belgium only a few months to reconstitute her economic potential. Productive industry was soon at work again, raw materials were imported from all over the world, and Antwerp became Europe's commercial distribution center.

It was called a miracle, but this was not really the case. The Belgians had found a way of swiftly adapting their agriculture to the necessities of their food supply. They had profited from the short interval between September, 1939, and May, 1940 to import goods from all over the world in the hope of reselling them to their Allies. During the occupation these stocks had been, for the most part, concealed from the Germans. They had kept the Belgian market supplied for four long years through carefully organized underground channels, and the individualism of the Belgians, their spirit of initiative, and their resistance to all forms of tyranny, thus came into play against the occupying forces. The black market, a source of poverty and dislocation in other countries, helped Belgium to hide her stocks from the Germans and to distribute them to the population at all levels.

Agriculture was soon adjusted to the internal market. The winter of 1941 was difficult, but from 1942 onward the organization of production and distribution became more efficient, and the improvement continued in the two following years, while the rest of Europe was in the grip of food shortages. At the time of the liberation, Belgium still had considerable stocks and would no doubt have been able to continue the war for several months. She was thus able to get her economic system working immediately. The port of Antwerp, which had remained intact, was put at the disposal of the Allies and was able to make its contribution to the war effort and also to import the raw materials that were lacking.

The re-establishment of Belgian industry was made easier because of the Congo. For four years, the Congo had been supplying the Western Allies with oils and fats, food products, and such important minerals as copper, tin, cobalt, and uranium. It was because of the Congo that the new atomic industry was able to find the necessary supplies of radioactive material. The Belgian government in London had become a creditor of the world and had large credits at its disposal that enabled it to buy machines, food, and supplies.

By the end of 1944, Belgium's export trade was able to begin again. Imports were flowing into the country, and from there they were sent all over Europe. The country's recovery was beginning. The only danger was that the good results of the initial phase might be nullified by inflation and by the virtually inevitable relaxation of restrictions after the trials of the occupation. The realistic way in which the Belgian people faced the necessary sacrifices, so as to restore the equilibrium of the country, was worthy of a great nation. The political maturity of the people and their knowledge of the working of economic forces were made clear in the way in which all classes united to accept, with one accord, the measures that were necessarily enacted.

The finance minister, Camile Gutt, adopted the most courageous solution by freezing bank accounts, security holdings, and currency. Three-quarters of the Belgian population were thus put into uncomfortable circumstances, but the situation was made healthier and the country's recovery insured in conformity with the technique worked out during the war by Lord Beveridge in England, which was adopted shortly afterward in Germany by Chancellor Adenauer. The Gutt measures penalized people who were not receiving wages or salaries, but the cost of living was stabilized, the purchasing power of the public was maintained, and there was an immediate recovery in external trade that gave Belgium a favorable balance.

In this country, in which political and economic life were one and the same, everything depended on agreement between the government and the leaders of the trade unions. The same spirit prevailed in the reconstruction of the country, which was the collective work of all the citizens and required only a minimum of state interference.

At Antwerp, for example, whole streets had been destroyed by the German V-2's, but they were rebuilt by groups of local inhabitants who did not wait for government aid. The tradesmen realized that their interests were identical, and that their streets would become prosperous again only if all the buildings were rebuilt at the same time. It would have taken years to secure the necessary official credits and, in the meantime, the shops would have lost their trade. The inhabitants, therefore, preferred to take things into their own hands.

The internal structure of the country was still based on the two political parties—the Catholics and the Socialists. These two parties were crucially at odds in the "Royal Question," arising from the persistent hostility of many Belgians to Leopold III. The King had been taken into Germany as a prisoner, in 1944, and his brother, Prince Charles, had become regent of the kingdom in his absence.

A plebiscite was held, and 57 per cent of the electors voted in favor of the King's return. He still had many opponents, however, whose strength was the greater for the fact that they had behind them the great cities of the Walloon provinces. When the King returned in 1952, the Socialists refused to accept him. They showed again that they had not forgotten the art of mass agitation that they had so often used in the past.

After a few days of illusory calm, an intense campaign of agitation broke out from one end of Wallonia to the other. The demonstrations grew bigger daily, and the government, before it could adequately take stock of what was happening, had lost control of the situation. The demonstrators threatened a march on Brussels and, had this occurred, the forces of law and order would probably have refused to open fire upon them. The country was on the verge of civil war. Leopold III bowed before the storm and handed over his powers to his son Baudouin, who officially became King a year later. It was not long before the conflicting forces in the nation were reconciled.

In the 1950 elections, the Catholics obtained an absolute majority in Parliament for the first time since 1914. The education question, shelved for more than twenty years, again became pressing. The Catholic Party was now master of the situation and tried to solve the education problem to its own advantage, but in doing so it produced the inevitable reaction that resulted in a coalition of the two anticlerical parties. After their electoral victory, they undid the work of the previous Parliament (1954). Later, in 1958, there was a fresh swing of the balance and the Catholics were again returned to power. The school question was now settled by a compromise and, in 1959, the Belgians entered the Common Market representing the union of 165 million inhabitants of Western Europe.

Belgium's economic strength during the nineteenth century had depended on low wages and a low cost of living, but the country now followed the United States in becoming a land of high wages and strong industrial ogranization. The living standard of the working class had become one of the highest in Europe.

Belgium was also subject to the general world trend that was bringing different peoples toward unification. The Benelux Union, negotiated in London during the war, was a fusion of the Belgians, the Dutch, and the Luxemburgers into a single customs union that healed the split suffered by the economic union in 1830. In this new framework, Belgium's prospects were considerable. In the Congo, then on the threshold of independence, more than a third of the native population had been converted to Christianity within a few generations.

The industrial potential of the Limburg coal-mining area, with its

reserves of 8 to 10 billion tons of coking coal, enabled Belgium to produce at the same rate as Germany had done for half a century.

These trump cards, however, were nothing compared with the industry and creativity of the population. Belgium is still among the
leaders of world science, with mathematicians such as Canon Lemaître
(the author of the theory of the expanding universe and of the theory
of the primeval atom) and scientists such as Paul Janssens, who has
done such remarkable work in the field of analgesics.

Yet neither men of learning nor statesmen are the true soul of a
nation; nor is political strife, which is but foam on the disturbed surface of an age. And the material and economic life of a country is also
only a symptom. The real spirit of a nation is to be found in its heart,
its beliefs, its ideas, in its poetry and art.

The spirit of Belgium is to be found everywhere—among the missionaries who converted Africa and Asia, and among the artists whose
works reflect their innermost lives. It is to be found in Belgium's cities
—those vast museums of paintings and statues, towers and cathedrals.
In Antwerp, with its Cathedral of Our Lady, its market place and Town
Hall, its Van Eycks and Rubenses, Van der Weydens and Massys, its
Memlings and Ensors. In Mechlin, with its magnificent cathedral spire
and its Van Dycks and Rubenses. In Ghent, with its boatsmen's and
merchants' houses, its castle and its Town Hall, its soaring church spires
and the most magnificent of all Van Eycks, his "Adoration of the
Lamb." In Bruges, with its celebrated belfry, its canals and swans, its
Hôpital St. Jean—a huge Memling museum—its Van Eycks, Van der
Goes, Davids, and Pourbus, its richly ornamented churches and monuments, its patrician houses. In Liège, whose seven great churches are
storehouses of treasures—superb altarpieces, stained-glass windows, the
great Rénier de Huy font—and its archaeological museums. In Brussels,
the city of St. Gudule and Notre Dame de la Chapelle, the burial place
of Brueghel, with its corporation houses, its Town Hall and market
square, its museums housing some of the greatest treasures of Flemish
art. In Tournai, with its great cathedral, frescoes, statues, and Romanesque churches. In Mons, with its towers and statuary. In Louvain, with
Mathieu de Layen's Town Hall, its Dirk Bouts paintings, its wealth
of stained-glass windows, and the Beguinage. In Courtrai, with its Town
Hall, its Church of Our Lady and Church of St. Catherine de Beauneveu. In Huy, with its Collegiate Church containing the Rose and
Reliquary of Our Lady. And there is Oudenarde, with its luxurious
Town Hall.

It is not only the great cities, however, those capitals of the communes
of the Middle Ages and the Renaissance that make Belgium a world of
art and achievement. It is also in the little towns and villages of only

a few thousand inhabitants, where a whole host of treasures may be found. The spirit of Belgium is in Dinant, with its gothic portal; in Diest, with its thirteenth-century Virgin; in Furnes, with its Gothic church and houses; in Ypres, with the immense market halls; in Stavelot, with the relics of St. Remacle; in Nivelles, with those of St. Gertrude; and in Hal, with its statues and altarpieces.

It is often the smallest cities that have the finest works. In Zoutleeuw there are only a few hundred inhabitants, but the fine statues are more numerous than the men. Termonde has two pictures by Van Dyck; Aalst has a Rubens; Saventhem has another Van Dyck; Walcourt and La Gleize have their Virgins; Tancrémont has its pathetic Christ. All these treasures of past centuries are what has survived of many wonders that have been destroyed, but they are treasures that speak, beget others, dazzle the eye, and stir the spirit.

In this orchestration of art, where a thousand and one forms of beauty are interlaced, the listener may hear the voice of the country that brought a race of artists into being to build, not only its palaces and its churches, but the least of its burghers' houses; and through this concert of painters, sculptors, and architects may be heard, too, the voice of the true musicians: d'Ockeghem, Roland de Lassus of Grétry, and César Franck.

Perhaps one may also hear the voices of the invisible and nameless host of those who have felt the beauty of these works throughout the centuries, who have loved them, and left them here for us. The patrons, the rich burghers, the simple artisans, and perhaps a voice even more vibrant than the rest, the voice of the Belgian people.

For was it not the Belgian people who were the real creators of these masterpieces; who called them into being through the ages by a sort of secret link between life and art; who called them in answer to a deep inner need, a cry for beauty that was the counterpart of the people's own overflowing vitality; who would perhaps re-create such art tomorrow if it should be swept away in one of the cataclysms of humanity?

Historians are as a rule pessimists. They see the past only in terms of disasters and they are tempted to foresee still more disasters in the future. For them it seems that the security of mankind is never sure, success is never lasting, and history is no more than a lesson in discouragement. Yet history, viewed from another angle, is a living demonstration of mankind's extraordinary skill in adapting itself to every situation and in rising anew after every disaster.

The Belgium that has emerged in the course of twenty centuries is itself a paradox and a prodigious lesson in life. Its most striking feature has been its power to obtain, through work and the energy of its people rather than warfare, results that, for other countries, have required military adventures and dreams of power and glory.

The nation's history can only be understood by comparing it with that work of genius created on the soil of Greece by the Republic of Athens, in the fifth century B.C. The Attic world, like Belgium, began as a sterile land of bare rock and mountain, sparsely populated, and with soil that was almost worthless. It rose to greatness through ceaseless creative work and invention; by discovering the value of the olive tree; by selling the oil to pay for the grain it lacked; by organizing industry and a commercial fleet; and by settling all its internal problems by compromise.

Belgium in the tenth century was in even more unfavorable circumstances. Yet it transformed a land of marshes and dunes into a center of activity and intense vitality. Like Greece, it discovered solutions of its own for every problem: carrying its merchandise by canals; building inclined planes to link the navigable stretches of its rivers; setting up guilds for selling and export; tilling the fields by intensive cultivation; and, above all, uniting its people in elective institutions that enabled them to divert their energy toward external efforts.

The creative spirit of Belgium soon overflowed, as had that of Athens, from the world of wealth and commerce into the world of art. When the world changed and foreign competition threatened the country with ruin, it was supple in meeting the new situation, turning from the manufacture of woolen cloth to linen, expanding the port of Antwerp, and, through international trade, laying the foundations of yet another fortune. In the face of countless crises, the country kept going for a thousand years. In the nineteenth century it finally rose through its metal industry and became, in the twentieth century, one of the most advanced countries of the world.

The history of the Belgians is not so much a history as an epic. It is the epic of mankind with its energy and misery, its greatness, and the mystery of its inner power.

It is a history that has continued through the ages under every aspect: the intellectual ebullition of the Renaissance; the creation of a new social system that started from nothing in the tenth century; the stagnation of the Gallo-Roman world, and the world of the seventeenth century; and the industrial revolution of the nineteenth century. Behind it all lies a succession of disasters, suffering, triumphs, dazzling creation, and tragedy. It passes and repasses from joy to tears and from tears to joy, and its whole course embodies every aspect of the miracle of man.

What has made the history of the Belgians a great adventure, and their soil the battlefield of Europe for a thousand years, is that Belgium has always been the frontier between divergent ideas and conceptions, the center and the line of cleavage between beliefs. The strife fought out on her territory has been less the strife of armies and of nations than that of religions and concepts of the world.

Belgium's historic role as a land of experience and a melting-pot of ideas has been linked less with the facts of geography than with the great diversity of race, language, culture, and habits of life that are Belgium's characteristic feature. Its blood is both Latin and Germanic, and many conditions of thought and feeling are to be found there, side by side. It is a land of open frontiers, a sort of exposed beach in Europe, swept by the tides of many influences and beaten with the waves of every kind of civilization.

Its history sweeps onward with its children; its dreamers, adventurers, artists, and men of action; its apostles and its mystics. In the union of spirits and their wills, it forms this advancing force, this union of the real and the ideal, this living miracle and masterpiece: Belgium.